The Garland Library of the History of Western Music

One hundred eighty-five articles in fourteen volumes

General Editor
Ellen Rosand
Rutgers University

Contents
of
the
Set

Volume Thirteen

Criticism
and
Analysis

Garland Publishing, Inc.
New York & London
1985

Library of Congress Cataloging-in-Publication Data
Main entry under title:
Criticism and analysis.

   (The Garland library of the history of western music ; v. 13)
   Articles in English, including 1 in French, originally published
1956–1980.
   1. Musical analysis—Addresses, essays, lectures.
2. Music—History and criticism—Addresses, essays,
lectures   I. Series.
MT6.C797   1985   780'.9   85-16200
ISBN 0-8240-7462-9

The volumes in this series have been printed on acid-free,
250-year-life paper.

Printed in the United States of America

Contents

Acknowledgments

Adorno, Theodor W. "Modern Music Is Growing Old," trans. Rollo H. Myers, *The Score and I.M.A. Magazine*, No. 18 (December 1956), 18–29. Copyright © 1956 by *The Score*, reprinted by permission of Kraus-Thomson Ltd.

Carpenter, Patricia. "The Musical Object," *Current Musicology*, V (1967), 56–87. Copyright © 1967 by The Trustees of Columbia University in the City of New York, reprinted by permission of the publisher

Cone, Edward T. "Analysis Today," *The Musical Quarterly*, XLVI (1960), 172–88. Copyright © 1960 by G. Schirmer, Inc., reprinted by permission

Dahlhaus, Carl. "Issues in Composition," trans. Mary Whittall with Arnold Whittall, in *Between Romanticism and Modernism: Four Studies in the Music of the Later Nineteenth Century* (California Studies in 19th Century Music, I), trans. Mary Whittall (Berkeley: University of California Press, 1980), pp. 40–78. Copyright © 1980 by The Regents of the University of California, reprinted by permission of The Regents

Kerman, Joseph. "How We Got into Analysis, and How to Get Out," *Critical Inquiry*, VII (1980–81), 311–31. Copyright © 1980 by the University of Chicago, reprinted by permission

Mendel, Arthur. "Evidence and Explanation," in *International Musicological Society, Report of the Eighth Congress, New York 1961*, ed. Jan LaRue, II (Kassel: Bärenreiter, 1962), pp. 3–18. Copyright © 1962 by the International Musicological Society, reprinted by permission

Meyer, Leonard B. "Exploiting Limits: Creation, Archetypes, and Style Change," *Daedalus*, CIX/2 (Spring 1980), 177–205. Copyright © 1980 by *Daedalus*, Journal of the American Academy of Arts and Sciences, Boston, MA, reprinted by permission

Morgan, Robert P. "On the Analysis of Recent Music," *Critical Inquiry*, IV (1977–78), 33–53. Copyright © 1977 by The University of Chicago, reprinted by permission

Preface

The Garland Library of the History of Western Music, in fourteen
volumes, is a collection of outstanding articles in musicology that
have been reprinted from a variety of sources: periodicals, *Fest-
schriften*, and other collections of essays. The articles were selected
from a list provided by a panel of eminent musicologists, named
below, who represent the full range of the discipline.

Originally conceived in general terms as a collection of outstanding articles whose reprinting would serve the needs of students of musicology at the graduate and advanced undergraduate
level, the series took clearer shape during the process of selecting
articles for inclusion. While volumes covering the conventional
chronological divisions of music history had been projected from
the very beginning, several other kinds of volumes cutting across
those traditional divisions and representing the interests of large
numbers of scholars eventually suggested themselves: the volumes
on opera, source studies, criticism, and analysis.

Indeed, although the general objective of excellence remained
standard for the entire series, the specific criteria for selection
varied somewhat according to the focus of the individual volumes.
In the two on opera, for example, chronological coverage of the
history of the genre was of primary importance; in those on
source studies, criticism, and analysis the chief aim was the
representation of different points of view; and in the volumes
devoted to chronological periods selection was guided by an effort
to cover the various geographical centers, genres, and individual
composers essential to the understanding of a historical era.

The articles themselves were written over a period spanning
more than a half century of modern musicological scholarship.
Some are "classic" statements by scholars of the past or early
formulations by scholars still active today, in which musicological
method, intellectual vision, or significance for their time rather
than any specific factual information is most worthy of appreciation. Others represent the most recent research, by younger
scholars as well as more established ones. No general attempt has
been made to bring the articles up to date, although some authors

have included addenda and misprints have been corrected where possible.

Since no single reader could be fully satisfied by the selection of articles in his own field, the aims of this collection, by necessity, have had to be considerably broader: to provide not only a wide range of articles on a large number of topics by a variety of authors but to offer the student some sense of the history and development of individual fields of study as well as of the discipline as a whole. The value of these volumes derives from the material they contain as well as from the overview they provide of the field of musicology; but the series will fulfill its function only if it leads the student back into the library, to immerse himself in all the materials necessary to a fuller understanding of any single topic.

Ellen Rosand

Panel of Advisors

Richard J. Agee, The Colorado College
James R. Anthony, University of Arizona
William W. Austin, Cornell University
Lawrence F. Bernstein, University of Pennsylvania
Bathia Churgin, Bar-Ilan University
Edward T. Cone, Princeton University
John Deathridge, King's College, Cambridge
Walter Frisch, Columbia University
Sarah Ann Fuller, SUNY at Stony Brook
James Haar, University of North Carolina at Chapel Hill
Ellen Harris, University of Chicago
D. Kern Holoman, University of California at Davis
Robert Holzer, University of Pennsylvania
Philip Gossett, University of Chicago
Douglas Johnson, Rutgers University
Jeffrey Kallberg, University of Pennsylvania
Janet Levy, New York, New York
Kenneth Levy, Princeton University
Lowell Lindgren, Massachusetts Institute of Technology
Robert Marshall, Brandeis University
Leonard B. Meyer, University of Pennsylvania
Robert P. Morgan, University of Chicago
John Nádas, University of North Carolina at Chapel Hill
Jessie Ann Owens, Brandeis University
Roger Parker, Cornell University
Martin Picker, Rutgers University
Alejandro Planchart, University of California at Santa Barbara
Harold Powers, Princeton University
Joshua Rifkin, Cambridge, Massachusetts
John Roberts, University of Pennsylvania

Volume Thirteen

*Criticism
and
Analysis*

MODERN MUSIC IS GROWING OLD

Th. W. Adorno

If to assert that modern music is beginning to age were only a paradox it would not matter so much. But it would appear that modern music today is in danger of being mixed up with those so-called 'cultural activities and manifestations' whose object is to attenuate or camouflage *Angst* of any kind, whereas the very nature of this music and, indeed, the reason for its existence, obliged it to refuse any such compromise and to express and give form to the disquiet that marks our epoch. Reactionary observers are only too pleased to note that the 'modern' is becoming academic. And modern music, by definition, cannot be self-indulgent. To profess satisfaction would be to betray its own ideals; for music only became 'modern' when it announced its profound dissatisfaction with the state of musical affairs. That is why, during the 'heroic' period, the *Rite of Spring* or certain pages of Alban Berg seemed to those who heard them for the first time in Paris or Vienna so outrageous and so shocking. This music wasn't merely, as some faithful disciples would have us believe, strange and disconcerting at first hearing; it was disquieting because it was itself an expression of anxiety amounting almost to bewilderment and a sense of insecurity. To deny that and to assert that once the first surprise is over modern music is quite as beautiful as traditional music, is to deal it a knock-out blow—to offer it, in fact, a certificate of good conduct which it will spurn so long as it obeys its natural impulses.

But these impulses may weaken, and it is then that modern music begins to grow old. And then it contradicts itself, loses its aesthetic substance and doesn't ring true any longer. As early as 1927 there were signs that modern music was going to 'settle down' and enter the danger zone of safety; since then these signs have become more marked. And this does not mean, as is sometimes asserted, that after a period of fermentation contemporary music has mellowed deliciously in the bottle. It is no longer a question of genuine masterpieces, with all their angles rubbed off, taking the place of the experiments and excesses perpetrated by the pioneers and forerunners of yesterday. (To expect masterpieces of this kind is precisely one of those conformist illusions to which modern music should never have succumbed.) The truth is that the pseudo-modernists--their name is legion—have forgotten the real meaning of the movement to which they have attached themselves. Their works are becoming less good and less convincing. Tension has relaxed and imagination grown feebler. No one would pretend that what is being composed today is in any way better than *Pierrot Lunaire*, *Erwartung* or *Wozzeck*, or than Webern or the youthful ebulliences of Stravinsky or Bartók. It may be true that technique today is purer, style more homogeneous and that in the writing of music a certain degree of rigidity is now admitted and practised; it nevertheless remains to be seen whether, by dint of purging aesthetic values of all impurities and subjecting technique to an iron discipline, we may not be running the risk of injecting into music too strong a dose of puritanism—of something at once too definite, too artificial and too inartistic. In any case these technical acquisitions do not appear to have greatly improved the quality of the works in which they are exhibited. One would have indeed to be a fanatical believer in the uninterrupted progress of music not to admit that, since the twenties, whatever music may have done it has certainly not progressed; that, on the contrary, it has lost much ground, and that the majority of present-day compositions show much less originality and less invention than their predecessors of that period. If one has the cause of modern music at heart one must not refuse to face the facts. Indeed, this may well prove to be a better way of defending it than by deciding to come to terms with present-day trends no matter what these may be.

To admit that 'advanced' music is not making any progress concedes nothing to its adversaries who think that, now 'the danger of the atonal revolution is past', music will once more 'return to its traditional path'. Such a view would be no less superficial and banal than those 'stabilized scores' based on ancient models and enlivened by a sprinkling of false notes. Even where the past is concerned, over-simplified views of this kind are to be mistrusted. It is, for example, by no means certain that the eclipse of Bach in 1750 and the triumph of the *style galant* can be considered as a 'healthy evolution'. This new anti-polyphonic style certainly gave us Haydn and Mozart; on the other hand the disappearance of the Bach tradition, which was a matter of some concern to the great Viennese masters, was perhaps the cause of certain shortcomings (only too visible today) in the methods of these same musicians. In our own day there can be no doubt that the general tendency of contemporary music—the music for Festivals of contemporary music—is far from being the result of a new and vital taste being formed, as was the case when a new style made its appearance after Bach's death. Present-day music, on the contrary, is living on the discoveries made by modern music which it cultivates (inefficiently) dilutes, or distorts. Let us try to illustrate this point by an example taken from literary history. Some time ago a work (*Die letzen Tage der Menschheit*, by Karl Kraus) was published in Vienna; the frontispiece showed the execution of the Deputy Battisti, convicted of espionage, with a horrible photograph of the grinning executioner. In a recent edition of this work this frontispiece was omitted. This alteration, although exterior to the work itself, nevertheless considerably changed its impact and significance. In a less obvious way, this is what is happening in the music of our time; it uses almost the same tonal palette as thirty years ago, but the element of anxiety (*Angst*) so characteristic of its finest moments then has now been repressed. The anxiety motif has now grown to such proportions that its direct transposition into the language of art is no longer bearable; afraid of being afraid, modern music is allowing itself to grow old. But an art that accepts without discussion such a repression and is willing (because incapable of tragedy) to be nothing but entertainment, has given up trying to be true and has renounced what is, in fact,

3

the only justification for its existence. Excuses are sometimes made for art of this kind, by calling it 'detached' and placing it far above the rough and tumble of the lower forms of existence in the loftiest regions of the mind. But that amounts to congratulating it for having found an outlet for its bad conscience. A century ago Kierkegaard remarked that ever since the railway companies had built bridges over frightful precipices travellers got a thrill from gazing into their depths. This is exactly what is happening in music. And even if the ruthlessness of History makes it useless to resist, we must at least be free of any illusions with regard to an art that is ready to compromise, for such an art is neither what it pretends to be nor what those forces with which it has effected a compromise are quite glad to see it mistaken for.

It is not a question here of pseudo-modernists or second-rate musicians. The symptoms can be observed in the most gifted composers and in those who would personally be the least inclined to make concessions. Nor are we thinking of a Stravinsky or a Hindemith who have more or less explicitly abjured everything that made them so fascinating in their youth; in their determination to effect a classical restoration (comparable to a similar attitude on the part of certain repentant surrealist painters) they have rejected even the idea of such a thing as *modern* music, being obsessed with the mirage of a *musica perennis*. Even a Bartók, who had quite other ideas, at one time in his career detached himself from his past. In the course of a conversation in New York he once stated that a composer like himself, rooted in 'folk' music, would in the end be unable to do without tonality—a surprising statement for a man like Bartók who, in the political sphere, had resisted so successfully any nationalist temptations and had chosen exile and poverty at a time when Europe was plunged in Fascist darkness. And yet his last works—the Violin Concerto, for example—belong to traditional music. Not that they aim at one of those artificial 'returns' to something that has been done away with long ago. Rather do they represent an almost naïve continuation of the Brahms tradition. These works are certainly late-flowering and posthumous masterpieces; but they have been domesticated and contain nothing of a volcanic, savage or menacing nature. And this evolution in Bartók has a strange retroactive effect: thus, in some of his earlier works, even the most 'advanced' such as the first Violin Sonata, the music, looking back on it again, seems much more innocent; what used to seem like a sort of conflagration now sounds like a sort of czardas. And so, even among those who were once at the head of the contemporary movement, there was more than one, it would seem, who could not quite keep up with his own *avant-gardisme* and was living, so to speak, aesthetically above his means. A state of affairs for which, among other things, the naïveté of the professional musician is responsible. All he does is to exercise his profession, caring nothing about the Spirit of History. And so it is that the reason for the gulf between Society and contemporary music must be sought in the actual musical make-up of musicians themselves who feel obliged to produce 'contemporary music' as a duty, although their education and their natural taste revolt against such music. In their experience as musicians there are certain elements that refuse to coincide. Those especially who were first attracted by contemporary music because their knowledge of classical music was inadequate tend to capitulate as soon as they are confronted with the unattainable heights of the music of the past.

There is no doubt that the ageing of modern music is a more alarming phenomenon than the repentance of a few contemporary composers or the escapism of
the 'return to the classics'. To denounce the impotence of neo-classicism today is to
attack a cause that is already lost: the feebleness, insipidity and monotony of recent
examples of this kind of music is, it seems, quite enough to cause talented young
composers to keep clear of it. It is all the more urgent to ask ourselves what is
happening in the opposite camp which attracts the unsatisfied and anti-academic
school, the partisans of the twelve-note technique which today, historically speaking,
is still necessary and essential. But, like Schoenberg himself, one may have good
reasons for not being over-pleased at the growing popularity of this technique.
The fact is, the twelve-note method is only justified when it serves to introduce
order into some complex musical content which is refractory to other methods
of organization. Otherwise, this technique merely degenerates into an absurd system.
Sufficient proof of this is surely to be found in the fact that, on the one hand, *avant-
garde* music, and above all the music of Schoenberg, is generally hailed as being
'twelve-note' and instantly labelled and catalogued, one might almost say mis-
represented as such, while on the other hand a great deal of this music (and perhaps
the part which, from the point of view of quality, is the most important) owes nothing
to this technique or was written before it was perfected. Schoenberg himself always
refused to treat as something that could be taught a technique that was subsequently
and mistakenly turned into a system. We have only to think, for example, of Webern's
Five Pieces for String Quartet which are as vital today as when they were first written,
and have never been surpassed in technical perfection. This score was composed
forty-five years ago; its syntax shows no vestige of tonality and contains nothing
but what are known as dissonances; yet it is not in any way 'twelve-note'. Every
one of its dissonances is surrounded, as it were, with an 'aura' of apprehension. They
have never, one feels, been heard before, and their creator only introduces them
with fear and trembling; the circumspection with which the composer treats them
is reflected in every detail of the technique employed. He is reluctant to take leave
of each one of these strange sonorities and does not allow them to die out before
he has exhausted all their expressive *values*. He is careful not to handle this material
in a reckless manner, but treats his discoveries with the greatest respect. Thanks to
this attitude these edifices in sound retain all the freshness of their eager delicacy.
Of course, things cannot be expected to keep for ever the strength of their virginity,
which must be sacrificed: one must go further, and be willing for discoveries and
effects to be classified. It then remains to be seen, however, whether these chords,
having lost their singularity, will fit into other combinations where they will retain
their character or whether, on the contrary, they will lose it and allow themselves henceforward to be treated as if they had never meant anything in particular.

It is the levelling down and neutralization of the actual material of modern
music that show most clearly that it is growing old, and it is here that the arbitrary
nature of a radicalism that no longer has any value is most apparent. No value in
itself, internally, since these discords no longer cause either pleasure or concern to
composer or listener as they have become impersonal and emptied of their expressive
substance; and no value, externally, since the twelve-note technique represented

5

at all the festivals of modern music no longer shocks any audience. It is tolerated as something that only concerns the technicians—something that still has some cultural value, no one quite knows why, that disturbs nobody and can safely be left to the experts to deal with. What is forgotten is that twelve-note technique is without significance except in so far as it serves to bind together centrifugal, recalcitrant and more or less explosive musical forces. Unless accompanied by this corollary and contradiction this technique has no justification and is a waste of time. In the case of a lot of music, relatively simple both in form and content, which is served up to us today dressed in the twelve-note fashion, it is merely a useless luxury and therefore aesthetically wrong.

Then, again, there are the uncompromising extremists who would like, if possible, to go further than Schoenberg. Their attitude, curiously enough, is both sectarian and academic. It is, of course, not difficult to discover and denounce in the music of the great modernists, including Schoenberg, traditional features—features relating to the expression and, as it were, the internal composition of certain scores which seem to be in flagrant contradiction with the essentially subversive nature of the actual musical material. The fragments of Schoenberg's unfinished opera *Moses und Aron* recently performed in Hamburg are a striking example of this ambiguity. In spite of all the musical innovations, the traditional 'music drama style' is faithfully respected; and it is this style which here determines the expression, the relations between music, stage and text and, in some degree, the general conception of the whole thing. Not only that, but something very similar is to be observed at the very kernel of Schoenberg's methods of composition: Theme, Exposition, Bridge Passages, alternating Tension and Relaxation—all this is to be found even in the most advanced works of Schoenberg no less than in traditional scores such as those of Brahms, for example. This is because any compositional technique consists in the minute articulation of all the material employed: any other method is almost inconceivable. Now, the only means of doing this that have been available up to now have all been matured on tonal soil; and when they are applied to non-tonal material they lead to a certain incoherency, a break in the continuity between musical form and musical matter. Schoenberg, being a master, was able to overcome this difficulty, but it is no use shutting our eyes to the fact that this internal antimony has been discernible in his style, and that the young composers of today have escaped it. For all these traditional features which, as we have seen, Schoenberg preserved with such thorough-going naïveté (cf. the twelve-note *Fourth Quartet* where certain musical figurations are modelled on those of the tonal *Kammersymphonie* No. 1) cannot so easily be transposed from one style to another. Thus, for example, the Bridge, or Transition implies modulation—passing from one harmonic plane to another. And, apart from the tonality which engenders these harmonic relationships, a 'bridge' (which no longer has anything to connect) is in danger of becoming a sort of formal reminiscence. Even the 'theme', that essential concept, can only be retained with difficulty when, thanks to the 'series', all the notes are from the very beginning equally determined and equally 'thematic': often in twelve-note compositions the themes seem like survivals from another technique. And yet, on the other hand, it is precisely these retrospective elements that, in Schoenberg's case prevent him from ever losing sight of that essential aspect of music—'composition' considered as a technique that is something more than merely arranging notes in order. Schoenberg's conservatism did not mean a failure to carry things to their logical conclusion; on the contrary, it was the result of his anxiety to protect the art of composition from being swamped by the rising tide of pre-fabricated compositional materials. And when his recent successors imagine that they can easily dispose of that antinomy which Schoenberg rightly thought should not be resolved, their methods are in danger of being short-circuited. They are in a hurry to forget what Schoenberg always respected—the exigencies of music's essential meaning and its articulation. They believe that 'preparing an assembly of notes' is the same as 'composition', provided you do away with everything that makes the difference between 'assembling' and 'composing'.   This results, of course, in compositions that are abstract in a negative sense, that is to say, empty and care-free, and in composers who turn out, one after another, with the greatest of ease, immensely complicated scores in which, when all is said and done, nothing happens at all.

This evolution began with Webern. An almost skeleton-like simplicity is what makes the last works of this disciple of Schoenberg difficult: they try to get over the antinomy by effecting a kind of synthesis, a fusion between the essence of fugue and the essence of sonata form. In this way Webern tried to adapt the language of music to the new material—the *series*. And that meant for all intents and purposes renouncing musical significance. In the last resort it meant that music has now become identified with the series: what 'happens' on the musical plane is simply what has to happen on the technical plane. Expression is saved by becoming a kind of differential.

More recently a group of composers has gone still further along these lines. Pierre Boulez, their leader, is undoubtedly a first-class musician, extremely gifted and cultivated and endowed with a vitality which makes itself felt even when he is wringing the neck, as he is determined to do, of subjectivity in any form. He and his disciples aim at eliminating from their scores the last traces of traditional idiom, and would prohibit, as arbitrary, any free and subjective initiative in the process of composition. (Inevitably, according to this theory, since the moment a musician attempts to express 'himself' he is almost bound to employ terms borrowed from some tradition or other.) In consequence Boulez and his followers seek to extend the rigours of the serial system to the metric and other aspects of composition so that, in the end, the art of composing is replaced by a system of serial arrangements which guarantee objectively and control arithmetically, from one end of a score to the other, the exact position of every sound according to pitch, and every interval and metric or dynamic value. The result is nothing more nor less than an integral rationalization (apparently without precedent) of the art of composition. But it soon becomes evident that the regularity thus imposed is completely arbitrary, and that the objectivity attained by this process is only an appearance of objectivity. For all music, as it goes along, creates structural relationships which defy these regulations. No matter how ingenious a system may be, it is never quite ingenious enough. That is because it is based on a *static* conception of music: all the exact ratios of equivalence and symmetry decreed by extreme rationalization assume that the identical (or exactly analogous) things that appear in different places in the score *are*, in fact, identical (or exactly analogous) in the same way that figures placed to the right or to the left, high up or low down in space would be in a schematic design. There is, in other words, a tacit agreement to confound the symmetrical patterns that the ear is about to hear with the symmetrical patterns that the eye can see carefully set out in space in the score. But so long as music continues to happen in time (and not space) so long will it continue to be dynamic; the fact that it is moving through time will always mean that what appears identical to the eye will appear as non-identical to the ear—just as for the same reason the ear may apprehend as identical what to the eye seems different (an abbreviated re-exposition, for example.) It is on structural relationships of this kind, imperceptible to geometry, that what has been called, in great classical or romantic music, 'musical architecture' is firmly based. The 'ultra-constructivists', however, not only dispense with this architectural concept, which is fundamental to music, but are unable, as a consequence, to prevent their constructions from being (though far from wishing it) somewhat disturbed by the temporal element they have failed to take into account. And so, as a result of wishing to control everything they lose control in the end because the dynamism inherent in music, intolerant of a too precisely regulated static order, overthrows that order or at any rate renders it inoperative in the particular sphere in which it was primarily intended to function—namely the actual unfolding of music in time.

It would seem that these experiments in integral rationalization make a strong appeal to the young of today. For they clearly spring from the current widespread antipathy to any form of 'expression' in music. On this point the most advanced apostles of 'ultra-constructivism' see eye to eye with some of their adversaries whose staunch conservatism is unquestioned: the musicological interpreters of Bach, for example, or the advocates of a certain musical 'boy-scoutism'—choral singing and recorders. The mistake here, of course, is the confusion between expression as a whole and the kind of expression associated with old-fashioned romanticism and a form of post-romanticism already out of date: a false equation, thanks to which the anti-expressive attitude is assumed to be 'modern'. Expression is punished for the misdeeds of sentimental theatricalism and, rather than be duped by sentiments masquerading as 'human', people cultivate an attitude which is authentically inhuman. That is yet another aspect, another cause of modern music's ageing: the young no longer dare to be young. The anguish and sufferings of our time have proved too much for the individual soul. The result has been repression and this anti-expressive idiosyncracy—for expression implies suffering. As an afterthought, this retreat is excused by attributing it to a striving after a 'higher spiritual state' of which the ingredients are modesty and stoicism.

However questionable the basis of this postulated 'objectivity' may be, it certainly is a symptom of a state of mind current today, and there is no doubt that this general state of mind does account for the spirit underlying constructivism run amok. Among the products of this attitude of mind there are some which possess that force of suggestion characteristic, it would seem, of everything that—however absurd the result—pursues its own internal logic to the end. And, indeed, these compositions do end by becoming absurd, being, from a musical point of view, devoid of sense: their logic and coherence are found wanting when it comes to hearing the music in performance. Of course, modern music has always revolted against the concept of music considered as a 'language': it has always aimed at being very strictly 'pure'. In a case like Schoenberg's, however, the protest itself became a kind of 'speech' in its turn—and even non-sense in a musical structure may make sense by contrast, just as music can make the absence of expression a part of its expressiveness. But with the ultra-constructivists there is nothing of the kind: their programme attributes a positive value to the absurd. Sometimes they claim to be following the teaching of a certain existentialist philosophy: what they are trying to make people hear is not subjective intentions but the Being or Essence of music. In point of fact, however, this music, owing to the very nature of the abstractions by which it is ruled, is anything rather than an archetype: on the contrary, it is (and to what an extent!) subjectively and historically conditioned. What, then, is the use of this music which, though purified to excess, can never hope to become pure essence? The means of construction, schematic lay-out and logical development are here cultivated to the point of idolatry. All this exaggerated articulation of the actual raw material of music is not inspired by any artistic aspirations; on the contrary the manipulation becomes an end in itself. The palette takes the place of the picture. In the end the rationalization of form results in an absence of form—and this may be taken as a bad sign. It results, too, in the regression of music to the pre-musical, pre-artistic stage of raw sound; it is only logical that the next step should be concrete, or electronic music. To criticize in this way a recent school of thought is not to be construed as an arbitrary refusal to go further than Schoenberg, Berg and Webern and in so doing to incur the reproach of being a crypto-reactionary. Neither in the sphere of modern music nor elsewhere is there anything to be gained by concealing things on the pretext that by revealing them one may be carrying ammunition to the enemy's camp. These reservations are not dangerous, even though they may be cited with satisfaction by those who are hostile to modern music; the real danger would be to defend, without due reflexion, tendencies which are, to say the least, problematic. Evidently it would be absurd to propose a 'return to the twenties'—quite apart from the fact that in order to 'return' to them some advance would have to have been made since, whereas in fact there has only been a regression; thirty years ago the then new music raised innumerable problems which, in the meantime, no one has seriously attempted to solve. Moreover the geological upheavals that have occurred since then are such that nobody today would yield to the temptation of re-discovering an epoch which, though in those days it may have been considered a period of crisis, seems to us today, by comparison, to have been one of idyllic calm.

Nor can the critic be reproached for not *understanding* the products of this rationalization *à outrance* because, on their own admission, this school does not want its productions to be understood; all it wants is to show how right they are, and if anyone asks 'what does it mean', the answer is to expound the system in as great detail as anyone could wish. Should we console ourselves by thinking that, as in the 17th century, the object now is to concentrate on perfecting new technical methods for

9

the use of the composers of the future who will invest them with some musical significance? This possibility is not to be rejected *a priori*, although it is not easy to believe that all our accumulated experience in aesthetic matters can be discarded so completely as to make it seem plausible that the invention 'from scratch' of the means of an art will in future precede the discovery of its end. Furthermore, such a prospect would mean that the divorce between the *means* of expression and genuine expression would be final—a state of affairs that modern music had in past years been endeavouring to circumvent. For it is sheer barbarism to separate the raw material of music from its artistic aspects.

It is time the notions of 'musical progress' and 'musical reaction' were applied to something other than the mere material of music—although it must be admitted that this material has for some time past been a vehicle for progress. The fact is, the whole idea of progress becomes meaningless when by 'composing' is understood 'concocting' or 'piecing together', when subjective freedom—an essential condition of all modern art—is exorcized, and when an artificial and tyrannical mania for integration at all costs—not, after all so very different from other forms of totalitarianism—is in complete command. This results in the production of scores which, from a technical point of view, are, so to speak, fool-proof; each bar is a demonstration that the composer is fully conscious of what must be done to ensure that his music is immune from any conceivable reproach. He is, in fact, turning out the kind of music that is set for competitions, exemplary examples. All this is governed by unwritten laws as to what is or is not permissible, and the 'watchful control' (which is certainly very necessary when one is composing) is here the only thing that matters. In consequence this music sounds as if the only human impulse it contained was the composer's fear lest some young fellow-composer might discover some note, however insignificant, that might be open to criticism on the grounds that it had not been sufficiently 'purged'. Musical logic (a notion which has always been a butt for satire) has now become a subject for caricature; its only effect is to ossify and desiccate everything with which it comes in contact. From the very first bar the listener is resigned; an infernal machine has been set in motion which will allow him no respite until its destiny has been fulfilled.

It would hardly be an exaggeration, moreover, to say that today one of the first signs of a composer being really gifted is his ability to perceive and dread the existence of a dilemma of this kind. As witness, for example, in Germany Henze and, of the generation before him, Fortner. Pierre Boulez himself has dwelt in no ambiguous terms on the real and fundamental difficulty of this question; his remarks in his article *Recherches maintenant* in the *Nouvelle Revue Française* (November 1954) remind us that there is not always and inevitably a complete correspondence and perfect parallelism between an exact subjective perception of sound as such (with which in the last resort music and its destiny are bound up) and the mathematically objective precision of its notation. And it would seem that Boulez intends to free his ultra-constructivist aesthetic from the deadly rigidity which threatens it, without however making any concession as regards the necessity of maintaining a strict discipline.

Nevertheless there are many composers of the twelve-note school who do not observe such a high standard of uncompromising severity or show such a critical spirit.

They content themselves with applying the rules of serial composition—which, by the way, are more or less apocryphal—and they also juggle with the series considered as a substitute for tonality, thereby departing considerably from what Schoenberg and his early disciples understood by this technique. This school is, indeed, something of a paradox, and would not exist if modern music had not begun to forget its own traditions.

This is because the innovators—Schoenberg, Bartók, Stravinsky, Webern, even Hindemith, and their like—all derived their formation from traditional music. Their critical attitude—their spirit of contradiction, in fact—was shaped by this music, and it was through taking this as their yardstick that they evolved their own style. Those who succeeded them no longer have this compass to steer by, and make the mistake of wishing to adopt as absolute (and with insufficient effort) principles which are only valid as a basis for criticism. For this they can hardly be blamed. For the teaching they have received in the conservatories and academies is, with few exceptions, highly conventional and unlikely to make them capable of judging, even on technical grounds, what a modern score is worth and what it is aiming at. Consequently, in these matters they accept some 'impressive' work as being authoritative, and follow its example, although lacking the necessary experience which would enable them to be sure whether, by so doing, they have really grasped the true significance of their model, or whether they are merely contenting themselves with copying its external features and adopting its technique in too much of a hurry. This technique may be perfectly suited to the original work, but much less so at second hand.

Many so-called professional musicians do not even attempt to follow the new movement, and the critics are not to be relied on. Composers and critics rarely function on the same plane. Indeed the latter are even more incapable than the majority of professional musicians when it comes to judging whether some rather 'advanced' new work is really viable and assessing its strength, form and class. What musical criticism usually provides us with is a more or less competent 'reportage' on the degree of pleasure or the reverse with which a work may be listened to, its origin, the general impression it created, its stylistic tendencies and the personality of its author. Having said so much, the critic generally refrains from expressing a considered opinion. Some even would seek to invest the limitations of their own personal powers of comprehension with the sanctity of an aesthetic law, denouncing everything they cannot understand as abstract music, intellectual experiments or mere exercises. Others are more inclined to judge a work from the historian's rather than the musician's point of view. Others, again, abound in clichés concerning the moral duty of making music accessible to the masses—whereas in the world today one may seek in vain for a community that has any claim to be considered worthy of having music specifically composed for its benefit. But there is a certain kind of critic whose lack of comprehension is more than compensated by his fear of failing to note the appearance of a new genius. These are the ones who lavish their praises on anything that might—one never knows—turn out to 'be something'. All this

11

makes a fine mess of musical culture. And there is a horrible tendency today to take as a model a kind of 'moderate modernity'; any sort of bilaterally lame compromise between innovation and tradition is recommended; people get accustomed to modern dissonances as they do to drugs which soon lose their potency; and almost everyone forgets that, whereas traditional music might, in all innocence, make use of familiar material, the 'uniqueness' of a work and the refusal to hark back to it again is a law that modern music ought to have imposed upon itself in the process of freeing itself from pre-established forms. Apart from the ultra-constructivist school, most composers are content to go on producing works modelled on prototypes created by a Bartók, a Stravinsky or a Hindemith. They forget that in future no type of composition is expected to be a 'proto' for the purposes of mass production, and that what is more important is to create new types, or rather new characters.

Furthermore, modern techniques that have got out of hand and old techniques that have lost their significance now combine to form a kind of decadent syntax that results in works having a quasi-literary flavour, if only on account of that form of irony, as futile as it is facile, which has become one of their principal ingredients. But this pseudo-intelligent music, made up of knowing winks and shreds of past traditions, shallow and even technically inadequate, is in no way superior to the elucubrations of the serial engineers. It is therefore all the easier to produce and get performed.

The symptoms of the ageing of modern music are, sociologically, the reduction of freedom and the disintegration of the individual, which are accepted, endorsed and copied in private life by people who have lost their sense of direction and their individuality. In this respect the 'advanced' school, who are wholly concerned with 'pure material' and enthusiastically bent on doing away with anything that might suggest the presence of a composer, are tarred with the same brush as those who seek the shelter of decaying traditions or cling to the illusion, so dear to weak or timid characters, that they are cultivating an impersonal classicism. The truth is that no one feels capable of being daring or of taking a risk; they are all playing for safety. The brutal measures current under totalitarian régimes, where music is muzzled and any 'deviation' looked upon as decadent and subversive—these measures reflect, in a cruder form, what is happening more gradually and more subtly in other countries, as well as what is happening in the art itself and in the attitude of most people towards it.

This, unhappily, is the position today, and it would be folly to look for someone or something to take the blame for it. It is nevertheless a fact to be reckoned with that the gulf between music and public is so wide today as to threaten the very existence of those artists who refuse to abdicate. Everything combines to force them to make concessions which must inevitably be in vain owing to the nature of the trouble with which they have to contend. Life was already difficult for a Berg or a Webern, and if they were able to hold out, that was only because the Austria of their day was behind the times and even, in some respects, pre-capitalist, so that it was possible now and again to make a living out of values which were not quoted on the market. But the premature death of Alban Berg was not only a calamity but a scandal, since it could probably have been avoided had he been able to afford proper medical attention.

Unless one is content to sit back and look upon the ageing of modern music as something merely to be noted on the intellectual plane, its symptoms must be considered as a sign of actual human suffering—not the least serious aspect of which is the fact that, as Theodore Haecker has pointed out, from now on human beings will no longer have the right themselves to express or describe their own condition. Today it is impossible to conceive how a Webern or a Berg could possibly find a corner for themselves to winter in. If any musicians of their sort were alive now they would have either to 'play the game' and come to some sort of agreement with the principles that reign supreme, or else, at least, put themselves at the head of some doubtful league or sect; in other words, they would in any case have to toe the line and subscribe to some questionable form of collectivism.

The paralysis afflicting music today is a reflexion of the paralysis that inhibits all free initiative in a world gone administration-mad and intolerant of anything determined to remain outside that world or unwilling even to be integrated therein to the extent of forming part of the 'authorized opposition'. All this must be understood clearly and unambiguously if there is to be any chance of improvement—a slender chance, it must be admitted, because the very foundations of all art, not only of music, are tottering. It is by no means certain that matters appertaining to aesthetics can still be taken seriously. Ever since the European catastrophe culture has been vegetating like one of those buildings you see in a town that has been bombed, still standing up or patched up anyhow. Nobody really believes in it any more; peoples' minds are crippled and spineless, and if we fail to notice this and carry on as if nothing had happened, that means we are willing to crawl while pretending to walk upright. What works today could be considered authentic unless they reflect intense fear? And who, short of being a Schoenberg or a Picasso, feels genuinely strong enough to undertake such works?

And yet can we be sure that the artists who, through a sense of responsibility, may thus choose the path of renunciation and silence would still not be yielding to an insidious temptation—the temptation to conform—in the sense that to give up creative work would be equivalent to conforming to the present universal tendency to accept things as they are and make no attempt to break away. All the arts today, even if they feign innocence, have a bad conscience, as is inevitable. But that is no justification for their giving up the struggle. For in the world we live in there are always things for which art is the only remedy; there is always a contradiction between *what is* and *what is true*, between arrangements for living and humanity. Only he who has the courage to recognize that the art which the mind demands (and society too, in the last resort) must today be produced in a solitude from which there is no escape will find again, through his work as an artist, the strength to resist these tendencies. And this task must be performed spontaneously, and no illusions must be entertained as to its being either necessary or legitimate; then, perhaps, something better will be achieved than a mere mirror held up to isolation and disorder.

(Translated from the French
by Rollo H. Myers)

Patricia Carpenter, *The musical object**

I   (Music as object and music as process)

It is my concern here to focus attention on the quite ordinary notion of "a piece" of music. Usually when we speak of music today, we make (perhaps implicitly) what seems to me an interesting distinction between "music" and "a piece" of that music. It is this distinction and some of its consequences which I shall explore.

In the narrow sense, I shall take "a piece" to represent a particular way of conceiving musical form, which has been characteristic in the mainstream of the modern Western tradition. This might be compared, perhaps, to the way a painting in this tradition has been conceived as a piece of three-dimensional visual space, articulated upon a plane by clear relations between objects and calculated to be seen from a single point of view, i.e., in the manner of classical perspective. I think the chronological limits for this conception of form in the two modes of perception roughly coincide—from about 1420–30 to about 1910.[1]

I raise the problem of "a piece" in this sense for two reasons: whereas the kind of form to which this notion gives rise has seemed eminently natural to the mode of vision, it is difficult to see how it can be constructed for and grasped by the ear. What kind of a piece can be made out of so incorporeal a stuff as music? Secondly, many of the current controversies over musical form are rooted, I believe, in the assumption of this particular kind of form as an ideal, a norm that has been identified, in music as in other arts, with High Art. The self-conscious notion of the musical work and the cultivation of autonomous musical form both arose in connection with an early culmination of this formal ideal during the 16th century. Today this model of form is called into question. Current controversies concerning musical form reflect in a specialized way the change in conception of 'form' in general. But form is an aspect of object. And such controversies are complicated by a more deep-seated change in the conception of 'object' itself. They are interesting because they bring to light tensions between old and new ways of conceiving, and hence, of perceiving, the world.

Consider two examples which reflect two very different conceptions of the nature of music. One is a piece, in the narrow sense in which I have taken this notion; one is not.

Ionization, by Edgard Varèse, is an exploration of a new kind of musical

---

* A revised version of a paper presented at a joint meeting of the Greater New York and Princeton chapters of the American Musicological Society at Princeton, January 7, 1967.

matter. He considered music to be not so much the organization of tone as of all sound. Nevertheless, however revolutionary its stuff, this piece presents me with a familiar model of form: I grasp its shape much as I do the first movement of a symphony by Mozart, as a single unified gesture or motion— an introduction, first and second ideas, climax and release, coda. Or, in the terms by which Aristotle characterized the movement or plot of a tragedy, I follow a beginning, middle, and end. By way of contrast, music such as John Cage's *Variations for Orchestra and Dance* cannot be comprehended in this way. Cage is also interested in expanding the stuff of music. "If this word 'music'", he says, "is sacred and reserved for 18th- and 19th-century instruments, we can substitute a more meaningful term: organization of sound." But his set of variations, however familiar its title, is not, in fact, "a piece" (except perhaps in the sense that a Chinese painting, by serving as a sort of window, cuts out "a piece" of the endlessly extended visual world). In his notes for the performance of the *Variations*, Cage writes: "In recent years my musical ideas have continued to move away from object (a composition having a well-defined relationship of parts) into process (nonstructured activities, indeterminate in character)." To approach such pieces as objects, he says, is to miss the point utterly. They are, rather, "occasions for experience".

Although these two examples are eccentric, they illustrate very well two different—and I take them as polar—ways in which music can be said to be: as object and as process. A piece of music is, first of all, music conceived as an object. Any form is an entity; a piece of music is musical form highly stylized toward wholeness. The most obvious differences between these two examples involve those aspects of a work which we ordinarily class as "form"— features of the overall structure of the whole. The two examples illustrate differences between an articulated and a diffuse structure. Whereas the Cage is a random flow of musical happenings, the Varèse is tightly organized. It has clear relations of part to part and of parts to whole; its parts are highly articulated within the whole. Music thus conceived as object invites us by its clear overall structure to step back and look at its "objective" aspect, i.e., its form.

The difference in the degree to which these two examples are in fact objects entails another difference—a difference in the distance from which we experience the music. In order to hear Varèse's piece, I do indeed "step back", as it were, and its familiar formal structure helps me to place it as something I recognize, over there. Cage, on the contrary, seems to draw me into the musical process, as if he were concerned to break down the distance between the music and the listening subject, to obliterate the "otherness" of the musical object.

There is a fundamental difference between music in which one stands at the center and music to which one is "spectator". In a sense, Cage reverses a procedure which seems to have been self-consciously carried out during the early development of the autonomous musical work, that of placing it *there*, at a distance. The deliberate exploitation of physical space in music, as in Venice and Rome at the outset of the Baroque era, has the effect of specifically locating a piece of music in relation to the external world. The achievement of this fundamental requirement for objectivity (i.e., distance) can be seen, for example, in that exemplar of the autonomous piece, the fugue. I suggest that one of the primary differences between the so-called precursors of fugue (a ricercar of Adriano Willaert, for instance) and the fugue as it culminates in the works of Sebastian Bach is the distance from which we listen. The ricercar was written primarily for performance; the listener, as performer, participates to produce the whole from within the piece. The scale by which he listens is quite small; he follows best near-reaching relations of "texture". The piece is most satisfactorily grasped at the level of moment-to-moment unfolding of an activity. But the performer of the fugue presents a musical object intended for contemplation by someone who is removed and listening, someone who grasps more far-reaching relations of structure in his confrontation of the piece as a whole.

As in the examples of Cage and Varèse, structural differences between the pieces of Willaert and Bach illustrate, respectively, differences between a diffuse and articulated kind of construction. But there are further corresponding differences concerning distance. In respect of the functional relation within the musical situation between hearing subject and object heard, the music of Cage and Willaert might be said to be syncretic, as compared to that of Varèse and Bach, in the extent to which the relation between subject and object is fused.

In regarding a musical object, we can consider not only the mode of its construction and the manner in which it asks to be heard, but also other aspects of the heard thing—for example, ways in which it is related to space and time. For instance, the factor of distance dictates a difference in the space that music shapes and fills. Although the increasing hierarchization of the musical space by means of tonality is an important feature of the development from ricercar to fugue, the two contemporary examples, which use not tone but sound, still present two very different kinds of musical space. Varèse speaks of the spatiality of sound and molds it as if it were a very solid, palpable matter. Cage, on the contrary, exploits the most fundamental properties of the mode of hearing. He deliberately breaks down any sense of corporality or external spatiality and constructs—or better, induces—what has been described as an "acoustic" space. Time, consequently, is made manifest in two very different ways. Varèse shapes a single stretch of time which is outlined, framed, and conceived as one motion. Not so Cage, for whom there is no causality, no necessity—with respect to the sounds themselves, which are randomly produced, or with respect to their order, brought about by the improvisatory movements of dancers and sound engineers. Time is something that simply happens. Hence, there is no unity of content, no musical idea that is stated, developed, and summarized, as in the Varèse. Cage is not constructing the kind of musical discourse which has served as a model for familiar musical form from, say, the fugue of Bach, to the present day.

Early in the modern era, Johann Gottfried Walther aptly described what has happened to music in the Western world: the word 'musica', he says in his definition, has gone through a change in its usage from adjective to substantive (*Musicalisches Lexicon oder Musicalische Bibliothec*, Leipzig, 1732). A piece of music, in the narrow sense of musical form highly stylized toward objectivity, has been achieved by an application of wholeness on increasingly far-reaching levels, an increasing unification of the musical object in respect of both form and content. Composer and listener alike have learned, over greater spans of time, to keep a musical form present as a whole and cogent as a whole.

In the broadest sense, a piece of music is something like what the philosopher, Edmund Husserl, had in mind when he used music as a demonstration of our subjective consciousness of time. The first note of a piece of music, he says, is not over until the last has ceased to sound.[2] At the least, that is to say, the idea of a piece of music carries the requirement of some kind of wholeness. Indeed, it is a remarkable representation of wholeness, not only in the perception of music but also in the realm of perception in general. The basic fact about a piece of music is that the object heard is never actually there; yet actually, in our mode of hearing music strikingly tends toward wholeness, toward Gestalt. For this reason, the kind of hearing demanded by modern Western music has been called "antilogical perception", for it requires the ability to grasp the nonsimultaneous as simultaneous.[3] The apprehension of a melody demonstrates a paradox of simultaneity in successiveness. A melody, like a swing of my hand, for example, can be understood as made up of a series of instants or moments—in the case of the gesture, an infinite number of motionless hand stages; in the case of the melody, moments articulated, perhaps, by tones—each moment to the right of, or later than, the last. Yet the melody, like the gesture, is perceived as a single motion.

Now problems posed by the melody—or by the physical motion—are in miniature the most fundamental problems presented by the notion of a piece of music. These are problems concerning our apprehension of time itself, problems concerning continuity in change and a piece of time grasped as an entity. These problems are not new to the contemporary world. Zeno's ancient paradox of the arrow, for instance, presents the problem of continuity of motion. Augustine, concerned with time as perceived in the course of a poem, wrestles with the problem of a moment—a time-point *now* which has no extension. Aristoxenus of Tarentum placed the problem within the realm of music: we hear music simultaneously both as it is occurring and as it has occurred. Music owes its effect, he said, to the fact that in it there is not only a pure temporal becoming but also a spatial being. In the West, it would seem, it is these stable elements of "spatial being" which we have increasingly emphasized, until today a melody has become the paradigm for perceptual

17

form in general. The paradoxical nature of a melody focused, at the beginning of this century, a revision of old notions of perception away from the model of an entity as a bundle of sensations and associations, toward the recognition of the primacy in our perception of wholeness—of qualities and of structures belonging only to wholes. In contemporary theory of form, a melody is a model for a perceived object, a Gestalt, and for an object of a rather curious kind—a so-called "temporal object". A melody is an object in the sense of pure form (it can be moved from place to place within the pitch-space, and yet remain constantly itself); and it is an entity which is grasped as a whole (it is more than its successive parts); but it also includes temporal extension in its very nature (it is a shaped course of time). A melody is the simplest sort of a piece of music.[4]

But the very notion of a piece, applied to music, is somewhat paradoxical, for a "piece" is a loose or separated part or fragment—a portion of something, as it were, taken from or added to a concrete whole. If we piece something together, we make an aggregate, not a true whole. Yet a piece of art, of literature, of music may be taken to be an organism in the sense that to remove any one of its members is to deform it.

Therefore, I shall take the position that the notion of a piece of music is not really so ordinary an idea, but, on the contrary, rather extraordinary, emerging quite locally in the Western tradition and developing in a spectacular fashion during the past two centuries. There are musics which are primarily sheer process—unfixed expression, motor participation, magical incantation—but these are musics less differentiated than ours. In the West, music is microcosm, discourse, architectonic construction. A piece of music is finished work, *opus perfectum et absolutum*, a product brought to completion and detached, as it were, from the loom. Most music of the world is not primarily perceptual form, i.e., something to be listened to; our music is. In our central Western tradition, music has been gradually but steadily pried loose from its surrounding world of activity. And it is this process of differentiation that I want to investigate here.

Briefly, the gradual emergence of the piece of music might be described in two stages, as the transformation of music from process to product (*res facta*, a made thing) and from product to poem (in the modern sense of the word, a created thing). The self-conscious notion of the piece of music arises late, as compared to that of the poem, say, or drama. The new idea emerges in the humanistic climate of the 16th century and shows itself specifically in a new concern for the musical work. The phrase *opus perfectum et absolutum*, for instance, first appears in a textbook written by Nikolaus Listenius[5] in the 1530's in connection with the reformation of the schools in Germany. But the emphasis on the musical work was only a symptom of a striking change in attitude toward the nature and function of music itself. There is a cluster of new notions around this idea: for example, a new attention to the notated, published composition, which now stands independent both of practice and of its maker; a new role taken by the maker, who is now not only builder but also creator; concern for a new kind of expressivity in music; and a new significance given to the act of musical creation itself as a bringing-forth rather than a letting-be. The background for the work of art in music, as in the other arts, is the transformation of skill to expression, of know-how to genius, of *ars* to Art—i.e., the change in the conception of creation from sacred to secular.[6]

I am not concerned here with tracing the historical background of a piece of music except insofar as it illuminates the problems of form peculiar to this kind of music, problems of a thoroughly composed work, fixed with respect to substance and fixed with respect to form. Nevertheless, I do want to question our very conception of "a piece". The contraction of our contemporary world affords us insight into the extent to which different people and different cultures (and historians must add, different eras) differently conceive, structure, and constitute their worlds. For the sake of exploration, then, consider briefly some of the peculiarities of our Western habits of thought, for example, the kind of thinking that leads to the notion of "a piece".

II   (Object as entity)

'Piece' is an interesting sort of a noun. It has been maintained that the language (like the music) of a people reflects their reality. And nouns like 'piece' are not found in all languages. Indeed, such nouns are strikingly characteristic of the group of languages sometimes called Standard Average European. Let me spend a few moments on what kind of an object such a noun denotes, for such objects presumably are not found in all worlds.

Our Western way of speaking shows a striking tendency to objectify and spatialize things. A comparison made by Benjamin Lee Whorf of differences in structure embedded in the language of the Hopi Indians and Standard Average European brings to light very different fundamental conceptions of the world—especially of matter, space, and time—which point up our Western inclination toward objectification.[7]

We objectify many things which Whorf calls "imaginary" entities. For example, we objectify multiplicities. We use plurals not only for actual aggregates that can be given all at once (such as ten men) but also for "imaginary" aggregates (such as ten days). The Hopi does not use plurals in the latter case but would say, rather, "until the eleventh day" or "after the tenth day". In a similar way, we objectify phases of cycles. We treat nouns like 'summer', 'morning', 'hour' in much the same way as other nouns; we can say "at sunset", like "at the corner" or "in the orchard". In Hopi, phase terms are not nouns, but a kind of adverb, rather like "when it is morning" or "while morning-phase is occurring". This tendency to spatialize time is reflected in our language in other ways, as for instance, in our three-tense system of verbal forms, by which we are able to stand time units in a row, so to speak, in our imagination; and also in our widespread use of spatial metaphors in speaking of durations, intensities, and tendencies. (We use such words as 'long', 'short', 'heavy', 'light', 'high', 'low', 'rise, 'fall'.) The Hopi never speaks of space unless the space involved is actually there. But he has, on the other hand, a huge class of words denoting only intensities and strengths, how they vary, their rate of change, and so forth—ways of describing process and events so subtle and abstract that it is often difficult for us to follow him. We objectify even time itself. We speak of *a* time, a moment of time, a second, a year of time, like a bottle of milk or a piece of cheese. In Hopi, nothing is suggested about time except the perpetual "getting later" of it.

But "a piece" of time is merely an instance of yet another peculiarity of our language: our nouns of physical quantity. Whorf distinguishes two sorts of nouns in our way of speaking: individual nouns denoting discrete bodies with definite outlines (such as a tree, a stick, a man) and mass nouns (such as 'water', 'flour', 'wood', 'granite'). Mass nouns denote homogeneous continua without implied boundaries. Where it is desirable to indicate boundaries for a mass noun, we do so by such phrases as 'a pane of glass', 'a cup of coffee', 'a piece of soap', i.e., by a combination of a term for container or body-type with one for contents or matter. Hopi nouns, by contrast, always have an individual sense, even though the boundaries of some objects are vague or indefinite.

Our manner of speaking paves the way, Whorf thinks, for our notion of the world as a combination of form and substance (a notion, incidentally, which much of 20th-century thought has been engaged in refuting). In our Western way of speaking, we seem to assume a reality fundamentally made up of objects that persist and are recognizable through time. Our sentences can speak of subjects taking an action or of subjects to which qualities are attributed, but in both cases the subject is made of some sort of substance that endures. Even when the subject is not an object in this sense—for example, an event—we speak of it as if it were. Thus, as one commentator puts it, a mechanic will talk of fixing the timing on a car in much the same terms that he uses in speaking of fixing the tire, even though the timing is simply a relation of events, whereas the tire is a thing. Perhaps this is simply a metaphorical manner of speaking, but the metaphor proceeds via the conception of a stable physical object. A piece of music is like the timing on a car; it has been objectified.

Now there are many kinds of objects—material, immaterial, real, unreal, things, thoughts, events, states of mind. But however an object is constituted, there are three minimal requirements for its objectness. An object is, first of all, an other, not I; I grasp it as a part of that world which I encounter as there, not here. Also it is an entity: anything to be perceived at all must be perceived as a whole or a part of a whole, as something, for perception is fundamentally an act of integration. And finally, because perception also involves an act of categorization, an object is a certain kind of a thing: I grasp it as some kind of an identity which persists as a recognizable part of my world.

In a specific sense, we have been accustomed to distinguish object from process or event. Several sensations received simultaneously represent our idea of an object; received successively, of an event. Now this is not, in fact, so simple a distinction to make, because "simultaneity" is not a simple notion. Nevertheless, a piece of music is, of course, an event. Its connections are laid out in time; they come to pass and die away. But it is not sheer process, sheer succession; it is *an* event, *a* succession. Like discourse, a piece of music takes time to disclose its meaning; yet it can be comprehended in a single act of the imagination. Like a melody, a piece can be made to be a single image, which I grasp not only as a successive, but also as a simultaneous, whole.

Such a piece is exemplified by the Prelude in B minor, No. 24, from Bach's *Well-tempered Clavier*, Book I. What I hear first is an instrumental sound— a piece of *keyboard* music. And it sounds "baroque": I am immediately

Ex. 1 J.S. Bach, *WTC I*, Prelude 24.

struck by a familiar kind of continuity, the sense of "ongoingness" given by the walking bass. I am listening to a performance for harpsichord, so the single sounds are discrete and non legato, "atomistic". Yet the materials I hear are lines—two lines—although there is, in fact, no melody in the common sense of a singable line. In the left hand I hear a scale passage, part of the habitual vocabulary of any continuo player, a keyboard cliché; and in the right hand, a contrapuntal cliché, a duo of fourth-species suspension figures. But *as a whole* the piece is shaped like a melody. It moves like a melody—strongly anchored between points of tension and rest, exploiting the possibilities for pattern inherent in the musical system it manifests. I follow and grasp a single, continuous motion. The two lines never stop at the same time except at the half-cadence, which marks "antecedent" and "consequent" phrases. The momentum builds up relentlessly, through the knotted-up climax of sequences to its release at the final cadence. In its overall structure the entire piece is a "melody"-shape, even though it is made out of an "instrumental" kind of stuff—a two-strand line polarized into right- and left-hand material. At this most primitive level of form—i.e., of sheer sound *quality*—I grasp first this particular kind of texture. At ground, it is this texture which Bach has manipulated and I recognize this Prelude first as a certain kind of a musical object, made out of this kind of sound.

Consider the musical object. Musical hearing deals with what has been called a "pure" sensation, disembodied from its sounding source, which functions more like thought than like a thing. Nonetheless, a piece of music is something grasped, something encountered outside myself. There is a space between it and me: it is something that can somehow be laid hold of. And there is a relation between it and me: I bear on it and it also bears on me. A piece of music has an identity of its own. It is something fixed and embodied, which exists in its own right, past the death of its maker. It is a made thing—*res facta*, to use the 15th-century term which distinguished it from improvisation—notated and preserved like any poem or drama and meant to be heard and reheard. It is available for contemplation and analysis. As I learn to know it, I know it as a thing, quite apart from any single experience of it. I can "walk around it", so to speak, and am very much aware of its "other side". And if I know it well, I certainly know what it "looks like" as a whole, as if from a single point of view. Yet like any object, a piece of music is inexhaustible. My perception of it is never limited to a single aspect—for example, to one moment of creation or one unrepeatable performance. A piece of music is not sheer act of music-making, but a musical "thing", with its own depth, solidity, and volume. It is "räumlich"—and I borrow the sense of the word from Paul Klee—in that it is related to physical, intellectual, and imaginative concepts of space as well as of time.

And finally, a piece of music corresponds to something I recognize. Just as I cannot see a chair, a man, the letter A, without some sort of schema into which it fits, so also I cannot hear a piece of music that is not part of my world. In this regard, the importance of the great formal types of musical organization developed in our tradition cannot be discounted, for they serve as perceptual categories. They establish certain recognizable musical events which aid thus in the comprehension of a total form. If, for example, a "literate" listener should come in in the middle of a sonata, he knows where he is, where within the whole he is located. In some degree this can be said as well of a fugue after Bach. This kind of wholeness is one of structure.

But there is another kind of wholeness by which we recognize a sonata-sound or fugue-sound from the first few notes, just as we recognize a piece for keyboard, a baroque piece, a piece by Bach. We recognize a specific kind of an entity immediately and intuitively, for what it is. This, I should say, is the most primitive level of wholeness—on the level of sheer sound. Rather than a structure which is comprehended as a whole, this is a total, global quality, i.e., a quality of substance that pervades the whole. These two extremes of wholeness—a pervading quality of the whole or a well-articulated structure—delimit a continuum along which many kinds of musical wholes may lie.

The problems, then, of fashioning a piece of music have to do with wholeness and are twofold: those of any temporal Gestalt, and those of a sheerly musical nature.

The first are problems of connecting, grouping, and binding together a shape given only gradually in time. To make "*an* event", I must first of all give it an outline, so that it is finished, framed, somehow set apart; so that it has a shape and is indeed "a piece" within the course of time. This is the problem of temporal art in general: the integration of successive stimuli.

But strictly speaking, a piece of music is not just any happening or experience. It is isolated as to modality of perception; it is a part of a differentiated perceptual field, in this case, the auditory field; it is something to be listened to. If then, a piece of music is a piece of time, as is sometimes said, it is heard time, objectified time, not my own, subjective, lived time.

The specific problems of making and grasping a piece of *music* do ultimately lie in the stuff itself and have to do not so much with differences between a statically given structure and dynamic, unfolding process, as with the peculiar nature of musical objectivity, with difficulties that arise in trying to fix music and give it body. For the notion of a "piece", as we have seen, is modeled after the notion of a thing. But sound is notoriously evanescent, fragile, and intangible. The musical object is indeed *there*, something encountered, but it is easily internalized, difficult to keep at a distance and in self-repose. A piece of music presupposes, even before the attempt to create a shape in time, a step back, away from the stuff, so that its substance is clearly distinguished from my own mood, phantasy, feeling, activity. The ultimate problem of the musical work of art lies toward the negative side of autonomy, toward distance and isolation. It is not so much to free music from words, representation, or function, as to free it from ourselves, to externalize it. The musical object must not only be made whole, but also given body, located at a distance and kept there. It must be "spatialized", so to speak. The problem of musical form conceived as a piece is the making of the musical *thing*.

III   (The object as distanced)

When we speak of music as "a piece", then, we assume for it a particular mode of existence: it is an object, and an object of a certain kind. We assume that some kind of a form has been imposed upon an indefinitely extending substance, that is, upon music. Such a form, at a highly developed level, might represent a familiar formal type, such as a fugue or a sonata. But at the least, such a form is a limit, a boundary, an outline—some kind of a container, like a frame. For example, the early centuries of our history of music show progressive achievements in the fixing of sound, but they might be seen as well as steps in isolating and framing a piece of sound.

Now to conceive of reality in terms of form and substance, I have emphasized, is to construe it in the model of a thing, a stable physical object, which we step away from and view from without. This dichotomy is especially uncomfortable in regard to music, chiefly because its substance seems so intangible and so immediate. Precisely for this reason, I suggest, the dichotomy of form and substance has been important in music as it has come to exist in our Western world—as work of art.

True, an essential feature of the art work is the inseparability of form and substance. Nevertheless, the condition for Art is the articulation of form through a specific medium. And further, artistic form is not the result of internal forces that shape the thing, but, by definition, a form imposed upon the substance from without by its maker, whose mark the object bears. Thus, although the work of art does not exist in the world of things but in a realm of its own, the first step toward the art work is the step back, which distances it.

The notion of the work of art, in the sense of an object created for itself, is quite unique to our modern Western world, developing chiefly during the 18th century. It was Immanuel Kant, at the end of that century, who emphasized the requirement of distance for the work of art, that it must exist in another, the aesthetic, realm, isolated from the demands of both doing and knowing. The technical means by which the art object has been set apart in a spiritual space of its own, in the modern world, are collected under the idea of *Beauty*. Such an object is made to be clearly an image, not real: framing subdues the context of reality, idealizing the content removes it from reality, and concentration and intensification lift it out of the real world.[8]

Music by its very nature seems extraordinarily "distanced" in this regard; its ties to reality seem remote. But any particular piece may be more or less framed, isolated, idealized, concentrated, intensified. Bach's B minor Prelude, for example, is probably not a work of art in our modern sense; it was written for teaching purposes. Nevertheless, it illustrates certain means for achieving distance analogous to those which have been applied in literature or painting. It is a single, serious action, shaped as one intensely directed motion, clearly defined as to beginning, middle, and end, and unified as to content. The whole is an expansion of a single musical idea stated in the first measure—which is a remarkable sort of a "beginning": a precisely symmetrical division of the octave of the key, by scalar tetrachords in the left hand and fourths in the right—a motion left closed and without a leading-tone, stable, yet strongly impelled forward by the suspension formulae. This idea is thoroughly worked out in the middle and brought to resolution and summary in a perfectly placed climax.

Now this kind of a shape is self-consciously modeled after a conception of "good" rhetorical or dramatic form and has prevailed during the time, in our tradition, when music has been conceived as a kind of language—i.e., from about 1680 to about 1880. A piece of music became, according to this model, expressive discourse, a poem. But in a more general sense, our entire tradition of music in the West has been engaged in setting apart the musical object, in stabilizing the musical process into product. The means by which a physical object has been thus distanced, in order to exist for its own sake, is that which our culture has traditionally applied to the object of thought, i.e., *theoria*, contemplation. This is an ancient image: if life is compared to a fair, for example, in which some strive, while some are spectators, it is the philosopher who is contemplator and, in this fundamental sense, theorist. Objectivity in our music, too, has been achieved by heightening the traditional distinction between doing and knowing and, thereby, between the knower and the known.

To a child, for instance, or to a man who lives in a world more primitive than ours, music is primarily activity, something to do. In such a world, reality is organized in a syncretic manner; i.e., ideas, feelings, actions, objects are undifferentiated in a functional sense. The interaction between subject and world is more fused, more immediate. Experience is a sort of continuum, in which time and space exist in a more or less undifferentiated manner: space is a structure embedded in concrete activity, a space-of-action; time is a moment, a salient event in the concrete flow of action. Things are perceived differently than in our world: they do not stand out there, discrete and fixed in meaning with respect to the knowing subject. Things in that world are intrinsically part of the whole situation, which is itself essentially dynamic. Objects are things-of-action, signal-things—i.e., known and recognized by their functional and pragmatic character. A thing is, first of all, what you can do with it. A stick, for example, may be something to hit with, something to reach for something with, something to be held like a doll, or ridden like a horse.

In such a world, music, too, is embedded in the immediate, concrete, dynamic situation, deeply bound up with the activity of life. A free sound or a fragment of tune may be something to play with; a hypnotic chant or beat may be something to be used—to activate a magic connection between inner and outer, for instance, or to help sustain an effort. But primarily music is something to be responded to. To the infant, sound is one of the most primitive stimuli for the "startle" response. One of his strongest impulses is to kick in response to sound; and a motor response of the whole body cannot ordinarily be inhibited until adolescence. An interesting point has been made in this regard: that being musical is nothing else than being master of one's own transport under the influence of tones.[9]

The Western tradition, however, in even its earliest images of music, has shown an inclination to distance it—to rationalize, and hence to objectify, it. The West has placed music on the side of the mind—towards *logos*, knowledge, education, communication, expression. Western music calls on memory, retention, expectation. For us, music is primarily something to be learned, taught, achieved, accomplished, created. In the mainstream of our culture, the various conceptions of music reflect a progressive transformation of the nature of music from activity to object. In Antiquity, *mousikē* qualified a certain kind of activity, a certain know-how, a skilled way of making. The broad sphere of the Muses originally embraced a part of the arts of production, of *poesis*: those of the arts which produce not things, but images. As our tradition increasingly separated the acts of making and doing from that of knowing, music, too, was conceived as knowledge (in the broader sense of *scientia*) as opposed to its practice. But in our modern world music is no longer primarily either a certain kind of activity or a kind of knowledge, but a work of art. The piece of music, in this context, arose between the two realms of theory and practice—in the area of *poetica*, now reinterpreted as the production of real, not ideal, things. The modern world is concerned with the concrete, perceived musical form—with the actual realization before our eyes, so to speak, of a heard movement in space and time, here and now. In our contemporary way of thinking, a piece of music is a specific kind of an object, a made thing, a stylistically made thing, and ultimately, an object made for its own sake, a form of being-in-itself. On this view, "music", then, becomes the total collection of all its pieces, the imaginary museum of musical works.

Now I have sketched a picture of the gradual differentiation in our musical culture of a musical object in order to bring to bear on it principles of a more general nature having to do with perception. For that process of differentiation presents a rather remarkable resemblance, it seems to me, to the development in the growing child of a consciousness of an objective world, i.e., of his gradual reorganization, reconstruction, and transformation of experience itself. One might say that we have reconstructed the musical experience, learning to make and to grasp a musical object in something like the way the child learns to distance and comprehend the world around him. It is fruitful to look at the emergence of the musical object by analogy to genetic development—i.e., as an increasing differentiation of parts of the organism, on the one hand, and as an increasing hierarchization and subordination of the parts to the whole, on the other—because the analogy illuminates in a broad way perceptual problems that this particular kind of form presents in music. A piece of music, in this sense of music that has been highly stylized toward objectivity, exploits to a remarkable degree the principles of so-called "good" Gestalt, e.g., centering, regularity, smooth continuation, and the like.[10]

But as I have pointed out, a well-articulated structure is only one pole of wholeness in music. Characteristics of a more primitive kind of form are described by Heinz Werner in a study of some of the fundamental changes that come about through a primitivation of a given pattern.[11] Children of kindergarten age who were asked to reproduce a given pattern (either auditory or visual) showed a striking tendency toward leveling and closure, which results in two sorts of diffuse, nonhierarchical form: they produced, on the one hand, a radically homogeneous, global type of representation, with strong emphasis on qualities-of-the-whole (for example, figures made more uniform and indivisible, open figures closed, parts made alike and symmetrical, directions simplified) and on the other, a chain type of structure, characterized by a relative lack of definiteness in the relation of the parts (occasioned by the fact that these parts are experienced as multiple global units and not conceived as figurally related and strictly centralized). Kurt Koffka summarized the diffuse way in which the child shapes his world: because his categories are so highly dynamic, he can integrate into one sphere of being and happening things which have nothing in common except that they are

26

continuous in space and time. Children use juxtaposition, whereas adults use integration. Although syncretism, he says, means a firm cohesion of parts, the parts articulate very poorly with one another.[12]

Two criteria are helpful in a study of the musical object, as they have been in genetic psychology in regard to objects in general—the polar concepts of syncretic as opposed to discrete and of diffuse as opposed to articulated.[13] These concepts served as a framework for the earlier comparison of a highly articulated, distanced work by Varèse and a musical process, diffusely put together by Cage.

The first polarity describes a functional development in the relation of subject and object from a high degree of fusion to separation of ego and world— or, in regard to the musical work, from intense participation of the subject to extreme isolation of the musical object. This raises the question of the so-called "optimum distance" at which an art object should be contemplated in order best to be seen; for each such object dictates its own distance (the single point of view demanded by classical perspective is an exaggerated case of this). Further, to view the musical whole from a distance entails a progressive unification of the over-all field, or space.

The second polarity describes a development in structure from the diffuse kind of composition described above by Werner and Koffka to one in which the parts are well articulated and subordinated to the whole. Exemplars in perceptual theory are often drawn from music: a glissando exemplifies a diffuse structure; a melody, an articulated one.

But music presents us with many illustrations of these two polar kinds of form—for example, the highly structured, goal-directed kind of motion so effectively achieved by classic triadic tonality as contrasted to a mosaic sort of form put together by juxtaposition, as shown by canzonas of the early 17th century, many of the works of Debussy or Stravinsky, or contemporary experiments in musical collage.

Both of these polarities, of function and of structure, bear on the level in time at which a piece of music is organized as a whole.

IV (Hearing)

A piece of music is not only an object grasped, a perceptual form; it is an object heard, grasped in a specific way. At ground, the problems of musical form conceived primarily as something to be listened to are the problems of auditory perception. Before turning to the characteristics of a specifically heard thing, then, let me turn your attention to hearing itself and the quite remarkable place it occupies in the total sensorium, especially in view of the premium put today on the highly differentiated and specific sense of vision.

It has been maintained that a primitive syncretic state, in which sensorial, motor, emotional, and conceptual phenomena are inseparably fused, is the ground of experience for all of us. Only gradually do we distinguish in our experience between motor and sensory response, between an internal sensory and external mode of behaviour, and, indeed, among the senses themselves. For all of us, hearing remains close to that primitive global state.

The sensorium is progressively differentiated in two directions: toward increasing discreteness or clarity of distinction between internal and external world (tasting and smelling are said to be more primitive because of their inability to distinguish subjective and objective content) and toward increasing articulation in modes of perception (a visual act is less syncretic than hearing, tasting, or smelling, because it is characterized by a higher degree of specificity). Hearing in many ways remains close to an undifferentiated response of the total organism in both these directions.

For instance, hearing is close to the intersensory relationship known as "synaesthesia" (i.e., the arousal by a specific stimulus of a second sensation united with the first), the most common form being a coupling of color and tone perception. The following example of a total synaesthesia is the response of a subject under the effects of mescalin to a steady knocking on the wall: "I think that I hear noises and see faces, and yet everything is one and the same. I cannot tell whether I am seeing or hearing. I feel, taste, and smell the sound. It's all one. I, myself, am the sound." This kind of total response to sound, it has been shown, is prevalent among primitive and archaic peoples and, it is suggested, is potentially inherent in the mentality of all of us.[14]

Similarly, the interrelation between hearing and motor response is especially strong. Plato remarked on the fact that the young of all creatures cannot be quiet in their bodies or in their voices (arguing that therefore education is to be given first through music). And it has been pointed out that the imagination for motion, i.e., the ability to transform kinetic energy into kinetic imagery, is acquired only late in life.

For such reasons as these, perhaps, one view of music has traditionally placed it on the subjective side of our world—as the representation of our inner life, pure will, for example; or as an image of "pure duration", pure subjectivity. The tune, says Bergson, cradles us and pulls us back to the psychic state from which it comes.[15]

But the interesting fact about hearing, and especially musical hearing, it seems to me, is the peculiar way in which it mediates between inner and outer world. This is expressed in one of the oldest images of music, as *harmonia*, the perfect attunement between microcosm and macrocosm. And it is this—the peculiar relation between subject and object within the activity, the situation of music—that is an issue today.

The double nature of hearing with respect to the subjective and objective world has been emphasized by Helmut Reinold. If the senses are arranged in a hierarchy that reaches from the more object-related to the more subject-related sensory perceptions (at one end of the scale, the existence and condition of material objects; at the other, the fact that we feel this way or that), and if the acoustic mode is placed within this hierarchy, then the quite special and significant position of auditory perceptions, he says, becomes evident. Beyond their capacity of not being experienced as affects of a bodily part (as are taste and temperature experiences), auditory perceptions can become separated from their object, move to the forefront of experience, stand and hold attention by themselves, as, for instance, in music.[16]

The ambivalent nature of hearing is already seen in the earliest responses of the infant to sound. He has two very different responses. In general, his reactions to sounds are very diffuse, involving practically the whole body, a mass reaction described as "flight". But one of his earliest specific responses is, in fact, to sound: he turns his head in order to locate and fix in place a sound as an external object.

Different stages in the hierarchical position of sound relative to the internal and external world—what might be called a scale in the degree of immediacy by which we experience sound—have been demonstrated by Heinz Werner, who differentiates three levels in the experience of tone: instrumental tone, spatial tone, and what he calls "vital sensation". Let me summarize some of this work, my point being that in order to create a musical object, it is necessary to transform sound from vital sensation into tone that has an objective character.

If a series of tones is played on a piano, several stages of awareness can be shown to exist, which differ as to degree of subjectivity in the hearing of the tone. Commonly it is perceived as altogether outside the listener, as coming from a specifically defined source of sound and bound up with some particular object (for example, a musical instrument). Such a tone may be called an "instrumental tone". There is as well another type of tonal experience, in which the tone no longer seems to reside primarily in the object or instrument, but rather fills the space around it, occupying the entire room. This may be called a "spatial tone". Both of these possess an objective character. Yet there is still another way of experiencing tone, i.e., as actually vibrating within the hearer. (" I am filled with tone, as if I were a bell that had been struck.") It is tone experienced in this manner that Werner calls vital sensation. Vital sensations are devoid of the objectivity that characterizes the instrument or spatial tone; they are psychophysically undifferentiated and involve pervasive bodily reactions to the stimuli.[17]

A piece of music, as distinguished from sheer musical process or activity, articulates not only a piece, a stretch, of time, but also shapes and fills a kind of tonal space of its own.

Now I have suggested that the peculiar relation between listening subject and the world he hears—a connection of interpenetration and immediacy—has become a crucial issue in our contemporary world. I have maintained that the musical object, in the mainstream of our modern Western tradition, has been fashioned after the manner of a thing visually perceived. Our dominant conception of reality, as evident to the sense of sight, is, I believe, in a process of change. And the nature of this change is strikingly demonstrated, I think, in our music.

One of the more interesting ideas currently being explored is that our present view of reality, in which real things, persons, ideas, and events are spread out there, clearly and distinctly before us in a more or less continuous, uniform line, is essentially visual; that this view arose at the turn to the Renaissance, out of the "auditory-tactile" matrix of a less fragmented, more total (perhaps less civilized) earlier sort of a world, through the isolation of one thing at a time, one operation at a time, one sense at a time; and that this predominantly visual approach to the world is again giving way to a more global way of conceiving of the real. I have tried to show here that hearing in its essential nature negates this kind of a visual world. Yet the heard object, the piece of music, has become in this visual world the paradigm, not only for perceptual form, but also for artistic form. "All art", writes Walter Pater at the end of the last century, "constantly aspires towards the condition of music. For while in all other kinds of art it is possible to distinguish the matter from the form, and the understanding can always make this distinction, yet it is the constant effort of art to obliterate it."[18]

Pater conceives of music as "pure" language. But in this passage can be heard the ancient strain of music conceived as sounding number, pure form. And it echoes as well another version of this old notion, one which prevailed during the time about which Pater writes—the Renaissance. The model for beauty and wholeness, as described by Leon Battista Alberti, for instance, in the mid-15th century, was the harmonious proportion of an ideal body, so ordered that every part has its fixed size and shape and that nothing can be added or taken away without destroying the harmony of the whole. Music also served as paradigm for this conception of form. But this is form eminently separable from the matter it shapes—it is number, "organic geometry", abstract and priorly given, ideally existing beyond real time or space. Yet the image is concrete and corporeal. An "ideal" body was achieved by seeking after "the most fugitive aspects of things" and by putting together only the most perfect parts found in nature. But the harmonies generated were concretely seen (in the porportions of buildings, for example) and concretely heard. And the eye and ear were in agreement. Alberti borrowed his rules for harmonic relations from musicians ("to whom this sort of numbers is extremely well known") for an interesting reason: "The numbers by means of which the agreement of sounds affects our ears with delight are the very same which please our eyes and our minds."[19] His statement might be taken as *terminus a quo* in the career of a piece of music, for it indicates a turning point at which real space, indeed, was "musicalized"—but where real music, in turn, was spatialized.

V   (The heard thing)

I have spent some time on the matter of isolating and externalizing a musical object and setting it at a distance—on the problem, that is, of making it discrete in an objective world. Let me turn now to the matter of distinguishing it as a specifically heard thing, an object made out of sound. This will concern the problems of giving such an object body and keeping it present. What are the differences in objects, as they are seen, heard, and felt?

Hearing has been defined as acoustic successiveness. And, on this basis, a distinction has been drawn between an object given simultaneously in space and one given "only" in time. A painting, it is said, presents itself to me all at once as a meaningful whole, so that I am able to grasp it in a single moment or to contemplate it at my leisure. But like any object that unfolds in time, a piece of music is never simultaneously *there*. It comes to me only one sound at a time; one moment after another passes the time-point *now*. The musical object thus is discontinuous, fragmentary, and scarcely lays claim to existence at all. On this view, painting has been taken to exemplify being, and music, the process of becoming.[20]

Now I do not want to raise here the venerable issue of the unity or division of the arts, but I do want to point out that such a one-sided view of hearing is misleading in its emphasis and gives rise, therefore, to several problems. The first concerns what a piece of music is made of. Music as physical thing might, perhaps, be said to be made up of sound (and the absence of sound). But what we perceive as object, in both time and space, is not a bundle of sensations, given either successively or simultaneously, but an organization of stimuli. And, at the level of aesthetic object, an element in a piece of music is already formed material. Such an object is not made up of instants or of single tones, but of concretely sounding forms in motion.

Another question concerns succession or, broadly, our perception of time. In experience the present is not an unextended point of time—"now". On the contrary, we hold, in the present, a bit of time, "just as you can hold in your hand a certain amount of water from a flowing stream", as it has been put.[21] Although that amount of time varies, its upper limit is ordinarily about 5 or 6 seconds. How, in music, do we connect a succession of such "nows"?

A third question concerns simultaneity or, broadly, our perception of space. It is not the case that, in time, we hear one thing at a time. The sense that comes closest to dealing with one thing at a time is the sense of touch. A conception of space in which things are spread out one at a time in a line is the conception of tactile space. We *hear* many things at once—one *time*, it is true, at a time.

There are important differences between vision and hearing other than simultaneity versus successiveness. For example, vision separates, holds things apart in space, even as it holds them together in *a* space, simultaneously. But the things we hear are fused; we hear them all at once. And, as I have emphasized, vision distances, whereas hearing interconnects.

I cannot explore these questions adequately here, yet perhaps it is provocative to raise them. But I shall attempt to deal with them briefly by building up a picture of the musical object.

Let me begin at the most primitive level in an approach to the musical object, i.e., with a state of consciousness. Consciousness, it seems, is of a dual nature: it is both temporal and presentational. I am aware at a primary level of both the flow of time and the presentation of structures within that stream of time—i.e., experience always presents us with objects in contexts, not with bare sense-data. I cannot begin to build an object, then, from a pure sensation, such as "sound". The first operation of attention is to create for itself a field.

Consider first, then, structures within that field—within the temporal flow of consciousness. That is, consider simultaneity.

My field of awareness includes everything that is given as co-present, in various degrees of simultaneity and various degrees of vagueness: a problem with which I am concerned, shadows of possible solutions or consequences, a sense of my environment and of myself. If I am neither looking nor listening, for example, then either visual or auditory continuum is a sort of diffuse background—the sound of the ocean, the light of day. To grasp anything distinctly, to articulate that total field, I must categorize: first, by a mode of intending—this is something perceived, perhaps, or something imagined; then (since I am interested here in the perceptual field), by a mode of perception—this is something seen or something heard. Yet there are differences even at this level of awareness in the modalities of perception. For example, perhaps there are street noises outside, hums and creaks inside, a child singing in the next room—these may still be background sound, part of the auditory field. Like the visual field, the auditory field is unbounded and continuous. But it is peculiarly immediate. Even without my active attention sounds easily penetrate; the ear is passive. Yet without my active participation they do not readily remain; sound is evanescent and fragile.

Now suppose I actively attend to the sounds around me; I shut my eyes and listen. Then the vague, indefinite stuff of sound becomes an auditory world. As soon as I fix my attention, I fix "things" as well. Sounding objects emerge and isolate themselves as sounding things which are presented to my mind as things happening: a rustle, i.e., something rustling—a thump, i.e., something falling. Things are perceived differently in different modalities. If I feel a cube, for instance, I proceed in a line, grasping each surface as I go, collecting the information in my mind as I proceed. If I see a cube, what I see—i.e., three of its sides—is unclear, but the knowledge I have of simple cubeness fills out my perception and renders it clear. If I hear something, I immediately and clearly know a great deal about it: an approaching heavy truck; several children over there, at play.

Space perception, the visual perception of objects, separates things. It has to do with outlines, distinctions, articulation. My eye can follow a multiplicity of lines, extending in many different directions. At the same time, the background of visual space acts as a container, holding together a myriad of objects, all at once. The primary fact about visual space is that it is empty.

Perception of sound, by contrast, fuses things. The first observable fact about auditory space is that it is full. It is full of everything that is sounding *now*. I can easily hear two, three, a hundred sounds, but they tend to fuse into one event. Nevertheless, I collect a great deal of particular information about the external world through my ears. I can locate objects—quite accurately with respect to direction, less so with respect to distance. Sounds give me little information about the size and shape of a source, but can tell me much about its personality. And acuity for thresholds of perception of events in time (the difference between the instantaneous and the durable, for instance, and between simultaneity and succession) is a hundredfold sharper for hearing—and touch—than for vision.

Space, then, whether auditory or visual or tactile, I take to be the form of the world in the sense of its objectivity, its givenness. And auditory space is the sum total of my perception, through my ears, of the external world. Musical space is a piece of auditory space.

Suppose now I turn my attention to the child's singing, with the intent to listen. What happens now as the background song becomes foreground? If the child simply reiterates the same figure over and over, this is not yet temporal construction. Nevertheless, the music itself stands out against the background noises of the sounding world, which are now masked, as if part of a surrounding silence. There is a difference now between the silence of the background (which is probably not true silence) and the gaps of silence that articulate the music (these are indeed true silences and belong to its own continuity). The music is perceptually isolated; it has an outline; it makes and fills its own tonal space; it is *a piece* of music.

If the child is singing what we grasp as a melody, that melody comes forth as a nonspatial figure. It arises across the single tones and traces its outline upon a tonal space, against a background of silence. I am aware of what happens during the course of the melody, of its beginning, of points within it in relation to the beginning, of its completion. A melody in our modern sense is more than mere prolongation of musical matter, mere reiteration; it is a temporal object. And it is as well a *musical* object; it marks out, concretizes, fixes, embodies, enlivens a piece of musical space.

I have developed the notion of a piece of music as a piece of the concretely sounding musical field. Let me illustrate this idea by returning to the primary phenomenon in the articulation of any perceptual field, i.e., the differentiation between figure and ground.

Auditory space has been described as a sphere without fixed boundaries, as a space made by the thing itself, not a space containing the thing. It is not pictorial space, boxed in, but dynamic, always in flux. It has no fixed boundaries and no point of favored focus. Whereas the eye pinpoints, locating each object in physical space against a background, the ear favors sound from any direction and is indifferent to background.[22]

Now this is not entirely accurate, for the depth of the world is given to the ear, as it is to the eye. A sound-figure can move in a heard line against a background which is much like the flight of a bird, for example, seen against the sky. Sound, like sight, lays out planes of depth. The farthest seems at first to be made up of distant sounds, such as the recurring roll of the sea, but this is because distance blurs detail. In fact, if we listen to the space around us, we notice that continuous, homogeneous, undifferentiated sounds tend chiefly to make up the background: traffic sounds outside, a ticking watch nearby, the hum of my typewriter. It is the shaped sounds—characteristic, isolated, discretely outlined—that stand out from the background as figure.

This is a phenomenon we, as musicians, know well, for in music background and foreground are not usually constituted by actual distance, but by formal features. When we speak of different "textures", we are usually speaking of differing relations of figure and ground. Sixteenth-century polyphony, for example, tends toward an undifferentiated field. The beauty of the Renaissance line lies in the manner in which it contributes to the whole organism. To remove one line is like taking one thread from a tapestry or one member from a body. The separate strands are generally neutral, typical, idealized parts. The Renaissance musical space is not a container for a motion or a figure; figure is minimized and the line is leveled to a smooth part. The musical space becomes solid and homogeneous.

To some extent this relation of part to whole holds for the Bach B minor
34 Prelude; each line is equally central in our attention. But each is highly characteristic in nature; each now has the quality of "figure". Much of the movement in the piece comes about as one or the other of the lines comes forward as foreground, a shift in focus which is produced by the slightest shift in pattern. And we are strikingly aware of the tendency of a continuous motion to become background (as in the bass) when it is relieved for a moment at the half-cadence.

Ex. 2 Frederic Chopin, *Three Etudes* (posthumous), No. 2

In a texture which is clearly what we call "homophony", however, it is exactly this relation between figure and ground that the composer manipulates. Compare to the Bach, for instance, a piece by Chopin—the "Moscheles" Étude in A-flat Major. This is also essentially a single melodic line, which is reflected in its triadic support and rhythmically distorted in a subtle manner. The melody itself is, in fact, so simple that it recedes into the background and is absorbed into the total stream of sound, which is shaped (harmonically and rhythmically) by the standing-forth of one figural distortion after another. In the "Funeral Scene" in Wagner's *Götterdämmerung*, the framework is also a simple melody, consisting of five quite regular phrases, marked by a half-cadence to the tonic major and framed by material which sets the scene. Here, too, the melody and its "scenic" setting continually shift in position in depth. One of Schoenberg's piano pieces, Op. 19, No. 5, is an interesting reproduction in miniscule scale of the shape of Wagner's scene: it is a four-phrase melody, articulated chiefly by background material, which "moves out" at the joints and thickens the cadences. In contrast to this, the several mosaic-like figures which make up Debussy's Prelude, *Voiles*, for example, are put together in such a way as to minimize the difference between figure and ground. This piece, as compared to the Wagner or Schoenberg, might be said to be quite "flat" and two-dimensional.

The freedom to manipulate background and foreground is achieved in classic tonal homophony by an extraordinarily systematic organization of an integrated musical space. Continuity no longer depends upon a thread-like connection from one tone to the next, but rather upon more abstract functional connections between simultaneous triadic units. These functional relations support a space so clearly organized in itself that only the skeleton need be indicated, over which motifs, rhythms, and themes may be quite freely thrown. To hear in this "tonal" manner, I must stop perceiving the whole freely and circumscribe my hearing. I subordinate the musical world to a single point of view, as in the analogous way of looking at a visual space organized by classic perspective. Both ways of perceptual organization depend upon so-called "natural" relations—holding among triads, on the one hand, among objects, on the other. Both assume a "common-sense" manner of hearing or seeing, clearly and distinctly reflecting in perception the evident, and hence, "natural" order of the real world.

VI (Heard time)

Now let me turn briefly to our perception of time, in order to emphasize one point: that we organize time differently at different levels. What holds together "a piece" of time?

Perhaps our most fundamental sense of time is indeed one of continuity, of an irreversible flux, in which the separate moments of lived experience fuse and interpenetrate, growing dim as they recede into the past. This inexorable flow is marked, especially for the Westerner, by the point at which he stands and the perspective this throws on past and future. But time, even for the Westerner, does seem to be, above all, a stream.

However, in order to *perceive* time, we must perceive change—either a change that has happened or a change taking place. We do not perceive sheer duration, independently of something that endures. And a duration, either filled or empty (as a gap) is a definite interval, grasped only in relation to change, i.e., to succession. Further, we do not perceive succession itself in terms of its elements or the intervals between them, but rather as a schema of relations, an organization—i.e., a rhythm. Especially in music, time, as we hear it unfold in a melody, for instance—"musical" time—has to do with distinction and order as well as interpretation and fusion. The comprehension of succession requires some sort of similarity among its elements, some sort of differentiation between them, and a certain limit during which they can be grasped.

There are two facts about the perception of time which are especially interesting in regard to music: First, we perceive differently continuous change and discontinuous change, as transformation or as succession, respectively. Secondly, we perceive discontinuous change differently, according to its rate of speed, as flicker or as true succession.[23] Although we tend to group any recurring stimuli into an organization, we group such forms at various levels according to these basic differences in perception. In music, we group, for example, at the level of figure, at the level of theme or line, and at the level of piece or object.

Ex. 3 Claude Debussy, *Préludes*, Bk. I, No. 2, "Voiles"
Modéré (♪=88) *(Dans un rythme sans rigueur et caressant)*

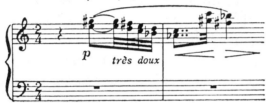

How then do we hear *a* succession? To perceive mere succession as such requires the perception of *before* and *after* as somehow simultaneous, i.e., as occurring within a single mental present; it is a multiple apprehension. Now

Ex. 4 Edgard Varèse, *Ionisation*

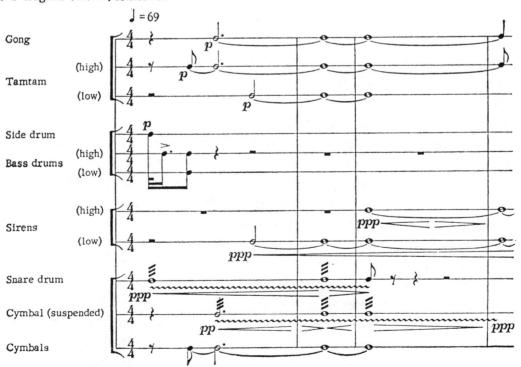

perception is an act of integration which itself takes time; an instant is not a durationless point. We can grasp as whole a series of changes provided the interval that embraces them is not too long. This length of time depends on various factors, chiefly the direction of our attention and the possibilities given in the stimuli for organization. Ordinarily, as I have said, its upper limit is about 5 or 6 seconds. What I grasp, even in this instant, is an entity—a musical element, for example—a motif, a rhythm, a configuration of sound, a splash of tonal color. A musical figure fills an "instant"; a melody extends it. Listen, for example, to the opening ideas in a few of the pieces I have mentioned: The first figure of Debussy's *Voiles* is clocked by the composer at about 4 seconds. The first figure of *Ionization* is marked at less than 2 seconds, but the sustained background sound moves forward, fills the space, and extends it to about 11 seconds. The first phrase of Chopin's Étude (which is, in fact, a piece of a melody) takes about 8 seconds. The opening measure of Bach's Prelude spans an interval of about 7 seconds (and remarkably divides it, in time as well as space, in a symmetrical way).

The apprehension of musical form involves at least two distinct levels of integration: At the level of smallest unit or formal element are those musical events which are grasped as whole within a single mental act—a figure, a gesture, a phrase. But these elements are in turn gathered up into larger wholes—a melody, an action, a discourse. 37

The primitive condition for an extended form which is grasped as whole, whether it be an area in space or a stretch of time, is a bounded field with possibilities for organization. Such a field is neither sheer continuity (such as a grey fog or the distant roll of the ocean) nor uninterrupted pattern (for example, a child's endlessly reiterated bit of melody or an expanse of grillwork). A true Gestalt lies somewhere in between. A musical whole, like any other, can be stylized in either direction.

For example, let me indicate how these two polar possibilities for form apply to repetition. In any temporal form, repetition both extends and articulates matter. Its essential function is not to produce symmetry or closure, as in spatial form (although it can indeed serve this purpose), but rather to establish an identity, an element, which thereby differentiates itself and persists in time, remaining somehow constant under change. In music, any parameter of sound can generate such an entity; two of the most familiar are durational pattern and patterns of pitch. But not all music is essentially repetitive. And further, any kind of repetition can be constructive or non-constructive and, if constructive, tight or loose.

The different effects of different kinds of repetition reflect differences in the way we perceive any change. At the most basic level, we perceive continuous stimuli differently from discontinuous stimuli. Rhythm in the restricted sense of a regular reiteration of pattern is an obvious example of our tendency to organize any stimuli given as discretely separate: we tend to group regularly recurring stimuli (given at a moderate rate) into patterns of two's or three's. But there is as well a rhythm of continuous change, a rhythm of transformation, growth, motion. Rhythm in this wider sense is the preparation of one event by the last—the way in which one wave or one gesture, for instance, arises out of another.

Immediate repetition (reiteration) has been distinguished from repetition that returns after some time (recurrence), and these organize succession on two different levels. Reiteration emphasizes differences; it focuses attention on small-scale detail, on "texture". Recurrence emphasizes similarities and articulates more far-reaching relations of over-all structure. The one is absorbed with the moment-to-moment passage of time; the other tends to stabilize time for contemplation. In this way, repetition may stylize a musical whole either toward process or object, toward the pole of becoming or toward that of being.

Consider again differences between any of the ricercari of Willaert and a fugue of Bach (say, No. 2, Bk. I of the *Well-tempered Clavier*). I have suggested that one of the principal differences between them is the scale by which we listen, as that is dictated by the distance the object demands. And I have maintained that ultimately this distance is determined by the level in time at which the object is organized as a whole. In these two examples fugal repetition is used in very different ways in order thus to organize the whole.

The ricercar is essentially nonrepetitive music, depending for coherence on the musical properties of consonance and dissonance to hold the lines together and to propel them along—a more or less "Klang-by-Klang" procedure. There is no single recurrent, unifying theme, but rather a moment-to-moment stringing together of little fugal expositions—a reiteration, that is to say, of fragmentary passages, which seem to grow organically out of one another by a subtle kind of motivic reminiscence. The continuity of the ricercar might be described as the rhythm of continuous change, i.e., transformation. Bach's subject-matter, by contrast, exploits reiterative pattern in the most obvious ways: a relentless motor rhythm, a few unchanging figures that permeate the entire fugue. Yet the engaging repetition is the recurrence of the theme itself—constantly the same, although always in a different context—which brackets and structures the over-all course of time. And the *flow* of time, consequently, seems relatively unimportant in Bach's fugue, which is essentially timeless, grasped as a whole outside of and independently of time. The fugue represents, I should say, a musical illusion of the kind of wholeness we associate with a thing visually perceived: it is the presentation of a single bit of musical matter from many different aspects, in many different lights, moved bodily from place to place; but the matter itself (unlike the germ of a symphony of Beethoven, for instance, or the motifs in Willaert's ricercar) remains solid, static, and unchanged.

Bach's fugue exemplifies "a piece" of music—a musical object, a heard thing, a thing ultimately made to be perceived for its own sake, something sheerly to be listened to. I have stressed, for two reasons, that such a piece of music is form stylized toward objectivity.

First, this kind of form in music emphasizes similarities common to all perceptual form rather than differences specific to temporal form. In his fugue, Bach exploits the principles of "good" Gestalt: clear articulation of parts, grouped by similarity and proximity and subordinated to the whole. The ricercar, on the other hand, approaches the diffuse sort of form characteristic of less developed organization—i.e., a homogeneous, chain-like construction of parts which are themselves leveled and simplified, put together without any strong direction toward a goal. These are formal principles which apply equally to auditory or visual form and can be considered quite apart from the ingredient of "time".

And secondly, in thus abstracting from time, we can see the extent to which "a piece" of musical time depends upon the exploitation of simultaneity. Western music exploits simultaneity in two senses: It pushes further and further the amount of time to be grasped as "now", and it juxtaposes in an increasingly dense way the number of musical events that occur at the same time. Increasing hierarchization of parts dictates distance in both these respects, for it allows for a density of events which can be grasped the better if we step back. Bach's fugal form is not only well articulated, but also very dense. It extends the "now" to about a minute and a half, and at any point within this "moment" much is happening at once. Nevertheless, we apprehend it by a single act of the imagination. The rather undifferentiated structure of the ricercar, by contrast, is not clear from a distance.

In the extent to which a piece of music exploits simultaneity, it is also stylized toward spatiality. It requires not only a coherence through time but also a particular conception of musical space. At the least, this is a two-dimensional field that is framed and bounded; at the most, it is a space highly organized. And differences in the conception of musical space, as well as of time, are also a dimension of style. In these examples fugal repetition contributes differently to the organization of space. In the ricercar, repetition helps to build a homogeneous and highly fused tonal body, laying out equal, comparable lines, modeled after an ideal of the human voice, a pleasure to sing, smooth to grasp—lines that unfold organically out of simple connections between adjacent tones. In Bach's fugue, by contrast, repetition serves to focus and polarize the forces of a musical field, in order to contain and concentrate the expansion of a single musical idea. The cohesive force in the ricercar operates not so much *within* the line, which unfolds in a somewhat lazy way, but rather between homogeneous layers. Bach, on the other hand, sets up an intensely directed musical motion, within a tightly defined musical space, an organized field of abstract tonal functions.

And finally, a piece of music ordinarily has been unified by a single pervading idea, what Arnold Schoenberg has called its *Grundgestalt*. A musical idea can determine in the broadest manner how the space is shaped, "wie der Grund gestaltet wird". Space in this sense has been described by Schoenberg: "The two-or-more-dimensional space in which musical ideas are presented is a unit. Though the elements of these ideas appear separate and

39

81

independent to the eye and the ear, they reveal their true meaning only through their cooperation, even as no single word alone can express a thought without relation to other words. All that happens at any point of this musical space has more than a local effect. It functions not only in its own plane, but also in all other directions and planes, and is not without influence even at remote points."[24]

This passage might be taken to describe as well the unified picture-space or dramatic-space with which we are familiar in our modern Western tradition.

FOOTNOTES

(The following notes were not incorporated in copies of the paper sent to the commentators.)

[1] Maurice Merleau-Ponty, in the following contrast to "spontaneous vision", elaborates some implications of the mode of seeing "in perspective": "Sometimes Malraux speaks as if 'sense data' had never varied throughout the centuries, and as if the classical perspective had been imperative whenever painting referred to sense data. Yet it is clear that the classical perspective is only one of the ways that man has invented for projecting the perceived world before him and not the copy of that world. The classical perspective is an optional interpretation of spontaneous vision, not because the perceived world contradicts the laws of classical perspective and imposes others, but rather because it does not insist upon any one law and is not of the order of laws . . . [If I want to 'see' things in perspective], I must stop perceiving the whole freely. I must mark what I call the 'apparent size' of the moon and the coin on a standard of measurement I hold, and, finally, transfer these measurements onto paper. But during this time the perceived world has disappeared, along with the true simultaneity of objects, which is not their peaceful co-existence in a single scale of sizes . . . Now I reconstruct a representation in which each thing ceases to call the whole of vision to itself . . . then my glance, running freely over depth, height, and width, was not subjected to any point of view, because it adopted them and rejected them in turn. Now I renounce that ubiquity and agree to let only that which could be seen . . . by an immobile eye . . . figure in my drawing. (A deceptive modesty, for if I renounce the world itself . . . I also cease to see like a man, who is open to the world because he is situated in it. I think of and dominate my vision as God can when he considers his *idea* of me.) Then I had the experience of a world of teeming, exclusive things which could be taken in only by means of a temporal cycle in which each gain was at the same time a loss. Now the inexhaustible being crystallizes into an ordered perspective . . . a perspective within which nothing holds my glance and takes the shape of a present. The whole scene is in the mode of the completed or of eternity" (Maurice Merleau-Ponty, "Indirect language and the voices of silence" in *Signs* [Northwestern U. Press, 1964], pp. 48f., trans. by Richard C. McCleary from *Signes* [Paris, 1960]).

Evidence of the revolution in perception which occurred at the beginning of this century is seen in all fields. I cite one example, concerning architecture, from Sigfried Giedion's *Space, time and architecture* (Cambridge, Mass., 1962, 4th ed., p. 26): "Up to 1910 architects tried many ways of arriving at a new feeling for space . . . they could never quite break through. Around 1910 an event of decisive importance occurred: the discovery of a new space conception in the arts. Working in their studios as though in laboratories, painters and sculptors investigated the ways in which space, volumes, and materials existed for feeling. The speculations of the mathematical physicists seem very far removed from reality and from practical affairs, but they have led to profound alterations in the human environment. In the same way experiments of the cubists . . . gave the architects the hints they needed to master reality in their particular sphere . . . [offering] objective means of organizing space in ways that gave form to contemporary feelings."

Marshall McLuhan studies the cultural change in general (see esp. his *Gutenberg galaxy* [Toronto, 1962]).

Zofia Lissa, in "On the evolution of musical perception" (*The journal of aesthetics and art criticism* [*JAAC*] 24:273–286 [1965]), discusses methodological problems that arise when contemporary research attempts to examine the thesis that musical perception changes from one historic period to another.

Leonard B. Meyer, in "The end of the Renaissance?" (*The Hudson review* 16:170–186 [1963]), considers the period of music here at stake in terms of his distinction between teleological and anti-teleological music. He concludes that if predictability and choice are impossible, art cannot be a form of communication, for communication requires that the artist predict how others will interpret and respond to the images he produces.

Gerhard Albersheim, in "Mind and matter in music" (*JAAC* 22:289–294 [1964]), develops the same thesis on the basis of the breakdown of the spatial structure (in the sense of pitch-space) operating in tonal music, by the means of which music has been actively comprehended by the listener, and the renunciation of which relegates him to the role of passive receiver, thus destroying the possibility for communication.

Here I juxtapose a passage from Merleau-Ponty (*op. cit.*, p. 51):.There are two possible interpretations, he says, of that tolerance for the incomplete shown by the moderns: either "that they have given up the *work* and no longer look for anything but the immediate, perceived and individual; or else, completion in the sense of a presentation that is objective and convincing for the *senses* may no longer be the means to a work that is really complete, because henceforth expression must go from man to man across the common world they *live*, without passing through the anonymous realm of the senses or of Nature. . . . The accomplished work is thus not the work which exists in itself like a thing, but the work which reaches its viewer and invites him to take up the gesture which created it and . . . rejoin . . . the silent world of the painter, henceforth uttered and accessible. Modern painting presents a problem completely different from that of the return to the individual: the problem of knowing how one can communicate without the help of a pre-established Nature which all men's senses open upon."

[2] Edmund Husserl, *The phenomenology of internal time-consciousness* (Bloomington, 1964), (trans. by James S. Churchill from "Vorlesungen zur Phänomenologie des inneren Zeitbewusstseins", ed. Martin Heidegger *Jahrbuch für Philosophie und phänomenologische Forschung* [1928]), esp. Sect. 39.

[3] V. von Weizäcker, cited by Helmut Reinold ("The problem of musical hearing" in *Reflections on art*, ed. and trans, by Susanne K. Langer [Baltimore, 1958], p. 268. From *Archiv für Musikwissenschaft*, 1954), who points out the extent to which music has contributed to the revolution in the theory of sensations: not only did von Ehrenfels take the nature of a melody as starting-point for his dissertation *Ueber Gestalt-qualitäten* (1890), but also Erwin Straus helped to refute the mechanistic conception of the senses by means of the musical phenomenon of the complete rest, the "problem of the void", in *Von Sinn der Sinne* (Berlin, 1935).

[4] Robert W. Lundin gives a concise summary of modern theories of melody in *An objective psychology of music* (New York, 1963), Chap. V. Friedrich Kainz, in *Aesthetics the science* (Detroit, 1962), trans. by Herbert M. Schueller from *Vorlesungen über Aesthetik* (Vienna, 1948), makes available an enormous amount of technical material, especially from German aesthetic theory during the first half of the century. His own point of view is that of Gestalt theory.

Husserl (*op. cit.*, pp. 43f.) develops Brentano's analysis of a melody as model for a temporal object (i.e., an object which is not only a unity in time, but also includes temporal extension within itself) and applies it in an extended sense to temporality conceived as form for perception, fantasy, imagination, memory, and recollection.

The conception of melody as a motion which requires a musical space is a prevailing model for musical form in general. See Ernst Kurth, *Musikpsychologie* (Bern, 1947), esp. Part II, Chap. I and II; Victor Zuckerkandl, *Sound and symbol*, trans. by Willard R. Trask (New York, 1956); and Reinold (*op. cit.*, p. 271), who refers this notion to the interrelation between hearing and

41

motor response. The application of this notion of form to an extended piece of music descends from Hanslick through such writers as Pratt, Langer, and Meyer (all of whom conceive of form in music as in some way mirroring psychological "movement", i.e., tension and release).

Jean G. Harrell, in "Issues of music aesthetics" (*JAAC* 23:197–206 [1964]) (interpreting issues raised by Hanslick), supports in an interesting way her thesis that "form" in music has been equated with the goal-directed motion achieved by tonality, and "expression", with the breakdown in tonality.

Silence as the background for melody (and ultimately for music itself) is considered by Gisèle Brelet in "Music and silence" (in Langer, *op. cit.*, trans. from *La Revue Musicale*, 1946), who gives a number of observations on how the musical image is molded as an entity against this background in the imagination of the listener.

Zofia Lissa, in "Aesthetic functions of silence and rests in music" (*JAAC* 22:444–454 [1964]) deals with the same problem.

The priority of perceived form over actual pitch material receives increasing attention. Zuckerkandl (*op. cit.*, pp. 79ff.) describes an experiment designed to determine whether singers use just intonation or equal temperament, which demonstrated, rather, that they not only "simply sang unimaginably off pitch", but, more significantly, that it required the intervention of a measuring instrument to reveal these pitch distortions.

Fritz Winckel, in *Klangwelt unter der Lupe* (Berlin, 1952) presented experimental evidence for the fact that the pitch-stuff is not clearly represented tones but "deflecting Klänge". For an application to electronic music and recent bibliography, see his "The psycho-acoustical analysis of music applied to electronic music" (*The journal of music theory* 7:194–246 [1963]).

See also Charles Shackford: "Some aspects of perception" (*JMT* 5:162–202 [1961], 6:66–90 and 295–303 [1962]); and Paul C. Boomsliter and Warren Creel: "Extended reference: an unrecognized dynamic in melody" (*JMT* 7:2–73 [1963]).

5 Nikolaus Listenius, *Musica* (Nürnberg, 1537), Facsimile from the 1549 ed., *Musica Nicolai Listenii*.

6 The importance of *musica poetica* to the modern idea of the musical work was first emphasized by Hermann Zenck in *Sixtus Dietrich* (Leipzig, 1928). For convenient reviews of the topic and recent bibliography, see Martin Ruhnke: *Joachim Burmeister* (Kassel, 1955), pp. 100–170; and Paul Matzdorf: *Die "practica Musica" Hermann Fincks* (Frankfurt am Main, 1957), Chap. II–VI.

Walter Wiora, in "Musica poetica und musikalisches Kunstwerk" (in *Festschrift Karl Gustave Fellerer* . . . [Regensburg, 1962]), discusses the specifically musical work, its ingredients and the milieu in which it arises—an important article which reviews the literature and sources.

For two interesting interpretations of the change in the conception of the nature of music, from medieval to modern, see Hermann Zenck: *Numerus und Affectus* (Kassel, 1959); and Walter Eggebrecht: "Musik als Tonsprache" (*AfMw* 51:73–100 [1961]).

For the general background, see the following:

Ernst Curtius (in *European literature and the latin Middle Ages* [New York, 1953], trans. by W. Trask from *Europeanische Literature und latein Mittelalter* [Bern, 1944], formulates the change as the "transformation of the canon" from Imitation to Creation, from "*thesaurus* as warehouse of tradition to Walter Pater's 'House Beautiful'" (esp. pp. 396f.).

Paul O. Kristeller, in "The modern system of the arts" (reprinted from *The journal of the history of ideas* [1951] in his *Renaissance thought II* [New York], 1965), traces the origin of the term "Art" in its modern sense and the related term "Fine Arts" in the 18th century.

7 Benjamin Lee Whorf, "The relation of habitual thought and behaviour to language" (reprinted in *Language, thought and reality*, ed. John B. Carroll [Cambridge, Mass., 1956]). Paul Henle develops this material in "Language, thought, and culture" (Chap. I of a study by the same title, ed. Henle [Ann Arbor, 1958]).

For further material on the relation between language and world see:

Martin Heidegger, "Die Sprache" (in *Unterwegs zur Sprache* [Tübingen, 1955]) and rele-

42

84

vant passages (esp. Sect. 34) in his *Being and time* (New York, 1962, trans. by John Mac-Quarrie and Edward Robinson from *Sein und Zeit* [7th ed., Tübingen]).

Mikel Dufrenne, *Language and philosophy* (trans. by Henry B. Veatch [Bloomington, Ind., 1963]).

Albert Hofstadter, "Language as articulation of human being" in *Truth and art* [New York, 1965], Chap. IV.

For some points of comparison between a piece of language and a piece of music (considered as language), see my essay on the meaning of music in *Art and philosophy*, ed. Sidney Hook (New York, 1966), pp. 289–306.

[8] Kant, in *The critique of judgment* (1790), takes the first moment of the judgment of taste to be disinterestedness (Sect. I, Bk. I, "Analytic of the beautiful"). Although the term 'distance' is not new, the modern theory stems principally from two authors:

Edward Bullough, in "'Psychical distance' as a factor in art and an aesthetic principle" (*The British journal of psychology* 5:87–111 [1912]), maintains that "objectivity" and "subjectivity" when applied to art as a pair of opposites soon lead to confusion. Such opposites find their synthesis in the more fundamental conception of distance (obtained by putting the object out of gear with practical needs), which has both a negative and positive aspect. This "distanced", yet personal relation, one of the fundamental paradoxes of art, he calls the antinomy of distance.

José Ortega y Gasset, in "The dehumanization of art" (*Symposium* 1:194–205 [1930]), works out a scale of psychic distance which is somewhat misleading because it implies that distance leaves out feelings.

P. A. Michelis, in "Aesthetic distance and the charm of contemporary art" (*JAAC* 18:1–45 [1959]), develops the idea, describing distance as "the road of the mind itself, in which it must wander in order to meet and recognize itself, as if it were another" (p. 45).

[9] H. Plessner, "Zur Anthropologie der Musik" in *Jahrbuch für Aesthetik und Kunstwissenschaft*, 1951, p. 120—cited in Reinold (*op. cit.*, p. 270).

[10] Kurt Koffka, in "Perception: an introduction to the *Gestalt-theorie*" (*Psychological bulletin* 19:551–85 [1922]), summarizes the principles of Gestalt theory for English readers. (Reprinted in *Classics in psychology*, ed. Thorne Shipley [New York, 1961] and excerpted in *Experiments in visual perception*, ed. M. D. Vernon [Baltimore, 1966]).

Two recent articles review Gestalt theory:

Julian E. Hochberg: "Effects of the Gestalt revolution: the Cornell symposium on perception" (reprinted from *The psychological review* [1957] in *Readings in perception*, ed. David C. Beardslee and Michael Wertheimer [Princeton, 1958]); and Rudolph Arnheim, "Gestalten—yesterday and today" (trans. by the author from *Gestalthaftes Sehen* [Darmstadt, 1960] in Mary Henle, ed., *Documents of Gestalt psychology* [Berkeley, 1961]).

Arnheim's *Art and visual perception* (Berkeley, 1954) is the classic demonstration of Gestalt principles in visual art.

Georgy Kepes, in *The language of vision* (Chicago, 1948), in his concern to re-educate visual experience, applies these principles to the "grammar" and "syntax" of vision.

In music, these principles were first applied by the so-called "energists", Kurth (*op. cit.*), and Zuckerkandl (*op. cit.*). See also Helmut Federhofer, *Beiträge zur Musikalischen Gestaltanalyze* (Graz, 1950).

Leonard B. Meyer, in *Emotion and meaning in music* (Chicago, 1956), develops a theory of meaning in music utilizing Gestalt theory.

Charles M. H. Keil, in "Motion and feeling through music" (*JAAC* 24:337–349 [1966]), commenting on Meyer's book, stresses the importance of performance in music: every piece of teleological music, he says, involves not only syntax, but an elusive quality which he designates as "process".

James Tenney, in *Meta+Hodos* (New Orleans, 1964), applies Gestalt principles to the materials of 20th-century music.

[11] Heinz Werner, *A comparative study of mental development* (New York, 1948), pp. 122f.

43

[12] Kurt Koffka (*The growth of the mind*, trans. by C. K. Ogden [London, 1924], pp. 359 ff.) summarizes here Piaget's discussion of the original close connectedness in the child's experience of substance and force.

[13] I use the contrasts "syncretic-discrete" and "articulate-diffuse" as they have been developed by Werner (*op. cit.*, pp. 53f.).

[14] Werner (*op. cit.*, pp. 92f.).

[15] Henri Bergson, *Essai sur les données immédiates de la conscience* (Paris, 1889), trans. by F. L. Pogson as *Time and free will* (London, 1910), esp. pp. 100f. Gabriel Marcel, in "Bergsonism and music" (trans. by C. K. Scott Moncrieff from *La revue musical* [1925] in Langer, *op. cit.*), disagrees with Bergson on this point, maintaining that we speak of the beauty of a melodic line not as applied to an inner progression, but to a certain "non-spatial" figure (p. 146).

[16] Reinold (*op. cit.*, p. 263).

[17] Summarized by Werner from previous work, *op. cit.*, pp. 96f.

[18] Walter Pater, *The Renaissance* (New York, n.d., First ed. London, 1873).

[19] Alberti gives two definitions of beauty in his *De re aedificatoria*, Bk. VI Chap. 2 and Bk. IX Chap. 5. The quotation is cited by Rudolph Wittkower in *Architectural principles in the age of humanism* (London, 1952), Part IV, p. 97, in which he studies the relation of music and geometry in the Renaissance.

William M. Ivins, Jr., in *Art and geometry* (Boston, 1946), Chap. V, develops the thesis that the differences between metrical and perspective geometry can be traced back to the differences between the tactile-muscular and the visual intuitions of space, focusing the contrast between Greek and modern spatial thinking on Alberti's essay.

[20] Gisèle Brelet, in *Le temps musical* (Paris, 1949), has laid the groundwork for current studies of musical time. Music, she maintains, is temporal form *par excellence*. She considers arguments for and against correspondences in the arts and takes musical time to be a synthesis of time lived and time thought, immanent to the music itself.

Walter Wiora, in "Musik als Zeitkunst" (*Musikforschung* 10: 15–28 [1957]), using Brelet's study as a starting-point, reviews the background of the field and presents a comprehensive bibliography.

Susanne Langer, in *Feeling and form* (New York, 1953), pp. 115f., gives a brief outline of the history of the notion of "musical time".

Andres Briner, in *Der Wandel der Musik als Zeit-Kunst* (Vienna, 1955), structures the problem in terms of two polarities which recur throughout the literature on time, especially in regard to the contemporary change in the conception of time.

For some of the issues concerning music as temporal art see also Joan Stambaugh: "Music as a temporal form" (*JP* 61:265–280 [1964]) and my comment, "Musical form regained" (*JP* 62:36–48 [1965]).

Étienne Gilson, in *Painting and reality* (New York, 1957), develops the complementary view in regard to paintings, that the kind of reality proper to them is the mode of existence (vs. becoming).

Concerning problems in regard to time in general see also:

G. J. Whitrow, *The natural philosophy of time* (London, 1961); Paul Fraisse, *The psychology of time*, trans. by Jennifer Leith (New York, 1963); J. T. Frazer (ed.), *The voices of time* (New York, 1966).

The notion of space is related to music in several different ways and the literature is extensive. Edward A. Lippman collects, reviews, and discusses the literature in his *Music and space* (Ann Arbor Univ. Microfilms, 1952).

Albert Wellek (*Musikpsychologie und Musikästhetik* [Frankfurt am Main, 1963], pp. 294ff.) gives a recent review of the topic (from his own point of view).

Robert Hall, in "Heidegger and the space of art" (forthcoming in the *Journal of existentialism*, Fall, 1967), provides with his notion of space as "the form of World" a theoretical ground for discussions of musical space. The unifying principle of World provides for the nature of its component objects in conjunction with the basic kind of events that can take place within it. The space of that World is the potentiality for its objects giving rise to those events. The work of art is seen to be a unification of certain experiential effects so organized that they create a virtual space which exactly parallels the actual space of World.

21 The necessity, for the perception of change, of a "specious" present was first formulated by E. R. Clay in 1882 and developed by William James as a certain saddle-back of time with a certain length of its own, on which we sit perched and from which we look in two directions into time (William James, *Principles of psychology* [New York, 1891], I, p. 609). Psychologists refer to this by various names, "the sensible present" the "mental present" the "perceived present"; the metaphor quoted is Henri Pieron's. See Fraisse, *op. cit.*, pp. 85f., and Whitrow, *op. cit.*, pp. 70f.

22 Edmund Carpenter and Marshall McLuhan, "Acoustic space" in *Explorations in communication* (Boston, 1960), pp. 67f.

23 Fraisse (*op. cit.*, Chap. III).

24 Arnold Schoenberg, *Style and idea* (New York, 1950), p. 109.

ANALYSIS TODAY

By EDWARD T. CONE

THE analysis of music—especially of traditional music—is one of the most respected of theoretical disciplines, but the respect in which it is held would do it a disservice if it prevented the periodic re-evaluation of the subject. What is analysis, or what ought it to be? What are its purposes? To what extent are traditional concepts and methods applicable to new music? What are the relations of analysis to performance and to criticism? My title refers to a discussion, from the point of view of today, of these questions; it is in no way meant to imply that I have a new system to promulgate, or that I have made startling discoveries about new music.

I

Rather than presenting at the outset a naked definition of the term under consideration, let us begin by looking at a familiar example. The first few measures of *Tristan* have performed many services other than their original one of opening a music-drama; let them serve yet another and open the argument here.

Ex. 1

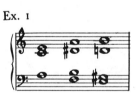

This chordal sequence can be accurately enough described as a minor triad on A, a French sixth on F, and a primary seventh on E; but such a description, revealing nothing of the relationships among the three chords, involves no analysis whatsoever. If, however, one

refers to the passage as I_3^5-$II_{\substack{\#6\\4\\3}}$-$V_{\#}^7$, he has performed an elementary analytical act: he has related each of the chords to a tonic, and hence to one another. He has made a discovery, or at least a preliminary hypothesis to be tested by its fruitfulness in leading to further discovery. But the analysis as such ceases with the choice of the tonic; once this has been made, the assignment of degree numbers to the chords is pure description. If, on the other hand, one points out that the second chord stands in a quasi-dominant relation to the third, he is doing more than simply assigning names or numbers: he is again discovering and explaining relationships.

Ex. 2

Turning now to the actual score, the analyst might begin a program note thus: "The rising leap of the 'cellos from A to F is succeeded by a chromatic descent, followed in turn by . . ." He need not continue; this is pure description. But when he points out that Example 1 represents the chordal skeleton of Example 2, he is once more on the right track. He can go still further by showing that all the appoggiaturas have half-step resolutions, and that the motif so created is augmented in the motion of the bass, and paralleled in the alto, in such a way that the chordal progression of measures 2-3 becomes an amplification of the melodic half-step of measure 1.

Ex. 3

The fact that in the above diagram no such analogy has been pointed out in the half-steps E-D♯ and A-A♯ is in itself an important though negative part of the analysis, since it implies by omission that these progressions, if relevant at all, are incidental and subordinate.

Going one step further, one might claim that, from a serial point of view, the opening sixth is imitated in the third E-G♯ (see Ex. 4). This is the point at which analysis proper passes over into what I call

47

Ex. 4

prescription: the insistence upon the validity of relationships not supported by the text. In the above case, for example, the orchestration implies the wrong-headedness of the suggestion, since the opening interval, played by the 'cellos alone, is heard as a unit, whereas the E-G♯ is divided disparately between 'cellos and oboe.

Analysis, then, exists precariously between description and prescription, and it is reason for concern that the latter two are not always easy to recognize. Description is current today in the form of twelve-tone counting—necessary, no doubt, as preliminary to further investigation, but involving no musical discrimination whatsoever. Prescription, on the other hand, is obvious in the absurd irrelevancies of Werker's analyses of Bach but is equally inherent in some of Schenker's more dogmatic pronouncements and in those of his followers.

It should be clear at this point that true analysis works through and for the ear. The greatest analysts (like Schenker at his best) are those with the keenest ears; their insights reveal how a piece of music should be heard, which in turn implies how it should be played. An analysis is a direction for a performance.

In order to explain how a given musical event should be heard, one must show why it occurs: what preceding events have made it necessary or appropriate, towards what later events its function is to lead. The composition must be revealed as an organic temporal unity, to be sure, but as a unity perceptible only gradually as one moment flows to the next, each contributing both to the forward motion and to the total effect. What is often referred to as musical logic comprises just these relationships of each event to its predecessors and to its successors, as well as to the whole. The job of analysis is to uncover them explicitly, but they are implicitly revealed in every good performance. Description, restricted to detailing what happens, fails to explain why. Prescription offers its own explanation, referring to an externally imposed scheme rather than to the actual course of the music.

One more familiar example may clarify this view of logical — or, as I prefer to call them, teleological — relationships.

The recapitulation of the Prestissimo from Beethoven's Sonata Op. 109 bursts in upon the development in such a way that the II♯ (V of V) is followed immediately by I. From a narrowly descriptive point of view one could call this an ellipsis, pointing out that the normally expected V

Ex. 5

49

has been omitted. Looking ahead, however, one will find that the first phrase of the recapitulation ends on V, and its consequent on I. The puzzling II♯, then, only temporarily and apparently resolved by what immediately follows it, actually points ahead in such a way that the whole passage is bound together in a cadential II-V-I. The propulsion thus generated is given an extra spurt by the compressed II-V-I at the end of the consequent, and the forward motion is renewed with fresh energy by the elision that sets the next period going.

Ex. 6

I need hardly mention the obvious effects of such an analysis on the performance of this passage. Whatever doubts one had as to the proper placing of the main accent in these phrases when they first appeared can now be resolved; the exposition can be reinterpreted, if need be, in the new light of the recapitulation.

II

It should be apparent at this point that analysis — and hence performance as it has been discussed above — cannot apply to certain types of composition in vogue today. When chance plays the major role in the writing of a work, as in Cage's *Music for Piano 21-52,* logic as defined above can take only an accidental part. The same is true of music written according to a strictly predetermined constructivistic scheme, such as Boulez's *Structures.* In neither case can any musical event be linked organically with those that precede and those that follow; it can be explained only by referring to an external structure — in the one case the laws of chance and in the other the predetermined plan. The connections are mechanistic rather than teleological: no event has any purpose — each is there only because it has to be there. In a word, this music is composed prescriptively, and the only possible or appropriate analytic method is to determine the original prescriptive plan. This is not analysis but cryptanalysis — the discovery of the key according to which a cipher or code was constructed. (If we are lucky, the composer or one of his initiates will spare us a lot of hard work by supplying us with the key.)

A third category that does not permit analysis is represented by Stockhausen's *Klavierstück XI,* where improvisation is given such free rein that it actually creates the form of the work anew at each performance. Thus *Klavierstück XI* does not exist as a single composition and cannot fruitfully be treated as one. Each new rendition can be discussed on its own merits, to be sure; but the relationship of all such versions to the abstract idea of the piece as a whole, and the decision as to the esthetic value of such an experiment — these problems can be argued endlessly. At any rate they are far afield from the practical considerations that are our concern here. (It need hardly be pointed out that improvisation as traditionally applied to the framework of a Baroque concerto, for example, had purposes quite different. A cadenza served not only to show off the soloist's virtuosity but also to punctuate an important cadence; the soloist's elaboration of a previously stated orchestral melody clarified the dualism inherent in the form. The quality of a given realization depended on its appropriateness to the compositional situation; the performance did not, as in many present-day examples, create the situation.)

III

The analysis of music of the periods closely preceding our own — the 18th and 19th centuries — has almost always assumed the applicability of certain familiar norms: tonally conditioned melody and harmony, periodic rhythmic structure on a regular metrical basis. Naturally such standards cannot be applied uncritically to the music of our own century, but on the other hand they should not be dismissed without examination. I contend that, in a more generalized form, they are still useful. Regardless of vocabulary, linear and chordal progressions still show striking analogies to older tonal procedures, analogies that are in turn reinforced by rhythmic structure. Only in those rare cases where the music tries to deny the principle of progression (as in the examples cited in the immediately preceding section) are such analogies completely lacking.

This point of view is more generally accepted with regard to harmony than to melody, perhaps because harmonic analysis is the more firmly entrenched discipline. After all, for many musicians theory is synonymous with harmony, melody being supposedly a free creative element, neither in its composition nor in its perception subjected to rule. (They forget, of course, that the object of the study of counterpoint is primarily the construction, and only secondarily the combination, of melodies.) Whereas Hindemith's enlargement of traditional harmony to encompass present-day vocabularies is generally known and often applauded, his attempt to find a melodic framework, actually a much less questionable procedure, is often ignored.

Another reason for shunning melodic analysis is that it is not always easy or even advisable to abstract the purely linear element from a progression. Wagner, in such motifs as the *Wanderer* and the *Magic Sleep*, is writing passages in which the melodic aspect is an incidental result of the chordal motion. A little later, Debussy offers examples (like the opening of *Reflets dans l'eau*) in which a linear phrase is dissolved into an atmospherically dispersed harmony that implies without actually stating the expected melodic resolution. Hyper-impressionistic pages, like parts of the *Night-Sounds* from Bartók's *Out-of-Doors* Suite, fragmentize the melody to such an extent that the progressive element is heard to be the increase and decrease of density as the motifs follow one upon the other, rather than the specifically linear aspect, which is here reduced to a minimum. Nevertheless, wherever there are successive differentiations in pitch there is melody of some kind, and wherever there is melody the ear will try to hear it in the simplest possible way.

This is not meant to imply that we must expect to find behind contemporary melodic lines the simple stepwise diatonic framework that Schenker has pointed out in Classical examples. But the ear will naturally connect each tone with those nearest it in pitch. The adjacent pitches may be diatonic or they may be chromatic; they may be actually **adja-**

51

cent or displaced by one or more octaves; they may be present by implication only. In some cases motivic associations or peculiar scale-formations may enforce the acceptance of a larger module — as in the simple case of bugle-calls, the adjacent tones of which are a third or a fourth apart. (In the case of microtonal music, smaller modules may be in effect, although it is doubtful to what extent even present-day ears can accept them.) In every case the ear will do the best it can with the available intervals. It is the duty of the analyst to show the pattern of connections by which an educated ear — his own — makes sense of the total melodic flow.

Even less than in traditional melodies must one assume that there is one uniquely correct way of hearing. Rather, the best analysis is the one that recognizes various levels functioning simultaneously, as when a tone resolves once in the immediate context but turns out to have a different goal in the long run. Two very brief examples may help to clarify this point of view.

52

Ex. 7

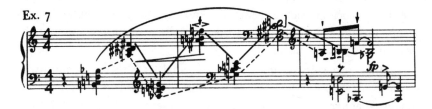

The first is the opening of Schoenberg's *Klavierstück* Op. 33a. Chordal rather than melodic in conception, its linear structure is nevertheless clear. Despite the octave displacements, a line can be traced in the uppermost voice from the F♯ in the first measure to the B in the third. (Notice, however, that at one point two adjacent tones are presented simultaneously instead of successively.) At the same time, the original B♭ leads, through various voices but always at the original octave-level, to the same tone of resolution. At this point the entrance of the F, repeating the climactic F of the second measure, begins a new motion that is carried forward through the succeeding phrase.

Ex. 8

The second passage is from the second of Sessions's piano pieces *From My Diary*.[1] Here both the F in the first measure and the Gb in the third are associated with upper and lower chromatic neighboring tones. But what of the cadential motif? Why is the pattern altered? And why is the linear descent from the Cb in the second measure broken at this point? There are several possible answers, all of which are probably relevant. First of all, the most prominent bass-note in each of the four measures — as indicated by its repetition and by its quarter-stem — is an F, which can be heard as a resolution, at another level, of the hanging Gb — a resolution confirmed by a direct Gb-F in the bass. But at the same time, there seems to be an implied E filling the space between the Gb and the D in its own voice — a tone suggested by the original association of E with Gb, and by the prominent whole-step motion in the melodic descent. In this case the line gradually increases its pace as it descends.

Ex. 9

But if it seems far-fetched to introduce an unstated, understood element, one can hear the skip Gb-D as a way of emphasizing the cadence, and point out that the motif of neighboring tones aims each time more directly towards its resolution: the first time the neighbors follow the principal; the second time they precede it; and the last time the principal takes the place of one of its own neighbors. Finally, it should be noted that the next phrase takes off from the dangling Gb in a subtle motivic reference to the beginning.

Ex. 10

It is of course impossible to do justice here to the role of such details in the total melodic structure, but on examination one will find

53

the same kind of connection at work in the large. Note, for example, how much of the first theme of the Schoenberg piano piece is controlled by the high F already mentioned — whether in its original octave or in another — and by its association with the adjacent E. It is again this F, in its highest register, that prepares for the recapitulation; and it is the E that, returning first with the tranquil second theme, later closes the motion in a lower octave in the final measure. In sum, modern melody can not get rid of stepwise motion, because that is the way we hear melody; but it can and does expand (or on occasion contract) the distance, both temporal and spatial, between successive steps. From this point of view even Webern is found to be no pointillist, but a draughtsman of subtle and fragile lines.

The role of harmony in the music of our century, although more extensively explored, is perhaps more difficult, complicated as it is by many factors, such as the frequent exploitation of the static, sensuous effect of the chord in addition to or even at the expense of its progressive functions. As a result, one can no longer assume the easily defined functionality of obviously tonal music. Chords can no longer be precisely named, nor can their identity be maintained in differing contexts. But it is important to realize that, even in stubbornly non-triadic music, the concept of the chord remains, by analogy at least. The composer can set up arbitrary simultaneities that, by their commanding position or by repetition, are accepted as the controlling sonorities — the chords — against which other tones can function in the manner of traditional non-harmonic tones. Bartók's *Improvisations* Op. 20 show how by such a technique quite complicated sonorities can be used to harmonize simple modal folk-tunes. In the following example from the last of Sessions's *Diary* pieces the metrical position and the half-step resolutions suggest that the first chord is an appoggiatura to the second; this supposition is confirmed by the appearance of the root-like D in the bass, and by the clinching repetitions that ensue.

Ex. 11

In fact, only where the contrapuntal aspect becomes so strong that every element of each sonority is heard primarily as a point in a moving line, or at the other extreme, where the texture is completely pointillistic, is the chordal concept seriously challenged. In such cases one further assumption of traditional harmony that must then be questioned is the primacy of the bass. Contrapuntally or coloristically, of course, it will have gained in importance, but at the expense of its role in defining the harmony. A beautiful example of this process already at work over a century ago is shown in the opening of Liszt's *Vallée d'Obermann,* where the melodic action of the bass clouds the harmony. Not until the return of the theme adds a new bass underneath the original one is the situation made clear. A further step in this direction is taken by Mahler, who by his polyphonically opposed chords points the way towards polytonality in the magical cowbell passage in the first movement of his Sixth Symphony. A more thoroughgoing example is Stravinsky's *Symphonies pour instruments à vent,* a more truly polytonal work than any of Milhaud's often-cited *Saudades,* which in fact present only extended and elaborated harmonies over a single real bass.

There are other forces at work undermining the primacy of the lowest voice. Impressionistic parallelism, which reduces its role to that of coloristic doubling, is too well known to require citation. Less frequent, but possibly more important in the light of later developments, is the masking of the true harmonic bass by a decorative voice below it, a technique seen clearly in the repetition of the opening of *La Fille aux cheveux de lin.* Another device, common to the Impressionists and Mahler, is the *ostinato.* From one point of view the persistent voice is emphasized, but at the same time it is removed from the sphere of action. In Debussy, as later in Stravinsky, the *ostinato* results in harmonic stasis; in Mahler there is a constant tension between the harmony implied by the motionless bass and those outlined by the moving voices and chords above it. In both cases the functional role of the bass is called into question.

So far no specific reference has been made to the problem of tonality. Except in comparatively rare cases, such as passages in *Le Sacre du printemps,* where an almost completely static tone or chord of reference is set up, tonality is created not by harmony alone, nor even by harmony and melody, but by their relationship with the rhythmic structure: in a word, by the phenomenon of the cadence. A discussion of certain rhythmic aspects, then, can no longer be postponed.

IV

Much of the vitality of the music of the Classical period derives from the constant interplay of meter and rhythm, the former determined

55

by regular beats and measures and the latter by constantly varying motifs and phrases. This tension between the abstract and the concrete begins to break down during the 19th century, when phrase articulation is often either slavishly tied to the meter or else so completely liberated that the sense of the meter is almost lost. The retention of the measure in much Impressionistic music is purely conventional, and it is no wonder that later composers have abandoned the effort to keep an abstract pattern when it would conflict with the actual rhythm. For this reason the regularity of the meter in such composers as Webern must be carefully examined. Is it to be felt as a constantly present control? Is it a pure convention? Is it, as some would have us believe, an evidence of the composer's numerological superstitions?

The answers to such questions must always be given with specific reference to the text involved. When, as in the case of Example 11, the motif sets up a clear cross-rhythm, the explanation is relatively easy. Webern's Piano Variations, on the other hand, present the problem in an acute form. What has happened here, I think, is that the composer has called on a complex set of interrelationships of rhythmic, metric, dynamic, and textural factors to compensate for the tenuity of melodic and harmonic interest. In the first twelve measures of the last movement, for example, I find at least seven different time-divisions simultaneously functioning. These are set up by the meter (3/2), a possible cross-meter (5/4), the rhythm of the two-note motifs, the rhythm of the phrases, the tone-row, the dynamic alternations, and the linear pattern (Ex. 12).[2]

The really important question to ask in all such cases — and even in cases where the composer has deliberately tried to get rid of all traditional metrical measurement — is, can we locate the structural downbeat? If we can, then we can proceed with analytic concepts in some way analogous to those of the traditional rhythm and meter, phrase and cadence. If not, some completely new rhythmic theory must be devised. Some musicians, like Stockhausen, are trying to do this, but I have as yet seen no satisfactory one emerge.

By structural downbeat, of course, I do not mean the arbitrary accentuation of the first beat of every measure; I mean rather phenomena like the articulation by which the cadential chord of a phrase is identified, the weight by which the second phrase of a period is felt as resolving the first, the release of tension with which the tonic of a recapitula-

Ex. 12

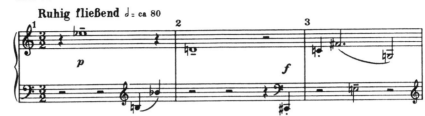

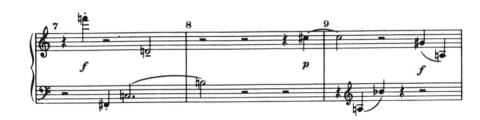

tion enters. (In the Webern example, I hear the downbeat as the E♮ at the beginning of measure 12; and I consider it no accident that it occurs at the beginning of a measure, preceded by a *ritardando*.)

It is just here that the importance of rhythm to the establishment of tonality emerges, for the cadence is the point in the phrase at which rhythmic emphasis and harmonic function coincide. It would be partly true to say that the cadence creates tonality, but it would be equally true to say that tonality creates the cadence. Where the cadence exists, it is impossible to hear music as completely atonal, even though one may be unable to define the key in conventional terms.

We know the signs by which a cadence can be recognized in traditionally tonal music: its position at the end of a phrase, the melodic
resolution, the change of harmony. The actual downbeat may not always
exactly coincide with the cadential point, but such unusual cases arise
most often when the phrase is rhythmically prolonged (the feminine
ending) or when it points ahead so clearly that the next phrase acts as
a huge cadence to the first (as when an introductory section is followed
by a main theme). In any case, keys are defined by the appearances of
strong, cadential downbeats — whether clearly on the tonic as in most
Classical examples, or on deceptive resolutions, as notably in the Prelude
to *Tristan*.

The extent to which analogous principles govern the structure of
contemporary music is surprising. A few examples will show them at
work.

The opening of the second movement of Bartók's Fifth Quartet may
prove puzzling until it is heard as an upbeat. The first downbeat comes
on the D in measure 5, clinched by an even stronger cadence on the same
tone (now supported by its fifth) in measure 10. The digression that
follows suggests the key of C, but this tonality is not confirmed by the
cadence, which, when it arrives in measure 20, is again clearly on D.

The first page of Sessions's Second Sonata for Piano is much less
triadic; yet when the downbeat comes in measure 11, the harmony of B♭
is clearly established. Not only the V-I implied by the progression of fifths
in the bass, but the melodic resolution to D, accented by the downward
leap, points towards this tonal center, which is confirmed by what follows.
In the second movement, no such clear downbeat is presented, but the
two important feminine cadences of measures 177 and 190 both suggest
an unstated resolution to E. The important downbeat of measure 191,
coming as it then does on F, is in the nature of a neighboring harmony;
and not until much later, at measure 213, does the expected E occur, its
extension as a pedal for ten measures compensating for its long postpone-
ment. The last few measures of the Lento act as an upbeat released in the
return of B♭ in the opening of the finale. But this in turn, after a long
battle with conflicting elements, gives way at the last to the key of C,
on which a downbeat is firmly established in the final chord.

Stravinsky is sometimes referred to as a "downbeat composer," by
which I suppose is meant that he often emphasizes the beginnings rather
than the endings of his phrases. This results in a weakening of the
cadential sense, it is true, the phrases so accented being as it were huge

feminine endings to their own opening chords. A typical example is the opening of the *Sérénade en la*. The harmonic progression would be described in traditional terms as VI $^6_3$-I $^5_3$ in A minor; actually the F of the first chord is heard as hardly more than an appoggiatura resolving to the E of the second. This would appear to be no progression at all, in which case the phrase should be a huge *diminuendo*. Yet we cannot be too sure: in a similar situation at the beginning of the third movement of the *Symphony of Psalms,* the composer, by changing the mode and the orchestration at the cadential word *Dominum,* creates a clear accent even though the chord has remained essentially the same (C) throughout the phrase.

In any event, whatever we may decide about the reading of his phrase-accent in detail, Stravinsky is perfectly capable of producing a big structural downbeat at precisely the point where it is required. I need only point to the huge deceptive cadence that opens the Symphony in Three Movements, the dominant G of the introduction resolving finally upward to the A of the *ostinato* theme (rehearsal number 7); or to the way in which the Interlude acts as an upbeat to the C major of the finale.

More controversial is the attempt to find traces of tonal form in avowedly atonal compositions; yet I do not see how music like Schoenberg's, with its usually clear cadential structure, can fail to arouse certain traditional associations and responses. The previously cited *Klavierstück* Op. 33a begins with six chords, of which the second through the fifth are very easily—although not necessarily—heard as forming a progression referring to E minor. This in itself is nothing, but when the opening phrase is heard as an upbeat resolved in the third measure, and when the resolving sonority is recognized as a seventh on E, a tonal analogy is set up. The first section of the piece concludes even more unmistakably on E, with the added emphasis of a *ritardando;* and the theme that follows in measure 14 gives the effect of a sudden shift of key. In the recapitulation, the *ritardando* of measure 34 again calls attention to the following downbeat, where the E appears in the upper voice, but supported in the bass by A—in the manner of a deceptive cadence on IV. It remains for the final cadence to confirm the E, which is so strong that it is not dislodged by the dissonant tones with which it is here surrounded.

Several objections can be made to the above account: that it picks

59

out isolated points without reference to the movement between them, that the "cadences" on E are a result of the fact that the row ends on that note, that such analysis is irrelevant to music in this style.

To the first count I plead guilty. I have indeed picked out isolated points, because these seemed to me to be the important "full-cadences" of the piece. (Important "half-cadences" occur at measures 9, 24, and 32.) The movement between them cannot, I grant, be explained in simple tonal terms. At some points, linear or contrapuntal motion dominates—in which case the melodic principles suggested above will indicate the logic of the chosen cadences. At other points the sonorities themselves dominate—and these can of course be shown as derived from the opening chords. As a result the entire piece can be heard as a development of its original cadential progression—that is, as analogous to a traditional structure.

I agree that the cadences are partially due to the use of the row. Depending on one's point of view, this effect is a virtue or a vice of Schoenberg's twelve-tone technique. It may even have been one of the points persuading him to turn towards the system, away from freer atonal methods. In no case can the argument invalidate the actual musical result.

To the charge of irrelevancy, I answer that one who cannot indeed hear such cadential phenomena in this music must judge the analysis to be prescriptive and inapplicable. But one who does hear them must admit to that extent the validity of the approach. He may counter that one ought not to hear the music in this way; but he is then criticizing the music, not the analytical method. Unwanted cadential effects would be as great a flaw in atonal music as the chance appearance of a human figure in a non-representational painting.

V

The last point suggests that there is a relation between analysis and criticism. It is not a simple one. Analysis can often reveal flaws in a work, it is true — often but not always. If it were dependable in this regard, we should be able to decide definitively between the disputed C♯ and C𝄪 in the last movement of Beethoven's Sonata Op. 109 (measure 55) or whether the famous A♮ in Schoenberg's Op. 33a is indeed an A♭ (measure 22). But unfortunately such cases all too often work both ways: the C𝄪 that from one point of view prepares for the advent of D two measures later might have been avoided in order not to anticipate it; by the same token, although the A♭ seems more logical in the row-structure (in spite of the A♮ lacking in the left hand), it may somewhat spoil the freshness of the A♭-E♭ fifth that comes soon after. The ear must be the ultimate judge of such subtleties, but insofar as analysis trains and sharpens the ear it makes its contribution to the final decision.

It would be tempting to go further and state that analysis can demonstrate the quality of a work, but this requires a faith in rationality that I am unable to summon. Judgment of final excellence must be fundamentally intuitive. If analysis leads one to condemn a work he nevertheless continues to hear as good, he must conclude that there is something wrong either with his ear or with his method. Since he cannot dispense with the only pair of ears he has, upon whose evidence the examination should have been based in the first place, he must blame his method. He must then find a new one based on his own hearing, one that will substantiate, not contradict, his musical judgment. He may then claim that analysis has established the excellence of the work in question, but he will be wrong; his own judgment will have established the analysis.

One positive point emerges here, and it is a crucial one. The good composition will always reveal, on close study, the methods of analysis needed for its own comprehension. This means that a good composition manifests its own structural principles, but it means more than that. In a wider context, it is an example of the proposition that a work of art ought to imply the standards by which it demands to be judged. Most criticism today tacitly accepts the truth of this statement and sets about discovering the standards implied by a given work and testing how well it lives up to them. For investigation of this kind, analysis is naturally of primary importance.

Criticism should take a further step, however, and the best criticism does. It should question the value of the standards. A work that sets no clear standard denies or defies the possibility of evaluation; one that does set its standard fails or succeeds insofar as it measures up to it; one that measures up completely is at least flawless — but its value cannot exceed the value of its own standard. It is this final step that is completely beyond the confines of analysis.

The music of Webern is a prominent case in point. No serious critic denies the perfection of his forms and the complete consistency of his style. Its paucity of normal melodic and harmonic interests has been mentioned above, but in connection with other values that, replacing

61

these, uniquely characterize his manner. What is seldom questioned is the significance of the style itself — of the restrictive standard (for it is a restrictive one) that Webern set for his own music. Are the limits too narrow to permit accomplishment at the very highest level? Only a decision of this point can determine one's final evaluation of the composer. It is a decision that depends on one's beliefs about the limits and aims of art in general and is thus not exclusively musical, although it must at the same time be peculiarly musical. It must be made on faith, and it must be accepted or rejected in the same spirit.

Issues in Composition

1. The musical idea

Richard Strauss once observed that the melodic ideas which provide the substance of a composition seldom consist of more than two to four bars; the remainder is elaboration, working-out, compositional technique.[1] The aesthetic crux that he touched on here is one which occupied the Greeks and has not lost its teasing character with age: the perennial question of the priority of reflection or inspiration, *ars* or *ingenium*, technique or genius. The aesthetic discussion has to be located in a historical context, however, if it is not to remain on a plane of abstract speculation. Certainly the limited dimensions of the kind of thematic inspiration to which Strauss referred are characteristic not so much of all musical creativity at all times as of composition in the latter part of the nineteenth century. It is no exaggeration to say that the difficulties faced by composers after Beethoven were due in no small part to the brevity of their musical ideas: these difficulties were shared by Wagner, Liszt, Bruckner, and even Brahms, although their solutions differed. Nietzsche's axiom that it was necessary to close one's

1. R. Strauss, "Vom melodischen Einfall," in *Betrachtungen und Erinnerungen,* 2d ed. (Zurich, 1957), p. 165.

eyes to Wagner the "al fresco painter" if one was to discover
the true Wagner—"our greatest musical miniaturist"[2]—
employs a metaphor to describe something that could be expressed as the contradiction between the brevity of the musical ideas and the monumentality of the formal designs.

It could be argued that brevity of musical ideas was a
characteristic not of the later nineteenth century alone but
of Beethoven himself, at least in the symphonies, but this
was not the case; the *Eroica* and the Fifth Symphony may
spring to mind, but Wagner's formal problems are different in kind from Beethoven's. The eight-note theme—or
"motto"—of the first movement of the *Eroica* is determined
by the overall design and not vice versa: the form is not built
up out of the theme. The motto is not so much stated or
expounded and then developed as brought forth by the symphonic process in which it has a function to fulfill, and the
musical "idea" is the symphonic process itself, not the
theme. The opening of the Fifth Symphony is analogous: as
Heinrich Schenker demonstrated,[3] the belief that the first
four notes constitute the thematic substance of the movement is, however popular, mistaken. The melodic idea is not
what is contained in the first two bars, repeated sequentially
in the third and fourth (more than that would have to be
taken into account, if one wished to define the "idea" in the
Beethovenian sense); it is the whole of bars 1–4, the twofold
descending third (G–E♭ and F–D) which in the subsidiary
theme becomes a descending fifth, also repeated (B♭–E♭ and
F–B♭). (The structural similarity of the thematic openings
indicates that the sequential working belongs to the thematic idea and not to the elaboration.) But the error as to
the structure of the theme—one shared by even Wagner
himself[4]—is historically revealing. What to Beethoven was
a part, a component, was understood later in the nineteenth
century to be an independent, self-sufficient musical idea,

2. F. Nietzsche, *Der Fall Wagner*, in *Werke*, 2:918.
3. H. Schenker, *Beethoven: V. Symphonie* (Vienna, n.d.), pp. 3ff.
4. Wagner, *Gesammelte Schriften*, 8:282 (*Über das Dirigieren*).

because the composers of the day looked for and found in Beethoven what they themselves practised. The original melodic unit represented by bars 1—4 was broken up and described as model and sequential repetition, so that it conformed to the pattern which was fundamental to the musical syntax of thematic openings written by Wagner and Liszt, whereas in the early nineteenth century sequence was a technique employed in elaboration and development, never in exposition. Of course Beethoven's theme can be described, in terms of its technical elements, as a model and sequential repetition, but the important distinction is whether the theme is understood primarily as a unit, whose sequential structure is a secondary factor, or whether, erroneously, the first four notes are treated as an idea complete in itself, which is then elaborated sequentially. In Beethoven formal ideas and melodic detail come into being simultaneously: the single motive is relative to the whole. By contrast, in the later nineteenth century the melodic idea acted as a motive in the literal sense of the word, setting the music in motion, and provided the substance of a development in which the theme itself was elaborated. Musical form now presented itself primarily (though by no means exclusively) as a consequence drawn from thematic ideas, not as a system of formal relations.

At least one reason for the extreme concision of the musical idea and for the consequent need to distinguish between the initial idea and its elaboration is to be found in the social and intellectual preconceptions of the time. The concept of originality which grew up in the later eighteenth century established itself in the nineteenth as an unquestioned aesthetic doctrine, whereas the idea of *ars inveniendi*, the theory of musical invention which was taken for granted in the seventeenth century and earlier in the eighteenth, was condemned in the nineteenth as if it were a blasphemy against the cult of genius.

Until the end of the eighteenth century a musical idea could be a platitude, something quite commonplace, with-

66

out attracting the charge of being meaningless; convention—recognizable dependence on precedent—was still regarded as aesthetically legitimate. That is not to say that no one could distinguish between an individual and unusual idea and a well-worn cliché, but the quality of an entire movement was not considered to depend entirely on the originality of the idea expounded at its start.

The thematic technique of classical composers around 1800 represents a transitional stage, achieving a balance, at once felicitous and precarious, between opposing aesthetic principles. The originality for which Haydn and Beethoven undoubtedly strove and the amount of formal convention which was still acceptable complemented each other without contradiction, since the dichotomy—which is often apparent aesthetically—was not the decisive structural factor. As yet the single idea was still understood primarily as a corollary of the whole, and not as the essential sustaining substance, whose individuality or conventionality determined the overall form and was the only grounds on which its quality might be judged. Both Wagner and Schoenberg complain about the mere padding to be found in Mozart's music, even in some of his principal themes, but this is almost unavoidable when the musical form is made up of corresponding, well-balanced parts which of themselves delineate the whole movement. Such form resembles the metrical pattern adopted in a poem, by contrast with the musical "prose" which results when melodic ideas are expressed plainly without periphrasis. In the first movement of Mozart's C major Symphony K.551, the continuation of the first thematic period—a tutti described by Hans Georg Nägeli as "shallow" and "trivial"[5]—can be justified by its function, which is to provide a counterbalance to the opening of the movement, even if it is indefensible in terms of melodic or harmonic invention, of which it has none. Classical form could survive banality in some (not all) of its

5. H. G. Nägeli, *Vorlesungen über Musik mit Berücksichtigung der Dilettanten* (Stuttgart, 1826), pp. 164f.

parts: the banal did not become intolerable until the idea of a balance of parts distinguished by their functions was replaced by the principle of developing ideas, the concept of musical form as something which presented the history of a musical theme.

During the course of the nineteenth century, for socio-historical reasons among others, it became virtually obligatory for themes, or their initial ideas, to be original, because form itself fell into a state of one-sided dependence on the musical idea. Schematic forms, of the kind predominating in short character pieces for piano, were sustained exclusively by the quality of the initial idea, the individual character of which compensated for the conventionality of the overall outline. (The fact that the differentiated formulation and development of ideas can be accommodated in conventional ABA formal patterns in the piano music of Schumann or Brahms would be an almost irreconcilable contradiction, were it not that the formal outline serves no other purpose than to present and arrange the musical "content.") Individualized form is the polar opposite of schematic form (the tendency to create it can be observed in some of Liszt's symphonic poems); it represents the consequential unfurling of the initial musical idea (which, for its part, is determined programmatically), and its success in formulating and presenting the musical content can be measured by how well it conceals the fact that it is doing so.[6]

In a form in which every part or detail is supposed to be an original idea or the consequence of an original idea, conventional material is bound to be regarded as superfluous padding, and a work in which platitudes are conspicuous will be condemned aesthetically as derivative hackwork. No phrase in a theme or its continuation should be empty of meaning, the mere formulaic expansion of the essential musical idea to a regular verse-like period (symmetry and rounding-off, the essential premises of a form conceived of as a "poetic"

6. Wagner, *Gesammelte Schriften*, 5:187f (*Über Franz Liszts symphonische Dichtungen*).

metrical pattern on a large scale, are almost unimaginable without conventional components and interpolations). By contrast, when musical ideas are wholly original, significant at every instant and expressed without padding, as Richard Strauss said, they are apt to be extremely short. Leitmotivs as long as the Siegfried motive are the exception in Wagner, not the rule; the Sword and Spear motives are representative of the norm.

The type of motive represented by the Curse motive in *Der Ring des Nibelungen* and the Day motive in *Tristan und Isolde,* a type which was regarded in the later nineteenth century as the paradigm of a musical idea in the emphatic sense of the word, is not subject to the laws governing the distinction between "open" and "closed" syntactic structures; the usual categories do not apply to it. On the one hand these motives come to an end without a perfect or imperfect cadence; harmonically undetermined, they suggest that more is to follow. On the other hand their rhythmic outlines are so clear-cut that continuation is unnecessary as a means of giving them syntactic sense or identity. Thus the motive is neither a complete period in itself, nor will it tolerate the construction of a consequent clause to make it up to a period. The idea that the Yearning motive in *Tristan* needs a motivically analogous and harmonically complementary clause to "complete" it is inexpressibly trivial; the only suitable means of continuing the motive is sequential repetition, which leads it into tonally remote regions.

2. Real sequence and developing variation

The technique of real, "literal" sequence, which effects an interruption or an actual change of the initial key, acquires in Wagner and Liszt—and Liszt's symphonic poems seem to have had some influence on Wagner[7]—a formal significance which is different in principle from the "same" procedure as used by Haydn or Beethoven. In classical symphonic or

7. C. Dahlhaus, *Wagners Konzeption des musikalischen Dramas* (Regensburg, 1971), pp. 111ff.

sonata movements, "real" (or modulatory, but not tonal) sequence was used primarily as a developmental technique, one part in the process of musical working-out, which had invariably been preceded by an exposition section where the themes had been stated in a form both tonally and syntactically complete. (The fact that sequential models are drawn into expansive modulatory processes in the course of a development section is closely connected with their melodic formation out of fragments of a theme or of several themes: the dissolution of the harmonic and tonal outlines is felt to be the correlative of melodic and syntactical dissolution. The unrest of the modulation, like the thematic instability, corresponds to the transitional stage reached in the formal process.)

In Wagner and Liszt, on the other hand (and sometimes in Bruckner too, e.g. the beginning of the Sixth Symphony), real sequence is an expository procedure, a means of elaborating a musical idea which in itself—like the Yearning motive in *Tristan*—needs no continuation and would not tolerate conventional "rounding-off" in a closed period. In Liszt's symphonic poem *Hamlet*, the principal section of which is no less than 159 bars long, the principal theme (bar 105) is the goal and the outcome of an extended development which relies essentially on acceleration of tempo and transformation of themes. The individual musical ideas are spread out in sequences, either real or modulatory, according to a tonal pattern which seems at times excessively schematic. (In bars 9ff. the model, which is repeated, modulates from C minor to A♭ minor, and the sequence modulates from E♭ minor to B minor; the principal theme is stated complete in B minor and D minor, and fragments are then transposed to A♭ minor, E minor and D♭ major.) It might be thought that the sequential structure is determined and justified at the start by the introductory character of the parts, and in the main theme by the merging of exposition and development (the transposition of the theme from B minor to D minor both prepares and starts the evolution).

The form is unusual: an expansive introduction eventually arrives at a principal theme which, after a brief moment of actual "exposition" in the sonata-form sense, moves on into development. Yet it seems as though the sequential structure is not a product of the unusual form but, on the contrary, the form is a consequence of the sequential structure, which is itself motivated by the brevity of the musical ideas. This lends more support to the theory that conceptions of musical form are based, in each era, on the characteristic types of thematic material, of melodic invention, than to the opposing notion, that thematic types are produced by formal ideas.

It would be wrong to dismiss the change in the function of modulatory sequence from a developmental technique to an expositional technique as an event of merely peripheral significance in the history of composition. Changes in the functions of musical techniques are historically of no less (even if less apparent) importance than the substantial, material developments—such as the growing prominence of chromaticism and the exploration of remoter tonal regions—which are normally regarded as the signs of musical progress in the nineteenth century. If the importance of a change is measured in terms of its influence on musical form, understood as the sum of the associations between all the elements in a composition, it is by no means possible to assert *a priori* that the invasion of expositional processes by modulatory sequence had a less profound effect than the chromaticization of harmony.

In Wagner and Liszt the change in the function of real, modulatory sequence is the formal outcome of the kind of thematic writing epitomized by the leitmotiv, which does not permit the formation of regular periods or submit to the regulations of large-scale metrical patterns. Brahms, faced like them with the difficulties caused by the concision of the basic thematic substance under the pressure of the all-pervading insistence on originality, sought a different solution in the procedure that Schoenberg was to call "develop-

71

ing variation." The latent unity of the music of the age is demonstrated by the fact that essentially the same problem faced Wagner, Liszt *and* Brahms; it is not reflected in stylistic unity or uniformity, however, since individual stylistic traits, which develop in the course of working out solutions, are not contingent on separate initial problems. The difference between these composers is discovered in the methods which they employed to resolve or annul the discrepancy between the narrow dimensions of thematic ideas and the tendency towards large, expansive, monumental forms: a tendency that Brahms the symphonist—an aspiring symphonist even in the structure of his chamber music—shared with Wagner the composer of music dramas. Real (modulatory) sequence and developing variation are alternatives to each other in practical musical terms, without mutually excluding each other in principle. As expositional procedures they can be said to represent the practices of what Franz Brendel in 1859 dubbed the "New German" school of composition on the one hand and the "conservatives" on the other (although, as the progressive consequences that Schoenberg drew from Brahms's techniques demonstrate, the latter were by no means as backward-looking as may have appeared in 1870 or 1880).

In his own way Brahms was as much a "musical miniaturist" as Wagner and Liszt, nurturing the same ambitions to use large, all-embracing, "Beethovenian" forms. The serenades and the First Piano Concerto are milestones on his way towards the symphony, the monumental demands of which he did not feel himself ready to meet for another two decades. Beginning with thematic substance that was reduced—one might almost say shrunk—to the utmost, he had to evolve a technique of formal elaboration which would carry over wide spans without subsiding into vacuous academic discursiveness.

The use Brahms made of developing variation as an expositional procedure (that is, in a formal function similar to that of modulatory sequence in Wagner and Liszt) is exemplified in the first movement of the G minor Piano Quartet op. 25. The material of the principal section (bars 1–27) derives from two motives of the utmost brevity and, in themselves, no great significance: the first consists of four notes, the second of two. The first part of the theme is based on the motivic shape which appears as D–B♭–F♯–G in bar 1, transposed in bar 5, and freely inverted, either as in bars 2–3 and 6–8, or with the two middle notes played simultaneously (bar 4: F♯–C♯–E–D):

The second part of the theme consists of nothing more than a descending second, which is repeated sequentially and imitatively (bars 11–13) and appears in all manner of rhythmic shapes: in half-notes (bars 11–13, 20) and dotted half-notes (bars 17–18), in eighth-notes (bars 13–15) and in quarters (bars 15–16). Compositional economy, the building of musical interest out of minimal capital, was taken to extremes by Brahms.

The process of developing variation bestows on both the basic motives and the material derived from them—insofar as it is recognizable as such—a meaning that they would not have in themselves, as isolated figures. The whole significance of the musical instant, unimportant in itself, is that it points the way forward to something greater. Even if it is agreed, however, that the musical meaning of the individual phrases is dependent on the relationship in which they stand to each other and to the initial idea, this is still not enough to characterize the material; as in the case, already mentioned, of the first tutti of Mozart's "Jupiter" Symphony, it is only the relationship to the opening period

73

that gives the music its aesthetic justification. But in
Mozart's case the musical form can be compared to architecture (and was, by Friedrich Schlegel), whereas in Brahms it is
like the development or elaboration, both logical and rhetorical, of a process of thought. Mozart does not by any means
despise using his initial ideas as a source of further thematic
and motivic material, but doing so always serves a function.
It is subordinated to the principle of balance which dominates and controls his forms of whatever order, from the subordinate clause to the overall outline of the whole: the
motivic correspondence between a first-subject group and a
transition, as much as the motivic contrast between a
second-subject group and a closing section, is a procedure
intended to balance corresponding parts. (The provision of
links and analogies between a first subject and a transition is
of lesser importance: it does not constitute a structural principle but is merely an expedient—for which others could be
substituted—for demonstrating that the sections are complementary.) With Brahms, on the other hand, the elaboration of a thematic idea is the primary formal principle, on
which depends the integration of the movement as a whole,
preventing it from appearing as a mere pot-pourri. Musical
form takes the shape of a discourse in sound in which motives develop out of earlier motives like ideas, each of which
is a consequence of its predecessors.

The differences in the technical procedures adopted by
Wagner and Liszt on the one hand and by Brahms on the
other are of course, like the stances taken up by opposing
parties in the musical life of the later nineteenth century as
a whole, closely connected with the differences between the
preferred genres—between music drama and chamber music; this has always been recognized. (Wagner's chamber
compositions are mere parerga—curiosities with no real
bearing on the central part of his oeuvre—and likewise it is
no accident that Brahms never carried out his operatic
plans.) Sequential writing on the scale and in the manner in

which it occurs in Wagner and Liszt, if found in the exposition of a piece of chamber music, would strike the listener as unwelcome tonal discursiveness and pompous rhetoric. Developing variation, for its part, would fall flat in music drama: it would be nothing but a pedantic self-indulgence by the composer, it would not penetrate the listener's awareness in performance, and aesthetically—in any bearing it might have on the realization of the drama—it would still be ineffectual even for someone reading the score who was able to see the latent associations. Wagner's technique of motivic transformation, such as the growth of the Valhalla motive out of the Ring motive during the transition between the first and second scenes of *Das Rheingold*, is a procedure that is an exception rather than the rule in music drama. It is imposed on the music by the dramatic program and is not at all the same thing as the unobtrusive, yet completely convincing, musical logic of the developing variation in Brahms's G minor Piano Quartet.

The symphony can be said to occupy a middle ground, stylistically, between the large canvas of music drama and the intimate discourse of chamber music, and in it the divergent techniques characteristic of those two contrasting genres in their most typical manifestations tend to overlap and blend. It has always been recognized that Brahms's symphonic writing is rooted in the premises of chamber music, but there has never been any question of regarding it simply as chamber music in disguise: rather it is a matter of transformation. The process undergone by the "motto" of the first movement of the Third Symphony is a paradigm of developing variation when transferred from chamber music to the monumental dimensions of the symphony. The motive expounded in the introduction, which is the fundamental musical idea of the movement, though it does not function as the principal subject, constantly recurs in changing harmonizations wherever there is what could be called a "hinge" in the form. The variation of the harmony is not

75

coloristic in intention, but corresponds functionally to the various changes in the situation and significance of the motto (establishing the basic key at the beginning; providing the bass line in a harmonically ambiguous antecedent clause; preparing the second subject by modulation); it can therefore be described as a "developing" variation—one, that is, which affects the formal progress, and not simply one which provides transient coloring. On the other hand, the motivic shape of the motto is always recognizable, so that it can continue to fulfill the role of establishing connections over the wide span of a symphony.

If Brahms was attempting in his Third Symphony to combine the pregnant significance of the leitmotiv, which strictly speaking cannot develop, with the principle of developing variation, Bruckner at the beginning of his Sixth Symphony introduces the Lisztian practice of using modulatory sequences in thematic exposition. This works in a symphonic poem like *Hamlet*, because there the distinction between exposition and development is ultimately unimportant, but the basic form of a symphonic movement still rests on the traditional distinction. The "dynamism" of incessantly modulating sequences contradicts the essentially "thematic" importance of the exposition, which should create the background against which development can take place. But if such conflict sometimes occurs in the symphony, in the middle ground between the poles of chamber music and music drama, and puts the form at risk, it confirms rather than refutes the correlation between a musical genre and its "ideal type" of expositional technique.

3. "Musical prose" and "endless melody"

The shrinking of thematic ideas created problems for composers all the greater because it coincided with the later nineteenth century's obsession with ever larger forms. This was a tendency for which it is hard to find inherent historical musical reasons, so an explanation must be sought in social and cultural history. (That is not to say that interpretation on socio-historical lines should, as a matter of principle, take over where the history of compositional procedures breaks off: in one sense each offers an alternative to the other, but there is also a stage at which one approach is transformed into the other.) The fact that thematic material was reduced during the course of the nineteenth century from the period to the motive was the result, as has been said, of the principle that a musical idea, to be worthy of the name, had to be original and meaningful throughout; a platitude lost the aesthetic right to exist that it was still allowed to enjoy as a component in a larger figure in Beethoven (in spite of the dominance of the doctrine of originality). Particles that lacked any special melodic character or content, but met a functional need insofar as they rounded off a musical idea to bring a phrase or a period to a formal conclusion, could no longer be tolerated. Such aesthetic rigor was linked with the emphasis that the age of romanticism, with its cult of genius, laid on inspiration, but it threatened to undermine traditional musical syntax and the regular periodic structure which provided the framework of musical form—that is, of form conceived of as a large-scale metrical pattern. "Quadratic compositional construction," as Wagner scornfully called it—in a failure to appreciate the architectural nature of a formal principle based on the idea of balance, a principle which Alfred Lorenz wrongly asserted to be the "secret" of Wagnerian form—is scarcely imaginable without some melodic filling-out.

In an essay with the provocative title "Brahms the Progressive," Arnold Schoenberg, whose initiation of the atonal techniques of the New Music in 1908 signified not only a break with the past but also, and simultaneously, one of the ultimate consequences of the compositional trends of the nineteenth century, spoke of "musical prose."[8] The term

77

8. A. Schoenberg, *Style and Idea* (New York, 1950), p. 72 [2d ed., 1976, p. 415]; cf. also Dahlhaus, "Musikalische Prosa," *Neue Zeitschrift für Musik,* vol. 125 (1964): 176 ff.

should make it plain that the rhythmic and metrical irregularity of which the New Music was accused—and which was as great a hindrance to its acceptance as atonal harmony[9]—was not a sign of wanton destructiveness but the necessary outcome when composers undertook to express a musical idea directly, without circumlocution or ornament. (Schoenberg shared Adolf Loos's hostility towards ornamentation.) Periodic structure, the musical equivalent of "verse" form, is open to the charge of creating opportunities for empty rhetoric and interpolations which express little or nothing. Melody, as popularly conceived, is characterized above all by rhythmic regularity, by the use of symmetry and repetition: this was a "formula," in opposition to which Schoenberg set up the musical "idea," which is expressed "like prose" (*prosaisch*). "This is what musical prose should be—a direct and straightforward presentation of ideas, without any patchwork, without mere padding and empty repetitions."[10] The traditions of which Schoenberg was the continuer and which he took to their ultimate consequences were those of the nineteenth century; this is his justification for applying to earlier works the categories that doubtless originated in his own compositional experiences although he developed them in analysing Brahms and Mozart. These categories represent an extreme statement of their case and therefore should not always be taken literally, but some of the essential facts and associations in nineteenth-century music cannot be revealed or explained by any other means.

The rejection of what were felt to be empty melodic formulas and the consequent tendency towards rhythmic and metric irregularity (that is, the recoil from both symmetrical periods and the filling-out necessary if symmetry was to be achieved) are closely connected with the conception of melody for which, in the essay *Music of the Future*, Wagner invented the term "endless melody."[11] The concept's sub-

9. A. Berg, "Warum ist Schönbergs Musik so schwer verständlich," in W. Reich, *Alban Berg* (Vienna, 1937), pp. 142ff.
10. Schoenberg, *Style and Idea*, p. 72 [p. 415].
11. Wagner, *Gesammelte Schriften*, 7:130.

sequent terminological career obviously owes less to a precise understanding of its original meaning than to the vague
associations that have attached themselves to it.[12] Bemused
by the word "endless," people have forgotten to enquire
what Wagner understood by "melody."

In Wagner's vocabulary "melody" is primarily an aesthetic category, not a technical compositional one: what is
musically eloquent and meaningful is "melodic" in this
positive sense, what is formulaic and inexpressive is "unmelodic." Schoenberg's reputedly "unmelodic" musical
language is consistently "melodic" by Wagner's criteria. A
melody is "narrow" (to use the terminology of *Music of the
Future* again) if the truly melodic is forever breaking off, as
in Italian opera, to be replaced by "unmelodic" filling-out. In
Wagner's historico-aesthetic scheme of things, Italian opera,
as exemplified by Rossini, is at the opposite pole to the symphonic writing of Beethoven. (In a context where Italian
opera is not the subject under discussion it is permissible to
ignore the stylistic dualism of the nineteenth century, that
is, to overlook the fact that it makes no sense historically to
judge the tradition of Rossini by the criteria of the Beethovenian tradition, or vice versa.) Wagner was convinced that
any listener whose musical sensibilities had not been
blunted by too much "narrow" operatic melody of the kind
that amateur enthusiasts took for the quintessence of
melody was bound to "acknowledge that every note in the
harmony, yea, every pause in the rhythm [in a symphony by
Beethoven] has melodic significance."[13] The principle of expression, of eloquence *(das redende Prinzip)* is what determines Wagner's concept of melody.[14] He once demonstrated
this concept to Felix Draeseke by singing as much as he
could of the first movement of the *Eroica* before he ran out

12. F. Reckow, "Unendliche Melodie," in *Handwörterbuch der
musikalischen Terminologie* (Wiesbaden, 1973).
13. Wagner, *Gesammelte Schriften,* 7:127 *(Zukunftsmusik).*
14. A. Schering, "Carl Philipp Emanuel Bach und das 'redende Prinzip'
in der Musik," in *Vom musikalischen Kunstwerk,* 2d ed. (Leipzig, 1951),
pp. 213ff.

79

of breath, and judged by that criterion the movement, since not a note of it is superfluous or inexpressive, is indeed "nothing other than a single, perfectly coherent melody."[15]

The single, uninterrupted melody that Wagner found embodied in Beethoven's symphonies is a forerunner, even the prototype, of the "endless melody" that he himself realized in music drama. (The essential difference between Beethoven's works and his own, as Wagner saw it, lies in the transition from the indeterminate "meaning" of the melody in Beethoven to the meaning it derives from the drama in Wagner.) Thus the primary meaning of the term "endless melody," which is often misused and should by no means be treated exclusively as a technical expression, is not that the parts of a work flow into each other without caesuras but that every note has meaning, that the melody is language and not empty sound. The technical characteristic, the absence of formal cadences, is merely a consequence of the aesthetic factor: cadences are regarded as formulas, syntactic but not semantic components—in short, they express nothing and are therefore to be avoided or concealed.

There would seem to be no way of accommodating the idea of "endless melody" to the precarious concision that we have seen to be characteristic of melodic ideas in the music of the later nineteenth century, but if we ignore terminological externals, we can recognize that the former is the correlative of the latter. Their all-important common premise is a rejection of ornament and filling-out. In an age in which musical form had ceased to be regarded primarily as a matter of large-scale metrical patterns, the formal function carried out previously by ornamentation and filling-out was almost forgotten.

If, in the words of Wagner's dictum, "an endless melody" has to be "perfectly coherent," it means that the individual musical events and shapes ought to proceed out of each other, instead of being arrayed side by side, linked by mean-

15. Wagner, *Gesammelte Schriften*, 7:127 (*Zukunftsmusik*).

80

ingless padding and with no inner relationships. Brahms,
sharing Wagner's concern to "justify" musical processes,
would certainly have endorsed his postulate. Freedom from
inconsequentiality can either be a matter of formal logic, as
in Brahms's chamber music, or, as in Wagner's music
dramas, it can obey a logic transmitted primarily (though
not solely) by "content." (The invention of a polarity between "formalism" on the one hand and "the aesthetic
theory of content" on the other was a typical piece of nineteenth-century silliness and created a spurious dogmatic
conflict between parties, both of which shared a concern
with the whole nature of music. The dialectics of form and
content and the historical shifts in the definitions of the two
terms mean that the conflict could at best be a matter of
altering the emphasis on one or the other. Nevertheless, the
polarity has its uses in furnishing a provisional means of
identifying tendencies in formal creative processes which
are bound up with differences between genres.)

An inherent postulate of the idea of "endless melody" is
that throughout the course of a piece of music each instant
will possess a "significance" equal to that of every other
instant. This resulted in the shrinking of the thematic
period—part of which was necessarily formulaic in composition—to the short, as it were "prose-like," shape of the
individual musical idea. And the apparently mutually contradictory factors, brevity and endlessness, can be reconciled—on the basis of their common aesthetic premise—so
long as the composer succeeds in mediating between the
individual parts and the whole, between the original idea
and the wide span of his form. But in the later nineteenth
century opinions about the methods of mediation—the
structural principles—adopted by composers were colored
by aesthetic prejudices and partiality, which blinded the
adherents of both sides to the fact that the composers' problems were fundamentally the same. The primarily "formal"
elaboration of musical ideas in Brahms was regarded by
those Wagnerians hostile to him not as a process in which

81

one could acknowledge the "melodic significance" of every note but as inexpressive musical academicism. Similarly, the "formalists" in the anti-Wagner camp would not acknowledge that the role played by "content" in linking a series of leitmotivs constituted melodic continuity. With their restricted concept of music as something to which "drama" or a "program" could only be an external, non-musical addition, they regarded the concatenation of motives which sometimes diverged abruptly from each other as mere cobbling.

But if the historian keeps aloof from the partisan squabbles of the later nineteenth century and, in obedience to the maxim that every musical phenomenon must be interpreted in the light of its own premises, recognizes that formal development in Brahms is the development of ideas (not the mechanical spinning of formulas) and, conversely, that the developments in Wagner which are transmitted by content are developing ideas (and not mere cobbling), he will perceive that the compositional issue that lies beyond the aesthetic, stylistic and formal cruxes is the same. Wagner and Liszt, no less than Brahms, conceived of music as discourse in sound, in which every detail should be an original idea (or the outcome of one) and the whole a logically constructed chain, every link justified by what has preceded it.

As he wrote with polemical emphasis in *Nietzsche contra Wagner*, Nietzsche saw "endless melody" as something which threatened to dissolve rhythm, by which he understood the perceptible ordering of musical motion, not merely durational structure. While earlier music walked or danced the new music tried to "float" or "hover." " 'Endless melody' sets out to disrupt all regularity of duration and accent, and in doing so it makes mock of them."[16]

Musical verse-form, the regular period composed symmetrically of antecedent and consequent clauses, was dissolved in Wagner's music dramas from *Das Rheingold* on, if

16. Nietzsche, *Werke*, 2:1043.

not into prose then into a kind of *vers libre* (the upsurge of which in French poetry cannot be wholly unconnected with the Symbolists' enthusiasm for Wagner). The decline of traditional musical syntax did endanger that classical or classico-romantic concept of musical form to which periodic structure—the relation of "proposition" *(Aufstellung)* and "response" *(Beantwortung)*, to use Hugo Riemann's terms—was fundamental. The balance of complementary parts—from the relationship between upbeats and downbeats to the answering of an antecedent clause by a consequent, from the relationship between exposition and development within one subject group to the contrasts between subject groups as a whole—was the fundamental principle of musical form in the eighteenth and early nineteenth centuries. The transition to "logical" form, form determined by the development of musical ideas, is half accomplished in Beethoven; he did not, however, jettison architectural form altogether but held the divergent principles poised in a precarious balance. Even in Wagner's *Lohengrin*, which the composer was terminologically and historically quite correct to call a "romantic opera" and not a music drama, the music consists for long stretches at a time of periods, the regularity of which ensures formal coherence.[17]

With the dissolution of regular periodic structure, music drama from *Das Rheingold* onwards used in its place a much more fully developed leitmotivic technique. Leitmotivs had already been used in *Lohengrin* to emphasize and comment musically on isolated elements in the drama, but now they were spread over entire works in a dense network of motivic relationships: that is, the technique assumed the function of creating the musical form. It took a long time for anyone to acknowledge that musical form can be a polythematic network, a "web" or "woven fabric" *(Gewebe)* as Wagner called it himself, instead of having to be either architectural or the extended elaboration of a few thematic ideas. For didactic

17. Dahlhaus, *Wagners Konzeption des musikalischen Dramas*, pp. 50ff.

reasons, theorists of form tended always to favor simpler kinds of schematicism, and even in the 1920s Alfred Lorenz,[18] intending to refute the incessantly repeated charge that Wagner's music was amorphous, expounded what he regarded as the "architectural" principles underlying Wagner's form: for the most part these "principles" are figments of Lorenz's own imagination, conjured up in apologetic zeal.[19] There is as much aesthetic virtue in "reticulation" as in "grouping" and "elaboration" as means of creating musical form.

Thus leitmotivic technique plays a formal, structural role in Wagner equivalent to that of regular periodic structure in other music: the leitmotivs create the framework of the form instead of being interpolated, for dramaturgical reasons, into a structure that rests on other foundations. The replacement of the one formal principle by the other marks the transition from "romantic opera" to "music drama." (In a brief historiographic outline it is hardly necessary to say that an "ideal type" is here being constructed to describe a process which was far more complex in musico-historical reality; that is, it is not being claimed that leitmotivic technique plays no structural part at all in *Lohengrin*, nor that there is not one regular period in *Das Rheingold*. Groups of four and eight bars are not, of course, banished from the *Ring:* they are not even particularly infrequent, but they no longer provide the framework of the musical form as they did in *Lohengrin*.) Differentiation between regular and irregular syntax almost ceases to be of any formal importance or to exert any formal influence in the *Ring;* one could very well make an analogy with the "emancipation of dissonance" and speak of the emancipation of the metrically irregular phrase—which hereupon ceases to be irregular:

18. A. Lorenz, *Das Geheimnis der Form bei Richard Wagner,* 4 vols. (Berlin, 1924–33).
19. Dahlhaus, "Formprinzipien in Wagners 'Ring des Nibelungen'," in *Beiträge zur Geschichte der Oper,* ed. H. Becker (Regensburg, 1969), pp. 95ff.

84

whereas irregularity was previously an exception to a norm of regularity, a license, the purpose of which was understandable only by reference to that norm, emancipated irregularity exists in its own right. The "emancipation" does not mean that there is no longer any difference to be discerned between consonance and dissonance, or between "quadratic" and "non-quadratic" syntax, only that the difference is no longer an integral part of the musical structure: it exists, but it is no longer an element in the construction of the form. When there is continual alternation of "quadratic" and "non-quadratic" phrases—and the latter are not such as can be reduced to fit into quadratic structure—they do not add up to make periodic groups conforming to a large-scale metrical pattern; the effect of the "quadratic" phrases remains locked in the moment.

It is mistaken to suggest that the periodic framework of classical form was preserved intact by the "classicist" Brahms. Although his conservative tendencies can scarcely be denied, they do not mean that he revered the fundamentals of tradition while making modifications in some of the details, but rather that he radically rethought the traditional principles in the altered circumstances of the second half of the nineteenth century. Sonata form takes on a different meaning from the one it originally had when motivic development, the elaboration of thematic ideas, becomes the primary structural principle, in place of the pattern of key relationships and the construction of symmetrical groups. The form is "conserved," but by means which eventually made possible Schoenberg's development of atonal sonata form.

The principle of originality which was the reason for the brevity of musical ideas resulted, in the music of Brahms, in the technique of developing variation, used as a means not only of development but also of exposition. The opening of the B major Trio op. 8 is paradigmatic. The essential thematic idea is given in bars 1–2; bars 3–4 are instantly recognizable as being related by inversion to bars 1–2; bars 5–8

85

transpose the melody of bars 1–4 up a third with a modification in bar 8; and in bars 9–10 material derived from bars 6
and 7 is placed at the beginning of a phrase, so that what
were originally the second and third bars in the metrical
structure are transformed into the first and second—this is
variation achieved by metrical means. Those who, in the
heat of musico-aesthetic battle, decried Brahms's "formal"
motivic development as "empty" or "poverty-stricken" in
content were quite wrong, however. It is precisely the consequences, the events to which it leads, that first give color
and character to the modest little motive that opens op. 8
and, far from being overstretched in the process of development, it expands accordingly. The emphasis given by the
transposition in bars 5–8 and the intervention of the metrical variation in bars 9–10 are expressive traits which are the
result of the motivic evolution, that is, of a "formal" procedure. (See example below.)

86

The spinning of broad melodic paragraphs out of one small motive can become monotonous, however, no matter how variously the material is presented, unless it is alleviated and balanced by constant harmonic variety. The enrichment of the fundamental bass is the correlative, both technically and aesthetically, of developing variation. (In op. 8 Brahms begins with a persistent pedal point and does not begin to enrich the harmony until bars 17–20, when the effect is explosive; this is a special form of differentiation, not simplicity. The pedal point does not represent further simplification of harmonies that are poor in themselves but complication—like a kind of additional dissonance.) However, the enrichment of harmony by increasing the number of degrees in regular use endangers periodic structure as it was understood in about 1800, when its harmonic foundations were simple cadential models such as I–V–V–I or I–(V)II–V–I. (Whether auxiliary degrees and secondary dominants and subdominants are integrated into the model or not, whether they differentiate the pattern or disrupt it and finally destroy it, depends to no small degree on the metrical position of the chord; harmonic analysis is an abstract procedure if no reference is made to the metrical function of the chord.) It is not impossible to encase enriched harmony in a regular periodic structure; as some works by Reger demonstrate, it can be done with violent imperfect and perfect cadences, but the procedure is self-defeating as long as the technical and aesthetic criterion is the rule that development of all the elements of the composition should be analogous.[20] In order to avoid discrepancies between harmony and syntax, Brahms often followed the example of Bach and constructed tripartite groups which owe their form not to the correspondence (motivic analogy and harmonic contrast) of antecedent and consequent clauses but to the evolution of an initial phrase by means of a harmonically enriched developmental passage, not tied down to a quadratic structure, which concludes with a cadential

20. Dahlhaus, *Analyse und Werturteil* (Mainz, 1970), pp. 59ff.

epilogue.[21] (The principal theme of op. 25 is tripartite:
the initial phrase comprises bars 1–10, the evolution bars
11–20, and the epilogue, which refers back to the initial
phrase without there being any question of ternary form,
bars 21–27; but the evolution differs from the typical Bach-
ian procedure of a series of sequences and comes about, as
has been shown [p. 49], through the uncommonly differentiated development of a two-note motive, the descending
second.) This is not the restoration of something that belongs to the past; it is a derivation or an analogy made under
fundamentally different historical conditions.

Different—even contradictory—as the solutions worked
out by Brahms on the one hand and by Wagner and Liszt on
the other were, it is surely beyond question that their initial
problem was the same, arising from the difficulty of recon-
ciling constricted melodic ideas with the desire to work in
large forms and from the undermining of classical form by
the technical consequences of the brevity of the thematic
substance. It is the sameness of the problem which marks
the second half of the nineteenth century as an essentially
unified epoch in musical history, in spite of the stylistic
contrasts it embraced.

4. "Expanded" and "wandering" tonality

The individual elements of musical composition—harmony, counterpoint, motivic technique, and musical syntax
—are not mutually independent: each one individually can
be described, its functions defined, only with reference to
the others and to the effects each has on the others. Any
attempt to write a history of harmony which dealt with
pitch relationships in isolation would be too abstract to have
any useful application: "*schlecht abstrakt*" in Hegel's
phrase. Their correlationship makes harmony and syntax
inseparable, just as harmony and meter are, or harmony and
voice-leading.

21. W. Fischer, "Zur Entwicklungsgeschichte des Wiener klassischen
Stils," *Studien zur Musikwissenschaft* 3 (1915): 24–84.

The difference between the Wagnerian (or Lisztian) and the Brahmsian methods of stating and continuing a musical idea caused a divergence in harmonic procedure which has been noted by some commentators, but has never really been studied in the context which gave rise to it. With the Wagnerian procedure of modulatory sequences, chromatic alteration and the undermining of tonality by fragmentation became the principal characteristics of the harmonic writing, while Brahms's use of developing variation, with the enrichment of the fundamental bass, preserved tonal integrity.[22] Later, around 1900, Arnold Schoenberg forced the two trends to come together again, but that does not alter the fact that originally, in the nineteenth century, they represented alternatives: different solutions to the problem of establishing a harmonic technique appropriate to the process of motivic development and the structure of the syntax.

The analyst Schoenberg—whose theoretical conclusions were drawn from the composer Schoenberg's urge to reunite divergent trends—included both Brahms's enrichment of the fundamental bass and Wagner's undermining of tonality in his concept of "expanded tonality."[23] The weakness of the concept is that it conceals an important difference between the Wagnerian and the Brahmsian techniques, and while the analyses of Brahms on which Schoenberg bases his theses are illuminating, some of his analyses of Wagner are questionable.

If the term "expanded tonality" is given its full value, one of its postulates is that, far from being disrupted or suspended by the Wagnerian procedure of modulation towards some tonally remote region, the listener's awareness of the tonality is actually strengthened by it. For if the formal or syntactical association, the music's inner coherence, is not

89

22. Schoenberg, *Harmonielehre* (Vienna, 1911), p. 416 [*Theory of Harmony*, trans. R. E. Carter, based on 3rd ed. (1922), London, 1978, p. 370].

23. Schoenberg, *Die formbildenden Tendenzen der Harmonie* (Mainz, 1954), pp. 74 ff. [*Structural Functions of Harmony*, 2d ed., London and New York, 1969, pp. 76ff.].

to become unrecognizable, the listener's tonal awareness is tested and compelled to perceive the tonal relationship of even the remotest excursion. Schoenberg shared with Alfred Lorenz[24] the view that, in Wagner, tonality—the relation, capable of retention by the consciousness, of all harmonic processes to a tonal center—is structural in the wider context. Insofar as this is so, reluctance to hear Wagnerian harmony over long stretches as "centripetal" signifies a rejection of a means of proper formal understanding.

An alternative interpretation of Wagnerian tonality is possible. As they change in quick and often "rhapsodic" succession, the keys, or fragmentary allusions to keys, do not always relate to a constant center, around which they are to be imagined as simultaneously grouped; they should rather be seen as joined together like the links in a chain, without there necessarily being any other connection between the first and third links than the second. In the light of this theory, the characteristic function of Wagner's use of harmony is to establish not hierarchies but an order of succession. This is not to claim that there are no examples in Wagner of tonality which is both "expanded" and yet still clearly related to a tonal center, or even that such examples are rare, but merely that that particular harmonic procedure is not the first that should be cited as representing the principles of Wagnerian form.

If a valid assessment of the merits of these two opposing theories is to be made, it will not be by reference to listeners' reactions (whose validity would have to be measured in turn, thus setting up a vicious circle) but solely by means of formal analysis (though there will still be scope for questioning its intersubjective validity): not, that is, by a psychological process but by a phenomenological one. The question of whether the consciousness needs to retain the sense of a fundamental tonic throughout long modulatory passages in

24. Lorenz, *Der musikalische Aufbau des Bühnenfestspieles "Der Ring des Nibelungen" (Das Geheimnis der Form bei Richard Wagner*, vol. 1), p. 9.

90

Wagner will not be decided by reference to statistics about the effects the music has on the listener, but only by an investigation of the formal function of Wagner's use of harmony, and that function will be discovered in the relationship of the harmony and the musical syntax. If the absence of a change of key is irrelevant to the listener's grasp of the form of a particular passage, then the postulate that awareness of the tonic must be retained is shown to be redundant.

Schoenberg[25] interprets an eight-bar passage from Act I of *Tristan*, "War Morold dir so wert", as a tonally integrated period in B minor (with the dominant F♯ minor as an "extension," signifying no change of key):

Gb⁶	C⁶	ab⁶	eb⁶	b⁶	C⁶	G⁶		f♯⁶₄	C♯	f♯
b:V	IIN	VI	III	I	IIN	f♯: IIN		I⁶₄	V	I
1	2	3	4	5	6			7		8

Schoenberg's analysis is ingenious but not particularly illuminating. Some of his premises are theoretically unsound: it is doubtful whether the listener will hear the reversal of the familiar, well-worn chordal progression IIN–V to V–IIN (bars 1–2) (he will involuntarily hear Gb–C as IIN–V, re-

25. Schoenberg, *Formbildende Tendenzen*, p. 104 [*Structural Functions*, pp. 107f.].

91

lated to F minor); it is equally doubtful whether he will hear
the chromatic alteration of the roots of the chords VI and III
(bars 3–4). (If the postulate of chromatic alteration of
roots—which rests on a dubious interpretation of the chord
of the Neapolitan sixth and an even more dubious generalization of the outcome of that interpretation—is taken to its
ultimate conclusion, the consequences would be absurd:
every chordal progression could be related to any and every
key.) But above all, Schoenberg's assumption that the passage is harmonically integrated is not born out by formal
analysis. The passage may be eight bars long but its syntactic structure does not rest on a periodic schema representing
a formal correlative to the principle of tonal centrality; it is
created by sequential repetition, a linear and successional
procedure. (Moreover the sequences are real and the intervals equidistant: F–A♭=G♯–B; symmetrical division of the
octave, to which Liszt was particularly prone, is a procedure
alien to tonality and undermines functional tonality:
C–F♯–C; C–E–G♯=A♭–C; C–E♭–F♯–A–C; C–D–E–F♯–
G♯=A♭–B♭–C.) There is admittedly some modification of
the sequences, but there is no difficulty in recognizing the
basic form to which the others must be related if they are to
make sense: the latent original shape I–V is replaced or
"represented" first by IIN–V in F minor, then by I–V♭³ in
A♭ minor, and finally by I–IIN in B minor. Thus the tonal
fragments are not held together by the persistence of a single
underlying key functioning as a central point of reference
throughout, but by the linear process of sequential repetition, allied to the harmonic reinterpretation of individual
notes, which, being held in common by certain chords, me-
diate between remote keys or fragmentary tonal allusions.
Thus one expects the A♭ in bar 3 to become the mediant of
F minor (after F minor: IIN–V), and the B in bar 5 to become
the mediant of G♯ minor (A♭ minor); but instead the A♭ acts
as the root of a chord of A♭ minor, and the B as the root of a
chord of B minor.

The tonality characteristic of Wagner, unlike that of
Brahms, is not an "expanded," centripetal one, integrating

remote degrees and regions in one secure tonic to which modulations can always be related, but a "wandering" or "floating" tonality.[26] The fragmentation of classical tonality, with its ability to delineate form across wide spans, into brief tonal particles which follow each other in line, connected like links in a chain rather than assembled round a common center, by no means represents aesthetic weakness, the relinquishment of harmonic function; it is rather the precise correlative of a sense of form which is concerned less with the clearly perceptible grouping of separate parts than with the weaving of an ever denser network of motivic relationships. Wagner envisaged musical form as resembling a woven fabric, as he described it in *Music of the Future*,[27] not an architectural structure. One could refer to it as a dynamic form, which draws the listener into it during its course, whereas one observes an architectural form from the outside. When the listener is sufficiently aware of classical form, all the musical events of a movement can ultimately be perceived in an imaginary simultaneity.

In contrast the tonal centrality created by the enrichment of the fundamental bass and regional connections in the music of Brahms, the complementarity of differentiation and correspondence, express an idea of form that strives for complete and absolute integration—not the integration that comes as a matter of course from following a plan prepared in advance, but integration that must be won, often by force, from recalcitrant material. The structural role of harmony in Brahms is never so much in evidence as where he appears to be adopting Wagnerian and Lisztian expositional procedures but then transmutes them to serve his own idea of form.

The opening of the G minor Rhapsody for piano op. 79, no. 2, appears at first to be a paradigmatic example of the kind of "wandering" or "floating" tonality that is more characteristic of Wagner or Liszt than of Brahms. The first period is tonally unstable, containing fragmentary allusions

26. Schoenberg, *Harmonielehre*, p. 430 [*Theory of Harmony*, p. 383].
27. Wagner, *Gesammelte Schriften*, 7:131f.

93

to D minor: I–IIN (I merely an upbeat); to F major: V–I; and
to G major: IV–VII–I.

94

It is not imperative but it is possible to relate all these tonal
fragments to G minor: for one thing G minor is, so to speak,
their common denominator, and for another the chromatic
motion through the fourth, D–Eb–E–F–F♯–G, pointing towards G minor, provides the melodic framework (Heinrich
Schenker would have called it an *Urlinie*, if he had permitted an ascending *Urlinie*) of the chordal succession. However, the fact that it continues in bars 5–8 as a real sequence
transposed a major third upwards disturbs the listener's consciousness of the tonality: centrality has been replaced by
linearity. At the end of the principal thematic group (the
rhapsody is in sonata form) there is a faint suggestion of G
minor (bars 11–12) as a chromatic variant of the G major of
bars 9–10; the second subject group is in the key of the dominant, D minor. If the principal key is merely hinted at in the
exposition section, it is fully expounded, contrary to convention, in the development section (bars 61–85).

The sequential construction and the tonal instability of
the opening spring from the paradoxical formal concept of a
sonata-form rhapsody. To begin with, the tonality is allowed

to float in a rhapsodic fashion, later it is pinned down by the conventions of sonata form.

Although the principal subject group recalls the expositional procedures of Wagner and Liszt in its syntax and tonality—and in the correlation of sequential structure and "wandering" tonality—it must bear a different interpretation from what would be appropriate in a music drama or a symphonic poem. The fact that G minor can be taken for the common denominator of the tonal fragments in bars 1–4 of the rhapsody is of essential importance for considerations of musical form. (Schoenberg's analogous interpretation of the eight-bar passage from Act I of *Tristan*—the B minor that Schoenberg posited as the underlying tonic is also a common tonal denominator—was wrong, as has been shown, insofar as it mistook the formal nature of the period.) The opening of the rhapsody, at first sight "roving"—to use Schoenberg's alternative to "wandering"—in obedience to no laws, demands to be interpreted tonally because the work is in sonata form (in the nineteenth century sonata form became virtually second nature to listeners with any sense of form). After the advent of the second subject group, which is in the dominant (to be more precise: the key of which is unambiguous and is recognized as the dominant because experience has taught that second subjects are normally in the dominant), it is possible to look back and recognize the opening as the principal subject group, and the scattered suggestions of G minor coalesce, under the influence of formal awareness, to form a tonic. The listener's understanding and recognition of formal conventions intervene in his grasp of the harmony; "rhapsody" is made subject to "sonata form."

5. The "individualization" of harmony

In the sonata, harmony and rhythm are the pre-eminent structural forces, the themes are the material and in the classical sonata they are of less value. There is a real distinction to be made here between an active and a passive role for thematic

95

material, dominant and active in fugue, subservient and suffering—even to the point of suffering deprivation—in the sonata, while harmony and rhythm have priority.[28]

The kind of musical form outlined here by August Halm is the "architectural" variety based on the equilibrium of the parts—which is all that Halm means in this passage by "rhythm"; the equilibrium is observed in all stages of construction, from single bars to the outline of entire movements. (Whether the thesis is valid for the "sonata" in general—for the type, divorced from any particular historical manifestation; whether it applies equally to Beethoven's sonata form, of which Halm was thinking in the passage quoted, and to Mozart's, of which Halm held a low opinion; and whether the release of the themes from structural obligations in Mozartian sonata form did not actually enhance the melodic growth rather than cause it "deprivation"—these are questions that need not be answered here: by his equivocal use of the word "value" Halm equates the function fulfilled by an element of musical form with its aesthetic rank.)

The decline of "quadratic" syntax, the trend towards "musical prose" in the later nineteenth century, was the reverse face, or correlative, of a change in the function of musical thematic writing, which now took the place of "harmony and rhythm" as the primary structural principle (and in the twentieth century, in the music of Schoenberg, became the only structural principle). In order to do justice to the changed musico-historical circumstances, Halm's formula has to be reversed. The loss of structural significance suffered by rhythm (syntax) and harmony did not mean, however, that they became weaker or poorer in themselves but quite the contrary, they became richer. The breakdown or dissolution of quadratic rhythmic (syntactic) structure introduces greater subtlety (not in function but in substance—in respect of the isolated musical event and its

28. A. Halm, *Von zwei Kulturen der Musik,* 3d ed. (Stuttgart, 1947), p. 117.

momentary effect): since the musical structure is no longer determined primarily by the equilibrium of complementary (whether analogous or contrasting) elements, symmetry is no longer obligatory. (It must be admitted that aesthetic quality can suffer if irregular phrases are regarded as self-sufficient, irreducible entities rather than as modifications and transitional forms within a "quadratic" framework: subtlety in one direction is purchased by the loss of refinement in another.) And just as the tendency towards the "direct," prose-like formulation of musical ideas, untrammeled by the need for symmetry, enabled syntax to break free of regular, strophic structures, so harmony, too, was liberated from the traditional formulas and conventions, reused incessantly with occasional minor modifications, which could hardly be avoided so long as harmony had an important structural function to fulfill, as defined by Halm.

At the beginning of the nineteenth century simple patterns of key relationships, constructed on cadential models and with a recurrent generic similarity, provided the basis of all musical forms. But in the second half of the century, in the music of Wagner and Liszt—and in that of Brahms too in some respects—the role of harmony was almost completely reversed. In Wagnerian harmony, with its reliance on chromatic alteration and its consequent tendency towards "wandering" or "floating" tonality (that is, a linear succession of fragmentary allusions to keys), the accent falls on harmonic details—on single chords or unusual progressions—and there is such a degree of differentiation in the compositional technique (the interrelationship of harmony and instrumentation) that it is no exaggeration to speak of an individualization of harmony, which is hardly less important than that of thematic and motivic material. Some harmonic progressions and even some individual chords in Wagner have the same significance as a leitmotiv: the "mystic chord" in *Parsifal*, the expressive and allegorical functions of which were described by Alfred Lorenz,[29] or the

97

29. Lorenz, *Der musikalische Aufbau von Richard Wagners "Parsifal"* (*Das Geheimnis der Form bei Richard Wagner,* vol. 4), pp. 29ff.

major seventh chord which provides the greater part of the substance of the Day motive in *Tristan*. Relieved of the responsibility for the large-scale formal structures, the harmony serves instead to establish the unique identity of one instant in the music.

The structural function and the individualization of harmony represent alternatives which can, in particular cases, be reconciled. It is characteristic of Brahms—"the conservative" whom Schoenberg nevertheless hailed as "the progressive"—that on the one hand, as the contemporary of Wagner and Liszt, he strove to give harmonic details "unique identity," while on the other hand, as a composer who had made the tradition of Beethoven his own by exploring it from within, he did not wish to sacrifice the structural function that tonal harmony could perform over a wide expanse. There are times when Brahms succeeds not merely in preserving a precarious balance between the two contradictory tendencies but in actually making one of them the natural outcome of the other.

The D minor Piano Concerto op. 15 begins with an expansive and harmonically exploratory sequential passage (bars 1–24), at first sight analogous to the openings of Wagner's *Tristan* prelude and Liszt's *Hamlet*. But the purpose of sequential writing is different in Brahms from what it is in Wagner or Liszt. The opening of *Tristan* is harmonically "centrifugal": it is true that, in spite of the modulation of the sequences into tonally remote regions, one senses a relation to an A minor which nonetheless remains unheard, but all the time the movement is away from any center. But although the Brahms op. 15 begins on the tonal periphery the music's sole ambition is to reach its center (it does so in bar 25, but the tonality is established tentatively rather than triumphantly): the harmony is "centripetal."

A precedent for this procedure of establishing the tonic by approaching it from the outside inwards is to be found in the first subject of Beethoven's Piano Sonata op. 53, the "Waldstein." But in Brahms the harmonic details go far beyond the simple cadential schema followed by Beethoven. The first chord, prolonged over no fewer than ten bars, seems at first to be the inversion of a foreign dominant seventh chord (D–F–A♭–B♭), but the context, its position before the first inversion of the true dominant seventh (C♯–E–G–A), makes it quite clear (even if only retrospectively) that it is the inversion of the augmented sixth chord (i.e. D–F–G♯–B♭): this is a chord which, according to the letter of convention, cannot be inverted, so its inversion signifies an individualization of the harmony. Understood as D–F–G♯–B♭, the first chord acquires a "unique identity," which it owes to its function in the gradual presentation or establishment of the tonic.

The dominance of the idea of originality before all else affected even the use of harmony, which underwent a radical alteration in its formal significance during the later nineteenth century. The emphasis shifted from the general and structural to the particular and instantaneous, from providing a framework, which was its principal function in Mozart and, still, in Beethoven, to the individual characterization of detail, the harmonic "idea." That Brahms nonetheless achieved integration of tonality and syntax—partly, it must be admitted, through the construction of tripartite groups, remotely analogous to Bach's typical continuation procedure, that is, not always derived from the classical model of symmetrical periodic structure—is the outcome of "conservative" resistance to the "tendency of the material," as Adorno would call it. Brahms must surely have felt that tendency and he was sometimes able to do it justice, as at the beginning of his op. 15, where he individualized the harmony by working with (rather than against) formal harmonic functions.

6. Conclusion

So long as one is not afraid of making broad generalizations, fastening on the salient points in tendencies and constructing "ideal types"—and the writing of any kind of history

99

would be severely impeded if methods which have a footing
in the empirical but venture beyond its frontiers are to be
condemned on principle—it becomes clear that the music
of the middle and later nineteenth century is conditioned by
the close and intricate relationship between the aesthetic
principles and the technical compositional issues that have
been examined in the foregoing. These are the pre-eminence
of originality, the shrinking of thematic material in inverse
proportion to the ambition to create larger forms, the reces-
sion of classical periodic structures and of architectural
methods of construction based on the principle of equilibrium and exemplified in large-scale metrical patterns, the
conversion of developmental techniques like developing
variation and real, modulatory sequence to expositional
uses, and finally the "individualization" of harmony, which
was now liable to produce either superabundant chromaticism resulting in "floating" or "wandering" tonality or else
tonal integrity achieved by means of centripetal harmony
and enriched fundamental basses. These factors amount to a
problem nexus which provides a single, unified background
to the music of the whole epoch, far outweighing the significance of stylistic differences and the partisanship of
composers and their adherents.

This is not to deny the existence of "external" factors, or
to detract from the significance of the effect they had on the
development of music. As has already been said, there is no
intrinsic technical explanation in the history of composition
for the general trend of the music of the second half of the
nineteenth century towards ever larger, monumental forms;
and there can be no doubt that a sociological study of the
audiences which lent their support variously to the musical
and musico-political institution established in Bayreuth[30]
and to Brahms's chamber music[31] would be not merely per-

30. W. Schüler, *Der Bayreuther Kreis* (Münster, 1971).
31. K. Stahmer, *Musikalische Formung in soziologischem Bezug:
Dargestellt an der instrumentalen Kammermusik von Johannes Brahms*
(diss., Kiel University, 1968).

tinent: it is urgently needed. That there are social implications in the works themselves, in the very conception of the *Ring* and in the idea of absolute music embodied in the string quartet,[32] cannot seriously be denied, although the prospect of deciphering them is one to daunt any scholar whose ambitions go beyond facile categorizations (such as "bourgeois culture") on the one hand and the construction, on the other, of merely verbal analogies, analogies which rest exclusively on the words and not on the matters that they are supposed to represent.

It is accepted that a history of music which examines the subject primarily from the standpoint of compositional issues is one-sided and requires augmentation. The aesthetic and technical terms of reference are inadequate in their exclusiveness but they are equally essential, as a first stage that must on no account be skipped over. However, while it has always been asserted that the fragmentary nature of such description results in an intolerable distortion of the reality it is intended to describe, because one should encompass the whole in order to grasp the individual detail, there has never been any really illuminating substantiation of the claim. (The fundamental rule of hermeneutics, the platitude that the context must always be taken into consideration, remains a shadowy ideal so long as there is a shortage of suitable criteria to help one to decide in any individual case just how large the context is that one needs to consider if one is to come up with a meaningful explanation or interpretation of one particular phenomenon; in any event, the assumption that the context of musical works is always society as a whole is an exaggeration, dogmatic in origin.) The nexus of aesthetic and technical issues that has been outlined here is only part of the history of music in the later nineteenth century, a subject which cannot adequately be reduced to the history of compositional technique in the period. However, the "totality" invoked by methodologists, sitting in judg-

101

32. Dahlhaus, "Brahms und die Idee der Kammermusik," *Neue Zeitschrift für Musik* 134/9 (1973): 559ff.

ment on studies that are confined to only one, or some, of
the aspects of a historical period, is a demand that has not
yet been met, and all its attractions do not amount to a
guarantee that it ever can be met to a degree consistent with
scholarly requirements.

On the other hand the attempt to discover the common
ground underlying the contradictions and differences in the
music of the later nineteenth century is by no means an en-
dorsement of the dogmatic claim that what unites, what is
common to things is *a priori* more important and has a more
general significance than what separates and distinguishes
them, that foundations amount to more than the building
that rises on them. When trying to comprehend a period in
the history of ideas, one must resist the temptation to award
the homogeneity of the problems posed priority over the
multiplicity of the solutions that were explored, if the only
reason for doing so is the powerful tradition that encourages
historians to reveal the inner coherence behind the contradictions that rend an epoch. Tracing divergent trends
back to their common root is not the only way of relating
them to each other comprehensibly: like a primary unity, a
polarity can also be understood and explained as an ultimate
instance, fundamental, irreducible, and meaningful in itself.
So far as the history of music in the later nineteenth century
is concerned, however, any eventual need to progress beyond the reconstruction of a fundamental unity of compositional issues underlying the stylistic polarities—in the full
expectation of discovering new contradictions in a lower
stratum—is not yet in sight.

How We Got into Analysis, and How to Get Out

Joseph Kerman

As a matter of general usage, the term "criticism" is applied to music in an anomalous and notably shallow way. This is regrettable but not easy to change so long as the usage has the consent of musicians and non-musicians alike. When people say "music criticism," they almost invariably mean daily or weekly journalistic writing, writing which is prohibited from the extended, detailed, and complex mulling over of the matter at hand that is taken for granted in the criticism of art and especially of literature. Journalistic writing about music is posited on and formed by this prohibition. The music critic may accept it grudgingly, keeping a higher end in view, or he may depend on it to hide what may gently be called his lack of intellectual rigor; in any case, the prohibition is central to his métier. The music critic's stock-in-trade consists of the aesthetic question begged, the critical aphorism undeveloped, the snap judgment.

In fact a body of less ephemeral, more accountable professional criticism does exist in this country and elsewhere: which is the first thing I wish to argue (or just point out) in this paper. The discipline in question is called by musicians "analysis," not criticism, and by nonmusicians it is seldom recognized or properly understood—this for a number of reasons, one of which is the simple matter of nomenclature. In conjunction with music theory, musical analysis enjoys a relatively long academic history going back to the nineteenth-century conservatory curricula.

In a slightly different form, this paper was first read as one of the 1978–79 Thalheimer Lectures in Philosophy at Johns Hopkins University. It will be published with the four other lectures in a forthcoming volume by Johns Hopkins University Press.

Today all university as well as conservatory musicians are into analysis. They all have to study it and generally do so with much respect. Many practice it, either formally or, more often, informally. They do not, however, like to call it criticism—and one reason for *that* may be traceable to phobias in the profession at large caused by prolonged exposure to journalistic critics.

Thus even those who have dealt most thoughtfully with music criticism in recent years have shown a marked reluctance to affiliate criticism and analysis. I am thinking of such commentators as Arthur Berger, Edward T. Cone, David Lewin, Leonard B. Meyer, Robert P. Morgan, and Leo Treitler. Indeed, some words of my own, written about fifteen years ago, can perhaps be taken as representative:

> Criticism does not exist yet on the American music-academic scene, but something does exist which may feel rather like it, theory and analysis. . . . Analysis seems too occupied with its own inner techniques, too fascinated by its own "logic," and too sorely tempted by its own private pedantries, to confront the work of art in its proper aesthetic terms. Theory and analysis are not equivalent to criticism, then, but they are pursuing techniques of vital importance to criticism. They represent a force and a positive one in the academic climate of music. . . .[1]

Fifteen years later, I can only regard this as waffling. According to the *Harvard Dictionary of Music,* the true focus of analysis, once it gets past the taxonomic stage, is "the synthetic element and the functional significance of the musical detail." Analysis sets out to discern and demonstrate the functional coherence of individual works of art, their "organic unity," as is often said, and that is one of the things—one of the main things—that people outside of music mean by criticism. If in a typical musical analysis the work of art is studied in its own self-defined terms, that too is a characteristic strategy of some major strains of twentieth-century criticism. We might like criticism to meet broader criteria, but there it is. Perhaps musical analysis, as an eminently professional process, fails to open access between the artist and his audience,

1. Kerman, "A Profile for American Musicology," *Journal of the American Musicological Society* 18 (Spring 1965): 65.

Joseph Kerman, professor of music at the University of California, Berkeley, is the editor of *Nineteenth-Century Music.* His books include *Opera as Drama, The Elizabethan Madrigal, The Beethoven Quartets, Listen* (with Vivian Kerman), and *The Masses and Motets of William Byrd.*

104

and perhaps it does indeed fail "to confront the work of art in its proper aesthetic terms"—such failures, too, are not unknown in the criticism of literature and the other arts. Many tasks are ritually urged on criticism that cannot be incorporated into the concept of criticism itself. In other words, I do not see that the criteria suggested above can be included in a definition of criticism that corresponds to the practice of modern critics. We may consider it very desirable that criticism meet these criteria, but we cannot reasonably insist on it. What we have here is a matter for adjustment between music critics of different persuasions rather than some sort of stand-off between adherents of distinct disciplines.

It may be objected that musical analysts claim to be working with objective methodologies which leave no place for aesthetic criteria, for the consideration of value. If that were the case, the reluctance of so many writers to subsume analysis under criticism might be understandable. But are these claims true? Are they, indeed, even seriously entered?

Certainly the original masters of analysis left no doubt that for them analysis was an essential adjunct to a fully articulated aesthetic value system. Heinrich Schenker always insisted on the superiority of the towering products of the German musical genius. Sir Donald Tovey pontificated about "the main stream of music" and on occasion developed this metaphor in considerable detail. It is only in more recent times that analysts have avoided value judgments and adapted their work to a format of strictly corrigible propositions, mathematical equations, set-theory formulations, and the like—all this, apparently, in an effort to achieve the objective status and hence the authority of scientific inquiry. Articles on music composed after 1950, in particular, appear sometimes to mimic scientific papers in the way that South American bugs and flies will mimic the dreaded carpenter wasp. In a somewhat different adaptation, the distinguished analyst Allen Forte wrote an entire small book, *The Compositional Matrix,* from which all affective or valuational terms (such as "nice" or "good") are meticulously excluded. The same tendency is evident in much recent periodical literature.

But it scarcely goes unnoticed that the subject of Forte's monograph is not a symphony by Giovanni Battista Sammartini or a quartet by Adalbert Gyrowetz but a late sonata by Beethoven, the Sonata in E Major opus 109, a work that Forte accepts without question as a masterpiece—without question, and also without discussion. Indeed, this monograph sheds a particularly pure light on the archetypal procedure of musical analysis. This branch of criticism takes the masterpiece status of its subject matter as a donnée and then proceeds to lavish its whole attention on the demonstration of its inner coherence. Aesthetic judgment is concentrated tacitly on the initial choice of material to be analyzed; then the analysis itself, which may be conducted with the greatest subtlety and rigor, can treat of artistic value only casually or, as in the extreme case of

Forte's monograph, not at all. Another way of putting it is that the question of artistic value is at the same time absolutely basic and begged, begged consistently and programmatically.

In fact, it seems to me that the true intellectual milieu of analysis is not science but ideology. I do not think we will understand analysis and the important role it plays in today's music-academic scene on logical, intellectual, or purely technical grounds. We will need to understand something of its underlying ideology, and this in turn will require some consideration of its historical context. Robert P. Morgan is an analyst who has reminded us on a number of occasions that his discipline must be viewed as a product of its time—a corollary to his conviction that it must also change with the times. The following historical analysis owes something to Morgan's but is, I think, framed more radically or at any rate more polemically.

2

By ideology, I mean a fairly coherent set of ideas brought together not for strictly intellectual purposes but in the service of some strongly held communal belief. Fundamental here is the orthodox belief, still held over from the late nineteenth century, in the overriding aesthetic value of the instrumental music of the great German tradition. Of this, the central monuments are the fugues and some other instrumental compositions of Bach and the sonatas, string quartets, and symphonies of Mozart, Beethoven, and Brahms.

Viennese or Pan-German in origin, and certainly profoundly guided by nationalistic passions, this ideology took hold in other countries depending on the strength or weakness of their native musical traditions. It took no hold in Italy, some hold in France, strong hold in Britain and especially in America. The ideology drew to itself many familiar currents of nineteenth-century thought about art and music. Among these were an essentially mystical notion of spontaneity and authenticity in musical performance, a romantic myth (owing much to the example of Beethoven) which cast the artist as sage and suffering hero, and—most important for the present purpose—a strain of Hegelian aesthetic philosophy, which now runs from Schopenhauer to Susanne K. Langer with an important backtrack by way of Eduard Hanslick.

For Hanslick, instrumental music was the only "pure" form of the art, and words, librettos, titles, and programs which seem to link music to the feelings of ordinary, impure life were to be disregarded or deplored. Music, in Hanslick's famous phrase, is "sounding form in motion." Later aestheticians such as Langer have labored to preserve this central insight without denying, as Hanslick did, that music was anything more than that. The concept is an important one for the essential criterion of value that is built into the ideology. For if music is only "sounding form," the only meaningful study of music is formalistic; and while Hanslick was not an analyst, later critics took it on themselves to analyze music's sounding form in the conviction that this was equivalent to its content. To these analyst-critics, needless to say, content (however they defined it) was not a matter of indifference. The music they analyzed was that of the great German tradition.

The vision of these analyst-critics was and is of a perfect, organic relation among all the analyzable parts of a musical masterpiece. Increasingly sophisticated techniques of analysis attempt to show how all aspects or "parameters" or "domains" of the masterpiece perform their function for the total structure. Critics who differ vastly from one another in their methods, styles, and emphases still view the work of art ultimately as an organism in this sense. From the standpoint of the ruling ideology, analysis exists for the purpose of demonstrating organicism, and organicism exists for the purpose of validating a certain body of works of art.

I do not, of course, ignore that broader philosophical movement of the late eighteenth and early nineteenth centuries which focused on organicism and which some musicologists have recently been trying to relate to the development of musical style. But together with this historical process went an ideological one, in the service of which the concept of organicism began to lead a charmed existence. Organicism can be seen not only as a historical force which played into the great German tradition but also as the principle which seemed essential to validate that tradition. The ideological resonance of organicism continued long past the time of its historical impetus.

The origins of the ideology can be traced back to the famous biography of Bach published in 1802 by J. N. Forkel, director of music at the University of Göttingen and the first real German musicologist. "Bach united with his great and lofty style the most refined elegance and the greatest precision in the single parts that compose the great whole, . . ." wrote Forkel in his exordium to this work. ". . . He thought the whole could not be perfect if anything were wanting to the perfect precision of the single parts; . . . And this man, the greatest musical poet and the greatest musical orator that ever existed, and probably ever will exist, was a German. Let his country be proud of him; let it be proud, but, at the same time, worthy of him!"[2] We can see the concept of the musical organism taking form with the new attention given to fugue in the early nineteenth century. There was a swift Viennese co-option only a few years later, when E. T. A. Hoffmann began to view Haydn, Mozart, and Beethoven with much the same reverence we do today and began to

107

2. Johann Nickolaus Forkel, "On Johann Sebastian Bach's Life, Genius, and Works," in *The Bach Reader*, ed. Hans T. David and Arthur Mendel (New York, 1945), pp. 352–53.

marvel at the way works such as Beethoven's Fifth Symphony seem to grow from a single theme as though from a Goethean *Urpflanz*. The first great ideological crisis was precipitated by Richard Wagner—Wagner, who could not launch a paper boat without making waves, let alone a revolutionary theory of opera. As Wagner asserted his claim to the Beethovenian succession, the youthful Brahms and his imperious friend Joseph Joachim proclaimed their opposition to symphonic poems, music-dramas, and other such novelties. Hanslick had already closed ranks around the concept of purely instrumental music. He soon came to support Brahms, the most instrumental-minded as well as the most traditional-minded of all the great nineteenth-century composers.

But the ideology did not receive its full articulation until the music in which it was rooted came under serious attack. This occurred around 1900 when tonality, the seeming linchpin of the entire system, began to slip in Germany as well as elsewhere. Lines of defense were formed at what Virgil Thomson used to call "the Brahms line," first in opposition to Richard Strauss and then to Arnold Schoenberg. The situation was exacerbated after 1920 when Schoenberg, in an astonishing new co-option, presented himself and his music as the true continuation of the Viennese tradition. It is against the background of this new crisis that we must see the work of the founding fathers of analysis.

Schenker was born in 1868, Tovey in 1875. The first significant writings of both men, which appeared shortly after 1900, are peppered with polemics and were obviously conceived as a defense against the new modernism. Tovey was no Viennese, of course—Balliol was his beat, and before that Eton—but over and above the general reliance of Victorian England on German music and musical thought, he himself was deeply influenced by the aging Joachim. Concentration on the sphere of harmony and the larger harmony, namely, tonality, led Tovey ultimately to the organicist position, though he was never as dogmatic in this regard as the Germans. In his major essays on the Schubert Quintet and the Beethoven Quartet in C-sharp Minor opus 131, he went beyond his usual terminus, the individual movement, and saw tonality inspiring the whole work, with each "key area" conceived of as a functional element in the total structure. And in what he called the "superb rhetoric" of Bach's F-sharp-minor setting of *Aus tiefer Noth* in the *Clavierübung*, part 3—a chorale in which the melodic and rhythmic substance of the given cantus firmus is drawn into all of the polyphonic voice parts according to a rigorous system, so that every note is practically predetermined by an external scheme—Tovey found unshakable evidence that form in art is equivalent to content. "The process miscalled by Horace the concealment of art," wrote Tovey, "is the sublimation of technique into aesthetic results."

In many ways Tovey was a typical product of the *litterae humaniores*

108

at the Oxford of Benjamin Jowett and F. H. Bradley. He came by his neo-Hegelianism honestly. Schenker, on the other hand, was a typical product of the Vienna Conservatory, where the great systematic theorist Simon Sechter had been the teacher of Bruckner, himself the teacher of Schenker. Slowly, stage by stage throughout his career, Schenker labored to construct a grandiose general theory to account for all the music of the great tradition. Tovey's analytical method may be said to involve a reduction of the melodic surface of music to the level of the articulated system of tonality. Schenker's method involved a much more systematic reduction to the level of a single triad, the tonic triad. In his famous series of formalized reductions, he analyzed music on "foreground," "middleground," and "background" levels—the latter comprising the *Urlinie* and the *Ursatz,* a drastically simple horizontalization of the vertical sonority of the tonic triad. (We shall see an example of such an *Ursatz* later.) The concept of hierarchies or levels and the technique of their manipulation constituted Schenker's most powerful legacy to the structuralist future.

Beethoven occupied the dead center of both Schenker's and Tovey's value systems. Schenker's most exhaustive studies concern Beethoven's Third, Fifth, and Ninth Symphonies and the late piano sonatas. Indeed, the list of some fifty compositions which Schenker discussed formally and at full length presents a striking picture of musical orthodoxy. With a few exceptions (including most honorably those late sonatas), they are drawn from the stable of symphony orchestra war-horses and from the piano teachers' rabbit hutch. In his tacit acceptance of received opinion as to the canon of music's masterpieces, Schenker exemplifies more clearly than any of its other practitioners one aspect of the discipline of analysis.

His work looms so large in academic music criticism of the recent past that analysis is sometimes equated with "Schenkerism," as it is called. The movement is much broader, however, and therefore more significant than any intellectual current which was the province of just one man and his followers could be. Schenker is not the only impressive and influential figure among the older analysts. I have already mentioned Tovey. Rudolph Réti, a disciple at one time of Schoenberg and later an emigré to America, developed a nineteenth-century strain of analysis based not on tonality, line, or triad but on motif. Réti's demonstrations of the hidden identity of all themes in a musical composition—a sort of poor man's organicism—has had a particular impact in Britain. Alfred Lorenz, also originally from Vienna, extended organic analysis over a larger span than had been thought possible and into forbidden territory, the four great music-dramas of Wagner. While modern Wagner scholars seem not to tire of disproving and rejecting Lorenz's work, it receives sympathetic attention from the

109

Verdians, among others. It is possible that both Réti and Lorenz have been written off a little too hastily by modern American academics.

More important—indeed, crucial—is the role of Schoenberg himself in our story. In his relatively limited body of writings on music, Schoenberg showed himself to be a brilliant theorist and critic, and, justly enough, the fact that he was the composer he was gave those writings immense authority.

Schoenberg's really decisive insight, I think, was to conceive of a way of continuing the great tradition while negating what everyone else felt to be at its very core, namely, tonality. He grasped the fact that what was central to the ideology was not the triad and tonality, as Schenker and Tovey believed, but organicism. In his atonal, preserial works written just before World War I, Schoenberg worked out a music in which functional relations were established more and more subtly on the motivic, rhythmic, textural, and indeed the pitch level, with less and less reliance on the traditional configurations of tonality. So for Schoenberg, Brahms was the true "progressive" of the late nineteenth century—Brahms, who had refined the art of motivic variation, rather than Wagner, who had refined and attenuated tonality to the breaking point. Twelve-tone serialism was not far off, and indeed in retrospect one can see implicit from the start the ideal of "total organization" which was to be formulated by the new serialists after World War II.

Schoenberg himself was never interested in developing the sort of analysis that has subsequently been practiced on his own and on other serial music. But once he had entered his formidable claim for inclusion within the great tradition, it was inevitable that a branch of analysis would spring up to validate that claim. For analysis, I believe, as I have already said, exists to articulate the concept of organicism, which in turn exists as the value system of the ideology; and while the validation provided by analysis was not really necessary for the Viennese classics, it became more and more necessary for the music of each succeeding generation. What Schenker did for Beethoven and Lorenz did for Wagner, Milton Babbitt and others did later for Schoenberg, Berg, and Webern.

The universal impetus behind analysis was expressed with particular innocence by Réti when he recalled asking himself as a young student why every note in a Beethoven sonata should be exactly *that* note rather than some other. Réti dedicated his career as an analyst to finding an objective answer to this question. And questions of the sort can indeed be answered in respect to the totally organized serial music of the 1950s. Every pitch, rhythm, timbre, dynamic, envelope, and so on can be derived from the work's "precompositional assumptions" by means of simple or slightly less simple mathematics. Whether this derivation provides the *right* answer—that, to be sure, is another question. But the answer provided by serial analysis is, undeniably, objective.

110

3

I come at last, after this lengthy historical digression, to the current state of music criticism in the American academy. Analysis, as I have already indicated, is the main, almost the exclusive, type of criticism practiced in music departments today. I believe also that analysis supplies the chief mental spark that can be detected in those departments. Musicology, a field considerably larger and better organized than analysis, involving mainly historiography and quasi-scientific scholarly research in music, is also cultivated; but American musicology in its academic phase—which has now lasted about thirty or forty years— seems to me to have produced signally little of intellectual interest. What it has assembled is an impressive mass of facts and figures about music of the past, codified into strictly nonevaluative histories, editions, bibliographies, and the like. One is reminded of the state of literary studies in the 1930s. Musical analysis has also reminded many observers of the New Criticism which arose at that time. This analogy, though it is not one that will survive much scrutiny, does point to one of the constants of intellectual life as this applies to the arts: as intellectual stimulus, positivistic history is always at a disadvantage beside criticism. It is precisely because and only because analysis is a kind of criticism that it has gained its considerable force and authority on the American academic scene.

Still, as the years and the decades go by, the predominant position of analysis grows more and more paradoxical; paradoxical, because the great German tradition of instrumental music, which analysis supports, no longer enjoys the unique status it did for the generation of Schenker and Tovey and Schoenberg. There is no need to enlarge on the various factors that have so drastically changed the climate for the consumption and appreciation of music today: the wide variety of music made available by musicological unearthings on the one hand and recording technology and marketry on the other; the public's seemingly insatiable hunger for opera of all sorts; the growing involvement with non-Western music, popular music, and quasi-popular music; and also a pervasive general disbelief in hierarchies of value. It is not that we see less, now, in the German masters; but they no longer shut out our perspective on great bodies of other music, new and old.

Another factor contributing to this change in our musical climate stems from the crisis in which musical composition has for some time found itself. Heretofore the great tradition had been felt to exist in a permanent condition of organic evolution, moving always onward (if not always upward) into the future, into what Wagner confidently called "Die Musik der Zukunft" and what we were still calling "New Music" with the same upbeat accent in the 1950s. Forkel saw the German tradition originating with Bach; Hoffmann saw Beethoven following from Haydn and Mozart; and Schumann, when he turned resolutely from songs and piano pieces to fugues and symphonies, tactfully added his own name. Less tactfully, Wagner did the same. Hanslick countered with Brahms, Adorno nominated Mahler and Schoenberg, and it was still possible in the 1960s to think of Karlheinz Stockhausen, followed at a discreet distance even—who could tell?—by some non-German figures. Now that there are no candidates from the 1970s, a void has been discovered very close to the center of the ideology.

The paradox has been working itself out in recent American analysis. True, a newly published anthology of *Readings in Schenker Analysis* holds primly to the traditional core of J. S. Bach, C. P. E. Bach, Mozart, Beethoven, Schubert, Schumann, and Brahms. But for more and more analysts it has become a matter of importance—perhaps of supreme importance—to extend the technique to all the music they care deeply about. That is the impetus behind serial analysis, the most impressive American contribution to the discipline at large, which was developed under the general inspiration of Babbitt at Princeton in the late 1940s and '50s. It is the impetus behind efforts such as those of Morgan and others to extend analysis to the so-called nonteleological music of the 1960s and '70s. At the other end of the historical spectrum, analyses of pre-Bach, pretonal music were published as early as the 1950s by Felix Salzer, Schenker's most influential follower in this country. Salzer has also sponsored other such analyses in the current periodical *Music Forum.* More or less Lorenzian methods have been applied to the Verdi operas. Not only opera but also other music with words and programs has been subjected to analytical treatment: the Schumann song cycle *Dichterliebe,* for example, and the Berlioz *Requiem* and *Symphonie fantastique.* The blanket extension of analysis to genres with words and programs has important theoretical implications, of course. For in spite of Hanslick, the verbal messages included with a musical composition have a strong prima facie claim to be counted in with its content, along with its analyzable sounding form.

These new analyses are, as always, conducted at different levels of sophistication and insight. Even the best of them leave the reader uneasy. They come up with fascinating data and with undoubtedly relevant data; yet one always has a sinking feeling that something vital has been overlooked. For however heavily we may weight the criterion of organicism in dealing with the masterpieces of German instrumental music, we know that it is less important for other music that we value. This music may really not be "organic" in any useful sense of the word, or its organicism may be a more or less automatic and trivial characteristic. Its aesthetic value must depend on other criteria. Cannot a criticism be developed that will explain, validate, or just plain illuminate these other musical traditions?

The obvious answer would seem to be yes, and indeed one can point to a number of recent efforts along these lines. These efforts have not been followed up to any significant extent, however—at least not yet. Musicians in the academic orbit have always dragged their feet when it comes to developing alternative modes of criticism. This is as true of the musicologists as of the analysts and of the large, less clearly defined group of musicians whose inclinations may be described as broadly humanistic and who care about musicology and analysis without having made a full commitment to either (one could point, for example, to the constituency of the College Music Society). Among these many people, it is not uncommon to hear criticism invoked, discussed in general terms, sometimes praised, sometimes even practiced, and occasionally even practiced well. But there seems to be a general disinclination or inability to formalize—much less to institutionalize—the discipline on any scale broader than that of analysis.

There is a real problem here which I do not believe can be attributed entirely to some massive failure of imagination or intellectual nerve. I should prefer to believe that at least part of the problem stems from the prestige of analysis—or, to put it more accurately, from the genuine power of analysis which is the source of that prestige. For analysis, taken in its own terms, is one of the most deeply satisfying of all known critical systems. ". . . music has, among the arts, the most, perhaps the only, systematic and precise vocabulary for the description and analysis of its objects": that is an envious quotation from Stanley Cavell, a philosopher and critic well versed in music, who knows how much more fully one can fix a melodic line as compared to a line in a drawing, or a musical rhythm as compared to a poetic one, or even an ambiguity in harmony as compared to an ambiguity of metaphor. The discipline of analysis has made a very good thing out of the precise, systematic vocabulary which music possesses. But as Cavell goes on to remark, thinking of the nonexistence of what he calls a "humane criticism" of music,

> Somehow that possession must itself be a liability; as though one now undertook to criticize a poem or novel armed with complete control of medieval rhetoric but ignorant of the modes of criticism developed in the past two centuries.[3]

The liability must stem from the power of analysis and its consequent seductiveness. Its methods are so straightforward, its results so automatic, and its conclusions so easily tested and communicated that every important American critic at the present time has involved himself or implicated himself centrally with analysis.

Not all these critics would consider themselves primarily analysts,

3. Stanley Cavell, "Music Discomposed," *Must We Mean What We Say?* (New York, 1969), p. 186.

113

and some would probably be begrudged that epithet by the analysts themselves.[4] Charles Rosen, for example, prefaces *The Classical Style: Haydn, Mozart, Beethoven* with a critique of analytical systems en masse: the limitations of Schenker, Tovey, Réti, and others are cataloged incisively. Nevertheless, Rosen's procedure in the book is basically analytical, if by analysis we mean the technical demonstration of the coherence of individual pieces of music. He also presents a trenchant, controversial, historical interpretation and a steady stream of brilliant aperçus on all aspects of music. But at heart his book is a wonderfully readable and original essay in musical analysis. Rosen speaks not of organicism but of "balance" and "coherence," and it is his sensitivity to the harmonic and melodic determinants of these criteria that provides *The Classical Style* with its greatest power.

Leonard B. Meyer, in his impressive first book *Emotion and Meaning in Music,* proposed a comprehensive theory of musical aesthetics. A wide-ranging scholar, he moves on in his fourth book, *Explaining Music,* to spell out his recipe for criticism. Again there are telling arguments against Réti and Schenker, and again the proof of the pudding turns out to be analysis—a detailed exemplary study of the first twenty-one bars of a Beethoven sonata according to the author's own analytical principles. (An even more detailed analysis of another German masterpiece has since appeared in *Critical Inquiry*.)[5] Meyer sees musical events as embodying multiple implications for other events that will ensue, implications which are realized or not in various ways. This follows perfectly the model of an overriding system of relationships between all musical elements which has always animated analytical thinking.

To turn now from the sublime to the confessional, my own criticism has returned repeatedly and, as I now think, immoderately to the manner and method of Tovey. There have been digressions to the left and to the right, but in its biggest manifestations, my work, too, has been centered in a kind of analysis.

Finally, I cannot resist mentioning the recent *Beyond Schenkerism: The Need for Alternatives in Music Analysis* by a new young writer, Eugene Narmour. This is probably the sharpest, most comprehensive attack on Schenker that has ever appeared; and it culminates in the modest proposal of a new analytical system developed by the attacker. The musician's instinctive tendency is always to choose among rival analytical sys-

4. "Work . . . by 'one-off' analysts like Rosen or Kerman [is] frequently held to be suspect in its theoretical focus," writes Jonathan M. Dunsby. "They seem to embed the most penetrating and original insight about specific musical objects in an all-embracing cultural critique that can be ultimately confusing, without the deep-rooted convictions— often hard to live with but always comprehensible—of the Schoenbergian analytical tradition" (review of David Epstein's *Beyond Orpheus: Studies in Musical Structure* [Cambridge, Mass., 1979], *Journal of the Arnold Schoenberg Institute* 3 [October 1979]: 195).

5. See Leonard B. Meyer, "Grammatical Simplicity and Relational Richness: The Trio of Mozart's G Minor Symphony," *Critical Inquiry* 2 (Summer 1976): 693–761.

tems or principles rather than to look for a broader alternative to analysis itself. Where we should be looking is not only Beyond Schenkerism but also Beyond Narmourism.[6]

4

I dislike seeming to preach in the abstract, especially when I seem to be preaching against, so I shall now sketch out some conceivable alternatives to analysis in reference to the criticism of one particular short piece of music. I have chosen a familiar, standard German-masterpiece-type example, hoping to show how much can and should be done even in the area where analytical methods traditionally work best.

The piece is from Schumann's song cycle *Dichterliebe*, the second number, "Aus meinen Thränen spriessen" (fig. 1). The poem is from Heine's *Lyrisches Intermezzo* in the *Buch der Lieder*. I have chosen it partly because, in the somewhat overheated words of the analyst Arthur Komar, "In recent years, the song has aroused an extraordinary amount of interest, much of which can be attributed to its selection as the principal illustration of Schenker's analytic technique in Allen Forte's important introductory article on Schenker's theories."[7] In my view, Schenker's analysis of this song, which bids fair to attain exemplary status, shows up the limitations of the discipline as a whole with exemplary clarity. It constitutes a strong argument for alternatives.

Those unacquainted with the Schenker system will be interested to see his analysis of the song (fig. 2).[8] From the "foreground sketch," on the bottom line, more than seventy-five percent of the notes in the actual

6. Another widely discussed new analyst, David Epstein, prefaces his *Beyond Orpheus* (see n. 4 above) with this statement about "the limitations imposed on the [analytical] studies that follow": "First, they are concerned with music written within the era commonly known as classic-romantic, in effect from Haydn and Mozart through the middle nineteenth century, as delimited by Brahms. Secondly, these studies are restricted to music written in what might be called the German-Viennese tradition—the most seminal body of music that emerged during this broad period. Third, they are confined to absolute music. . . . A fourth and final limitation: the matter of 'expression' in music is beyond the confines of these studies" (p. 11). One hears the sound of windows closing.

7. Arthur Komar, "The Music of *Dichterliebe:* The Whole and Its Parts," in *Dichterliebe*, ed. Komar (New York, 1971), pp. 70–71. "Schenker's Conception of Musical Structure," one of Forte's earlier articles, first appeared in *Journal of Music Theory* 3 (April 1959): 1–30, and has since been reprinted in Komar's casebook (*Dichterliebe*, pp. 96–106) and as the first item in *Readings in Schenker Analysis and Other Approaches*, ed. Maury Yeston (New Haven, Conn., 1977), pp. 3–37. In a graded list of "Initial Readings in Schenker" prepared by another leading analyst, Richmond Browne, for *In Theory Only* 1 (April 1975): 4, Forte's article appears as the second item from the top.

8. From *Free Composition (Der freie Satz)* by Heinrich Schenker, edited and translated by Ernst Oster. Copyright ©1979 by Longman Inc., New York. Reprinted with permission.

Fig. 1

Fig. 2

116

song have already been reduced away. Only those considered structurally most important remain, with their relative structural weight indicated by the presence or absence of stems, by the note values—half-
note forms are more important than quarter, and so on—and by the
beams connecting certain groups of quarter- and half-notes (in this
sketch). Above it, the "middleground sketch" carries the reduction one
step further, and above that the "background sketch" completes the
process. The basic structure of the song is indicated by the unit at the top
right of this *Ursatz:* a simple three-step arpeggiation of the A-major
triad, going from the third degree C-sharp to the tonic A by way of B as a

passing note in the middle. The unit at the left shows the original thrust toward this same *Urlinie* interrupted at the midpoint; the motion is then resumed and completed as shown at the right. Every middleground and foreground detail can be seen to play its organic role as subsumed by the *Ursatz*. And indeed the *Ursatz* is indicative of organicism on a higher level yet: for the *Ursätze* of all musical compositions in the great tradition are essentially the same. Although naturally the interruptions differ, and sometimes the tonic triad is arpeggiated $\hat{5}$-$\hat{3}$-$\hat{1}$ or $\hat{8}$-$\hat{5}$-$\hat{3}$-$\hat{1}$, rather than $\hat{3}$-$\hat{1}$, as here, in principle the *Urlinie* always consists of a simple downward arpeggiation of the tonic triad, which Schenker took to be the "chord of nature."

It seems interesting, incidentally, and possibly significant that this apparently simple song still leaves room for debate as to the precise location of the principal structural tones. Schenker put $\hat{3}$ on the upbeat to bar 1, $\hat{2}$ on the upbeat to bar 9, $\hat{3}$ on the upbeat to bar 13, $\hat{2}$ and $\hat{1}$ in bar 15. Forte proposed a modification: the second $\hat{3}$ on the C-sharp in bar 14 (beat 2). Komar accepts this and proposes another modification: the first $\hat{3}$ on the C-sharp in bar 2. More serious interest might attach to this debate if someone would undertake to show how its outcome affects the way people actually hear, experience, or respond to the music. In the absence of such a demonstration, the whole exercise can seem pretty ridiculous.

As is not infrequently the case with Schenkerian analyses, the fragile artistic content of this song depends quite obviously on features that are skimped in the analytical treatment. The song's most striking feature—practically its raison d'être, one would think—is the series of paired cadences in the voice and then the piano at the conclusion of lines 2, 4, and 8 of the poem. How are these rather haunting, contradictory stops to be understood (or "heard," as musicians like to say) at the two points within the body of the song? And how are they to be heard at the end? From Schenker's foreground sketch one gathers that in bars 4 and 8 he counted the voice's half-cadences as primary, whereas in bar 17 he counted the piano's full cadence. But there is no explanation for this disappointingly conventional interpretation, nor any appreciation of the whole extremely original and suggestive situation, nor indeed any relic of it on the middle- and background levels. The *Ursatz* confuses the issue, for in bars 4 and 8 the cadences lack status because they are regarded simply as details of prolongation, along with many others, and in bars 16–17 they are trivialized because true closure is conceived as happening a bar earlier.

Forte and Komar, with their *Ursatz* revisions, do nothing to help the situation. Ambiguities such as those set up by Schumann's cadences are likely to strike a critic as a good place to focus his investigation, to begin seeing what is special and fine about the song. The analyst's instinct is to reduce these ambiguities out of existence.

117

Another prime feature of the music skimped by Schenker is the climax at the words "Und vor deinem Fenster soll klingen," in line 7. This Schumann achieved by a classical confluence of thickened piano texture, intensified rhythms, a crescendo, and harmonic enrichment by means of chromaticism; for a moment the emotional temperature spurts up into or nearly into the danger zone. Schenker's foreground sketch, so far from "explaining" the chromaticism here, barely acknowledges its existence. Once again his very first reduction employs too coarse a sieve to catch something of prime importance. Schenker seems often to have derived a sort of grim pleasure from pretending not even to notice certain blatant foreground details in the music he was analyzing.

In this case, the pretense was too much for Forte, and he draws attention to what he rightly calls a "striking" chromatic line, an inner line, and to its parallelism to others in the song. The emotional temperature, however, does not interest him any more than does the symbolism (of which more later); he is interested only in the fact that the line serves as "an additional means of unification." Forte finds a particularly vexing problem in the G-natural of bars 12–13. Komar too dwells on this as the "major analytic issue" of the whole song.

118

Neither of these analysts troubles to say (though they surely must see) that both this chromatic G-natural and also the chromatic F-natural in bar 14 give the word "klingen" a richer emotional coloration than "spriessen" and "werden" at the parallel places earlier in the song. Sooner or later we shall have to retrace the course taken by the composer himself and peek at the words of the poem:

> Aus meinen Thränen spriessen
> Viel blühende Blumen hervor,
> Und meine Seufzer werden
> Ein Nachtigallenchor.
>
> Und wenn du mich lieb hast, Kindchen,
> Schenk' ich dir die Blumen all',
> Und vor deinem Fenster soll klingen
> Das Lied der Nachtigall.

"Klingen" is a verb applied by the man in the street to coins, wine glasses and cymbals; poets apply it to the song of nightingales. Was Schumann trying to insist on the poetic credentials of this verb? He certainly declaimed it strangely: the vowel should be short, as of course he knew perfectly well. Also harmonized very richly is the parallel word in the previous couplet—the assonant and no doubt hugely significant word "Kindchen." So presumably the curious accents in lines 2 and 4 on the words "spriessen" and "werden" (rather than on "Thränen" and "Seufzer") were planned with "Kindchen" and "klingen" in mind. Schumann's personal reading of the poem begins to take shape. That reading may fairly be suspected of having influenced his musical decisions.

A good deal more can be done along these lines. Musico-poetic analysis is not necessarily less insightful than strictly musical analysis, whether of the Schenkerian or some other variety, as is evident from the subtle and exhaustive analyses of Schubert songs by Arnold Feil and the late Professor Thrasybulos Georgiades in Germany. In America, unfortunately, the one serious recent study of the German lied is valuable mainly as shock therapy. In *Poem and Music in the German Lied from Gluck to Hugo Wolf,* the late Jack M. Stein prods all the great nineteenth-century lieder composers for their misreadings of poetry; our song, for example, he dismisses on account of its "mood of naiveté and sentimental innocence." There is often something in what Stein says. But while Schumann certainly comes dangerously close to sentimentality in his setting of the word "klingen," we should also reckon on the clipped and dryly repetitious musical phrase that returns unvaried for "Das Lied der Nachtigall." Does this not effectively undercut the sentimental tendency? On this occasion, at least, Schumann has not smoothed away the celebrated irony of his poet.

Komar's criticism of Schenker and Forte as regards the *Ursatz* stems from his reading of the song in conjunction with the preceding song in the cycle, "Im wunderschönen Monat Mai," the beautiful and well-known opening number. He is right as far as he goes, though he does not go so far as to make the obvious point that since "Aus meinen Thränen" directly follows the famous C-sharp-seventh chord on which that opening song is left hanging, its first few notes do not announce an unambiguous A major, as Schenker so brutally assumed, but rather, for a fleeting moment, the expected resolution in F-sharp minor. So even the first half-prominent gesture in the song, the articulation of "spriessen," sounds more poetic and less naive, less sentimental, than Stein would have us believe.

Komar says that Schumann forged the two songs "virtually into a single entity" from a strictly musical standpoint. If so, that shows that, unlike his analysts, Schumann cared that the two poems also form a unit:

119

> Im wunderschönen Monat Mai,
> Als alle Knospen sprangen,
> Da ist in meinem Herzen
> Die Liebe aufgegangen.

> Im wunderschönen Monat Mai,
> Als alle Vögel sangen,
> Da hab' ich ihr gestanden
> Mein Sehnen und Verlangen.

Aus meinen Thränen spriessen
Viel blühende Blumen hervor,
Und meine Seufzer werden
Ein Nachtigallenchor.

Und wenn du mich lieb hast, Kindchen,
Schenk' ich dir die Blumen all',
Und vor deinem Fenster soll klingen
Das Lied der Nachtigall.[9]

The "Knospen" of the first song open into "blühende Blumen" in the second, the "Vögel" identify themselves as "Nachtigallen," and so on. In terms of critical methodology, Komar's emphasis on the cycle's continuity merely transfers his organicist investigation from the level of the song to the higher level of the cycle. Still, there is some use to his procedure in that it indicates a broadening out, and one may ask what the real subject of the critic's attention should be—that G-natural which Komar calls the "major analytic issue" of the song, or the total music of the song, or its music taken together with its words, or the full sixteen-song *Dichterliebe* cycle, or perhaps the entire output of Schumann's so-called song-year, 1840. As is well known, *Dichterliebe* was composed along with about 120 other songs in a single burst of creative energy lasting for eleven months, a period which encompassed the composer's marriage, after agonizing delays, to Clara Wieck.

All the songs of 1840 were written for Clara, and many of them were written directly to her. *Dichterliebe* begins in the way that Schumann's earlier Heine song cycle, opus 24, ends: with a song of dedication. The poet-composer offers his work to his beloved, work that is formed out of his love and his longing. Heretofore, however,

---

9. Heine's poems appear in *Dichterliebe*, ed. Komar, with translations by Philip L. Miller:

In the lovely month of May,
when all the buds were bursting,
then within my heart
love broke forth.

In the lovely month of May,
when all the birds were singing,
then I confessed to her
my longing and desire.

From my tears spring up
many blooming flowers,
and my sighs become
a chorus of nightingales.

And if you love me, child,
I give you all the flowers,
and before your window shall sound
the song of the nightingale.

[Pp. 15–16]

Schumann had been transforming his longing not into nightingale songs but into piano pieces—which suggests a new irony to the word "klingen," a double (or by now a triple) irony if one thinks of the shallow virtuoso pieces by Herz and Pixis on which Clara was making her reputation as a pianist while Robert was attacking them angrily in his journalism, crippling his hand in a mechanism designed to strengthen it, and bit by bit relinquishing his own ambitions as a performer. The sixteen songs now dedicated to Clara speak of love's distress, not of love's happiness. Clara, incidentally, was twelve years old when Robert first turned up as her father's student, already a sick man and a rather alarmingly dissolute one. "Aus meinen Thränen" is the only one of Schumann's love songs which includes the word "Kind" or "Kindchen."

The comprehensive study of the Schumann songs published ten years ago by the English critic and cryptographer Eric Sams has not been much noticed in this country. Sams takes a strong antianalytical line and also puts people off by his somewhat brazen pursuit of a special theory about Schumann's compositional practice. This theory centers on the composer's use of a complicated network of private musical symbolism; thus Sams identifies several secret "Clara themes" in "Aus meinen Thränen," among them the expressive descending-scale figure on the word "Kindchen" which was mentioned above. The analysts cannot do anything with data of this kind. As far as they are concerned, the same notes in the same musical context ought always to produce the same sounding form, whether written by Schumann or Schubert or Mendelssohn. But it is not unusual for composers to nurture private musical symbols. Berg is a famous case in point. Schumann is unusual, perhaps, only in the large number of studied clues he left around for future decoders. No doubt Sams goes too far. But if what we value in an artist is his individual vision, rather than the evidence he brings in support of some general analytical system, we shall certainly want to enter as far as possible into his idiosyncratic world of personal association and imagery.

Looking again, more broadly yet, at Schumann's songs and the tradition from which they sprang, one must come to a consideration of characteristics inherent in the genre itself. An artistic genre has a life of its own in history; criticism cannot proceed as though history did not exist. The nineteenth-century German lied began with a firm alliance to a romantically conceived *Volksweise*, and while from Schubert on the history of the genre is usually seen in terms of a transcendence of this ideal, composers have never wished to transcend it entirely. Evocations of the *Volkstümlich* were handled excellently, in their different ways, by Beethoven, Schubert, Brahms, and even Wolf, to say nothing of Mahler. But Stein was right: Schumann's evocations are always tinged with "sentimental innocence." Some further examples may be cited: "Volksliedchen" opus 51 no. 2; "Der arme Peter" opus 53 no. 3; "Marienwürmchen" opus 79 no. 14; "Lied eines Schmiedes" opus 90 no. 1;

"Mond, meine Seele Liebling" opus 104 no. 1; and "Hoch, hoch sind die Berge" opus 138 no. 8.

Sams makes the same point and also stresses that in addition to word cyphers and musical quotations, Schumann was also addicted to disguises, of which the impulsive Florestan and the introspective Eusebius are only the most public—so much so, that in works like *Carnaval* and *Dichterliebe* one sometimes feels impelled to ask the real Robert Schumann to please step forward. In *Dichterliebe*, by contrast with the song cycles of Beethoven and Schubert, not all but very many of the songs seem to assume different personae: think of "Aus meinen Thränen" in contrast with "Ich grolle nicht," "Wenn ich in deine Augen seh'," "Ich hab' im Traum geweinet," and others. Schumann's self-consciousness as regards the implications of genre and subgenre must be taken into account for any comprehensive understanding of his artistic intentions.

The term "persona" has been borrowed from literary criticism by a musician whose commitment to analysis has never blinded him to what Cavell calls a "humane criticism of music," Edward T. Cone. In his latest book *The Composer's Voice,* Cone's argument, which ultimately goes much further than the lied repertory, begins with Schubert's *Erlkönig.* He first inquires who it is that sings the various "voices" in this well-known song and next invites us to distinguish the vocal persona or personae from that of the piano part which underlies and binds the whole together. This seems a fruitful line to take with "Aus meinen Thränen." At first the vocal and instrumental parts run closely parallel, but they pull apart at those ambiguous cadences to which attention was drawn earlier. The voice and the piano stop in their own ways and in their own sweet times; how are we to conceive of their coordination? A highly suggestive question that Cone asks about songs is whether the pianist hears the singer and vice versa (more precisely, whether the instrumental persona hears the vocal persona). There is no doubt that the pianist hears the singer in bar 12 of "Aus meinen Thränen." But I am less sure that he does so in bar 4 and pretty sure he does not in bar 17. At this point, the attention of the instrumental persona is directed elsewhere, toward some arcane and fascinating musical thought process of his own.

Can analysis help us here? Cone always likes to address his musical criticism to musical performance, and I believe that a resolution of this question of the vocal and instrumental personae will also resolve one performance problem with this song, this small, fragile, and haunting song: namely, the treatment of the fermatas in bars 4, 8, and 16.

5

The alternatives that I have suggested to traditional musical analysis—in this case, to Schenkerian and post-Schenkerian analysis—are not intended, of course, to exhaust all the possibilities. They are merely examples of some lines along which a more comprehensive, "humane," and (I would say) practical criticism of music can and should be developed. Nor is the term "alternative" to be taken in an exclusive sense. One cannot envisage any one or any combination of these alternative modes of criticism as supplanting analysis; they should be joined with analysis to provide a less one-dimensional account of the artistic matters at hand. What is important is to find ways of dealing responsibly with other kinds of aesthetic value in music besides organicism. I do not really think we need to get out of analysis, then, only out from under.

As I mentioned above, there are a number of pressures today leading to a new breadth and flexibility in academic music criticism. Of these, one of the most powerful emerges from efforts to come to terms with the newest music. The position of Morgan, for example, seems not far from that outlined in the present paper, though the way he formulates that position is certainly very different. The traditional concept of analysis as "the elucidation of a sort of teleological organism," Morgan feels—the language is derived from Cone—must be made broader; the analysis of new music

> must examine the composer's intentions in relation to their compositional realization, must discuss the implications of the compositional system in regard to the music it generates, consider how the resulting music relates to older music and to other present-day music, examine its perceptual properties and problems, etc. There is really no end to the possibilities that could enable this list to be extended.

Indeed, "a pressing responsibility of present-day analysis is to indicate how new music reflects present-day actuality."[10]

Within the narrow confines of the music-academic community, this call for analysis to examine, discuss, and indicate what it never thought of examining, discussing, or indicating before may well prove to be perplexing. Outside the community, the only thing that will perplex is Morgan's clinging to the term "analysis." What he seems clearly to be talking about is criticism, and he is talking about it in a way that must surely enlist sympathy.

10. Robert P. Morgan, "On the Analysis of Recent Music," *Critical Inquiry* 4 (Autumn 1977): 40, 51.

Evidence and Explanation

ARTHUR MENDEL, USA

The occasion for my choosing to investigate the subject *evidence* was the turning upside down of much of the chronology of Bach's works by Alfred Dürr and Georg von Dadelsen, the results of which appeared in the years 1951—1958, and which I had had the opportunity of observing at close range.

Here was a large corpus of works that had been generally available for over half a century. It had been studied carefully by Wilhelm Rust and even more comprehensively by Philipp Spitta, who had laid out a chronological scheme for it in considerable detail. It had been the subject of many monographs and studies, based on both internal and external evidence, in the form of books, articles, and critical editions. It had had devoted to it some forty-three annual Bach-Jahrbücher.

In 1951, Dr. Dürr's *Studien über die frühen Kantaten J. S. Bachs*[1] had shown that an extension of Spitta's own methods could be made to confirm, amplify, and even in some cases correct Spitta's results. But the two studies by Professor von Dadelsen published in the *Tübinger Bach-Studien*[2] and the one by Dr. Dürr that appeared in the *Bach-Jahrbuch* for 1957[3] use other though related methods to effect one of the most drastic revisions ever made in a chronology which at the same time pertained to so famous a corpus, had been so long established, and had been previously questioned with so little success.

Where had Spitta gone wrong? This question brought a whole sequence of others in its train, all of them having to do with the evidence used by Spitta and by Dürr and Dadelsen. What kinds of evidence? Evidence of what? Evidence to what purpose? And these questions have led me to a re-examination of some of the bases of music history, a re-examination perhaps naïve in that others have probably asked the same questions I now asked myself and found answers at least as satisfactory as I have found, mostly in writings about general history. But not since Guido Adler's *Methode der Musikgeschichte* (1919), to my knowledge, have these questions and answers been examined systematically in public in connection with music history, so I felt justified in re-examining them without claiming that my results are either original or exclusive or complete.[4]

*

Why do we inquire into the history of music?

"... All historical work," says Henri Pirenne, "is only a contribution to the history of human societies conceived as a whole, and ... the value of historical work consists in the degree to which it promotes the advancement of history as a whole."[5]

But why do we study history?

---

[1] Alfred Dürr, *Studien über die frühen Kantaten J. S. Bachs* (Leipzig 1951).
[2] Georg von Dadelsen, *Bemerkungen zur Handschrift Johann Sebastian Bachs, seiner Familie, und seines Kreises* (Trossingen 1957) and *Beiträge zur Chronologie der Werke Johann Sebastian Bachs* (Trossingen 1958).
[3] Alfred Dürr, *Zur Chronologie der Leipziger Vokalwerke J. S. Bachs* (Leipzig 1958).
[4] A brief discussion of some of these points, based principally on Maurice Mandelbaum's *The Problem of Historical Knowledge* (New York 1938) is contained in Glen Haydon's *Introduction to Musicology* (New York 1941) Chapter VIII. See also footnote 34, *infra*.
[5] *What are historians trying to do?*, METHODS IN SOCIAL SCIENCE ed. Stuart A. Rice (Chicago 1931) pp. 435—445, reprinted in *The Philosophy of History in Our Time: An Anthology Selected, and with an Introduction and Commentary* by Hans Meyerhoff (New York 1959) p. 89.

1 *

One of the common answers to this question is an explanation in terms of utility. I study history in order to learn from the past lessons about the consequences of certain types of behavior, or ways of accomplishing certain results, which comes to the same thing. If we consider that history must include *all* histories—of politics, economics, social organization, science, manners, literature, art, music, and so on—then the utilitarian answer might do as an explanation of our studying the history of music. We should then maintain that we study music history in order to understand history in general, which, in turn, we study in order to learn from the past what to do about the future.

But in actual fact those who inquire into the past are in general not those who do a great deal about the future; and the most active doers are not in the habit of inquiring deeply into the past or of being guided by the inquirers. The amount of energy we historians put into finding out what man has done, compared to the amount we put into using our results to decide, or help others decide, what man may do and should do, suggests that our primary reason for making a profession of studying history is not utilitarian.

This is true as concerns history in general, and it is specifically true as concerns music history. To the extent that composers ever used rules of harmony and counterpoint, for example, as guides, those rules were based mainly on speculation and were prescriptive rather than descriptive; that is, they were mainly not rules arrived at from observation of the past conduct of composers. By the time harmony and counterpoint became descriptive sciences composers had stopped obeying their rules, and begun to make new rules for themselves, again based mainly on speculation rather than observation. And we need not confine the argument to those things that have been codified as systematically as harmony and counterpoint.

Composers undoubtedly learn something of value in choosing types of compositional procedure from their observation of the procedures of composers in the past. But few would maintain that Beethoven, whose knowledge of the music of so recent a figure as Bach was small, and Bach, who knew no Beethoven, show the disadvantage of their inferior knowledge of music history as compared with Brahms or Wagner or Verdi, who could know much of both Bach and Beethoven.

No—our primary reason for studying history is not utilitarian; it is, I hope, the same as the primary reason why the best minds study anything: because we have a passion for understanding things, for being puzzled and solving our puzzles; because we are curious and will not be satisfied until our curiosity rests. "Man, who desires to know everything, desires to know himself." [6]

What is it that we are curious about? In music history it may be a great sweeping question like why around 1600 polyphony was crowded into the background or displaced by accompanied monody; or a more technical question like whether and to what extent modal rhythms were applied in mediaeval melodies; or a narrowly factual question like whether these three staves of a chorale in the manuscript viola part of a Bach cantata are in the hand of copyist X or copyist Y.

But music-historians have another type of interest, different from any of these. Apart from the fascination of establishing facts, and relations between facts, we are interested in musical works themselves—as individual structures and as objects of delight. Our interest in Mozart's Jupiter Symphony is different from the political historian's interest in Napoleon or the social historians's interest in the steam engine. I shall return to the implications of this special characteristic of the history of an art, as contrasted with other types of history.

---

[6] R. G. Collingwood, *The Idea of History* (Oxford 1946) p. 205.

Meanwhile, having thus briefly considered the purposes of the historian in general and the music-historian in particular, I turn to a consideration of various theories of history as such.

*

At least since the time of Descartes, much attention and much controversy have been devoted to the question of whether history is a science or an art.

"After all," writes Mr. Sebastian Haffner,[7] "history is not a science but a branch of literature. The merit of an historical book is to be measured by the artistic pleasure and the intellectual profit it provides to the reader and student." Croce[8] goes so far as to say that history "does not use induction or deduction, it does not demonstrate, it narrates." Oakeshott claims that in history "the conception of cause is . . . replaced by the exhibition of a world of events intrinsically related to one another in which no *lacuna* is tolerated."[9]

On the other hand, a number of philosophers have tried to show not only that historical inquiry is or may be scientific but to what extent it may be so.

When we read in Collingwood[10] that history "generically belongs to what we call the sciences: that is, the forms of thought whereby we ask questions and try to answer them," or that "Science is finding things out: and in that sense history is a science," we begin to wonder whether the whole question is not a matter of definition.[11] I think actually some of the controversy is false, and does arise from differences of definition.

Let us begin, then, with a quite pragmatic and often quoted definition of history — "History is what historians do." What do historians do? They find out, says Collingwood, about *res gestae:* actions of human beings that have been done in the past. By finding out about these actions, Collingwood means establishing not just what the actions were (the "facts") but what the thoughts behind them were.

How does the historian learn the facts? To throw his answer into relief, Collingwood first describes the man-in-the-street's mistaken idea of history as compounded of memory and authority — the idea that history consists in believing someone else (the "authority") when he says that he remembers something. This is what Collingwood calls scissors-and-paste history, and is of course not really history at all. "In reality," says Collingwood, "as natural science finds its proper method when the scientist, in Bacon's metaphor, puts Nature to the question, tortures her by experiment in order to wring from her answers to his own questions, so history finds its proper method when the historian puts his authorities in the witness-box, and by cross-questioning extorts from them information which in their original statements they have withheld, either because they did not wish to give it, or because they did not possess it." That is, he treats their testimony as evidence, to be weighed along with other available evidence in deciding the issue at hand. The other available evidence may consist of documents throwing light on the events in question only incidentally or only by implication, or of monuments and other artifacts — things which become evidence only when the historian makes them so by "putting them to the question."

What criterion does the historian use to decide when to believe what his sources tell him, or, if they conflict, which of them to believe? F. H. Bradley, in a famous essay, *The Presup-*

[7] In a review of A. J. P. Taylor, *The Origins of the Second World War*, THE OBSERVER (London, April 16, 1961).
[8] As paraphrased by Collingwood, *The Idea of History*, p. 194.
[9] M. Oakeshott, *Experience and its Modes* (Cambridge 1953) p. 143.
[10] Collingwood, *The Idea of History*, p. 9.
[11] The matter is complicated, too, by the fact that the word science does not always denote exactly the same things in English as its equivalents *Wissenschaft, Science* [Fr.], and *Scienza* [Ital.], all of which may at times be better rendered in English by the words knowledge, or learning, or scholarship, and that some of our usages have their origins in translation.

positions of a Critical History,[12] considered that this criterion consisted in the historian's experience of the world, which teaches him that some kinds of things happen, and others do not. Collingwood objects to this criterion on two principal grounds: (1) that it "is a criterion not of what did happen but of what could happen"; (2) "that the historical as distinct from the natural conditions of life differ so much at different times that no argument from analogy will hold." To be sure, Bradley's criterion cannot prove his sources right; it can at best only prove them wrong. But verification is always at least a more difficult matter than falsification. And while it is certainly true that there is danger in arguing from one's own limited experience as to what could have happened—since historical conditions do change, and with them some of the habits of mind that we are too ready to think of as "human nature"—this only means that the criterion is never a perfect tool, but can always be improved by ever greater experience, including the experience of the historian as historian, of what can and could have happened under an ever greater variety of conditions.

Collingwood suggests that what is needed is not only a criterion for testing what the sources tell us, but also a means of constructing statements to interpolate between the statements provided by direct evidence. "Thus our authorities tell us that on one day Caesar was in Rome and on a later day in Gaul; they tell us nothing about his journey from one place to the other, but we interpolate this with a perfectly good conscience." This imagining of the journey is necessary; it is, says Collingwood, *a priori*. "If we look out over the sea and perceive a ship, and five minutes later look again and perceive it in a different place," it is the *a priori* imagination, Collingwood says, that obliges us "to imagine it as having occupied intermediate positions when we were not looking."

Collingwood's reduction of this aspect of the historian's activity to these very simple terms seems to me most useful, but I think one must consider closely just what is *a priori* about the historian's imaginative act of interpolation. The statement that the ship has traveled through intermediate positions follows from the statements that it occupied one position at one moment and another position five minutes later *by logical deduction*—only in this sense *a priori*. For the logical deduction follows from the two statements of the ship's position only in conjunction with two other statements of things we have learned by experience: (1) that an object that occupied one position in the past and occupies another position now must have traveled through intermediate positions in the meanwhile; (2) that when we see what appears to be the same ship in one position at one moment and in another position five minutes later, and when the distance between the two positions is such that a ship of the type in question could have covered it in those five minutes, it is much more probable that what we are seeing the second time is the same ship than it is another ship similar enough to be mistaken for it. So our criterion consists both of experience and of the deductions that follow necessarily or with high probability from the comparison of that experience with the events to be historically connected. It is *a priori* or nearly so in the sense that it is logically necessary or nearly so; but not in the sense that it does not rely, as Bradley said it does, on our experience of the world, prior to our attempt to understand a particular historical event or sequence of events.

Imaginative interpolation of events less directly attested by our evidence from those more directly attested is necessary not only to the logic of our account of the events, but even to our interest in it. A mere chronicle of successive events is of no interest to anyone except as he imagines the links between them, or the links connecting them to other events not mentioned. A little analysis will show that we pay attention to any narrative—even the merest conversational narrative—only as far as it shows, or we can infer from it, either how one

---

[12] In *Collected Essays* by F. H. Bradley, vol. 1 (Oxford 1935).

event flowed from another, or how, surprisingly, the expected consequence of the earlier event did not occur. In the latter case our curiosity impels us to ask why it did not occur—what there was in the concatenation of events that could account for their unexpected issue. This is true even of tales of "pure fantasy," in which the explanations we seek have to include magical or other supernatural "causes." To be significant to us, an event must be connected in some convincing way with a prior or subsequent event: it must flow from the circumstances, or some other event must flow from it.

Collingwood's analytical primer of historical activity continues to be useful when it goes on to show that just as the historian's "authorities" are not fixed points, so neither are his data. Or, if he has data, these are not events in the past, but pieces of paper, inscriptions on stone, artifacts, existing in the present. In order to establish the history of the events "they reflect," he must first establish the history of these objects of his immediate perception, and thus *make* of them evidence of the events, *make* them reflect these events. It follows, then, Collingwood rightly says, that "historical knowledge can only grow out of historical knowledge," that the first stage of historical activity consists in establishing the history of our sources, and inferring the events which they reflect—the "facts."

If we look a little more closely at the logical process by which our criterion, Collingwood's *a priori* imagination, works, we see that it proceeds from what it accepts as data (in Collingwood's example, the successive appearances of the same object at two different points in space), through general statements about how such appearances can and must occur, to a conclusion about how they did occur. This explanation is now generally referred to as an explanation by "covering laws." Hempel has described the model for such explanations as consisting of (1) a statement (or set of statements) of events, setting out antecedent conditions; and (2) a statement (or set of statements) expressing a law or laws that conditions of the kind specified are always followed by events of a certain other kind specified. From these two types of statements a statement of the event of the second kind specified in the laws follows as a logical consequence. The model is represented by Hempel as follows

$$\frac{\begin{array}{l} C_1, C_2, \ldots, C_k \\ L_1, L_2, \ldots, L_r \end{array}}{E}$$

where C_1, C_2, etc. are statements of antecedent conditions, L_1, L_2, etc. are statements of covering laws, and E is a statement of the type of event to be explained, which for convenience Hempel calls the *explanandum*. [13]

We need to notice several things about Hempel's model.

---

[13] I am helping myself from the contents of several essays, here listed in chronological order: (1) Carl G. Hempel, *The Function of General Laws in History*, in THE JOURNAL OF PHILOSOPHY 39 (1942) as reprinted in Feigl and Sellars (Eds.), *Readings in Philosophical Analysis* (New York 1949); (2) Carl G. Hempel and Paul Oppenheim, *The Logic of Explanation*, in PHILOSOPHY OF SCIENCE 15 (1948) as reprinted in Feigl and Brodbeck (Eds.), *Readings in the Philosophy of Science* (New York 1953); (3) Carl G. Hempel, *The Logic of Functional Analysis*, published in L. Gross (Ed.), *Symposium on Sociological Theory* (Evanston 1959); (4) Carl G. Hempel, *Deductive-Nomological vs. Statistical Explanation* (1960), to be published in Feigl *et al.*, MINNESOTA STUDIES IN THE PHILOSOPHY OF SCIENCE 3 (Minneapolis 1962); (5) Carl G. Hempel, *Explanation in Science and History* (1961), to be published in Colodny, R. G. (Ed.), *Frontiers of Science and Philosophy*, UNIVERSITY OF PITTSBURGH PUBLICATIONS IN THE PHILOSOPHY OF SCIENCE 1 (publication expected 1962). I am greatly indebted to Professor Hempel for letting me read the two last-named articles before publication, as well as for help in private conversation and correspondence. I make no further specific acknowledgments to Professor Hempel because it will be clear to anyone who consults his essays how much this paper owes to them; but of course he is not responsible for anything I say.

First of all, it should not be thought inadequate as a model of causal explanation simply on the ground that the cause of one effect must itself be the effect of some earlier cause. "Is B not a cause of A simply because C is a cause of B?" asks Ernest Nagel, Professor of Philosophy here in Columbia University. And he answers: "... the fact that one problem may suggest another, and so lead to a possibly endless series of new inquiries, simply illustrates the progressive character of the scientific enterprise."[14] "Explanation consists," as N. R. Campbell puts it, "in the substitution of more for less satisfactory ideas,"[15]—in the substitution of "more satisfactory ideas," not of "completely satisfactory ideas." Explanation reduces a situation to elements that we accept "so that our curiosity rests," said the late philosopher-scientist P. W. Bridgman.[16] "It is part of the logic of 'explanation' that if something can be explained, there is something else which does not require explanation. But the reason it does not require explanation is not necessarily that we know its explanation already."[17]

In the second place, although Hempel's model works for causal explanation, it is not restricted to causal explanation. The thing to be explained may itself be a law, and the explanation may consist of subsuming it under a more general law or laws, in which case one cannot call the more general law the "cause" of the more specific law subsumed under it. At any rate, the relation between the explanandum and the antecedent conditions is always such that they are functions[18] of one another, in the sense that they are so related that when one varies, the other varies correspondingly. Thus when antecedent conditions vary so does the explanandum, and *vice versa*.

130The order in which they are arranged is not fixed. We can *explain* an event on the basis of antecedent conditions. We can use present conditions to *predict* future events. And we can *infer* (or "retrodict") earlier events (antecedent conditions) from later ones.

Prediction as such is not a task for historians, but it is worth noting that as Hempel says, a causal explanation is not complete unless it might as well have functioned as a prediction. That is, if the antecedent conditions are sufficient, one can logically infer from them the consequences; if they are insufficient, one cannot: and this irrespective of whether the consequences have already taken place or are still in the future. But by explanation we usually mean something more than a statement of sufficient conditions: what we want to explain is not only whether a set of known conditions was sufficient to cause a known event, but whether all these conditions were necessary or only some of them, and whether some of the conditions had a more important influence than others.

It is not possible to treat briefly here the relative importance of various conditions, since what is involved is the meaning we attach in each case to the word "importance," a question that has been analyzed by Professor Nagel in the essay I have previously quoted. But the question of necessary conditions brings us to the first and most elementary part of the historian's task: inference, or "retrodiction" of antecedent conditions from observed events. The simplest kind of observed events are mostly words (and, in our case, musical notation) written on pieces of paper which exist in the present, from which we retrodict the antecedent conditions that account for what is written on them: they are the existing evi-

---

[14] Ernest Nagel, *The Logic of Historical Analysis*, THE SCIENTIFIC MONTHLY 74 (1952); reprinted in Feigl and Brodbeck, *Readings*, and in Meyerhoff, *Anthology*.
[15] N. R. Campbell, *Physics, The Elements* (New York 1948) p. 37.
[16] P. W. Bridgman, *The Logic of Modern Physics*, as quoted in W. Dray, *Laws and Explanation in History* (Oxford 1957) p. 77.
[17] Dray, *Laws and Explanation*, p. 72.
[18] The relation of the concepts of cause and effect to that of function is explained by Bertrand Russell in *Mysticism and Logic* (New York 1918) pp. 180—205, reprinted in Feigl and Brodbeck, *Readings*.

dence from which we establish what we call the facts. To do this we use an inversion of the model: we start from the observed event, and by means of a law which states that this event could not have taken place without certain antecedent conditions we infer those conditions.

Thus prediction and retrodiction require two different types of law, and both are simpler than the kind of explanation historians mostly seek. The type of law we need for *prediction* is one that states that certain kinds of antecedent *conditions* are *sufficient* to bring in their train certain kinds of *events*. The type of law we need for *retrodiction* states that certain kinds of *events* are sufficient to infer the existence of certain kinds of antecedent *conditions*; or, in other words, that certain kinds of antecedent *conditions* are *necessary* for the occurrence of certain *events*. *But* the type of *explanation* historians seek is usually a combination of retrodiction from a later event to an earlier one and of what one might call "pre-dated prediction" from an earlier event to a later one. For this type of explanation we need at least both kinds of laws: one kind stating that certain conditions are necessary, so that they can be, or could have been, retrodicted from the observed events, and one stating that certain conditions are sufficient, so that the observed events could have been predicted from them.

Sometimes, in the absence of a law adequate for retrodiction, we construct a hypothesis which could account for the observed event, and accept it provisionally because any other hypothetical explanation seems less likely. At any rate, the form of the explanatory model is not affected by the question of whether any of its members is considered to be true or only hypothetical. From hypothetical antecedent conditions or hypothetical laws the logical procedure to either a true or a hypothetical explanandum is the same as that from true-to-fact antecedent conditions and true-to-fact laws.

It has been widely objected that historical explanation does not follow such models — is, in fact, not scientific at all. Many historians and philosophers have rejected the idea that history is concerned with either the discovery or the operation of general laws.

This is not the way historians think, they say. A historian does not arrive at his conclusions by inductive or deductive reasoning: he is led to them by "bringing to bear" on the evidence a special faculty called "judgment," or sometimes specifically "historical judgment." Now it is perfectly true that historians do not in practice always go through the steps indicated in our models, any more than a geologist does in "recognizing" a rock, or a physician in diagnosing an ilness. Is this because he "knows" what he sees by a special process of "*Verstehen*" which he could not reduce to orderly, logical steps? Perhaps at times it is: a gifted diagnostician may jump to a diagnosis through his sense of smell, or in other ways of which he feels it would be impossible to give a completely logical verbal account. "All scientists," said D. H. Lawrence in a remark to Aldous Huxley that has become famous, "are liars . . . I don't care about evidence. Evidence doesn't mean a thing to me. I don't feel it *here*." And, reports Huxley, "he pressed his two hands on his solar plexus."[19] But what the diagnostician smells, or "senses" by a combination of perceptions which he may not be able to analyze fully, *is* to him evidence, just as truly as the quantitative measurements that are made in the laboratory. The smell, or the combination of perceptions, is to him an event, in the sense of our model of retrodiction; in his experience this event is regularly associated with an antecedent condition, a particular disease; and he has made for himself (though perhaps not consciously formulated) a law to the effect that this combination of perceptions never occurs except in the presence of a particular disease — that this disease is an antecedent condition necessary to account for this combination.

He may be wrong; he may be proved wrong by the further progress of the case in a manner characteristic of a different disease and clearly showing his diagnosis to have been mistaken.

19 Aldous Huxley, Introduction to *The Letters of D. H. Lawrence* (New York 1932) p. xv.

131

In that case what he thought was a law turns out not to have been one, and he will have to base his future judgment on a wider generalization, which states that the combination of perceptions he has taken to be indicative of only one disease may in fact be accounted for by either of two diseases.

But this simply illustrates the fact that empirical laws are arrived at on the basis of a finite number of experiences and can be proven false whenever an event occurs which contradicts them.

Nothing I have read in any of the attempts to prove the "historian's judgment" exempt from analysis by deductive reasoning seems to me any more successful than such attempts would be on behalf of the physician's art of diagnosis.[20]

It is true that I have somewhat simplified the case of the diagnostician, and that he may not simply choose from among a limited repertory of abstract entities known as separate diseases. He may, rather, "freely invent" a hypothetical combination of factors, and only then investigate, by the process I have called "pre-dated prediction," whether these factors would be sufficient to bring about the patient's symptoms, and, by retrodiction, whether they must in fact be present. The historian and the scientist, too, may arrive at their explanations by first "freely inventing" a hypothesis and then testing it. This "free invention" is identical with what Collingwood calls the "*a priori* imagination"; it presumably does not invent anything for which its possessor's experience has not prepared it; or, if it does, like the composer's "inspiration," it does so for the natural scientist just as for the historian. And the hypothesis itself is based on the hypothetical sufficiency of the antecedent conditions, that is, upon a hypothetical law.

The invention of hypotheses is doubtless usually an art, not a completely orderly, logical process of deduction, in both natural science and history; the testing of the hypothesis— even that informal, preliminary testing that its inventor gives it in his own mind before advancing it as an explanation—must take place, in history as in natural science, under covering laws.

But in history, unlike physics, the objectors say, one does not construct laws on the basis of many instances; one is concerned with explaining individual events. If general laws enter at all, it is only that one sometimes applies them to explain individual events. But so one does, of course, in some aspects of geology, astronomy, and medicine, which apply the laws of such sciences as physics, chemistry, and biology to the explanation of individual rocks or mountain ranges, stars or galaxies, illnesses or epidemics.

Yes, they say, but history deals not with kinds of events, but with individual events, every one different from every other. "To formulate laws to cover them," it is claimed, "you would have to have a different law for every work, and then these would not be laws at all, which by definition deal with classes of things, not with individuals."

To put it another way, every advance in precision of statement takes us farther away from the crude uniformities which are first observed, into greater differentiation of antecedent and consequent, and into a continually wider circle of antecedents recognized as relevant. As soon as the antecedents have been described sufficiently fully to enable the consequent to be calculated with some exactitude, the antecedents have become so complicated that it is very unlikely that they will ever recur. But if the set of antecedent conditions is unique, no law can be made, since "a 'law' with only a single case" ought not to be called a law.[21]

[20] Some of the most serious of these attempts are: W. Dray, *Laws and Explanation in History* (Oxford 1957); A. Donagan, *Explanations in History*, MIND (1957) reprinted in P. Gardiner (Ed.), *Theories of History*; M. Scriven, *Truisms as the Grounds for Historical Explanations*, printed in the same Gardiner collection, which also contains an extended bibliography of its subject.
[21] Cf. Dray, *Laws and Explanation*, pp. 37—44.

But most of what I have just said is a quotation; and it is taken not from comments on historical explanation but from a passage written by the philosopher-mathematician, Bertrand Russell, about scientific explanation. Let me now read the passage again, restoring what I omitted in reading it the first time—the phrases that show that what Russell is discussing is the uniqueness of each sequence of antecedents and consequents in science.

"What I deny," Russell says, "is that science assumes the existence of invariable uniformities of this kind, or that it aims at discovering them. All such uniformities . . . depend upon a certain vagueness in the definition of 'events'. . . . Every advance in a science takes us farther away from the crude uniformities which are first observed, into greater differentiation of antecedent and consequent, and into a continually wider circle of antecedents recognized as relevant.

"The principle 'same cause, same effect', which philosophers imagine to be vital to science, is therefore utterly otiose. As soon as the antecedents have been given sufficiently fully to enable the consequent to be calculated with some exactitude, the antecedents have become so complicated that it is very unlikely they will ever recur. Hence, if this were the principle involved, science would remain utterly sterile."[22]

Every drop of water is unique, as is every human action. But this does not prevent us from comparing drops of water *in those respects* in which they appear alike, or from generalizing about them *in those respects*.

What seems a more powerful objection than any of these is that frequently the only generalizations that can be made are statements of statistical probability, which can never account for individual cases. Such laws state that in the long run antecedent conditions of a particular kind are followed a certain percentage of the time by events of a particular kind.

Statistical laws are arrived at by essentially the same procedure as universal laws—on the basis of a large but finite body of evidence. But there is a basic difference in what they *assert*: A universal law asserts that in specified circumstances a specified type of event always occurs; a statistical law asserts only that in specified circumstances a specified type of event occurs in a specified proportion of any larger number of instances.

A law of high statistical probability may be phrased: "It is almost certain that, given antecedent conditions of the types C_1, C_2, . . ., C_k, an event of type E occurs." While such a law will not provide the link necessary for a water-tight prediction of an individual event from a statement of the antecedent conditions, it will provide for a prediction of the type which itself begins with the words "It is almost certain that . . ."[23] But it will not provide the link necessary for retrodiction of any type, since there may be another statistical law which says: "It is almost certain that, given antecedent conditions C_m, C_n, . . ., C_y, an event of type E follows," and then there is no way of knowing whether from the establishment of event E we are to retrodict C_1, C_2, . . ., C_k or C_m, C_n, . . ., C_y. What we need for a retrodiction of the type "It is almost certain that" is a law of low statistical probability, which may be phrased: "It is almost certain that in the absence of conditions C_1, C_2, . . ., C_k an event of type E does not occur." From the establishment of event E we can then draw the conclusion that "It is almost certain that antecedent conditions C_1, C_2, . . ., C_k are present."

Another objection is two-fold: it states that history is concerned with men's actions only as embodiments of their thought, purposes, motives. With this we can agree. But, says the objector, thought, purposes, motives, cannot be brought under law. This is to say that psychology cannot succeed in establishing laws of mental and emotional behavior. Everyone

---

[22] Bertrand Russell, *On the Notion of Cause*, reprinted in Feigl and Brodbeck, *Readings*, pp. 391—392, from *Mysticism and Logic*.
[23] The logical distinction between the conclusions to be drawn from universal laws and from laws of statistical probability is explained in the Hempel essays listed as (4) and (5) in footnote 13.

133

will admit that psychology has not had great success so far in establishing such laws. But how much success has meteorology had? Do its laws tell us whether it will rain this afternoon? Can we predict *a priori* the futility of the attempt to establish laws for mental phenomena?

The second part of this objection is that to call motives causes would be to say paradoxically that the future can provide antecedent conditions for the present. But a moment's analysis suffices to see that it is not the future, but men's ideas of how they may affect the future, entertained prior to their actions, that "motivate" them to those actions.

Finally, consider a more inclusive objection as stated by Sir Isaiah Berlin[24]: "'History is what historians do', and what historians aim at", Professor Berlin writes, "is to answer those who wish to be told [for example] what important changes occurred in French public life between 1789 and 1794, and why they took place. We wish, ideally, at least, to be presented, if not with a total experience—which is a logical as well as a practical impossibility—at least with something full enough and concrete enough to meet our conception of public life ... seen from as many points of view and at as many levels as possible, including as many components, factors, aspects, as the widest and deepest knowledge, the greatest analytic power, insight, imagination, can present. If we are told that this cannot be achieved by a natural science—that is, by application of models to reality, because models can only function if their subject matter is 'thin' and consists of deliberately isolated strands of experience, and not 'thick' in the texture constituted by the interwoven strands—then history is not in this sense a science ... We can make use of scientific techniques to establish dates, order events in time and space, exclude untenable hypotheses and suggest new explanatory factors, but the function of all these techniques, indispensable as they are today, can be no more than ancillary, for they are determined by their specific models, and are consequently 'thin', whereas history is necessarily 'thick': that is its essence, its purpose, and its reason for existence."

There is no denying that one part of the historian's task is to write the "thick" type of history Professor Berlin describes. Nor can we pretend that history is able to construct the kind of general historical laws that would govern the interweaving of the infinite number of strands of which his thick texture consists.

But to include among the resources on which the historian must draw not only knowledge and analytic power but insight and imagination is to state that history consists not only of what we "know and can prove" but of what we feel and imagine and cannot prove. When we look closely even at what we say we "know and can prove" we invariably find that we don't quite know it and can't quite prove it. Even the most universal, scientific "laws of nature" are true only until proved untrue. "If you insist on proof (or strict disproof) in the empirical sciences," writes Popper[25] "you will never benefit from experience, and never learn from it how wrong you are .... The empirical basis of objective science has nothing 'absolute' about it. Science does not rest on rock-bottom. The bold structure of its theories rises, as it were, above a swamp. It is like a building erected on piles. The piles are driven down from above into the swamp, but not down to any natural or 'given' base; and when we cease our attempts to drive our piles into a deeper layer, it is not because we have reached firm ground. We simply stop when we are satisfied that they are firm enough to carry the structure, at least for the time being."

In history we erect far more detailed and elaborate (in Professor Berlin's sense, "thicker") hypotheses than in the natural sciences, on the basis of the piles we have driven down into the

[24] Sir Isaiah Berlin, *History and Theory, the Concept of Scientific History*, HISTORY AND THEORY 1 (1960) p. 23.
[25] Karl R. Popper, *The Logic of Scientific Discovery* (New York 1959) pp. 50, 111.

swamp—the so-called facts we think we have established. All the more reason why the structures will not stand long if we have not taken account of all the available relevant facts, and have not carried strictly logical reasoning from them as far as it will go.

But that is not far enough to write the kind of history Berlin describes, or far enough for most historical purposes, and we have to add material supplied by "insight and imagination." What is the nature of this material? It consists of things that could have happened, motives that could have operated, reasons and causes that could explain. Now the name for what could have happened but may not have is historical fiction. Historical fiction is not necessarily false (here *ficta* is not a synonym for *falsa*); it is just not necessarily closely bound to the "known facts." The writer of historical novels may use as little fact and as much fiction as he pleases; the historian, although he cannot get along without the fictive element, is bound to restrict it to the minimum necessary to connect the "facts" in a convincing pattern. But in this, too, history does not differ from science. Any hypothesis when first entertained is fictive; the task of the investigator is to constantly decrease the proportion of the part that is fictive to that part that is securely based on piles driven into the swamp.

*

What are the practical lessons to be drawn from the claim that the nature of historical inquiry is scientific? It seems to me they are clearly indicated by Hempel when he says: "Any explanation of scientific character is amenable to objective checks; these include

  (a) an empirical test of the sentences which state the determining conditions;
  (b) an empirical test of the universal hypotheses on which the explanation rests;
  (c) an investigation of whether the explanation is logically conclusive, in the sense that the sentence describing the event to be explained follows from the statements of groups (a) and (b)."[26]

" . . . In trying to appraise the soundness of a given explanation, one will first have to attempt to reconstruct as completely as possible the argument constituting the explanation."[27] When the parts of the argument are thus reconstructed and examined, when "the assumptions buried under the gravestones 'hence,' 'therefore,' 'because,' and the like" are resuscitated, "it will often be seen that the explanation offered is poorly founded or downright unacceptable," as Hempel says. Equally, it will usually be seen that what we provisionally accept as an explanation contains only "a more or less vague [or incomplete] indication of the laws and initial conditions considered as relevant, [which] needs filling out" in the form of "further empirical research for which [what is advanced as an explanation] suggests the direction."

The processes necessary to identify the thinnest strand of what Berlin calls the "thick" texture of history and to grasp (that is, explain) the full thick texture are not different. To establish the fact that Ockeghem died in 1495 we have to establish through general laws the relations between observed events (our evidence) and an antecedent condition (the fact). To establish the historical relations between Josquin's lament, *Nymphes des bois*, and Ockeghem's death, or between *Nymphes des bois* and the chant melody of the *Requiem aeternam*, or between polyphonic settings in general and *cantus prius facti*, or between all compositions that make some use of preexisting material and that material, or between Josquin's style and Ockeghem's, we have to use the same processes. But the higher we go in the scale of generality, the harder it is to make the empirical tests Hempel specifies[28] and the more our explanation will assume the character of a hypothesis or an outline: a hypothesis

---

[26] In the essay listed as (1) in footnote 13, section 3.3.
[27] *Ibid.*, section 5.5.
[28] For most helpful criticism of the version of this sentence delivered orally on September 5, 1961, leading to its reformulation, I am indebted to Dr. Carl Dahlhaus of Stuttgart.

135

that may never become amenable to empirical tests, and so must forever remain purely speculative; or an outline that is at the same time an interim report on research in progress and a tentative program for further research.[29]

Music history, being a young science, is still, to a greater extent than some other forms of history, concerned with establishing basic facts. The location and the critical publication of the sources—evidence—for our knowledge of the history of music is still, or perhaps even not yet, in full swing. We shall for some time to come continue to be busy establishing what are called individual facts—the dates, authorships, and readings of individual works—by reasoning from the evidence: that is, mainly by the process of retrodiction.

Meanwhile, our curiosity will constantly drive us toward completing the explanatory process by "pre-dated prediction," and toward explaining more and more generalized statements of events. We are not satisfied with relating "factual events" by external evidence. We want to understand relations between works and styles, by internal evidence. But this presupposes not only an ability to formulate general laws, but also an ability to describe events and conditions—which in this case are musical works and styles—with a precision that is far beyond us. Our methods of reasoning even from external evidence need constant reexamination. But they are incomparably nearer precision than our methods of analyzing and describing musical works themselves.

And here we are led back to the special characteristics that differentiate the history of an art from other kinds of history. Theories of historical knowledge have taken as their object almost exclusively history-in-general, or history *tout court*—that is, the history of men's behavior mainly in the fields of politics, economics, and social organization, the history of the doers of deeds. Both the doers and the deeds have vanished, and the historian can deal only with their traces, from which he tries to reconstruct as vividly as possible the men and what they did. But the deeds with which we music-historians mainly deal have not vanished. What we have before us in an old manuscript or print—or in its modern reprint, for that matter—is much more than a trace of the doer: it is his deed itself.

In history-in-general, as Collingwood points out, what interests us about a deed is how it came to be done, the thoughts and feelings that impelled its doer, which we infer from the circumstances in which he found himself. The historian, Collingwood says, "is interested in the crossing of the Rubicon only in its relation to Republican law, and in the spilling of Caesar's blood only in its relation to a constitutional conflict." He "must always remember that the event was an action, and that his main task is to think himself into this action, to discern the thought of its agent."

Croce puts this idea most vividly. "Do you wish to understand the true history of a neolithic Ligurian or Sicilian?" he asks.

> Try if you can to become a neolithic Ligurian or Sicilian in your mind. If you cannot do that or do not care to, content yourself with describing and arranging in series the skulls, implements, and drawings which have been found belonging to these neolithic peoples. Do you wish to understand the true history of a blade of grass? Try to become a blade of grass; and if you cannot do it, satisfy yourself with analysing its parts, and even arranging them in a sort of ideal or fanciful history.[30]

---

[29] Hempel calls this type of explanation, which needs filling out, an "explanation sketch." Perhaps some of the indignation with which this concept has been rejected by several of his critics is due to the suggestion of shallowness and *insouciance*, of something tossed off in an idle moment, that the word *sketch* may evoke.

[30] Benedetto Croce, *Teoria e Storia della Storiographia* (Bari 1917) p. 119, as quoted by Collingwood, *The Idea of History*, p. 199, from the English translation, *Theory and History of Historiography* (London 1921) pp. 134—135.

"As concerns neolithic man, the advice," says Collingwood, "is obviously good. If you can enter his mind and make his thoughts your own, you can write his history, and not otherwise; if you cannot, all you can do is to arrange his relics in some kind of tidy order, and the result ...," Collingwood concludes, "is not history."[31]

What Collingwood implies, it seems to me, is that the relics and their arrangement are the bare bones of history with too little flesh; in Popper's figure, the piles driven into the swamp with too little superstructure; or in the language I have been using, the "factual data" with too little of the fictive element needed to give them coherence, intelligibility, and interest.

If we translate Croce's metaphors into musical ones, we might say: "Do you wish to understand the true history of the *Missa Pange lingua?* Try, if you can, to become Josquin Desprez composing the *Missa Pange lingua.*"

This raises several difficulties.

The first is the question of what has been called the "intentional fallacy," which is defined as using the supposed "design or intention of the author ... as a standard for judging the success of a literary work of art." It is pointed out that: "If the poet succeeded ..., then the poem itself shows what he was trying to do. And if the poet did not succeed, then the poem is not adequate evidence, and the critic must go outside the poem—for evidence of an intention that did not become effective in the poem."[32]

If as historians we are, in Collingwood's words, "seeking the thought" of the composer that lies behind the work itself, we are not "using the supposed design or intention of the author ... as a standard for judging the success" of the work; but we are trying to understand the intention itself, and how Josquin came to it. The "intention itself" consists, of course, of a great deal more than the mere idea of using the *Pange lingua* melody as a *cantus firmus;* it comprises an immense number of aspects of the work. We cannot be sure it comprises all aspects even of the work viewed as an isolated entity: there may be aspects of which Josquin was not conscious, and which therefore cannot be called a part of his design or intention. But at any rate our principal clue to his intention is the work itself, and we cannot understand the intention without understanding the work.

To what extent then, can we imaginatively "become Josquin Desprez composing the mass" and to what extent is it necessary that we should?

Can we do so by analysis of the work? Certainly we can learn a great deal about it in that way, by methods analogous to and as diverse as those used by such men as Jeppesen and Schenker. Some of what we learn in this way undoubtedly corresponds to some of Josquin's conscious intentions; to this extent we are imaginatively "becoming Josquin." But is that the limit of what we mean by "understanding" the work? To ask the question is almost to answer it. We know that no matter how far we carry the analysis of a work of art, there is something in our relation to the work that is beyond analysis. I cannot prove that it is theoretically and forever beyond analysis; but I cannot escape the feeling that it is: that if we should succeed in analyzing it, it would have ceased to exist. Perhaps our delight in the work consists partly in being baffled by it, and perhaps there is no theoretical reason to believe that analysis cannot eventually remove our bafflement; but then it would at the same time have removed our delight.

This presents us with a strange paradox. We know what we think of music-historians who are, as we say, "unmusical." And we know what we think of their musical opinions. We say they do not understand the music they are discussing. But to be "musical" means, among

---

[31] Collingwood, p. 199.
[32] W. K. Wimsatt, Jr., and Monroe C. Beardsley, *The Intentional Fallacy,* sewanee review 54 (Summer 1946), reprinted in Wimsatt's *The Verbal Icon* (New York 1954).

other things, to have this direct, unanalyzable, baffling relation with a musical work. And if this is true, then the "understanding" of a work must include being baffled by it. I do not think this paradox arises from a mere play on the word "understand." I think what we mean is that there are many ways of "understanding" music, and that this instinctive, unanalyzable way is a *sine qua non* for any other way—that no one who is aesthetically interested in a work understands it completely, but that anyone who has never experienced this baffling, aesthetic interest in a work has not even begun to understand it.

Santayana speaks of the history of art as "only remotely [affecting] our aesthetic appreciation by adding to the direct effect certain associations." "If," says Santayana, "the direct effect were absent, and the object in itself uninteresting, the circumstances would be immaterial."[33] But who can certify to the historian the direct effect of the work itself that makes it worth his while to seek the relations of this work with other works? No one but himself; he must himself experience it. And this means that in the music-historian the musician and the historian are inseparable and indispensable to each other.

Hempel and Oppenheim argue that in history empathy is neither necessary nor sufficient for an understanding of the behavior of the persons studied, though it may be of heuristic value in the devising of hypotheses that may turn out to be explanatory. To some extent, as they point out, the behavior of psychotics or of people of an alien culture may be explainable and predictable in terms of general principles, even though the scientist who establishes or applies those principles may not be able to understand his subjects empathetically.

I cannot establish, for that matter, whether the music-historian has any direct relation of the type I have described to the musical work, or—if that relation is to be called empathy with the composer, or at least with the composer in the rôle he has assumed in this work— how much emphasis is to be put on the prefix *em*, and how much on the root-part of the word, *-pathy:* that is, to what extent his feeling represents a true understanding of the work and to what extent it is purely subjective, individual, occasioned by the work but perhaps having no necessary connection with it. But while I cannot prove any of these things, I find that I cannot doubt that the aesthetic relation to the musical work exists and is necessary to the music-historian.

It is possible to imagine a music-historian who has analyzed the individual works whose relations he seeks to establish to the point where he fully understands them, and accordingly has lost all aesthetic interest in them. But then it is hard to imagine why he should stick at music history. For we must admit that—*pace* Pirenne— in actual fact it is probably not true that most professional music-historians study the history of music primarily as a part of their general historical studies, or out of pure love of history. And certainly we would not match Collingwood's statement by saying that the music-historian is interested in the *Missa Pange lingua* only in its relation to abstractions like the Phrygian mode or the *cantus firmus* mass. Our love of history is mixed (and we require that it should be mixed) in various proportions with the love of music. We study music in order to understand history; we also study history in order to understand music.

But while I believe that the unanalyzable, direct relation of the music-historian to the work is necessary, it is certainly not sufficient for explanation. It does not even provide evidence except to the person who experiences it and to others whose experience is similar, any more than the odor the diagnostician smells is evidence to those who do not perceive or recognize it. Even to the one who has this aesthetic experience, it is, when he thinks historically about it, evidence, which he must use by the application of covering laws. And

---

[33] George Santayana, *The Sense of Beauty* (New York 1891) p. 17.

the fact that there is direct aesthetic experience of one work at a time gives us no license to substitute some sort of instinctive judgment for reasoning in tracing the relations between two or more works.

Furthermore, when the music-historian addresses those to whom his aesthetic experience is not evidence he must speak about the demonstrably present characteristics of the music.

To form hypotheses we need not wait for the perfection of our methods of describing those characteristics—the internal evidence. Obviously, to do so would be to adjourn the attempt to establish relations between works or between styles *sine die*. Our methods are still primitive, perhaps, but, in compensation, the materials we have to work with are incomparably more vivid than those of other types of history. François Ier is, for all the liveliness of his character, the merest abstraction to us, formed from the fragmentary documents we can hold in our hand and from our fictive imagination. But the *Missa Pange lingua* is almost as complete and present to us as François Ier would be if he could rise from his grave and walk into the room. And the difference in precision between statements about external evidence and those about internal evidence is only one of degree. All statements, and so all explanations, when scrutinized carefully enough, turn out to be more or less incomplete. If they are sufficient to satisfy our curiosity, we call them "complete enough." We believe that Bach was baptized on the 23rd of March 1685 because an entry in a baptismal register survives to tell us so; we do not "know" that the register or the entry is authentic, but we see no reason to doubt it, or even to doubt that it means that Bach was born a day or two earlier; the retrodiction of the facts from the evidence is not perfectly complete, it is just complete enough to satisfy us.

But as historians we are not easily satisfied, and the level on which we must begin to doubt is hardly higher than this. I have myself just recently had to entertain a doubt almost on this level, in connection with the editing of a sinfonia which is an adaptation of the first movement of the Third Brandenburg Concerto. The surviving autograph of the Brandenburg Concertos contains the famous letter of dedication to the Margrave of Brandenburg, dated March 24, 1721. Any copies or adaptations of the material contained in these concertos made after 1721 must, then, have been based on some other manuscript, since this dedication autograph had been sent off to the Margrave in Berlin in that year. So, at least, we have reasoned until now. But had it been sent off to Berlin? Or had Bach perhaps only intended to send it, and then heard, say, that whatever circumstances had provided his original motive for sending it had changed? The explanation had always been good enough, because we had never needed to make any assumption that contradicted it. As soon as we entertain a contradictory assumption, however, the incompleteness of the explanation, though not necessarily its falsity, is exposed. On higher levels of generality and significance—and internal evidence involves much higher levels—explanations are correspondingly more incomplete.

Finally, about specific pieces of internal evidence we can make at best only retrodictions, not pre-dated predictions, since we do not understand creative activity to the point where we can say anything about sufficient conditions for its occurrence. For example, we tend to accept as a hypothetical law a statement that might be phrased as follows: what seem on first consideration to be sudden changes in style will usually be seen, on closer examination, to have taken place more gradually. On the basis of this generalization, and of a striking instance of an apparently sudden change of style, Rore's chromatic piece *Calami sonum ferentes*, published in 1555, we can say that it is highly probable that this piece must have had predecessors, even though we still cannot say what they were. But if we knew these predecessors they would of course not be sufficient to enable us to make a "pre-dated prediction" about their successor. [34]

*

We can formulate a moral that results from all our inquiry: The more general, the more significant the explanation we advance, the less stubbornly we should cling to it, for the more surely it will be incomplete, the greater will be the proportion of its fictive content, the more surely it will be at best the outline of an explanation—a program for further research. Perhaps we should teach our typewriters to inscribe at the top of every page this warning of Oliver Cromwell's to the Church of Scotland, which is couched in terms that may be more congenial to the humanist than those I have used: "I beseech you, in the bowels of Christ, think it possible you may be mistaken."

140

---

[34] The question of the rôles of internal and external evidence in establishing the authenticity and chronology of musical works is discussed with particular clarity in the first chapter of Jens Peter Larsen's *Die Haydn-Überlieferung* (Copenhagen 1939).

LEONARD B. MEYER

Exploiting Limits: Creation, Archetypes, and Style Change

Creation

FOR THE PAST THREE HUNDRED YEARS OR SO, the natural sciences have been conspicuously successful in formulating and testing theories that explain phenomena in the natural world. And they have had striking success in applying the knowledge gained through theorizing to other realms—for example, industrial, agricultural, and medical technology. As a result, the sciences have become the preferred paradigm not only for intellectual inquiry, but also for accounts of creativity, originality, and cultural change in all areas of human endeavor.

This paradigm has emphasized that the most significant and valuable achievements in the sciences have resulted from the falsification of existing theories and the promulgation of new ones based on previously unformulated concepts or unimagined relationships. Because they have become exemplary cultural heroes, the names of scientists who wrought such revolutions come readily to mind: Galileo and Kepler, Newton and Darwin, Mendel and Einstein. Whatever its validity for the sciences, this paradigm was transferred more or less intact to the arts. One result has been the assumption implicit in the title of this symposium—in the arts, as in the sciences, the creative act involves transcending limits.

Of course, much depends on what is meant by the phrase "transcending limits." But the prevalent view—which may serve as a reminder of the still-powerful presence of Romanticism in our culture—seems to be that expressed by Bronowski: "We expect artists as well as scientists to be forward-looking, to fly in the face of what is established, and to create not what is acceptable, but what will become acceptable."[1] This view, which is entirely compatible with common cultural scuttlebutt, implies that artistic change is the desirable and necessary consequence of experimentation (the scientific model is obvious) and that such experimentation results in revolutions in technical means and perhaps aesthetic ends as well. In short, what seems meant by "transcending limits" is the overturning of some prevalent style of art and the institution of a new one through a revolution comparable to those characteristic of the sciences. The conception of creativity posited by this view seems to me to be partial and strained. When applied to the arts, it is misleading and mistaken in significant ways.

177

It is misleading because it encourages historical distortion, for the model makes it necessary that artists acknowledged to be "great" be radical innovators. For instance, Beethoven, perhaps *the* exemplary artist, has to be seen as combining the defiant heroism of Prometheus with the conceptual boldness of Galileo: a revolutionary toppling the rules and, in so doing, freeing music from the stifling confines of convention.[2] But a sober study of his music indicates that, if his musical values are not confused with his seemingly equivocal political views, Beethoven overturned no fundamental syntactic rules. Rather, he was an incomparable strategist who *exploited* limits—the rules, forms, and conventions that he inherited from predecessors such as Haydn and Mozart, Handel and Bach—in richly inventive and strikingly original ways. In so doing, Beethoven extended the means of the Classic style. But extending is not transcending—it is not abrogating rules and overturning conventions.[3]

The association of the creative act with "transcending limits" tends to obscure a distinction of some moment, that between the historical importance of a work of art and its aesthetic significance or value. These are by no means the same. Because they initiated or strikingly exemplified a new rule or principle of organization, some works of art (or groups of works) are considered to have been of signal historical importance. Peri's *Orfeo* and the operas of the Florentine Camerata are such works. But few listeners, scholars, or critics would, I think, include these among the great works of Western music. Mozart's *Marriage of Figaro*, on the other hand, must surely be counted one of the masterpieces of world music. But its modest innovations are confined to recombining and extending existing means.[4]

A moment's reflection—an informal mental survey of familiar classics—makes it evident that there is something suspect about associating creativity with transcending limits, for few of the greatest artists have been promulgators of new principles. As Josephine Miles has observed—

> It is surprising to note, perhaps, that the so-called great poets as we recognize them are not really the innovators; but if you stop to think about it, they shouldn't be. Rather they are the sustainers, the most deeply immersed in tradition, the most fully capable of making use of the current language available to them. When they do innovate, it is within a change begun by others, already taking place.[5]

In music, the situation seems unequivocal. Though some composers have both invented new principles and devised new means for their realization, creating compositions of the highest aesthetic value—one thinks, perhaps, of the work of Monteverdi—many of those recognized as great masters have transcended no limits, promulgated no new principles. Rather they have been inventive strategists, imaginative and resourceful in exploiting and extending existing limits. This pantheon includes masters such as Josquin and Lassus, Handel and Bach, Haydn and Mozart, Schubert and Chopin, Brahms and Verdi, and even, as I hope to show in this essay, such supposed revolutionaries as Hector Berlioz.

If these observations have merit, it would seem that two different sorts of creativity—and, by extension, originality—need to be distinguished. The first kind, most clearly exemplified in the work of renowned scientists, involves the discovery and formulation of new theories that make it possible to relate different phenomena to one another in coherent ways. The second kind of creativity, that manifested in the work of many of the greatest artists, involves exploiting and extending the possibilities potential in an existing set of principles in order to make a presentational pattern.[6]

This suggests that the kinds of things created and, consequently, the modes of understanding and appreciation appropriate to each are different. Both kinds of creativity involve the use of particular phenomena and general principles, but they do so in quite opposite ways.

The kind of creativity that most often transcends limits makes use of particular phenomena observed in the natural world or in human cultures. However, instead of being of interest for their own sakes, such particulars—a falling star or a brilliant diamond, a chrysanthemum or a nesting bird, a supermarket or a Schumann symphony—are relegated to the role of data. They serve as means for the discovery, formulation, and testing of a theory. The theory, which is the goal and end result of the creative act, is a general proposition in terms of which diverse and divergent phenomena can be related to one another in coherent, understandable ways. And those theories are most highly prized, most admired, and, yes, most aesthetically satisfying that are most general, that encompass the widest range of phenomena within the simplest set of principles.

The second kind of creativity—that which exploits and extends limits, and the kind I will be concerned with in the remainder of this essay—works quite the other way around. What is created is *not* a proposition about phenomena or about the relationships among them. *Hamlet* is not a tract about the behavior of indecisive princes or the uses of political power; nor is Picasso's *Guernica* primarily a propositional statement about the Spanish Civil War or the evils of fascism. What the second kind of creativity produces is not a generalization, but a particular; not a propositional theory, but a presentational phenomenon—a specific set of relationships designed to be directly understood and experienced by culturally competent audiences.

What the second sort of creative act gives us, then, is an idiosyncratic pattern, presented in time or space: in short, a work of art. As we listen to Major General Stanley sing his song,

> And binomial theorem I am teeming with a lot of news,
> And many cheerful facts about the square in the hypotenuse,

what we enjoy and appreciate are not the binomial or Pythagorean theorems, nor the perplexing principles of prosody that constrained and guided W. S. Gilbert's choice of words. What we respond to and delight in are the deft exploitation of cultural and linguistic habits in the playful coupling of a prosaic vocabulary with high-falutin concepts and the rather preposterous extension of the conventions of rhyming.

General principles—laws, rules, and even conventions (for instance, rhymed couplets)—play an important role both in the creation of works of art and in our appreciation of them. For the artist, they constitute a set of constraints without which intelligent choice would be impossible; for the competent audience they function as the rules of the game that form the basis for understanding and evaluating the particular presentational relationships that are the work of art: for instance, the specific verbal, visual, and gestural patterning that *is* the play *Hamlet*, as actualized in some interpretation.

The implied analogy to games may serve to illuminate something about the nature of appreciation. In works of art, as well as in games, what we enjoy and respond to is not our knowledge of governing principles or rules, but the peculiar relationships discerned in a specific composition or the idiosyncratic play of a particular game. And just as our delight in the play of a particular game of football depends in crucial ways on our understanding of the constraints governing the game—the established rules, prevalent strategies, physical circumstances, and so on—so our enjoyment and evaluation of art depends on our knowledge (which may be tacit) of the constraints that governed the choices made by the artist and, hence, the relationships presented in the work of art.[7]

The analogy to games cannot, however, be sustained, and the point at which it breaks down is revealing. In games, the constraints (the rules, prevalent strategies, and so on) are explicitly known and conceptualized by all concerned—coaches, players, onlookers: "Three strikes and you're out!" "A bishop may move diagonally in either direction." In the arts, on the other hand, some of the most fundamental constraints governing aesthetic relationships may be *un*known or not be explicitly conceptualized, even by those most accomplished and imaginative in their use, that is, creative artists. They know the constraints of a style not in the sense of being able to conceptualize them or state them as propositions, but in the sense of knowing how to use them effectively. As with knowledge of a language, what is involved is the acquisition of a skill, the internalization of the constraints as unconscious modes of perception, cognition, and response. The same is true of most performers, critics, and audiences. They, too, know the constraints of a style—the laws, rules, and strategies that limited the composer's choices—in this tacit way.

What composers, performers, critics, and listeners—and, yes, musicologists—*do* know consciously and explicitly are particular realizations (often grouped into types or classes) of more general stylistic principles. And from such realizations, music theorists attempt to infer the general principles that constrained, but did not determine, the choices made by composers. As constraints have changed over time, so have the patterns that are the basis for style classifications. We readily recognize that certain melodies or harmonic progressions are characteristic of the Classic style, while others are typical of the Romantic; that this Crucifixion painting is Renaissance, another is Baroque.

There are cases, however, in which fundamental similarities of form or process transcend traditional stylistic boundaries. Some kinds of patterning seem, if not universal, at least *archetypal* within one of the major cultural traditions, such as that of Western Europe.[8] And the most patently archetypal patternings are, one suspects, those that couple compellingly coherent processive relationships with patently ordered formal plans.[9] An archetypal pattern may serve as the basis for countless individual realizations, each of which is the result of some newly devised strategy. And however modest and unprepossessing the novelty may be, it is nonetheless evidence of a creative act that exploited, but did not transcend, limits. Example of archetypes come readily to mind: quest/trial plots from Homer to Joyce; gap-fill melodies from Gregorian chant to "Somewhere Over the Rainbow."[10]

Archetypes are important because they establish fundamental frameworks in terms of which culturally competent audiences (creators and performers, critics and scholars, as well as members of the general public) perceive, comprehend, and respond to the playful ingenuity and expressive power of the idiosyncratic patterns presented in works of art.[11] They are important for other reasons as well.

Because they are coherent, orderly, and simple, archetypes are memorable and tend to be stable over time. Since they are general types, the number of archetypes is limited. For these reasons they are an important basis for stylistic learning. They are what children learn when they tediously reiterate nursery rhymes, intone tiresome chants, and make visual images that only fond parents delight in, psychiatrists regard as interesting, and Wordsworthian Romantics find profound.

Archetypes, therefore, are an important basis for cultural continuity. They are the cognitive-mnemonic schemas that Richard Dawkins called "memes," because he thought of them as the cultural counterparts of the units of biological trait-transmission.[12] Like genes, they tend to persist—but in culture rather than nature. And because they persist, archetypes may help to illuminate the nature of the changes that have occurred in the history of an art such as music. That is, using an archetype as a constant may enable us to perceive, and perhaps eventually to explain, the nature of the succession of different realizations that constitute the history of music.

It is this possibility that I plan to explore in what follows. Obviously, in an essay such as this I can do no more than discuss a few realizations of a single archetype, considering how, and perhaps why, the realizations changed over time. The relationship between the general scheme of the archetype and particular realizations of it will first be illustrated with instances from the *oeuvre* of Mozart. Then I will present an example of the way in which Beethoven realizes the archetype, and suggest the significance of some of his modifications. Finally, I will consider how Berlioz realizes the same fundamental schema, and attempt to relate the peculiarities of his actualization to what I take to be some of the significant facets of Romanticism in music.

The Archetype

Before particular realizations of the archetype are considered, the bare bones of the schema must be described and discussed, for to appreciate the similarities and differences among particular realizations, the salient features of the schema must be recognized and remembered. The basic pattern of the archetype is given in Example 1. The schema is divided into two parts, marked A and B in line *a* of Example 1. The parts are distinguished by differences in melodic pattern and by the harmonic and rhythmic closure that occurs when mobile dominant-harmony (V) resolves to stable tonic-harmony (I) at the end of Part A. In particular realizations, moreover, contrasts in texture (for instance, accompaniment figure) and dynamics often serve to emphasize the distinction between parts.

In the instances that I have come across, this scheme may be the basis for the patterning of a whole theme or parts of it. In the latter case, the archetype may structure both parts of a larger melody—as in an antecedent-consequent period

145

(A-A′); or the archetype may, as we shall see, structure only one part (usually the first) of a higher-level binary form (A-B).

Part A itself consists of two melodic/rhythmic entities, designated *m* and *m′* on line *b*. These are always similar in melodic contour and in rhythmic pattern.[13] As a result of this similarity, the morphology of the first part of the archetype is always in the proportion (1 + 1). The length of the second part is more variable; but as a rule, it is either equal to, or half again as long as, the first part. The whole pattern, then, is generally in the proportion (1 + 1) + 2 or (1 + 1) + 3.

The patterns *m* and *m′* may themselves be subdivided into motives *x* and *y*, and *x′* and *y′*, but as the parentheses (on line *c*) indicate, motive *x* is not invariably present. When it is, it usually centers around the fifth degree of the scale (5); at times, the third of the scale (3) is also part of the patterning of *x*; when *x′* is present, it usually centers on the second degree of the scale (2) and perhaps touches the seventh (7) as well.[14] Thus, though its presence may be characteristic, motive *x* does not define the first part of the archetype.

What defines the archetype are the melodic and harmonic relationships between *y* and *y′*. As indicated in Example 1, *y* consists of a melodic motion from the tonic (1 or 8) to the seventh degree of the scale, accompanied by a harmonic progression from the tonic triad (I) to a chord built on the dominant (V), or some substitute for it (vii); *y′* consists of a melodic motion from the fourth degree of the scale (4) to the third (3), harmonized by a progression from the

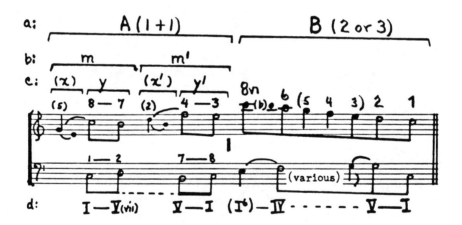

Note: The notation used in the analyses does *not* represent the duration of the stipulated pitches, but only their relative structural importance and their constancy as features of the archetype. These are notated as follows:

most important ⟶ least important

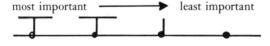

Example 1

dominant (or a substitute) back to the tonic.[15] Though what is crucial is its harmonic function, the melodic contour of the bass is usually the opposite of that of the melody: that is, when the melody descends, the bass ascends and vice versa. The most common bass pattern is that shown in the example: namely, 1 - 2 : 7 - 8.[16]

Part B of the archetype is considerably more variable in form and process than Part A. Melodically, it usually begins with the upper octave of the tonic, marked "8v" in Example 1. This note, which will be called the "upper tonic," is often harmonized by the first inversion of the tonic triad (I[6]). The first important structural pitch, however, is usually the sixth degree of the scale, accompanied by subdominant harmony (IV or ii[6]). Melodically, what most often follows is stepwise descending motion through the fifth, fourth, and third of the scale—with various possible harmonizations—to the second degree, harmonized by a dominant triad. This is resolved to the first degree of the scale harmonized by the tonic triad.

Conjunct descending motion is not, however, the only possible melodic patterning. To understand why this is so, we must consider the kinds of processes generated by motives y and y'. One of these is what I have called a "gap-fill" process.[17] When a skip occurs in a melodic pattern, we are aware, though perhaps unconsciously so, that some of the steps of the scale have been "left out." The sense of incompleteness created by such a gap implies a subsequent fill—a stepwise melodic motion that creates a sense of completeness by presenting the pitches previously skipped over.[18] And though ascending gaps are most often followed by descending fills, all or part of a fill may, as we shall see, consist of rising motion.

For the sake of later discussion, it is important to analyze the processes characteristic of the archetype in a bit more detail. Because y and y' are intervallically identical (each descends a half step) and are usually alike in metric placement, duration, and so on, we relate them to *each other* despite the fact that a different motive, x', may have come between them. Thus the skip from the end of motive y to the beginning of y' is understood as a gap implying conjunct fill.[19] As graph a of Example 2 shows, the fill begins when the fourth degree of the scale moves to the third at the close of motive y'. Further motion, through the second degree to the tonic, is, of course, implied. But such continuation is delayed until the end of the archetypal scheme. It is delayed because a second process, generated by the relationship between y and y', creates a further gap. This process is "sequential." The sequence consists of motive y and its repetition a perfect fourth higher (y'). This regularity implies continuation. And had the sequence been continued exactly, it would have been as shown in graph c of Example 2. The harmony, too, would have moved sequentially, as shown beneath graph c, to the subdominant—and perhaps beyond.

However, though the subdominant is characteristically the first structural harmony of Part B (see graph d), the sequence is broken. For instead of skipping in exact sequence to B-flat, y' is followed by a skip to the upper tonic. What remains of the sequential process is the structurally important motion to the sixth degree of the scale, harmonized by the subdominant.

The skip from the third of the scale to the upper tonic creates a second gap. But, as graph b indicates, the fill really begins with the sixth of the scale and descends to the third. Only then is the process generated by the first gap (graph *a*) completed by a fill that reaches the tonic.

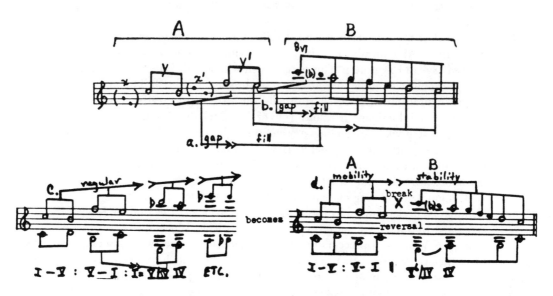

148

Example 2

From a syntactic point of view, the second part of the archetype complements the first. In Part B, that is, the implications generated in Part A are realized through the filling of melodic gaps, the curbing of harmonic expansion, and a general emphasis on stability. This "reversal" from the relative tension and uncertainty of ongoing mobility, present in Part A of the scheme, to the relative relaxation and certainty of arrival and provisional closure, characteristic of Part B, constitutes what I shall call the syntactic climax of the archetypal structure.[20]

Let us consider three instances of the archetype as they occur in the *oeuvre* of Mozart. The first instance (Example 3) is the beginning of the first movement of the Piano Sonata in G Major (K. 283). The theme exhibits almost all of the features said to be characteristic of the archetype. Its two parts are clearly differentiated by motivic pattern, direction of melodic motion, accompaniment figure, and dynamics. The structural lengths are (2 + 2) + 6. Though motive *x* and *x'* are unusually well-defined and discrete, lack of harmonic motion within them makes their subsidiary nature clear. The sequential gap-fill motion from *y* to *y'* is patent, as is the arrival at the upper tonic—though the high G is harmonized by a root position triad rather than one in first inversion. As indicated in the analytic graphs, the bass motion and harmonic progression are typical.[21]

The second instance, Example 4, is from the opening theme of the last movement of Symphony No. 29 in A Major (K. 201). The archetypal scheme structures both parts of an antecedent-consequent period—but only the consequent period will be considered here. In this instance, motive x consists of a single pitch, the fifth of the scale, which functions as an upbeat to motive y. As a result, x virtually loses its identity as a motive. Motive x', which is differentiated only rhythmically, is essentially absorbed into motive y'. Although subject to octave transfers, motive y and y' move unequivocally through the typical pattern (8-7, 4-3) accompanied by the usual harmonic progression and changing-note figure in the bass. Particularly in the consequent phrase, the conjunct descending fill as well as the contrast in rhythm, dynamics, and register differentiate the second part of the archetype from the first.[22]

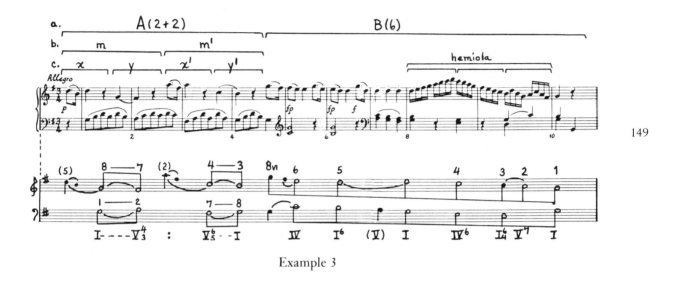

Example 3

Example 4

Example 5 is the first C Major section from the second movement of the Piano Sonata in C Major (K. 309). In this instance, x and x' are at least as patently shaped as y and y'. As in the archetypal model, the fifth is the most prominent tone in x, while the second of the scale is so in x'. Despite their relative brevity, there is no doubt that the cadential progression implicit in y and y' articulates the form and generates the process that structures this melody. Though the bass moves to the fifth in measure 35, the leading tone is present, and the harmonic progression is characteristic.

150

Example 5

Part B begins with the customary progression from I^6 to the subdominant (ii^6). But, instead of descending, the upper tonic is reiterated, while rising motion in a lower line begins the fill. As the analysis shows, the upper tonic ultimately descends as both lines converge on the sixth of the scale, the A in measure 39. Such emphasis is entirely appropriate, not only because A is typically a focal point in the archetypal scheme, but also because it begins the last in a series of conventional patternings suggesting closure[23]—a fact that will be important when the instance from Berlioz's music is considered.

Analyses abstracted from Mozart's realizations of the archetype are given in Example 6. For convenient comparison, all analyses are given in the key of C. The family resemblance is inescapable, though the realizations differ markedly in aural patterning—in foreground melody and rhythm, harmony and texture, meter and tempo. Faced with such underlying commonality, one cannot fail to ask what limits Mozart is here transcending. The answer, of course, is none. Rather, it is his genius to exploit his, and our, familiarity with the constraints, (the limits) of the classic style.

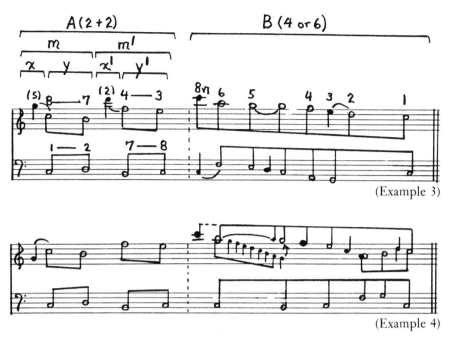

(Example 3)

(Example 4)

(Example 5)

Example 6[24]

Style Change

All of the preceding instances were composed during the 1770s. Now I shall discuss two instances of the archetype taken from works written more than forty years later. The first, one of the last works of the Classic style, was written by Beethoven in 1826; the second, one of the exemplary works of the Romantic style, was written by Berlioz in 1830.

The work from Beethoven's *oeuvre* (Example 7) is the theme of the fourth movement of the String Quartet in C-Sharp Minor, Opus 131. The theme is in two periods (labeled P[1] and P[2] in the example); each of the periods is repeated in somewhat varied form.[25] The first period (P[1]), an antecedentlike phrase, presents a version of the archetype. And Part A is an almost pristine distillation of the pattern—with no trace of an *x*-motive and no hint of harmonic elaboration.[26] Part B of the archetype begins typically with the upper tonic over first-inversion tonic harmony. The melody then descends linearly, developing con-

Example 7

152

siderable mobility as the result of a harmonic sequence that, following emphasis on subdominant harmony, closes on the dominant (m. 8 and 16).

Instead of a "proper" consequent phrase, however, what follows is a new sequence that, while maintaining the rhythmic figure established in P^1, moves from the second degree of the scale (B) back to the upper tonic.[27] (It is as though the fill of the second part of the archetype was not entirely satisfactory. In "compensation," the ascending line of the second period emphasizes the second and fifth of the scale, important tones touched only lightly (m. 7) in the descending fill of the first period.) In contrast to the first period, the rising sequence of the second makes reaching the upper tonic seem a more significant achievement. This is so for several reasons. First, rising lines generally engender a greater sense of effort than do falling ones. And this sense tends to be specially strong when the rising line is not only sequential, but what might be called "Sisyphean"—that is, when the motive, which is the basis for the sequence, itself rises (implying continued upward motion), only to fall back.[28] And the force of such upward goal-directed motion is heightened by the growth and decay of dynamics within measures 25 and 27. At measure 29 the sequence ends as the rising line moves directly to the high A. Again dynamics—the

crescendo in measures 29 to 30—help to heighten the sense of ascending motion, while the expansion of registral sonority (in the middle voices) and the appoggiatura, G-sharp, strongly stress the arrival of the A. Once this goal is achieved, dynamics die away, register and sonority return to normal, and the melodic line descends toward closure on the tonic.

This description calls attention to a distinction of importance, that between syntactic climax and statistical climax. A *syntactic climax* is a result of what was earlier called reversal: that is, a change in which forms and processes shaped by the primary parameters of melody, rhythm, and harmony move from a state characterized by relative mobility, ambiguity, uniformity, or irregularity, to one of relative stability, coherent process, and clear form. A *statistical climax*, or "apotheosis," on the other hand, consists of a gradual increase in the intensity of the more physical attributes of sound, the arrival at a tensional "highpoint," followed by a usually rapid decline in activity—a falling-away to quiet and closure. Because the intensity of the secondary parameters that shape such processes can be measured and quantified—for example, the increase or decrease in dynamics (intensity), in pitch (as frequency), rate of note succession, timbre, and tempo—they have been called statistical. One further point: though an intensification of secondary parameters—higher pitches, louder dynamics, and so on—often accompanies syntactic climax, such heightened activity is not a necessary condition for—but a concomitant, a symptom, of—such climax.[29] In a statistical climax, however, the highpoint of activity *is* the central tensional event—which either subsides to closure or "resolves" into a forthright affirmative musical assertion.

Returning now to Beethoven's theme, both periods are shaped by syntax, but in the second (P²), the syntactic climax in measures 29-30 is led up to and complemented by features characteristic of statistical climax: the gradual increase in intensity that results from the sequential rise, the crescendo, and the enlargement of registral sonority, all followed by a quick decline in intensity. This interpretation is supported by another difference between the first and second periods of the theme. Instead of occurring halfway through, as in the first period, the highpoint now occurs in the sixth measure—·three-fourths of the way through. For reasons that I will present later, such placement nearer to the end of a process is characteristic of the highpoint of a statistical apotheosis.[30]

The final actualization of the archetype that I will consider is the main melody, the famous *idée fixe*, from the first movement of Berlioz's *Symphony Fantastique* (Example 8). The work was written only four years after Beethoven's C-Sharp Minor Quartet, but Berlioz was Beethoven's junior by more than thirty years, and thus the difference in style is very striking.[31]

Despite significant differences, however, salient features of the archetype are unquestionably present. In what follows I will first show that Berlioz's melody is, in fact, a member of the class I have been describing. Then I will consider how and why Berlioz has modified the archetypal scheme, and attempt to relate such changes to what I take to be some of the leading currents of Romanticism in music.

That Berlioz's melody is a member of the archetypal class I have described seems indisputable—though not necessarily obvious. As the analysis given in Example 8 shows, the first part of the melody is divided into two long phrases that are comparable to those designated as *m* and *m'* in the archetypal scheme. Each phrase begins with a triadic pattern that prolongs a single harmony: these are the *x* motives. As in the instances already considered, motive *x* centers on the fifth of the scale (G), motive *x'* on the second degree (D). Typically, the first phrase (*m*) closes with a motive (here labeled *yᵃ*) that descends a halfstep from the tonic (C) to the leading tone (B); and the second phrase (*m'*) also closes with a descending halfstep (labeled *yᵇ*) that moves from the fourth of the scale (F) to the third (E). As in previous instances, the underlying harmonic plan is I—V : V—I.[32]

Berlioz's melody is certainly in agreement with my earlier observation that the second part of the archetype allows for greater variability than the first. Instead of beginning with the usual skip to the upper tonic, thus continuing the sequential gap process begun in Part A, the second part of the *idée fixe* (labeled B¹) first reaches the upper tonic (the C in measure 99) through a new linear sequence based on a motive (labeled *ss*) that was initially presented between motives *x* and *yᵃ*. In a sense, this first upper tonic occurs as part of the wrong sequence. Moreover, it is a mobile dissonance—an appoggiatura that calls for resolution. But in the archetypal scheme, and in all the instances of it presented, the upper tonic was relatively stable; usually, it was part of the tonic triad.

A satisfactory upper tonic does occur at the beginning of the last part of the melody (B^2). Harmonized, as it often is, by the first inversion of the tonic chord, the stable high C (m. 103) moves in familiar fashion to the sixth of the scale (m. 105). As in the second part of the instances already discussed, the remainder of B^2 descends to closure on the lower tonic. As shown in graphs G^1 and G^2, gaps generated earlier—from y^a to y^b, and from y^{b-3} to the high C (m. 103)—are filled by gradual descending motion. At the same time the fill also accommodates a succession of closing figures.

Though I do not doubt that the archetypal patterning is central to the form and process of Berlioz's melody, the need to argue the case at all suggests that salient features of the archetype have been obscured. The question is not only *why* the lineaments of the scheme have been veiled, but also *how* the particular changes made are related to the presumed need for disguise.

In my view, Berlioz's exploitation and extension of the archetype can be interpreted as an exemplary and revealing response to two of the beliefs central to Romanticism. The first is the belief that conventions, whether in human behavior or in the realm of art, are not merely deplorable, but are also somehow decadent and immoral. Habitually denigrated and disparaged as being impersonal formulae, calculated contrivances, or lifeless clichés, conventions were at the very least considered to be symptomatic of the detested fetters that, according to Rousseau, enchain mankind.

A number of different beliefs and attitudes characteristic of Romanticism can be related to one another through their common incompatibility with the conventional as it was understood at the time. The following are examples of attitudes toward the conventional that have a connection with the arts:

1. The personal expression of the artist-as-individual, assigned a position of prime importance in the aesthetics of Romanticism, could not easily be reconciled with the apparent impersonality and commonality of prevalent convention. Also, the artist's role as "revolutionary liberator," still with us here today, called on him to overturn rules and conventions—to transcend limits.

2. Inspiration, regarded with almost religious awe by devout Romantics, seemed diametrically opposed to convention. Far from being learned and culturally shared, as conventions were, inspiration was supposed to flow spontaneously from the artist's inmost being, as natural and unpremeditated art.

3. The perspicacity imputed to innocent infants (trailing their glorious clouds behind them) and the virtue patronizingly attributed to the uncorrupted honesty of presumably uncultivated primitives—these, too, testify to the low esteem in which culturally learned conventions were generally held.

4. The magical power of such Romantic heros as Siegfried and Parsifal is intimately connected with their cultural innocence—with the fact that they had not been defiled by the conventions of civilization.

As Charles Rosen and Henry Zerner point out, one of the deepest ambitions of Romantic artists was "the achievement of 'immediacy,' of forms of expression directly understandable without convention and without previous knowledge of tradition."[33]

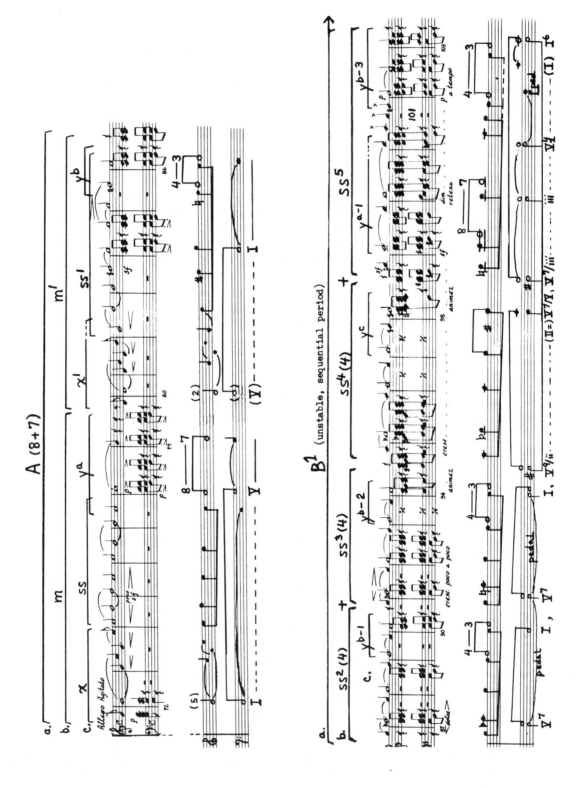

156

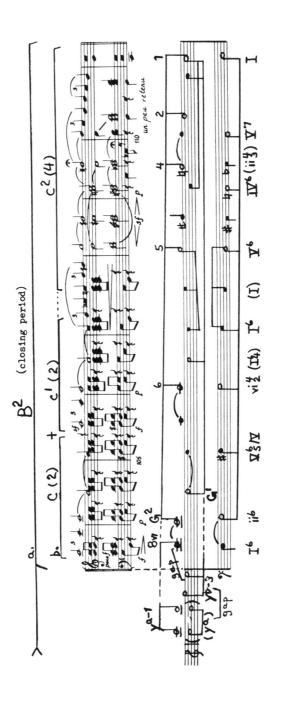

Example 8

157

Thus arises what I take to be a problem of signal importance for the history of music in the nineteenth century. From an ideological, conceptual point of view, the conventional, the formulaic, the archetypal is anathema—something strenuously to be shunned. But from a practical point of view, those who compose tonal music cannot do without conventions of grammar and syntax and the archetypal schemas that make relational richness possible.[34] While this dilemma was not satisfactorily resolved during the nineteenth century, a workable arrangement was reached.[35] Conventions, formulae, and archetypes were permitted in this arrangement, but they were to be veiled or disguised in some way. In music, one of the discoveries of Romanticism was how to hide your archetype and have it too!

A second belief central to Romanticism is a corollary of the deprecation of convention. It affirms the excellence and value of what is natural—of spontaneous action, unreflecting feeling, untutored genius, and informal, unarranged landscapes. This enthusiasm, at times reverence, for the natural can be related to an important characteristic of nineteenth century music: that is, the increasingly important role played by secondary parameters in the shaping of musical process and the articulation of musical form.

To understand this relationship it is necessary to recognize that the secondary parameters are, perhaps paradoxically, a more "natural" means for shaping musical processes and articulating musical forms than are the primary ones. For instance, the ritard and diminuendo, the thinning of texture, and the descending succession of pitches in measures 100 to 103 of Berlioz's melody all seem to foster and presage closure—even without help of the articulation created by melody, harmony, and rhythm. This is because the physical patterning of the sound continuum—of pitch frequency, concord and discord, dynamic intensity, rate of impulse, instrumental timbre, and so on—shapes states of tension and repose in an almost unmediated, direct way. However, the subtle, equivocal closure created (in the same measures) by the relationships among melody, harmony, and rhythm can be comprehended and experienced only by those who have internalized the constraints—have learned the conventions—of the style of tonal music.[36] Partly because they seemed more "natural," and hence compatible, with the prevailing ideology, secondary parameters became more and more important during the course of the nineteenth century. Complementing the increased importance of the secondary parameters in shaping music was a decline in the importance of large-scale tonal relationships created by the primary parameters.

A corollary of this change in emphasis was an increase in the importance of statistical climax, or apotheosis, relative to syntactic climax in the shaping of musical structure—until the former comes to overshadow the latter. Such statistical highpoints generally occur quite late in a form: roughly two-thirds rather than half the way through, as is commonly the case with syntactic climax. The reasons for this appear to be more or less as follows.

A syntactic climax need not, and usually does not, lead directly to closure. The reversal that articulates the climax is from a situation characterized by tonal ambiguity, unpredictability of uniform processes and weakened shapes, and uncertain formal organization, to one of secure tonal/harmonic orientation, strongly shaped patterns, and clear, formal organization. But tonal/harmonic processes may be coherent without being closed; patterns may be patently shaped, though some implications remain to be realized; and formal organization may be clear without formal structure being complete.[37] Because syntactic climax need not be directly followed by closure, it can occur as early as halfway through formal entity—as it does, for instance, in Mozart's realizations of the archetype.

The highpoint in any statistical climax, however, usually occurs fairly late in the pattern. Otherwise the falling-off toward closure, unsustained by syntax, will be too long, and boredom will ensue. The only way to "prolong" an apotheosis process is to begin a new buildup as the earlier one is subsiding. From this building up again and again arises the cumulative wave-form pattern quite common in the music of the nineteenth century. In fact, it was a miniature version of such a wave-form pattern that was earlier called a Sisyphean sequence. And this brings us back to Berlioz's melody.

One of the obvious differences between Berlioz's melody and the instances considered earlier is that it is four times longer. Thus motive m, which was two-measures long in all of the earlier instances, lasts for eight measures in Berlioz's theme.[38] This increase in magnitude, itself a characteristic of much Romantic music (particularly that for orchestra), acts both directly and indirectly to obscure the archetypal pattern. It obscures directly because the change in size increases the *absolute* temporal distance between the pattern-generating motives, y^a and y^b, making it more difficult for the listener to connect them. Indirectly, and more important, the change in size involves a change in structure, both within and between the parts of the archetype. The nature of the relationship of size to structure in music is at once of central importance for the history of music and still highly problematic. I can only suggest that D'Arcy Thompson's observations about the interdependency of size and structure in the natural world hold, with appropriate modifications, in the worlds of human culture. And just as one cannot simply increase the size of, say, a mosquito tenfold and still keep its functions and activities constant, so one cannot merely augment a musical pattern fourfold and yet maintain its functional relationships.[39]

From this point of view, seeing how Berlioz modified the archetype by amplifying (and thereby disguising) it may serve to illustrate some of the compositional problems of nineteenth century music. Phrases m and m' of Part A of the archetypal model are enlarged through both augmentation and addition. The model's motives x and y are augmented: each is two-measures, instead of one-measure, long. What is added is a new motive not previously encountered in instances of the archetype, labeled ss, for Sisyphean sequence. In internal construction it rises only to fall, and from phrase to phrase it is the basis for an ascending sequence. Motives ss and ss^1 tend to obscure the relationship between y^a and y^b (so fundamental for an understanding of the archetypal pattern) for three reasons. First, they add another item to be remembered. Second, it is unclear precisely where ss and ss^1 end and y^a and y^b begin. Finally, the relationship between y^a and y^b is weakened by the lack of parallel rhythmic patterning and by the shortening of y^b by one measure.

Harmonic usage also serves to disguise the archetype. Because dominant harmony (V) ends the first phrase *(m)*, and occurs as part of motive x', it is

159

196 LEONARD B. MEYER

understood to underlie the beginning of the second phrase *(m')*.⁴⁰ There is a resolution to tonic harmony in measure 84, but the context is wrong, as is the timing (see symbols under analytic graphs).⁴¹ Had the sense of dominant harmony persisted, the archetypal patterning

$$\frac{y^a}{I - V} : \frac{y^b}{V - I}$$

would have been more patent. But Berlioz subverted what might have been an unambiguous authentic cadence (V-I), probably because he sought to avoid even the slightest hint of the formulaic and the routine.

His distaste for the formulaic and the conventional—including authentic cadences—is evident throughout his writings, as these excerpts from his memoirs indicate:⁴²

> the appalling quantity of *platitudes* for which the piano is daily responsible; the *lure of conventional* sonorities (p. 41); hence those convenient vocal *formulas* . . . that eternal *device* of the final [authentic] cadence (p. 212); the deadliest enemies of genius are those lost souls who worship at the *temple of Routine* (p. 218); those *perfect cadences, recurring every minute*, account by themselves for some two-thirds of the score . . . [Cimarosa's] *Secret Marriage* is an opera fit only for fairs and carnivals (p. 317). *(italics added)*

160

This antipathy toward the conventional may help to explain why the force of other authentic cadences in this theme is enervated by tonic pedals (mm. 88-90, 93-94, 102-103), dissipated by silence (m. 89), and weakened by voice-leading (mm. 102-103). In fact, there is only *one* unambiguous, conventional authentic cadence in the forty measures of Berlioz's *idée fixe*, the one at the very end.

The next part (B¹) of Berlioz's melody is related to, yet independent of, the archetypal pattern. It is related to the pattern motivically. As if to compensate for the weak closure of *yᵇ* (and perhaps its shortened length as well), phrases *ss²* and *ss³* (each a normal four-measures long) end with reiterations of motive *yᵇ*; in the second of these (m. 93-94), no rest in the accompaniment weakens the connection between dominant and tonic.⁴³ More important, the essential intervallic structure of the first part of the archetype seems to guide the sequential progression. As Example 9 shows, the motion from one level of the sequence to the next involves the same intervallic pattern—that is, down a semitone, up a diminished fifth, and down a semitone—as is characteristic of the progression from *yᵃ* to *yᵇ*.⁴⁴

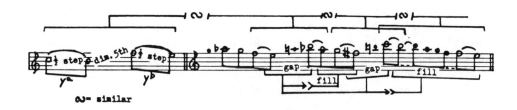

Example 9

Two considerations suggest, however, that though the second part (B¹) capitalizes on relationships borrowed from the archetype, it is essentially independent of the archetype. First, the similarity between the closes of Parts A (mm. 85-86) and B¹ (mm. 102-103) makes it clear that virtually nothing has happened. In terms of the processes generated by the archetypal pattern in the first period, we are literally, as well as figuratively, back at *Chord I*. Second, as was noted in the discussion of Part A, motive *ss* extends, and thereby obscures, archetypal relationships, but it does not alter them. And since part B¹ is based almost entirely on motive *ss*, it seems that it can, for purposes of analysis, be considered independent of the archetypal process. That this suggestion is not entirely implausible can be shown by an analytic experiment. If all traces of motive *ss* are removed from Berlioz's melody, and if measures 102 and 103 are substituted for measure 86 (which is not unreasonable, since they are equivalent), then the "melody" would be as shown in Example 10. And this pattern is not unlike that of, say, the second movement of Mozart's Piano Sonata in C Major (K. 309) (Example 5).

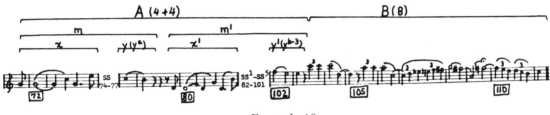

Example 10

This analysis calls attention to something of some significance. As suggested earlier, a growth in size has resulted in a change in structure. Instead of two parts, processively connected through the relation of gap-to-fill, there are now three parts. Part A generates processes: in addition to the gap sequence typical of the archetype, it begins the sequence that is continued in the second part (B¹), as Example 11 shows. In the second part (B¹) these processes are developed, reaching a culminating highpoint and then falling away toward closure. The third part (B²) creates satisfactory closure through, among other things, the realization of previously generated implicative processes (see Example 8).

Example 11

Though the sequential part (B¹) of the melody is not, properly speaking, an element in the archetypal scheme, it by no means follows that it is unimportant. It is obviously the longest and most continuous part of the melody. More significantly, it is the most intense and characteristically Romantic. Not only is the goal-directed striving of the Sisyphean pattern expressive of Romantic yearning, but many of the hallmarks of statistical apotheosis are patently present: the slowly rising sequence, the gradual crescendo and accelerando *(animez)*, the increased activity in the accompaniment (from two eighth-notes per measure to four), the sense of achieved arrival resulting from the relative stability of concordant resolution (to the E minor triad in measure 100), the placement of the highpoint about three-fourths the way through the melody, the falling-away from the highpoint through the diminuendo and the descending melodic line, and the broadening of the final phrase that results from the retention of the B (m. 100-101) and the ritard that accompanies it.[45]

The broadening of the final phrase of B¹ is significant because of its proximate effects and its remote relationships. Within B¹, the broadening at once stabilizes and emphasizes the achievement of apotheosis. The stretching of the phrase length from four to five measures also serves to maintain expressive tension even as the relaxation of the dying-away to closure is taking place.[46] The measure "added" to this phrase is, I suspect, also related to the shortened length of the second phrase of Part A *(m')*. For despite his avowed distaste for the regular and the routine, and Fetis's carping notwithstanding,[47] Berlioz evidently possessed a powerful sense of periodicity. This added measure not only contributes to the effectiveness of the last phrase of B¹, but also restores the balance disturbed by the measure removed from the end of the first period. As a result, the whole can be understood as a variation of the morphology more typical of the archetypal scheme: that is, (8 + 8) + 24. And the relationship, posited earlier, between y^b and y^{b-3} is made clear.

The scope and intensity of the second part are symptomatic of a significant shift in stylistic emphasis, from the syntactic to the statistical. Perhaps the nature of this shift can best be illustrated by considering the role of the upper tonic, as it has occurred in these examples. To put the matter much too briefly: in the instances from Mozart's *oeuvre*, the upper tonic, which occurs only once in each realization, serves as the root of a stable tonic triad and functions as part of the syntactic climax of the pattern. In the Beethoven (Example 7), the upper tonic occurs twice: first, as part of the syntactic climax of an antecedentlike version of the archetype and, second, as both the stable highpoint and the syntactic climax in the second part of the theme. Though features of apotheosis—the Sisyphean sequence, crescendo, and so on—are undeniably present, the fundamental processes are unequivocally syntactic.

Berlioz's melody also contains two upper tonics (Example 8). The first (m. 99) is the unstable highpoint of a cumulative, forceful statistical process. The second upper tonic (at the beginning of the final part, m. 103) represents what remains of the syntactic climax characteristic of the archetype. Not only has the preceding apotheosis overshadowed the syntactic function of the high C (m. 103), but the upward gap of a sixth (from E to C), which led to the reversal in the model and earlier instances, has here been masked by voice-leading. That is, the high C (m. 103) is perceived as following from the B over dominant harmo-

162

ny (m. 101) at least as much as from the E (of y^{b-3}), and the E tends to be heard as leading to the D in measure 104.

To summarize: in Beethoven's theme, syntactic climax dominates apotheosis; in Berlioz's melody, statistical apotheosis dominates syntactic climax. As noted earlier, throughout the Romantic period the importance of the secondary parameters in shaping musical process and form increases relative to that of the primary parameters. Thus, in a late Romantic piece such as the first movement of Mahler's Fifth Symphony, it is often difficult to find a single decisive syntactic climax to which lesser ones are related. Rather, there seems to be a succession of more or less equal, and local, syntactic turning points. But it is not difficult to discover the main statistical climax of the movement, for just before No. 29 in the Peters Edition, at a point of patent apotheosis, Mahler wrote "*Höhepunkt*" in the score![48]

Closure, which is the chief business of the final part, is established and enhanced in several ways:

1. The realization of implications generated by the archetypal pattern in the first part (A) fosters closure: for example, the arrival of the upper tonic (m. 103) and the subsequent filling of gaps.

163

2. Although initially undermined by irregular resolution, the patent motion from subdominant to dominant harmony (mm. 105-106; 109-110) strongly implies the decisive cadence that closes the melody.

3. Harmonic closure is complemented by rhythmic closure. The largely mobile phrase rhythms of Part A (8 + 7) and Part B¹ (4 + 4) and (4 + 5) are replaced by a closed, end-accented anapest grouping:

$$\underbrace{\overset{2}{\smile} + \overset{2}{\smile} + \overset{4}{\text{—}}}$$

4. But the most remarkable characteristic of this part is that, melodically, it consists of a succession of largely formulaic ending patterns. To recognize the conventionality of Berlioz's motives, it is necessary only to compare them casually with closing patterns from works by Mozart, which have, for the sake of convenience, been transposed into the key of C in Example 12. The first of the Mozart examples (A) is from the closing section of the slow movement of the String Quartet in D Major (K. 575); the second (B) is from the first movement of the Piano Sonata in C Minor (K. 457).

Given Berlioz's asserted antipathy to the formulaic and his avoidance earlier in this melody of the conventional, how is this overt use of almost stock patterning to be explained? The answer is, I think, that for Berlioz, the significant, expressive, and creative part of the *idée fixe* is over, and, for this reason, the closing period can—almost like a coda—employ conventional materials without disguise and without disdain. If this conjecture has merit, Berlioz's own compositional practice is, so to speak, behavioral evidence of his Romantic stance. For him, the heart of the melody lies not in syntactic relationships such as those of

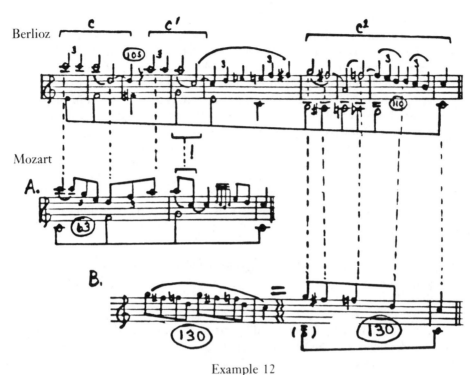

Example 12

gap-to-fill, but in the crescendo of activity characteristic of statistical climax—that is, in the excitement of culminating apotheosis.

*　　　　*　　　　*

It is now time for my own coda. I have sought to show that creativity in the arts need not involve transcending limits. The idea that a goal of the arts and a characteristic of their history is to overturn the rules of a prevalent style and institute new ones—as in scientific revolutions—rests on a confusion. The confusion is between the histories of conceptual theories and the histories of the phenomena that the theories are devised to explain. The histories of theories have evidently tended to involve revolutions that overturned prevailing paradigms. But the histories of the phenomena that such theories are designed to explain have not, for the most part, done so. What is comparable to the history of an art such as music is not the history of conceptual theories, but the history of some phenomenon, such as the forms of life. And just as natural history has been one of combining and recombining according to fundamental principles, so the history of music has, for the most part, involved the strategic manipulation of established rules. What François Jacob has said of biological evolution holds, I think, with minor reservations, for the history of music:

Evolution does not produce novelties from scratch. It works on what already exists, either transforming a system to give it new functions or combining several systems to produce a more elaborate one. . . . It is always a matter of using the same elements, of adjusting them, of altering here and there, of arranging various combinations to produce new objects of increasing complexity. *It is always a matter of tinkering.* [49] *(italics added)*

Though the idea of moving toward greater complexity seems suspect in the arts, regarding the history of music as having been largely a matter of "tinkering" is a salutary antidote to notions of history as dialectical necessity or as progress through revolution. And since archetypes are what composers often tinker with, understanding how they work may help us to understand and to explain the history of music. [50]

REFERENCES

[1] J. Bronowski, "The Creative Process," *Scientific American*, 199 (3) (1958): 64.

[2] In a comparable way, this model, coupled with a doubtful Hegelianism, leads Schönberg to transform Brahms into a "progressive," and encourages Webern to suggest that Bach anticipated the innovations of serialism (and was thus, despite customary belief, an innovator).

[3] This in no way denies that innovations transcending existing limits have at times changed the history of the arts.

[4] The failure to distinguish between historical importance and aesthetic significance has not only influenced our culture's view of the history of the arts, but has affected the history of the arts in our culture as well; for a considerable number of artists, as well as critics and historians, came to believe that the creative act, and, by extension, artistic originality, necessarily involved the invention and use of new syntactic means. As a result, the promulgation of new principles became a goal of art, until in an ultimate phase artists did not bother to make presentational works but simply presented the conceptual principles themselves.

[5] "Values in Language; or Where Have *Goodness, Truth* and *Beauty* Gone?" *Critical Inquiry*, 3 (1) (1976): 11.

[6] I have discussed elsewhere how these kinds of creativity—and their results: general propositional principles and particular presentational phenomena (works of art)—differ. "Concerning the Sciences, the Arts—AND the Humanities," *Critical Inquiry*, 1 (1) (1974): 163-216.

[7] Knowledge of prevailing constraints is indispensable, because understanding, enjoyment, and evaluation depend not simply upon perceiving what *actually* happens in a game or is presented in a work of art, but also upon the observer's ability to sense what *might have happened* or been presented. The significance of the road taken, to use Frost's metaphor, invariably includes an awareness of other possibilities that were not, but might have been, taken.

[8] In what follows it may occasionally seem that archetypes have been given a kind of Platonic reality or have been reified in some way. Thus it should be emphasized that, in my view, archetypes are cognitive constructs abstracted from particular patternings that are grouped together because of their similar syntactic shapes and/or formal plans. That is, archetypes are classlike patterns that are specially compelling because they result from the consonant conjoining of prevalent stylistic constraints with the neuro/cognitive proclivities of the human mind.

[9] As implied in this description, coherence of process can and should be distinguished from formal ordering. There are both archetypal processes (such as a circle of fifths progression in tonal harmony) and archetypal forms (such as strophic, ritornello, and binary kinds). An archetypal *pattern*, as I intend the term, combines such a process with such a form.

[10] Such archetypes are, I suspect, most unequivocally exemplified in music, because in music, syntactic process and formal structuring are explicitly presented. In this connection, see my *Music, the Arts and Ideas* (Chicago: University of Chicago Press, 1967), pp. 112-4.

[11] See my *Explaining Music: Essays and Explorations* (Berkeley: University of California Press, 1975), pp. 213-26, where I discuss the relationship of archetypes to understanding and enjoyment.

202   LEONARD B. MEYER

[12]In *The Selfish Gene* (New York: Oxford University Press, 1976), p. 206 ff, Dawkins suggests that "full-blown" tunes such as "Auld Lang Syne" are "memes." In my view, the archetypes of which the tune is composed are the units of cultural transmission.

[13]They are differentiated from each other by the very fact of melodic-rhythmic repetition, however varied, and by the presence of some sort of rhythmic, melodic, or harmonic articulation, however modest, separating *m* from *m'*.

[14]What is important here is emphasis, not order. Even though the third is heard first, as in Example 5, the fifth may predominate from a structural point of view.

[15]Or a substitute chord, for example, vi or $I^{7b} = V^7/IV$.

[16]This makes it evident that the archetype being discussed in this essay is a special case of a larger class—the class of changing-note melodies, whose first part is typically organized as follows:

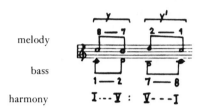

[17]L. Meyer, *Emotion and Meaning in Music* (Chicago: University of Chicago Press, 1956), pp. 128-35; and *Explaining Music*, pp. 145-57.

166

[18]Usually the gap and fill parts of such a melody move in opposite directions: if the gap is created by a rising motion, the fill falls, and vice versa. But this is not invariably the case. Occasionally, as we shall see, a rising gap may be followed by a fill, at least part of which also rises. What is essential is the relation of gap to fill rather than the direction of the motion.

[19]The implication is specially forceful in this case, because the interval of the skip—the diminished fifth from the leading tone (7) to the fourth (4)—itself requires, and strongly implies, resolution to the third of the scale (3).

[20]The term "reversal" is, of course, borrowed from Aristotle's *Poetics* and is, I think, used in an appropriately analogous way to refer to the process in which one moves from the tension and uncertainty of relative ignorance to the stability and resolution of relative knowledge. For a discussion of this process in music, see my *Emotion and Meaning in Music*, p. 93f. and *Explaining Music*, pp. 119 ff. and passim.

[21]The only other point that needs to be mentioned has to do with analytic technique. The high C in measure 8 has been analyzed as a structural tone in the descending fill because the octave transfers D-to-D (at the beginning of the measure) and C-to-C (ending after the first beat of measure 9) are unequivocal, given the patent hemiola meter.

[22]It should perhaps be noted that the fill is quite complete—except that the second degree of the scale is only weakly present. This is compensated for at the close of the second key area of the recapitulation (mm. 146-155), where a descent from the sixth degree of the scale to the tonic, guided by fourth-species counterpoint, strongly emphasizes the second degree through deceptive cadences.

[23]For instance, the end of the opening motive of this melody (part *a.*, below) is similar in significant ways to that which first closes the Rondeau theme of Mozart's Piano Sonata in D, K. 311 (part *b.*, below); and the falling seventh at the beginning of measure 37 (part *c.*, below) occurs quite often at closes, such as that near the end of the exposition section of the first movement of Mozart's Piano Sonata in B-Flat, K. 570 (part *d.*, below).

The cadential character of this realization of the archetype may be related to what appears to be a kind of formal ambiguity. When we first hear this melody, it is taken to be the main tune of the second key area of the movement. But when it returns in elaborated form after the main theme has been presented in the tonic (F major), it is not in the tonic, as it would be were this the second key area of a sonata without development; it is in the dominant, as when first presented. In other words, the theme really functions as a dominant prolongation. And it is perhaps to compensate for this disparity between form and function that the melody consists of a succession of cadential formulae.

[24]To facilitate comparison, the graphs given in the original examples have at times been slightly modified: the lowest level of structural tones has been omitted, and registers have been made more or less uniform.

[25]The overall structure of the theme, then, is P^1-P^1: P^2-P^2. Since the differences between the versions of P^1 and of P^2 are irrelevant for present purposes, only one version of each is given in the example: for P^1, measures 1-8; for P^2, measures 25-32.

[26]What is mostly responsible for the special savor of the theme is the unusual rhythmic patterning and the instrumental hocket that supports it. As line d of the example shows, the rhythmic group is one in which the mobile anacrusis is three times as long as the stable accent that follows it; that is,

[27]Notice that hints of the archetype are present in the foreground patterning of the bass (analysis line e).

[28]In this case, for instance, the B to C-sharp (m. 25) implies, but does not continue directly to, D. Similarly, the linear motion B—C-sharp—D (m. 26) implies continuation to an accented E, but the melody falls back to C-sharp on the first beat of measure 27, moving to an accented E only on the first beat of measure 28. A well-known instance of the sort of Sisyphean sequence I mean to describe can be found in the melody that begins the "Liebestod" from Wagner's *Tristan*.

[29]In theory, at least, a syntactic climax can occur at a low, soft, less active part of a structure *if* that is where ongoing processes are reversed and stabilized. See, for instance, the first Prelude in Bach's *Well-Tempered Clavier*, measures 20 to 24.

[30]In this connection, see George E. Muns, "The Climax in Music," (Ph.D. dissertation, University of North Carolina at Chapel Hill, 1955). I am grateful to my former student, Dr. John Chesnut, for calling Muns's essay to my attention and, more important, for suggesting through his own work on the shape of intensity curves in music, the distinction between what I am calling statistical and syntactic climax.

[31]In my view, it is *not* surprising that Beethoven's usage is more like Mozart's than like Berlioz's—even though the last of Mozart's works considered here preceded the C-Sharp Minor Quartet by forty years, while Beethoven's precedes Berlioz's work by only four years. What most affects compositional choices is the internalization of prevalent musical constraints, and such learning almost always takes place before a composer is twenty. In this respect, Beethoven and Mozart, who were born fourteen years apart, were near contemporaries; while Beethoven and Berlioz, who were born thirty-three years apart, were not. Beethoven's ingrained classicism seems evident in the high-level organization that unites the first and second periods, for it is an archetypal changing-note pattern, similar to that which structures the bass of Part A of P^1. This pattern is:

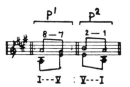

[32]Because it is at times doubtful which of Berlioz's bass-tones should be considered structural—for instance, in measure 78, is the G or the D the main structural tone?—I have treated the first eighth-note of Berlioz's succession of pairs as being structural, except where a patently ordered pattern preempts aural attention (as in mm. 95-101).

[33]"The Permanent Revolution," *The New York Review of Books*, 26 (18) (Nov. 22, 1979): 27. Antipathy toward the conventional may also help to explain the well-known, yet curious, penchant of Romanticism for the deformed and decrepit, the diseased and even the plain ugly. The point of such unsavory, even disgusting images seems to be that their Truth is guaranteed; that is, since no one would deliberately distort or disgust, representations of the repulsive must be "honest." Artifice cannot have masked their Truth. (Or, to put the matter in terms of the Romantic belief in the virtues of the natural: what is deformed, diseased, and so on, must be natural and, therefore "good.") The next step carries us to paradox. If Truth and Beauty are one, the equation is clear: ugliness, which is

natural and guileless, guarantees Truth; Truth is Beauty; therefore Ugliness and Beauty are, if not indistinguishable, at least not opposites.

[34]This problem is, I suspect, less pressing in literature and the visual arts, because novel subject matter can divert attention away from conventions of form and process. In architecture, and to some extent in the representational arts as well, the problem was ameliorated by adopting the conventions of a more remote past or of other cultures. Evidently, conventions seemed less oppressive when thus chosen. Music, too, followed this course, escaping the compulsive constraints of the immediate past by turning to folk music.

[35]The dilemma has been solved in the twentieth century—at least for those composers who have abandoned tonality. But this has created an even more formidable problem: that of devising viable constraints to replace those of tonality; for without constraints of some sort, choice is impossible. Thus, if the history of music in the nineteenth century can be understood as a continuing effort to reconcile the claims of the ideology of Romanticism with the practical need for conventional constraints, the history of music in the twentieth century can be seen, at least in part, as a succession of attempts to devise constraints that are at once nonconventional ("natural"? "logical"?) and artistically fruitful.

[36]It is important not to make the common mistake of supposing that because something is conventional it is necessarily arbitrary. To be experientially viable the constraints of a musical style must be consonant with the broad lawlike constraints of the physical, biological, and psychological realms. But different sets of conventional constraints may satisfy such requirements.

[37]To take a brief but clear case: in the first Prelude of Bach's *Well-Tempered Clavier*, a descending sequential process (mm. 5-20), guided by implied fourth-species counterpoint, is broken and reversed when a skip of a fifth (C down to F) in the bass is followed by chromatic rising motion which moves to the dominant (G) in measure 24. At this point the syntactic situation is clear; but closure is delayed for eleven measures through the prolongation first of dominant and then of tonic harmony. The statistical processes generated by secondary parameters cannot, however, delay closure in this way.

[38]These are a specially clear instance of what Edward T. Cone has called "hypermeasures." See his *Musical Form and Performance* (New York: W. W. Norton, 1968), p. 79ff.

[39]D'Arcy W. Thompson, *On Growth and Form,* abr. ed. J. T. Bonner (ed.) Cambridge, England: (Cambridge University Press, 1966), ch. 2. If one of the most important constraints governing the relationship of size to structure in the natural world is gravity, perhaps the comparable constraint governing relationships in human cultures are the principles of cognition—especially, I suspect, those of human memory.

[40]Edward T. Cone's discussion of this passage is illuminating. See his edition: *Berlioz, Fantastic Symphony* (New York: W. W. Norton, 1971), pp. 254-6.

[41]The context is wrong because the V/V suggested by the melody in measure 83 should lead to a I_4^6 chord in measure 84; instead, the tonic chord is in root position. The timing is wrong because the occurrence of tonic harmony at this point seriously weakens whatever sense of authentic cadence might have been experienced at measures 85-86. In my view, Edward Cone overstates the case when he asserts that the dominant is understood in measure 85 (p. 256). If it is so, it is largely in retrospect—after the closure in measure 86.

[42]*Memoirs of Hector Berlioz*, translated and edited by David Cairns (New York: Alfred Knopf, 1969); in each case, the page reference is given in parentheses after the quotation.

[43]However, as noted earlier, the conventional character of the cadence is veiled by the tonic pedal. It should perhaps be mentioned that the stronger closure created by this proximate connection, plus the striking change of harmony in the second half of measure 94, produces a (4 + 4) pattern in measures 87 to 98.

[44]Just as this pattern gave rise to a gap-fill process in the model, archetypal y—y', so it does here. And the resulting diminished fifth gaps (E—B-flat and F-sharp—C) are both followed by stepwise fills.

[45]In terms of function, Part B¹ is to the whole of Berlioz's theme as motive *ss* is to the first phrase (*m*) and motive *ss*¹ is to the second phrase *(m')*. I am grateful to my wife, Janet M. Levy, not only for calling this relationship to my attention, but for her sympathetic, yet scrupulous, criticism of this essay.

It is amusing, and not irrelevant, to observe that if the "experiment" of Example 10 were reversed—if motives *x* and *y* were deleted and only the succession of *ss* motives were presented—one would have something approximating pure apotheosis: that is, the quintessence of Romantic melody.

[46]As I hope to show elsewhere, "stretching" is an important expressive means in Romantic music. It can be a matter of interval as well as of duration. A very clear example occurs in "Träumerie" from Schumann's *Kinderszenen*, when what had been a perfect fourth (C to F, m. 2) in the first phrase is "stretched" to a major sixth (C to A, m. 6) in the equivalent point in the second phrase.

[47]cf. *Berlioz, Fantastic Symphony*, Cone, p. 219.

[48]Nor is Mahler the end of Romanticism: many of its characteristic traits are with us today. I do not mean merely in the music of such conservative composers as Samuel Barber, but in music that is often thought to be very "advanced." For what, after all, is the explicitly statistical music of a composer such as Xenakis (not to mention that of countless electronic composers), but Mahler without any syntax whatsoever?

[49]François Jacob, "Evolution and Tinkering," *Science*, 196 (4295) (1979): 1165.

[50]Though I had not planned to discuss another realization of the archetype, an odd coincidence leads me to do so. A few weeks before this essay was sent to *Daedalus*, my wife remarked, quite casually, that a Baroque realization of the archetype would probably be more continuous than any of the ones I had discussed in this essay. I was able to think of a Baroque instance right off because, as chance would have it, I had analyzed such an instance in *Explaining Music*—though without being aware of its archetypal patterning. The essential structure of the subject of the Fugue in F Minor from Book II of Bach's *Well-Tempered Clavier* is a slightly modified version of Part A of the archetype (*y′* descends a whole step instead of a half step), and the characteristic sequence *is* indeed continued (a possibility noted in Example 2, graph *c*) when the answer enters with the same archetypal pattern.

169

On the Analysis of Recent Music

Robert P. Morgan

Some fifteen years ago, in a frequently cited article entitled "Analysis Today," Edward T. Cone addressed himself to the questions: "What is analysis, or what ought it to be?" "What are its purposes?" and "To what extent are traditional concepts and methods [of musical analysis] applicable to new music?"[1] Cone's answer to the final question, concerning the analysis of new music, turned out to be largely determined by his answer to the first, concerning what analysis ought to be. Defining analysis as an attempt to explain rather than merely describe music, he states his position as follows: "In order to explain how a given musical event should be heard, one must show why it occurs: what preceding events have made it necessary or appropriate, towards what later events its function is to lead?" Turning then to new music, he says that in those cases where the music reveals what he calls an "organic temporal unity," a unity perceptible "as one moment flows to the next, each contributing both to the forward motion and to the total effect"—or expressed in rhythmic terms, where one is able to hear a "structural downbeat"—then one is able to "proceed with analytic concepts in some way analogous to those of traditional rhythm and meter, phrase and cadence."

In line with his conception of analysis as the elucidation of a sort of teleological organism, Cone concludes that analysis is no longer applicable to certain recent compositions, such as pieces that use chance procedures, those completely predetermined by serial operations, or those

This paper was presented as a contribution to a lecture series entitled "Current Trends in Musical Theory" at the music department of the University of Chicago in February 1977.

1. *Musical Quarterly* 46, no. 2 (April 1960): 172–88.

in which improvisation plays a significant role. (One might bring this list up to date by adding such things as, for example, the *Klangfarben* compositions of Ligeti and Penderecki, or the rhythmic phase music of Steve Reich.)

According to Cone, then, there is a great deal of music written today that is simply no longer susceptible to analysis. If this is true, it can mean one of several things. First, it may indicate that, although there are new compositions that one finds interesting and representative of the period in which we live, the music simply does not lend itself to analysis. Thus, even if we enjoy and admire this music, there is not much that we can say about it beyond perhaps a mere description—which I think most of us, along with Cone, would agree does not really constitute an analysis. I have the impression that many proponents of new music hold this view—that is, they feel that new music is understandable only through a sort of mindless apprehension of its sensory surface. But if this is a fair account of the situation surrounding new music, it seems to me to represent a very serious—and also depressing—state of affairs. For what it means, I suspect, is that new music does not lend itself to being thought about in any serious way at all; and if so, then new music is missing a crucial dimension—namely, an accompanying conceptual framework, erected through a body of critical and theoretical discourse, through which its meaning is defined and redefined as our thinking about music evolves. Indeed, this dimension forms—and has always formed—such an integral component of Western art music that its absence would seem to indicate that music, at least as we have known it, is in all likelihood dead.

Another possibility, in some respects similar to the previous one—and equally depressing in implication—is that somehow music has gone awry and is for this reason unanalyzable in Cone's terms. In other words, composition has gotten off the track, and until it gets back on again, the less we say about it—or analyze it—the better off we will be. If the preceding view is accepted by some proponents of new music, I suspect that this one is held by most of its detractors, who seem to feel that, given the extraordinary position into which composition has gotten itself, there is very little to do but maintain a polite silence and hope that sooner or later things will get better.

But there is a third possibility. The problem focused upon by Cone

Robert P. Morgan is professor of music theory and composition at Temple University. In addition to being a composer, he is active as a critic; his articles on contemporary music have appeared recently in several music journals and in *An Ives Celebration.* He is currently working on a book about differences between tonal and post-tonal musical thinking.

may not lie in new music itself, but in our conception of analysis. Indeed, our whole notion of what analysis is, or should be, may require rethinking in the light of what has happened in musical composition over the past quarter century.

Cone himself puts his finger on the problem when, near the end of his article, he points out that: "The good composition will always reveal, on close study, the methods of analysis needed for its own comprehension." This suggests that what analysis is is closely tied to—indeed, to a large extent determined by—the object toward which it is directed. And since analysis today forms a generally accepted area of musical study, about whose subject matter and methodology, at least in broader outlines, there is widespread agreement, it is useful to remember that its assumptions were largely shaped by the music composed during the period in which it developed as a discipline. Moreover, this music, as well as the analytic techniques it fostered, is itself incomprehensible—even inconceivable—outside of the larger cultural context within which they both flourished. My point, then, is that if things are changing—if music and its social role are undergoing transformation—it seems likely that analysis itself must experience some sort of analogous conversion.

With this in mind, perhaps you will permit me to retrace briefly—and in only its roughest outlines—the development of musical analysis over the past several centuries. Analysis as we know it today—as taught in our schools and practiced in our professional journals—is a relatively recent discipline that required for its maturation a cultural orientation placing great stress upon individual works of art, viewed not so much in terms of their function within a larger societal framework but as unique objects of aesthetic experience worthy of serious consideration as more or less independent entities. Although there are earlier indications of the emergence of this view, it did not appear in fully developed form until the eighteenth century; and it is only from this point that we can date the history of musical analysis in the modern sense of the word—as well as such related modern disciplines as musical criticism and aesthetics. Thus although one can point to certain isolated cases from earlier periods—such as Aristoxenus' detailed consideration of the Olympian nome of Athena as reported in Plutarch's *On Music,* the final chapter of Glareanus' *Dodecachordon* (1547), or, especially, Burmeister's *Musica Poetica* (1606), where the term "analysis" actually appears—it is only in the eighteenth century that such activity becomes a constant and irreplaceable feature of musical life and instruction.

One can point to the large number of analytically oriented articles that appeared in the newly surfacing *Musikzeitschriften,* penned by such figures as Mattheson, Marpurg, Forkel and Reichardt, who form part of a line that leads to such nineteenth-century analyst-critics as Hoffmann, Schumann and Berlioz. Similarly, in music theory, the analysis of passages from individual works to illustrate, clarify and justify theoretical formulations becomes increasingly common and gives rise to a parallel line, again beginning with Mattheson, that extends through Rameau, Riepel, Koch, Momigny and Riemann, to name only a few, to culminate finally in such twentieth-century figures as Schoenberg, Schenker and Ratz.[2]

Characteristic of this entire development is the presence of a circular relationship between the musical compositions and the analyses written about them. For the new discipline of musical analysis was not only made possible by a new attitude about the importance of individual works, it was actually required as a necessary support for that attitude. That is, when the musical work lost its functional role in a broader social context—and here one thinks above all of its increasing separation from the Church—and appeared as an autonomous phenomenon, it required a new kind of validation, one of an essentially internal rather than external nature. The work demanded, above all, acknowledgment of itself as a meaningful, logical and well-ordered musical statement.

It is not surprising, then, that analysis as we know it is largely concerned with pointing out such properties as consistency and well orderedness. The notion of "musical logic"—of music as a kind of perfectly structured language within whose terms meaningful statements can be made on the basis of widely accepted "grammatical" conventions—runs throughout the entire analytical tradition and indeed forms its central thread. The development of music theory during this period can thus be understood as an ongoing attempt to define the "laws" of musical grammar; analysis then attempted to clarify the various and constantly changing ways in which these laws were made manifest in individual compositions.

This close correlation between theory and analysis can hardly be overemphasized. Perhaps the most convincing way in which the individual composition could be justified was to show that it was not, in fact, an isolated statement at all, but rather partook of generally accepted conventions—that it was an instance of a widely understood language. The role of theory, then, was to define the relevant conventions and, at least for many theorists, to show that they were rooted in acoustical laws and thus explicable in more or less rigorous, scientific terms. Individual analyses were thus played off against, and supported by, a larger background of shared musical beliefs and assumptions that were ultimately reducible to explanations of an essentially technical—musico-grammatical—nature.

This brings me back to Mr. Cone, for it is clearly this type of analysis that he has in mind when he speaks of the need to clarify the logical, or as he puts it, "teleological" nature of musical discourse—its "organic

---

2. For a more detailed discussion of these developments, see Hermann Back, *Methoden der Werkanalyse in Musikgeschichte und Gegenwart* (Wilhelmshaven, 1974).

unity." Cone assumes that most of the music of the twentieth century can be analyzed in a way that is essentially similar to the way earlier music is analyzed, that it is still based upon those principles of musical logic—even if that logic is somewhat modified—with which earlier analysts concerned themselves. Exceptions, such as chance music or totally determined serial music, can be considered as departures—and presumably only temporary ones—from an uninterrupted and ongoing tradition dating back at least to the eighteenth century.

I should perhaps say at this point that I consider Edward Cone, with whom I happened to study, one of our most articulate and enlightening commentators on music today. Moreover, since his article was written in 1960, when the world and its music seemed quite different from the way they do today, one can understand his position. But the problem now is that, from our present perspective, it seems increasingly unlikely that those types of compositions barred by Cone from analytic scrutiny represent momentary departures. Chance and serial music, for example, though they are no longer practiced with the missionary fervor of twenty years ago, have—along with various other new approaches—become part of a larger mainstream carrying us into a new musical period in which our former analytical assumptions seem to have only marginal applicability. It is the music of this period, then, that I would like to focus upon from the point of view of the analyst. In doing so—and I do not pretend that I will be able to undertake more than some basic explorations—I would like to keep in mind Cone's maxim that a good composition will reveal the methods for its own analysis. Thus any answer to the question of what analysis should be must depend upon the work under consideration. And since it is characteristic of recent music that many of its most representative compositions seem to have very little to do with one another, answers may differ markedly from case to case. Nevertheless, I hope to identify at least certain general attributes of a meaningful analytical approach to musical composition today and to indicate that such an approach requires a definite reorientation of traditional thinking about the nature of the discipline.

I shall begin by considering the relationship between musical work and musical system, as it is here that one of the most dramatic changes in recent music has taken place. Once again it is helpful to consider first this relationship in earlier music. In discussing the interaction of theory and analysis with individual compositions of the common practice period, I suggested that these compositions could support such pronounced individual scrutiny only because they partook in a generally accepted musical system with a kind of independent life of its own. Thus the meaning of a work was determined precisely by its relation to an external set of norms, while its individuality was measured by the extent to which it reinterpreted these norms in new and unprecedented ways without completely undermining them. Indeed, it was widely felt that music could maintain its expressivity only through constant transformation of the surface characteristics of a still operative underlying syntax. (One thinks particularly in this connection of the use of more and more chromaticism, but it is also evident in other developments having to do with such matters as phrase and metric structure, formal organization, the role of timbre, etc.) It was the responsibility of theory and analysis, then, to reveal, on the one hand, the extent and individuality of these departures, and on the other, to show how, on some level, the agreed upon assumptions of musical order and logic remained nevertheless unimpaired.

This dialectic between work and system—between theory and analysis on one side and individual compositions on the other—forms one of the most essential factors in the evolution of musical composition during the eighteenth and nineteenth centuries. It accounts in large measure for the extraordinarily dynamic character of musical developments during this period, a period in which the most important works were, almost without exception, viewed to be those placing the greatest strain upon the accepted conventions. Indeed, the self-destructive nature of common practice tonality, viewed as an historical phenomenon, is one of its most characteristic features; it led of course eventually to a complete tonal breakdown—a breakdown that undermined the very foundation upon which the dialectic that had precipitated it had played itself out.

The need to recapture a lost order—to restore a basis for musical intelligibility in some way comparable to the old one—becomes almost immediately apparent after the collapse. The great bulk of music of the first half of the present century, as well as of the theoretical and analytical literature that accompanied it, is thus understandable as a concerted effort to maintain the old dialectic under what must have seemed insurmountable odds. One thinks of neoclassicism in its various guises, with its attempt to preserve aspects of tonal organization, phrase structure, etc., in some way analogous to those of earlier music. (It is of course just these aspects that Cone focuses upon in his article.) Perhaps most symptomatic of all is the twelve-tone system, which in its earlier stages was clearly thought of —certainly by Schoenberg—as a kind of replacement for tonality, as a new musical system for the next stage of a continuing evolution, with the same requisites of order and logic found in the old one. Thus most of its practitioners believed the new system would eventually attain general acceptance, much as had tonality in an earlier period.

Just how much things have changed is evident in the different view of the twelve-tone system that prevails today. Few composers still maintain that it is anything like the tonal system in regard to either the psychology of composing or that of listening. Nor is there any other compositional system that is viewed as constituting, even potentially, a common framework of shared conventions. Rather, the tendency is for each work to define, for its own unique purposes, a purely individual system with a validity thereby reduced to defining the characteristics of a single compositional structure.

From the point of view of the analyst this change becomes apparent in the difficulty of distinguishing between composition and compositional system, between what is composed and what is theoretical background, between the compositional process itself and its precompositional planning. In traditional analysis this distinction was fundamental and served to articulate an essential difference between what was unique in a musical work—its creative aspect, if you like—and what was general—the systematic framework within which the creative act was accomplished and through which it derived both meaning and justification. The blurring of this distinction has inevitably altered the nature of the analytic process.

There are, for example, many compositions of the past twenty-five years, including those of both a serial and aleatory persuasion, for which it seems that, once one has described how the piece was made—its rules of procedure, or more generally, the overall system through which it was generated—one has also described the composition itself. That is, the "content" of the composition seems identical to the musical system upon which it is based. The work, as Morton Feldman once said in a somewhat different context, rhapsodizes its own construction, exalts the intricacies of the structure through which it has acquired existence. Instead of revealing such properties as linear continuity, thematic and motivic development, formal cohesion, etc.—properties to a large extent jeopardized by the disappearance of a conventional syntax—the work reflects upon its own constitution. It is not surprising, then, that many composers establish systematic scaffoldings of great complexity on which to build their music, feats of dazzling virtuosity possessing considerable interest in their own right. The formal properties of the work become its true subject matter and thus a topic of primary interest. This explains, I think, why there is a tendency for each new work to have a system uniquely its own. This is perhaps overstated, yet if one thinks of a composer like Stockhausen, or even Ligeti or Xenakis, one sees that it touches upon an important facet of recent compositional thinking. The construction of the system has itself become an essential and inseparable component of the creative act.

For the analyst, this means that an important part of his activity involves the description and elucidation of precompositional planning, as distinct from the composition itself. This has brought about a definite shift of analytic emphasis: from the work to the manner in which it was composed. And since the latter is something the composer is himself probably conscious of and no doubt knows more about than anyone else, the analyst included, a great deal of what appears as analysis today is

177

undertaken only through the composer's direct aid. (One thinks of the articles that have appeared in *Perspectives of New Music*'s Younger American Composers series.)

This produces a distinct realignment of the traditional view of the relation between analysis and work. Looked at from the composer's point of view, analysis—to the extent that it presents his conscious formulation of the compositional, or precompositional, system for a particular work—represents an integral part of his composition. (This recalls Adorno's remark that the compositions of the Second Viennese School contain their own analyses.) What happens, then, to the so-called intentional fallacy, according to which the composer's attitudes about his own work are considered irrelevant to its analysis? The idea of such a fallacy could only have developed under assumptions concerning the relationship between a work and its interpretation similar to those found in the common practice period—that is, where general conventions prevailed against which the work could be judged and which lent it a sort of absolute objectivity beyond the reach of the personal attitudes even of the composer himself. But the intentional fallacy simply does not hold up—it is no longer a fallacy—when "conventions" are supplied individually for each separate work—which means that they are no longer conventions at all. On the contrary, the composer's intentions become an integral part of his overall conception.

One nevertheless has a sense of disquiet: if all the analyst is doing is reconstructing a compositional method, something that in all likelihood has already been done by the composer, then why should the composer not supply his own analysis and publish it as a necessary appendage to his composition? This, in fact, is what some have done—Messiaen, for example. But where does this leave the analyst? The answer, I think, is that he must go further: he must examine the composer's intentions in relation to their compositional realization, must discuss the implications of the compositional system in regard to the music it generates, consider how the resulting music relates to older music and to other present-day music, examine its perceptual properties and problems, etc. There is really no end to the possibilities that could enable this list to be extended. Speaking generally, however, one can say that the analyst must examine a composition, inclusive of its system, in the broadest possible context.

Let me take as an example Ligeti's justly famous analysis of Boulez's *Structures 1a* for two pianos.[3] Ligeti begins with a detailed and comprehensive description of Boulez's choice of materials, how these are regulated according to series of pitches, relative durations, dynamic levels and articulations, and, finally, how larger operations determine the order in which the series are used and how they are combined.

3. György Ligeti, "Entscheidung und Automatik in der Structure 1a," *Die Reihe* 4 (1958): 38–63. A translation appears in the English version of *Die Reihe* 4 (1960): 36–62.

(Much of this, incidentally, had been described by Boulez himself in a short article which he later—after the appearance of Ligeti's article—chose not to include among his collected earlier writings when these were published in book form.[4] Ligeti has acknowledged his debt to this article, and it is unlikely that he could have written his analysis at all without its help.) But Ligeti proceeds to discuss the compositional implications of Boulez's system—of what he refers to as "the automatically realized structure" that results when the elements and orderings "are thrown as if into a machine." That is, he focuses on the specifically compositional consequences of the system, and especially on how, despite the rigidly determined nature of the compositional processes, the effect is—and must be—one of chance in regard to individual details. He notes that this requires of the listener a shift in perception from the detail to larger, more comprehensive structures that are defined by easily identifiable characteristics of a "statistical" nature, such as overall dynamic level, frequency of attack and number of contrapuntal threads. Ligeti also identifies several "mistakes," or inconsistencies, in Boulez's realization of his system, suggesting that these may be "corrections" made by the composer in order to clarify those aspects of the piece that define it as an audible experience (although he does not rule out the possibility that the composer may simply have "had a bad day" while working on the section of the piece in which these inconsistencies occur). Finally, he indicates the limits of such a compositional approach, in which—as he puts it—the composer "leads himself around on a leash," and discusses the implications of this in terms of Boulez's development toward the more colorful and sensuous world of the *Marteau sans maître*, where such rigidities are at least partially abandoned.

Structures 1a is of course an extreme example—perhaps as extreme as any in the literature—and I have chosen it because it illustrates so graphically, even outrageously, the changing relation of the musical work to its underlying system. But to a large extent the point applies to a wide range of recent compositions by composers of such varying tempers as, say, Milton Babbitt, Peter Maxwell Davies and Steve Reich. Moreover, in examining the various individual musical systems with which composers are presently working, the analyst addresses himself to one of the most important questions in contemporary music: namely, what does the composer do—where and with what does he begin—when there is nothing left that he can take for granted as a conventional framework? Those who deplore Ligeti's kind of analysis as dry and "purely technical," to say nothing of solopsistic (since each work tends to require self-defined formulations), miss an important point: knowledge of a work's individual system is as important for analysis today as knowl-

4. Feldman, Boulez, Cage, Wolff: "4 musicians at work," *Trans/formation* 1/3 (1952): 69.

edge of the tonal system was in the case of earlier music. Again, such knowledge is of course not identical to analysis, but only supplies its necessary base. Unlike tonal analysis, however, the establishment of this base becomes a requisite part of the analytic process itself.

Let me now turn to some less extreme examples of self-imposed systematic constraints used by composers who are not serialists. I can begin with Ligeti himself, who, for the composition of his *Requiem*, devised a set of remarkably rigid "voice-leading rules." Among these are: two step-wise motions in the same direction are not allowed; two steps in opposite direction are allowed, but only if one is a major second and the other minor; a succession of steps and leaps is allowed without limitation if the direction changes, but if not, no more than two successive intervals are allowed.[5] In addition, there are rules of harmonic usage and rhythmic motion. What we have, then, is a sort of revised (and private) *Gradus ad Parnassum,* whose function, analogous to that of Fux's rules, is to control voice leading so as to achieve consistency of motion. In the case of Ligeti, the rules produce a dense, richly detailed polyphonic field, defined by a strictly regulated rhythmic web and equally strict intervallic structure. One hears a kind of cluster, but one in which—unlike those, for example, of Penderecki—the motion of individual voices is in some sense perceptible and serves to bring about extremely gradual, yet ultimately discernible, transformations of a tightly meshed polyphonic net. Thus, although one does not hear the individual voice motions per se, one hears their compositional result. Another example of this kind is the twenty-two voice canon that occurs in Ligeti's *Atmospheres,* used to effect a gradual reduction of the registral ambit from a very wide band to a quite narrow one consisting of only a few tones. The canon is, in this instance, a very efficient technique for creating a particular kind of slow cluster transformation. The fact that its function—and audible result—is completely different from that of traditional canonic practice in no way detracts from its effectiveness in this new context.

My next example is taken from Elliott Carter, in whose recent compositions very large-scale cyclical time-structures are used to govern the larger formal layout. Carter's Concerto for Orchestra, for example, has four separate and independent, though synchronized, textural layers that move simultaneously over different time cycles. Each one of these represents one of the "movements" of the piece, with its own tempo, character, etc. But in the Concerto—as in Carter's later Third String Quartet—these movements run concurrently, fading in and out in relation to one another according to a predetermined and carefully ordered plan of staggered cyclic entries. The plan as such is no doubt inaudible, but as with Ligeti's rules, it enables Carter to control a multileveled

5. The complete set of rules, quoted from Ligeti's sketches for the Dies irae section of the *Requiem,* can be found in Erkki Salmenhaara, *Die Musikalische Material und seine Behandlung bei Ligeti* (Regensburg, 1969), pp. 139–41.

rhythmic structure of extraordinary complexity. And the sonic result is obviously very different from what it would be without this plan. The listener is certainly aware of the varying grades of rhythmic tension that accrue from the coincidence of two or more strands and of the occasional conjunction of all levels at climactic moments. Carter's system—a word, incidentally, he would no doubt abhor—enables him to create varying degrees of regulated rhythmic tension over extended time spans without letting the whole fabric topple into chaos. (I might add, however, that I find the constant threat of disintegration, a threat only barely held within check, one of the most interesting—and exciting—features of Carter's music. Indeed, a precarious mediation between extremes of order and disorder strikes me as a characteristic feature of much recent music.)

A fourth example, the most general and least systematic of those I have chosen, is Berio's *Sequenza III* for solo voice. Here it is not so much a matter of a comprehensive system, or a set of rules, or even an overall formal-temporal plan but only of a general idea that governs the ordering of elements in the composition. In this work there is a tendency for the vocal sounds to become gradually more songlike—more lyrical, if you wish—as the piece progresses. Of the various types of vocal sounds employed—including speech, mouth noises and normal singing—the last of these becomes increasingly prominent until it finally takes over almost entirely in the final segment. At the same time, the text, which is subjected to various kinds of permutations, becomes increasingly unintelligible and ultimately consists only of individual syllables in which vowels—the speech elements closest to pitched sounds—predominate. In other words, the basic idea is that different types of vocal articulation, abruptly juxtaposed in sequential confrontation, gradually "resolve" into a single type—pure, textless singing. Although as far as I know there is no system determining the exact way this happens, the idea gives direction and meaning to the overall course of the piece. (It also illustrates *Sequenza*'s text, by the Swiss poet Markus Kutter, which offers a woman's singing as a kind of truth and an antidote to the banality of ordinary verbal discourse. The work also mirrors the text formally, since the latter already suggests the possibility of permutation through the interchangeability of its syntactic components.)

So far I have emphasized the purely musical, and thus essentially technical, implications of musical systems; but those systems also have a psychological function that is, I suspect, at least of equal importance. This brings me to the question of authenticity in recent music, a pressing one for both composer and analyst. What authenticates a musical composition when the previous validating agent—a shared musical syntax—is no longer available? Clearly if no outside agent exists, one must establish an internal, composition-specific one.

One of the most important of these agents is the musical system

181

itself; for there is a quality of authority, transcending the particular case, inherent in any system, be it public or private. Thus the system assumes a nontechnical, "extramusical" role for the work, which is legitimized by its adherence to principles that in some way transcend its own boundaries. There is, then, in spite of what was said previously, a sense in which, even for a work like *Structures 1a,* the system and the piece are actually not coextensive. The fact that the system may be private, perhaps even valid for only one work, does not completely undermine its capacity to authenticate. Indeed, even if the system is not revealed by the composer, and no one else is able to discover it, the mere belief in its existence lends the work a certain substantiality that would otherwise be missing. There is thus what might be termed a "psychological" relation between system and work that the analyst must also consider.

An example is provided by the music of Xenakis. The complex mathematical formulae Xenakis uses to generate his compositions not only enable him to achieve certain types of musical effects that might be difficult, if not impossible, to achieve otherwise, they provide a dimension that extends beyond the actual music to the realm of abstract human thought itself. Xenakis is given to emphasizing the status of mathematical equations as "universal laws" and as "treasures of humanity," an emphasis clearly revealing a wish to place the purely technical formulations upon which his music is based in the largest possible context.

Moreover, Xenakis speaks of mathematics not only as a "working tool" but as a "universal language," a phrase that—I think, not coincidentally—recalls those of composers and theorists of the tonal period concerning music as a kind of universal communications system. Nevertheless, it is significant that Xenakis' structural model is actually mathematical rather than linguistic. For, as I argued previously, composers have been forced to relinquish the idea of working within a linguistic framework. And it is not surprising, following the breakdown of a model of musical intelligibility based on conventions that were fundamentally linguistic, or more precisely, syntactic in nature (and it is above all the theorist Heinrich Schenker who has shown the extraordinarily precise sense in which this is true of tonal music), that composers should turn again to more mathematically oriented models, bringing their musical thinking closer, at least in this respect, to that of the Middle Ages and antiquity.

Stockhausen provides an interesting instance in his use of the Fibonacci series—a series that, through its "golden mean" proportions, easily translates its numerical properties into widely applicable spatial-temporal relationships, again of a more or less universal nature. In his *Klavierstück IX,* for example, the overall formal shape of the piece, as well as innumerable matters of detail, is derived from this series. This is the piece that begins with that notorious succession of 227 statements of the same chord; yet one's perception of that chord, as well as understanding of the piece in general, is transformed by the realization that the number of repetitions is determined by a decreasing series, derived from and closely related to the Fibonacci series, and relates logically to other appearances of the chord throughout the piece, all of which are controlled by this same series. Although one does not, of course, hear the series as such, its influence on the shape of the piece as a whole is if anything overly obvious.

Of course in discussing the role of mathematics in the music of Xenakis and Stockhausen, I am still talking about musical systems. But the question of authenticity, of the need to define musical meaning in terms surpassing the individual composition, leads us into a much broader area of consideration and to examples that are nonmathematical and less systematic in nature. A fascinating instance of what I have in mind is Messiaen's use of birdsongs. Messiaen has referred to birds as his "mentors" ("*maîtres*") and remarked that they provide him with "a means of working and progressing." Once again it is a matter of the composer having to begin somewhere, yet standing there empty-handed, so to speak, cut off from any externally conferred assumptions. For Messiaen, birds are as useful as mathematics (which he also employs): they provide a source of musical creation for which nature, rather than a humanly constructed system of abstract thought, supplies the basis of justification. Messiaen's method of "transcribing" birdsongs into melodic ideas playable on traditional instruments appears to be largely unsystematic, basically intuitive, and as far as I know no one has ever been able to identify on the basis of the music itself the birds he quotes—including professional ornithologists (as Messiaen himself once pointed out, with no apparent embarrassment, in an interview). Yet knowledge of Messiaen's use of birdsong is of the utmost importance for understanding his music. Not only does it explain much about the way the music sounds—especially the way the melodic components relate to one another, both in an absolute sense and in the specific sequential form in which they appear in a particular composition—but also tells us something about the "meaning" of the music that would otherwise be hidden.

A further illustration is George Crumb's use of symbolic notation in certain scores. There symbols, representing archetypical configurations embedded in human consciousness, establish associations that reverberate well beyond the particular piece. Moreover, they are not simply imposed upon the music but have a direct influence on its structure. Thus circular notations give rise to forms of a cyclic nature, while the various parts that make up other symbols—such as the two straight lines of a cross, to take the simplest example—correspond in length and placement to the analogous formal elements that shape the musical statement. Of course one does not hear a cross, any more than one hears a Fibonacci series, but the symbol's musical implications are perceptible and subject to study. And since the symbols lend those parts of the composition with which they are associated a special weight, Crumb can use them to support specifically compositional factors. Thus in the two pieces for solo amplified piano entitled *Makrokosmos I* and *II,* each of which consists of twelve pieces divided into three groups of four pieces each, the last piece of each group is notated in symbolic form. Another aspect of symbolic notation is its influence upon the performer. Not only must the symbolic pieces be memorized, since they are otherwise unplayable (which in itself removes them from their surroundings), the way in which they are learned—and thus the performer's entire conception of the music—is necessarily colored by the piece's special presentation.

There are other ways contemporary composers counteract the threat of isolation. The framework of a composition can be enlarged by establishing an explicit link with an older musical tradition through which it acquires a kind of historical resonance that extends beyond its own limited milieu. In Crumb's music, for example, evocations of earlier styles pervade the entire fabric (although actual quotations are rather the exception). Nineteenth-century models are particularly favored, but there are also frequent allusions to more remote sources drawn from medieval and non-Western traditions. Similarly, in Penderecki's vocal compositions, the appearance of chantlike material, conjuring the music of the medieval Church, forms an essential part of the musical substance.

184

The meaning of musical tradition, however, is thereby fundamentally altered. Instead of being something passed down in a continuous evolution from generation to generation, tradition itself becomes "contextual." Like the musical system, it is defined for each individual composition, which acquires its own unique historical correspondences. Although in Crumb and Penderecki these evocations do not normally determine the formal course of the music, there are many works for which an earlier composition provides the entire structural basis. The first of Lukas Foss' *Baroque Variations* is an example, as is the third movement of Berio's *Sinfonia.* In such cases the borrowed material is chosen arbitrarily, as it were, much as a musical system might be, and supplies an analogous precompositional base from which the composition can be generated.

In the Berio movement, for example, the Scherzo of Mahler's Second Symphony not only furnishes much of the musical material, it also provides a formal frame for the entire piece, a kind of structural container into which fragments of countless other compositions, ranging from Bach to Boulez, can be poured, achieving thereby unexpected transformations and interrelationships. Berio's piece might be taken as an elaborate allegory for the present musical situation: all types of sound objects, including music borrowed from various traditions, are conceived as representing "available material" and thus as being, in a fundamental sense, structurally equivalent to one another.

Attempts to legitimize new music through couplings with traditional material need not be of a specifically musical nature. John Cage, who himself has borrowed from Satie's *Socrate* in his recent composition *Cheap Imitation,* frequently employs the I Ching to arrive at compositional decisions, a procedure that curiously—despite its aleatory nature—removes his decision making from the realm of the arbitrary, the purely personal. The I Ching works acquire status, as it were, through their participation in an age-old divining process sanctified by its important role in a great non-Western culture. Again, universal laws—in this instance of a somewhat mystical or transcendental nature—are evoked to arrive at compositional decisions.

Another "extramusical" frame that has been used is the game—a universal activity for which essentially arbitrary rules are accepted as a necessary condition. Thus Mauricio Kagel's *Match,* a composition for two cellists and percussionist, is organized like a contest, with the cellists representing competitors and the percussionist a referee. The conventions of game behavior are so widely understood that Kagel is even able to introduce moments of humorous conflict by contradicting expectations, as when the cellists ignore the percussionist's rulings. (There is perhaps a distant analogy here with a tonal composer—say Haydn—who plays upon expectations conditioned by the conventions of common practice tonality.) The idea of a contest also serves as a basis for Xenakis' *Strategie,* a composition subtitled "Game for Two Orchestras." Unlike Kagel, Xenakis sets out his rules in advance ("precompositionally") and orders them in a typically complex matrix, with the form of the piece conceived as a series of tactics, or gambits, initiated by each orchestra in response to moves undertaken by the other group. (After the concert, a winner is even announced, followed by the presentation of a prize—"a bouquet of flowers or a cup or a medal.")

One way of putting all this is to say that much of the music written today is in reality program music. It is no longer absolute, as the necessary condition for absolute music—widely understood and generally accepted musical conventions—no longer exists. Thus the composer supplies a program—that is, another kind of framework, quite different from the syntactic one of the common practice period in that it is separable from the actual compositional elements. As in the nineteenth century, if the composer wishes his program to be understood he must supply it along with the composition; but what is new is that the program has become essential, both in a technical and psychological sense. For if previously the purely musical nature of the tonal system afforded even programmatic compositions an exclusively musical comprehensibility (and it is significant in this light that almost all nineteenth-century composers of program music—Wagner, a kind of program music composer, being here perhaps an exception—insisted that their music could, and indeed should, also be understood solely on its own terms), in today's

185

music the program represents the principal means of escaping from the confines of the isolated work. (The fact, however, that those nineteenth-century works that most severely strained the syntactic conventions were almost always programmatic should, no doubt, be understood as an early symptom of this condition.)

It is little wonder, then, that composers today feel called upon to write at length about their own music. One thinks of Stockhausen's prose writings, which collectively form a sort of running verbal commentary on everything he has produced, or of Messiaen's inclination to supply explanations of his compositional procedures as prefaces to his scores or even as indications within the scores themselves. Whether these commentaries take the form of technical, systematic explanations or assume a more metaphorical character (in Messiaen and Stockhausen, for example, both types occur more or less with equal frequency and are, in fact, often difficult to differentiate), the writings of composers have become a necessary appendage to their music, and it is just here that the analogy with nineteenth-century program music tends to break down.

Indeed, the distinction between musical system and programmatic metaphor is often blurred to the point of inseparability. Thus the program of Crumb's *Black Angels,* a purely instrumental piece for string quartet, determines such specific compositional matters as the number of movements, their symmetrical relationships to one another, the length of phrases and pauses between phrases, the works chosen for quotation, etc. Similarly, in Peter Maxwell Davies' *Antechrist,* the medieval concept of the Antichrist not only affects the choice of pre-compositional material (a thirteenth-century motet, "Deo Confitemini–Domino"), but also, as the composer points out, the compositional processes through which this material is transformed—the way it is "broken up and superimposed on related plainsong fragments, which both musically and with regard to the related implied texts, turns the sense of the motet inside-out." Thus, whereas the analyst of nineteenth-century music can, and usually does, to a large degree ignore programmatic aspects in order to focus on purely musical values, this is no longer possible. Or rather, the distinction is simply no longer clear. Consideration of the program—of the musical system behind a Xenakis work, of Cage's I Ching manipulations, of Kagel's game situation, or whatever—is a necessary part of the analysis. To take only Kagel's game format as a brief example, I would simply note that the entire character of *Match,* as well as its structure, is largely incomprehensible outside of this "extra-musical" context.

This said, however, I should not give the impression that traditional analytic categories are no longer applicable to more recent music. On the contrary, they are still absolutely necessary; for like the composer, the analyst cannot begin completely empty-handed. Nevertheless, to retain their usefulness these categories must now normally be transformed into

186

more general aesthetic ones. For example, traditional dualities such as tension-relaxation, motion-stasis, buildup-arrival, climax-denouement, etc., can be meaningfully applied to all but a very small portion of the output of the past quarter century or so. Thus the distinction between tightly structured musical units, with a high degree of periodicity and closure, as opposed to more loosely structured, open units—a distinction that forms a cornerstone of classical formal theory—remains valid in countless modern compositions. The chord repetitions in Stockhausen's *Klavierstück IX,* referred to previously, build tightly structured periodic units that are played off against others of a more loosely structured nature. The overall form of the piece is governed by a gradual reduction of the former units—controlled through the decreasing series I mentioned before—coupled with an increasing emphasis on the latter, which eventually take over entirely in an extended final section consisting of freely manipulated textural fields in the piano's highest register, with a rapid turnover of all twelve pitches, always in different order. The beautiful bell-like quality of this section depends very much upon what has gone before—that is, upon its being heard as the culmination of a process underway since the opening of the piece. The *Klavierstück,* then, contains structural analogies to traditional forms of an oppositional nature, such as the sonata or rondo. But here the overall shape, even in its most abstract outlines, does not represent a generalized formal convention, either for the listener or the composer. Indeed, Stockhausen's next piano composition, the *Klavierstück X,* reveals a formal plan that is in some respects its opposite: gradual motion from a state predominantly characterized by structural openness to one that is tightly ordered.

187

Similarly, in Penderecki's *Klangfarben* compositions, sections characterized by stasis and repose are opposed to sections of more complexity and surface activity, the mediation between and ultimate resolution of the two serving to shape the larger continuity. And in Xenakis one finds progressions from relatively permeable states, in which individual elements possess a high degree of independence and are audible as more or less distinct events, towards others in which the components are absorbed into a thick web, an overall sound field perceivable only as an indissoluble textural aggregate or Gestalt.

Even the concept of tonality remains applicable in much recent music. In Ligeti's *Lontano,* a *Klangfarben* composition not unlike *Atmospheres* in some respects, musical motion is shaped by transitions to and from stable tonal areas—consisting sometimes of only a single note, at others of a complex of several—that serve as structural pillars for the composition. There is thus a distinction between material of an expository, stable character and material whose function is to "modulate" from one area of stability to the next. Although these expositions are no longer thematic, they form points of tonal and formal cohesion, while the material concerned with the gradual dissolution of one such area and the eventual establishment of a new one, serves a transitional function.

Yet even when tonality is handled in a more traditional manner—in pieces that employ literal quotation, or in those that simply appropriate conventions from the common practice period without literally quoting, as in George Rochberg's Third String Quartet—its meaning is totally transformed. One cannot analyze the third movement of Rochberg's quartet simply as if it were a set of variations by Beethoven, despite the fact that to some extent that is what it sounds like. If one does, one misses what seems to me the real significance of the music, which is precisely the way it does *not* sound like Beethoven; and this is something that cannot be explained exclusively in terms of what appears in the score. For part of the reason—though only part—it does not sound like Beethoven stems from the fact that we know the quartet was written in the 1970s. The way we hear the composition—and thus understand it—is inevitably conditioned by this fact. Tonality simply cannot mean today what it did 150 years ago; it has a totally different relationship not only to the composer and listener but to the entire musical culture within whose context the piece exists and is experienced.

188

This brings me back to the question of context, a point I touched upon briefly before and that can now serve as a kind of summary for my remarks. For I suspect that our notion of what constitutes the proper context for the analytic consideration of a musical work requires, among all other matters, the greatest reorientation in the face of recent music. Of course, analysis has always been "contextual" in the sense that it has attempted to go beyond the particular piece, to relate it to a larger artistic environment. In traditional analysis, however, at least that of a technical nature, the environment has been understood primarily in musical terms. Compositions are analyzed in relation to conventional tonal language, or to other works of the same genre or those with a similar formal structure. Already in the case of earlier twentieth-century music, however, one must modify the notion of context, as this music is contextual in a decidedly different sense from that of tonal music. Here referential norms, at least those relating to pitch, are established uniquely for each composition—that is, by reference to, and within the confines of, the work's own internal context. This shift suggests that the problem of context has always been a pressing one for twentieth-century music. (Actually, the problem is already noticeable in earlier music, as I have myself tried to show in a study of the use of dissonant harmonic structures as referential norms in certain nineteenth-century compositions—structures that, viewed purely within the context of the tonal system, should have no independent value whatever.)[6]

6. "Dissonant Prolongations: Theoretical and Compositional Precedents," *Journal of Music Theory* 20, no. 1 (Spring 1976): 49–91.

But it is a striking feature of the contextual systems of most compositions predating the last quarter century that they are contrived to allow for the preservation of traditional notions of musical continuity—of linear progression, phrase structure, cadential arrivals and the like. Although these things can no longer be quite what they used to be, they nevertheless remain closely analogous (which is of course just the point Edward Cone makes in the article I cited earlier). And when theorists of this music fail to take such matters into consideration (as unfortunately frequently happens), their analyses seem curiously distorted.

Thus for this music, even though the structural context has narrowed, it is still possible to take an analytic approach that is, at least in its broader features, similar to that of traditional analysis. In the case of new music, however, where the specifically musical context threatens to shrink to the vanishing point, a widening of context, paradoxically, is required in the analyst's concerns. As each work tends to establish its own comprehensive contextual system—its own personal tradition, as it were, which it then irrevocably destroys—the relevance of context in the earlier sense becomes increasingly tenuous. Despite—or rather because of—the work's isolation, it is less and less possible, or meaningful, to consider it as an autonomous object analyzable solely in its own terms. One must take other factors into consideration and show how these relate to the work and how the work relates to them.

Thus a pressing responsibility of present-day analysis is to indicate how new music reflects present-day actuality. It is notable that today's composers more and more think of their own work in these terms—that is, not so much as solutions to technical, or even technical-expressive, problems but as responses to the conditions of modern life. The musical work seems to be in the process of being transformed from an object intended primarily for aesthetic appreciation to a kind of document, a position statement concerning contemporary existence. One sees this throughout virtually the entire spectrum of contemporary compositional activity. It is most apparent in works of composers like Frederic Rzewski and Christian Wolff, where the performance situation itself becomes a kind of laboratory for the cultivation of political awareness. But it is also detectable in even so traditional a work as Henze's Second Piano Concerto, a piece composed in 1967 that still reflects traditional concepts of pitch structure—both tonal and twelve-tone—and formal process, but about which the composer has remarked: "It is the work of someone who speaks of his discontentedness, his impotence, his wishes, within the conventions of so-called bourgeois custom, even within the terms and parameters of such norms, who observes all the possibilities and taboos and is only thereby able to make evident the progressive wretchedness and loss of freedom. In this piece there is no exit, and thus the form corresponds exactly to the content. It is a report of slavery and thus possesses an element of consciousness." To ignore these remarks is to

189

rob the work of one of its dimensions, and part of the analyst's job should be to consider how well the concerto reflects and makes musically valid the composer's stated intentions.

In his book on the sociology of music, Theodor W. Adorno states that the true goal of this discipline should be "the social deciphering of musical phenomena themselves, the clarification of their essential relationship to actual society, of their inner social content and their function."[7] Although there are facets of Adorno's program with which one can take issue, above all his apparent identification of music sociology with "social criticism accomplished through the criticism of art," it seems to me that he gives us a glimpse of a way out of what he refers to as the "inane isolation" of Western music. What is especially appealing about Adorno, at least for the analyst, is that he is concerned with the identification and interpretation of specifically musical processes, processes of a technical nature that are still susceptible to analysis in a more traditional sense. Mere identification and purely musical analysis are not enough, however, as he persistently points out, but should facilitate the consideration of the art work in the complex and evolving environment within which it exists.

It is no coincidence, I think, just at the moment when the musical work has retreated into itself, reaching a condition of solipsistic self-concern that threatens to reduce it to a state of total inaudibility, that we seem to be coming full circle, back to a point where musical meaning can be defined only by going beyond the individual musical object. To take one more extreme example, in John Cage's notorious piece, *4'33"*, in which the performer or performers are given a temporally defined span of silence during which no musical activity whatsoever takes place—that is, in which compositional inaudibility becomes an explicit reality—there is obviously nothing at all to say about the musical work itself, since there is absolutely nothing at all there. Here, obviously, significance and meaning can be considered only by passing beyond the work to consider its "comment" on larger musical and social conditions and its reflection of a tendency away from a conception of music as a structure of interrelated pitch and time events to one involving people placed in relation to one another and to the environment in which they find themselves.

The use of aleatory procedures in much new music, a subject I have avoided until now, provides another example. On the one hand, such processes can often be viewed in terms of their purely musical consequences—for example, as providing an efficient means for producing certain kinds of complex musical textures that would be difficult to achieve otherwise. These events can then be considered in regard to their own inherent musical interest, their relationships to other events in

7. Theodor W. Adorno, *Einleitung in die Musiksoziologie* (Frankfurt am Main, 1962), p. 208. This important work has recently appeared in English as *Introduction to the Sociology of Music,* trans. E. B. Ashton (New York, 1976).

the piece, etc. This is an approach that one might take, say, to a composition like Lutosławski's String Quartet. But aleatory procedures can also be thought of as a response to the tendency of Western music over the past few centuries to become an increasingly fixed commodity, communicable only through an ever more precisely articulated notational system. That the relationship of performer to composition has been greatly affected by this is obvious; and much aleatory music clearly reflects an interest in reestablishing a more process-oriented performance situation, as opposed to one in which a precisely defined result is reproduced as faithfully as possible.

Economics is often described as the dismal science, but the designation applies equally, I suspect, at least in the minds of many musicians, to the field of musical analysis. But if analysis is "dismal," it is so only because it is too limited and narrow in scope. There is certainly nothing inherently dismal about it; indeed, to be human is to be analytical, for I take it that part of what we mean by living a full life is being cognizant, as far as this is possible, of the nature and implications of our actions. Recent music may well have a lesson to teach in this regard: that the focus of the analyst's inquiries must exceed the parochial and ultimately encompass the entire range of human activity.

191

LANGUAGE MODELS AND MUSICAL ANALYSIS

Harold S. Powers

1. INTRODUCTION

The metaphor of music as language has three principal aspects, depending upon whether the focus is on semantics, on phonology, or on syntax and grammar.

1.1 Musical Semantics. First of all, music is often said to express or evoke something that might have been conveyed verbally. In certain restricted cases, like drum or whistle languages, something like music is even used as a referential coded substitute for language; the Tepehua "thought" songs described by Boilès (1967) seem to be the extreme case. But many musical cultures recognize conventionally coded induced associations of specific musical entities with persons, events, or things, in real life as well as in ritual or drama. In the most familiar cases the something that might have been conveyed verbally is emotive/expressive rather than cognitive/ostensive, and sometimes a more or less systematic doctrine of musical affect or musical ethos is found. In high cultures musical entities are often systematically correlated with non-musical phenomena, many of which may have strong expressive associations of their own. In some of the medieval North Indian systems of melodic types six superordinate types are correlated with the six seasons, which have strong affective connotations. In some sources of medieval European theory a similar correspondence is found between the four Galenic humors, the four Aristotelian elements, and the four pairs of plainsong modes (Gerbert 1784:218–19). Of course the linguistic metaphor need not be invoked in connection with musical ethos, but it often is. Individual affects, or whole classes of affect, are ascribed to musical entities like motives or tunes, or to musical features like rhythms or intervals, and these features or entities are then said to be units of discourse in a musical language of pure expression. The late Deryck Cooke's many times reprinted *The Language of Music* (1959) is an extended application of this aspect of the metaphor to Western music of the 15th to 20th centuries (see especially p. 89–90 and all of Chapter 3 "Some Basic Terms of Musical Vocabulary").

193

0014-1836/80/2401-0001$3.00

1

Most musicologists, however, are a little embarrassed by the notion that music is a language whose message is something other than itself. For instance, I confess to some discomfort over attempts by Keil and Keil (1966) and by Deva and Virmani (1968, 1974) to use the Osgood/Suci/Tannenbaum "semantic differential" method, with all its inductive paraphernalia of questionnaire and factor analysis, in order directly to find or confirm affective meaning to one or another individual North Indian *rāga*. There are simply too many uncontrollable variables. Not evaluative scales of good-bad, hard-soft, and active-passive, but rather paradigmatic scales of compatible-incompatible, same-different, and superordinate-subordinate seem to me the fundamental elements of a semantics of North Indian classical music, as I tried to show in "The Structure of Musical Meaning: A View from Banaras" (1977). Musical semantics may establish systematic relationships of meaning in musical discourse, but musical-verbal dictionaries of specific affects must be compiled ad hoc from exterior non-musical contexts. Those contexts may be verbal text or dramatic situation (as in Cooke 1959), or any other cultural (or even natural) event. The experience and expectations of fully enculturated listeners might well serve as a source too, though only one of many.

In "Language and Music: Areas for Cooperation" (1963:28), William Bright recognized that

> it is widely felt that music, like language, conveys something—that a musical performance, like a linguistic message, contains something more than the physical properties of the individual sounds which make it up.

But Bright too seems to have regarded the "content" of music as merely a function of what he called its "endosemantic" structure (p. 28–29). For Bright (p. 26),

> [the] two main types of link between language and music [are] their mutual influence in singing, and their structural similarity.

These are what I referred to at the outset as the phonological and the grammatical aspects of the music as language metaphor.

1.2 Phonological and Musical Shapes. Bright's own instance for the direct influence of linguistic phonology on musical sound was taken from South Indian classical music. He pointed out that there is a consistent pattern of correspondence between long and short syllables in a text and longer and shorter durations in its musical setting, and quoted a couple of lines from a Telugu *padam* to illustrate. I can confirm that the correspondences are exactly so in principle, though very much more complex in some circumstances. In Telugu compositions in South Indian classical *rāga*-s (melodic types) the relationships between text rhythms and musical rhythms are multiplex and heterogeneous, yet all musical rhythms can be derived in one way or another from Telugu prosody (itself multiplex and heterogeneous, incorporating both Dravidian and Sanskritic prosodic features at all levels, from syllable and foot on to stanza and beyond).

Of course, direct connection between phonological features in a language and basic features in the music associated with that language hardly constitute a metaphor. But to the extent that the vocal music of a culture is the model for instrumental music as well, the indirect influence of language-music connection may be easily discernible in musical practices having no connection with text. It is patently the case that rhythmic patterns in modern South Indian instrumental music are largely an outgrowth of the vocal repertory, which until recently has dominated South Indian practice. But this is in large part true for North Indian instrumental music as well, and not just in those very recent "*gāyakī aṅg*" fashions modeling their art on the vocal *khayāl* style. The oldest traditions of Hindustani solo instrumental music are for plucked strings, and the performance styles of the *sitār* seem originally to have been essentially independent of vocal influence, as in most Middle Eastern plucked string styles today. But the plucking patterns—the *mizrāb*—of all traditional genres, improvised and memorized alike, now reflect the quantitative relation of long and short syllables of language in varying degrees. Except in the case of the *jhālā*, in fact, the contrast of long and short is very much more evident than the motor accents of hand and finger movement so characteristic of Middle Eastern plucked string playing, such as Persian *chār-mezrāb*. *Sitār* playing has become "Indianized." Onto an original quasi-Middle Eastern accentual style in rhythm have been grafted quantitative features. These appear most obviously in the several varieties of *joḍ*, which seems to have come in from vocal *nom-tom* via the *bīn*.[1]

On a larger and more abstract scale too one can discern the connection of language forms and musical design in South Asia. Modern Indian performance practice in general is in considerable part connected with the mostly devotional post-classical literature of later Sanskrit poetry (beginning with the *Gītā Govinda*) and of the "medieval" and modern vernaculars. This poetry is characterized by refrain and stanza design, quite unlike the older classical Sanskrit poetry in which every quatrain is an independent entity. Furthermore, the poems are normally designed *en rondeau* semantically, and often even grammatically, in that the beginning of the independent refrain comes as a logical or even syntactic continuation and completion of the last words of the stanza. Finally, there is usually a matching rhyme of stanzas with refrain, sometimes even the

195

matching of a word or two; this ensures that not only the end of the stanza
but also the end of the refrain itself will flow easily back into the beginning, for the repetitions as well as for the returns of the refrain.

These three characteristic textual features have exact musical correspondences, not only in performance but in the abstract background
structures as well. As to performance, first, there is a fundamental part in
contrast with a second responding part, musically as well as verbally.
There is also continuous leadback, melodically as well as (often) syntactically, from the endings of both principal part and responding part to the
beginning of the principal part. Finally, at the end of each of the two parts
in the majority of cases there are sonically parallel passages, based on
syllabic rhyming or identity in the verbal domain and on equivalence or
identity of melodic contour in the melodic domain.

Here again, formal parallels between tune and text in themselves
hardly constitute a metaphor. But the three features that correspond—
contrast of two parts, use of leadback connections, and musical rhyme—
mark not only the characteristic shape of performance but are also built
into the still more abstract shape of the underlying musical substance.
Almost every classical *rāga*—that is, melodic type—is itself structured in
terms of these features: first, a clear contrast of two main registers, each
defined thematically as well; second, linear connections at the boundaries
from each register into the next, and especially in descent; third, parallelism between the nuclear motivic contours and/or intervallic contents of
each register.

Examples 1 and 2 are transcriptions (after V. N. Bhatkhande's
Kramik Pustak Mālikā) of two much sung traditional *khayāl*-s, originally
composed by Sadāraṅg (Niyāmat Khān) at the court of the emperor
Muhammad Shāh (r. 1719–1748). Both *khayāl*-s use the ubiquitous musical meter *tīn-tāl* and that most popular of all Hindustani melodic types,
the *rāg* called *darbārī-kānaḍa*. The *sthāyī* ("stable") section functions as
repeatable and recurring refrain, the *antarā* ("intervening") section is the
stanza.

The contrasting register with new themes at the beginnings of the
antarā-s are evident, and so also the leadback links and musical rhymes
that set up returns to the openings: . . . *more dātā, tuma sāī̃* . . . and
. . . *dunī ke dātā, tuma sāī̃* . . . in Example 1; . . . *māliniyā̃ bandhanavā*
. . . and *Mammada Sā pyāre ke ghara kāje, bandhanavā* . . . of the
sthāyī and . . . *saba sāyata sõ āje, bandhanavā* . . . of the *antarā* in
Example 2. These contrasts and parallelisms in turn reflect and are reflected by the underlying melodic type itself. Example 3 is a *calan* for the
rāg darbārī-kānaḍā; calan means "procedure," from the verb *calnā*
meaning "walk/go" (the relation is that of "*marche*" and "*marcher*" in

196

Example 1 (rāg darbārī-kānaḍā, tīn-tāl), after KPM IV, 669

Example 2 (rāg darbārī-kānaḍā, tīn-tāl), after KPM IV, 674

198

French), and it designates an outline epitome of the important configurations in a melodic type. I have constructed this sample *calan* from Examples 1 and 2, but it could serve as a summary for many other compositions in *darbārī-kānaḍā*, especially if a stipulation of certain possible (not all) octave equivalences is included. With one or two more optional units and restricted substitute motivic types it would be valid for nearly anything in *darbārī-kānaḍā*. More important, though, it can serve as a guide in making new melodic renditions in *darbārī-kānaḍā,* be they composed pieces to be memorized like *khayāl*-s, or extemporizations in one of the improvisatory genres like *ālāp*.[2] The parallel motivic types are marked with brackets and arrows. Rising and falling patterns alike turn on the shaken *A♭* and *E♭* in the contrasted registers. The parallel descending configurations epitomize the individuality of the melodic type: *F-G-b♭ F\E͡♭--- F-D* above and *B♭-C-D B♭\A͡♭--- B♭-GG* below.

Example 3 : a *calan* ("procedure") of rāg darbārī-kănaḍa

<u>1.3 Musicology and Linguistics</u>. Parallels between the formal patterns of sound and structure in text and music, whether concrete or abstract, are of course not unique to Indian music. I have myself used such structural parallels in dealing with the influences of word rhythm and textual form in 17th–18th century music composed to Italian texts (see especially 1962:82–90, and 1968:280–86, 308–09). Others will readily find instances from other areas, from Paris to Peking. It is an interesting area for study, with more subtleties than one might think. But nowadays the main focus of interest in the language-music connection is in the putative abstract structural similarities of language and music. Many have been encouraged to think that analytical models of linguistic structure may be heuristically relevant for the analysis of musical structure.[3]

The new literature of linguistics-based analysis of music is growing fast. Analyses and programmatic theories have come out of both the Western theoretical and the ethnomusicological traditions, and even more significantly, some musically competent linguists have interested themselves professionally in the subject. It is in this structurally oriented literature that the most interesting insights on the language-music connection are to be found, and at the same time the most faddish foolishness. The harsh criticisms of the foolishness that make up the bulk of Steven Feld's 1974 article "Linguistic Models in Ethnomusicology" seem to me thoroughly justified. But Feld seems not to have noticed the real insights available to musicology from a knowledge of the study of languages, or at

any rate not to have valued them very much, because of his own strong
theoretical bias against any consideration of "music sound" outside of its
cultural context. This bias comes from Merriam and Blacking (as expressed for instance in Merriam 1964:26–32, or Blacking 1973:25–27) and
given the kind of parochial notions they were reacting against, the bias is a
healthy one. But they overreact. It is of course true that (like language) no
music can exist without people who make it. It is also true that (like some
uses of language) some music may sometimes be more efficiently interpreted by discussing it as though it did have a life of its own. When and to
what extent any particular music ought to be interpreted out of context
depends in part, as it does in the study of linguistic phenomena, on the
purpose of the investigation, and in part it depends on the role of that
music in the culture in question—and of course this last question cannot
be resolved by music-analytical methods of whatever origin. Some musics
can be managed apart from cultural context more readily than others,
Western and Indian art musics being two notorious examples, while other
musics are so intimately tied in with a cultural or even material context as
to be incomprehensible except in that context. Ethnomusicologists need
not therefore denigrate abstract musical analysis merely on principle,
even abstract musical analysis inspired by linguistic models. Sociolin-
guists are not throwing out abstract linguistic analysis and abstract
models, they are merely incorporating them in their broader field (Labov
1972:186–87, 201–02).

To whatever extent methodological and theoretical imbalances in the
new literature on music as language arise from insufficient attention to
cultural factors in the societies being investigated, equal or greater imbalances arise from inattention to cultural factors in the society of the
investigators. In the sequel I propose to illustrate three broad areas in
which the reach of the new literature seems to be exceeding its grasp.

First, some of the more enthusiastic proponents of linguistics-based
musical analysis have not seemed very familiar with the analytical musicology they find inadequate. It may be, as some have suggested, that
musical analysis unaccountably or perversely lags behind other disciplines. It may also be that scholars working out of the by no means
negligible existing traditions have long been dealing with many of the
same kinds of problems as structural linguists, only in a more abstruse
and intractable domain, where the linguist's handy tool of "meaning,"
often used for rough work in the field if seldom acknowledged in fine
print, has not been available.

Second, there is paradoxically little comparative basis for the new
linguistics-based music-analytical literature, even though much of that
literature comes from ethnomusicologists. Comparisons in ethnomusi-

cology are seldom really cross-culturally multi-lateral but rather tend to be bilateral, and in a curious way. "Ethnic" musics are matched one at a time against theoretical models derived from various sources: field experience with one of them, anthropological theory, linguistics, or the investigator's notions of "Western" music or "standard" music theory, in varying proportions. But modern synchronic linguistics did not grow out of bilateral comparisons of a language with a model, or of an alien language with some aspect of the investigator's language. The now enormously influential *Cours de linguistique générale* (1916) of Ferdinand de Saussure, posthumously compiled by two of his students from their lecture notes and those of other students, is a seminal work of European structural linguistics and semiology. Saussure began his career, however, with the at the time equally influential *Mémoires sur le système primitif des voyelles dans les langues indoeuropéennes* (1879), a landmark work of comparative linguistics in the *Junggrammatiker* vein, and what little else Saussure actually published in his own lifetime was also in this field. Modern linguistics began with multilateral comparisons of languages in families, from Indo-European to Athabaskan, and their individually described grammars were matched not against borrowed models but against each other. A theoretical musicology inspired by linguistics could do worse than look to the history of linguistics in this regard, as well as to its latest fashions.

201

Third, the new literature seems uninterested in older traditions of language models for musical analysis. Yet those traditions are of value not only in their own right but even more because they have left significant residues in our modern notions of what constitutes musical analysis and even music itself. As is well known, there is not always agreement about what "music" is and about what is "music," not just across cultures but even within them. The very notion that music is something that can be segmented and analyzed, and the traditional terminology for doing so, have deep and particular roots in historical language models for musical analysis that are peculiar to Western European culture.

2. MUSIC MODELS AND LINGUISTIC ANALYSIS

Fondements d'une sémiologie de la musique (1975) by Jean-Jacques Nattiez is so far the most ambitious published attempt to synthesize techniques of musical analysis from models originating in modern linguistics. The author's intellectual acknowledgments are to Georges Mounin, Nicolas Ruwet, and Jean Molino, for their semiology, musicology, and epistemology, respectively (1975:13–15). In 1973 Nattiez (together with one of his students) had referred to two articles by the Belgian linguist Ruwet as "the new methodological paradigm that Ruwet has opened up" (1973:43). The articles are "Les duplications dans l'oeuvre de Claude Debussy" and "Méthodes d'analyse en musicologie," published in the *Revue belge de musicologie* in 1962 and 1966, and reprinted as Chapters 3 and 4 of Ruwet 1972. They were the musicological point of departure for the several analyses in Nattiez's *Fondements,* though by that time Ruwet himself had "disowned the originality of his musicological initiatives to return to the bosom of Chomskyan orthodoxy," as Nattiez has put it (1975:239). Nattiez was referring here to Ruwet's "Théorie et méthodes dans les études musicales" (1975), which Ruwet wrote after he had seen the typescript of *Fondements.* In the published version of *Fondements* Nattiez ascribes the initiatives of Ruwet's articles from the 1960's to "Ruwet I" and the disownings in 1975 to "Ruwet II" (1975:256–57, and see also p. 386ff. for further responses to Ruwet 1975).

In his 1966 article Ruwet demonstrated the formal analysis of four secular medieval monodies by segmenting them strictly according to internal repetition and recurrence, without regard to musical content, discussing (musical) transformations and substitutions only after completing the segmentation. The first analysis is of a *Geisslerlied* taken from Reese's *Music in the Middle Ages* (1940).[4] The three subsequent analyses, of troubadour and trouvère songs, have been less noticed semiotically, perhaps because transformation and substitution were rather flexibly incorporated into the demonstrations.[5]

The following excerpt from Ruwet 1966/72 briefly illustrates the aspect of "Ruwet I" that has appealed to semiologists of music, as well as giving a clear adumbration of "Ruwet II." The passage (1972:116–17) describes the method of displaying the musical examples and the real role of segmentation in analysis. (NB: All English versions of passages originally in other languages are mine unless otherwise noted.)

> A few words first about the graphic representation of the examples. It seemed to me illuminating, in the study of monodies, to take up a procedure that Claude Lévi-Strauss applies to the analysis of myths, being himself inspired by the musical notation of orchestral scores. Equivalent sequences are as much as possible written one under another in a single column, and the text must be read, omitting the empty spaces, from left to right and from top to bottom. Thus certain traits of structure are immediately apparent, at the same time, moreover, certain ambiguities. It would clearly be very difficult to apply the same procedure to polyphonic structures.
>
> One must stress the fact that in the analysis as it is actually done the diverse stages of the procedure do not necessarily follow in the order given. The procedure is much more a verification procedure, intended to see that the analysis is coherent, than a discovery procedure in the strict sense of the term. No doubt it would be possible to apply it rigorously in the order given, and one would obtain the same results, but it is much more economical and rapid to use it to verify the results of an analysis obtained, sometimes very rapidly, in an intuitive manner.

The second paragraph was then annotated with a quotation from Zellig Harris's "Introduction" to his *Methods in Structural Linguistics* (1951:1), in which an equivalent observation had been made regarding procedures of intuitive discovery and rigorous verification in descriptive linguistics. Ruwet 1975—Nattiez's "Ruwet II"—represents a further development along the lines of the pragmatic flexibility implicit in this paragraph, informed as well by a broader acquaintance with studies from the musical disciplines. Early in his essay, "Ruwet II" refers to "the structure of human languages" (1975:13) in terms of

> their richness and their real complexities (which the traditional grammarians saw very well in spite of the often very intuitive character of their theories and their methodologies).

This observation is valid not only because of but even in spite of its immediately Chomskyan genesis. A few pages later (1975:16) the expected parallel observation regarding music appears:

> There is no longer any reason to pass over other types of data, such as the various intuitions of good musicians, or even the data furnished by traditional musical theories.

The expansion of horizons evidenced by allowing some merit in older grammarians, of language and therefore of music, is followed later in Ruwet 1975 by a particularly telling riposte in the musical sphere to the observation on the complexity of human languages, to which I shall return in the next division of this essay. Now I want to take a closer look at some implications of the first paragraph quoted above from Ruwet 1966/72, Ruwet's introduction to his method for the graphic display of musical examples for analytic purposes. This is simply a point of departure; it is not my concern here whether or not this paragraph from "Ruwet I" reflects anything of "Ruwet II." It does graphically illustrate one of the central weaknesses in the new literature of linguistically inspired musical analysis. One has no call to cavil at a linguist's unfamiliarity with musicological and music-theoretical traditions. It is quite otherwise with members of the music scholars' guild, whose need for intellectual stimulus from outside seems to reflect not only admitted deficiencies in traditions of musical study but also ignorance of those traditions.

2.1 Syntax and Paradigm in Direct Display. To a musical scholar it should have seemed odd, for instance, that Ruwet needed to use Lévi-Strauss's chart of the Oedipus myth (see Table I below) as a model for the graphic representation of equivalence paradigms in his analysis of the *Geisslerlied* and the other monodies analyzed in Ruwet 1966/72. Whatever refinements of rigorous verification may have been desirable for confirming the analysis, the chart itself is a design long familiar to musi-

203

cologists, notably to those working in the two longest established fields of research in monodic music, folk-song scholarship and the study of Christian liturgical chant. If one is proposing that a number of different folk-song melodies are versions of the same tune, for instance, or members of the same tune-family, then to set them down one above the other in notation, gapped and stretched so that the claimed correspondences are vertically aligned, is an obvious way to show at a glance both overall similarities of Gestalt and individual likeness in detail (see for example Bayard 1954:18–19, Table II). An early use of this format in Christian chant studies may be seen in Wellesz 1920:142–44. In Gregorian chant scholarship the so-called "centonate" chants have often been shown as melodic types in this way. A particularly elaborate instance of the format is Table F "Melodic analysis by formulas of the first part of the Gradual responses of mode 2" appended to Suñol 1935 (note particularly the handling of "variant" and "additional" formulas, and see the discussion on p. 421–24). A comparative chart of 22 antiphons in mode 8 in Ferretti 1938 (after p. 112) illustrates another way of using vertical alignment to demonstrate individual tokens of a general melodic type.

204

Example 4 is taken from Table I of Helmut Hucke's "Musikalische Formen der Officiumsantiphonen," published in 1953. It is here given as an instance from the musicological tradition of a chart like Ruwet's charts of the *Geisslerlied* and other monodies. It is, like them, a graphic model in staff notation of the axis of combination (syntactic concatenation) and the axis of selection (paradigmatic equivalence). Six office antiphons in mode 1 are shown and claimed as members of a general melodic type.[6]

The criteria for segmentation and alignment are complex, and involve both text and music. Hucke's principal tool for separating melodic units syntactically was the syntax and sense of the words variously attached to a tune (1953:8):

> The text put to a melody is first of all significant for its form because it determines its articulation. . . The articulation of the text is above all determined through the segments of meaning.

His principal criteria for assigning segmented melodic units to the same paradigmatic class—given the prior establishment of the syntactic order—were register and direction (ibid.:24).

> Many times we find in Gregorian chant groups of melodies which exhibit the same succession of segments, with the same area of movement [*Bewegungsraum*] and the same direction of movement [*Bewegungsrichtung*], yet in particulars they can exhibit far-reaching differences.

Had only musical correspondences been considered, the alignment and assignment of some of the motives in the antiphons shown in Example 4 would have been somewhat different. The *clivis* neume *DC,* for instance, occurs at the boundary of a paradigmatic segment at three different places in Hucke's chart: I.3 ("-tro"), II.6 ("-um"), and III.1 ("in"). In the purely melodic syntaxis, however, they are all in the same position, after low-lying opening phrases that establish *D* and before a rising motive *F-G-a* that establishes *a* as the high point of the melodic line in all six antiphons. That the presence of the *clivis DC* is not a matter of mere concord, however, is shown by antiphon 2, which starts straight off with *F-G-a*, and antiphon 4, whose initial phrase ending on *D* is followed immediately by *F-G-a*; the *clivis FC* in antiphon 5 may be taken as a variant conditioned by the preceding *scandicus* neume *DEF*. Hucke's distribution of the *clivis DC,* as an appendage to initial phrases in I.3 and II.6 but as a preparation for the rise in III.1, is entirely a consequence of the divisions of the text.

The varying assignments of material in columns III and IV of the segmentation chart are more complex. The column III material establishes *a* from below, while the column IV material comprises the first descent from *a* to *D* in those antiphons where there are two descents from *a*. In principle *a* comes twice, as the culmination of the rise ending *F-G-a* and as the beginning of the nuclear descent pattern *a-G-(F)-E-(F)-G-(a)-F-E-D-(C)*; this is the procedure in antiphons 1, 4, and 6. In antiphons 2 and 3, however, the high point *a* occurs strongly and independently only once, at "lu-" and "tu" respectively, both ending the rise and beginning the fall. Hucke has parsed these antiphons in different ways melodically, again presumably because of the text. In antiphon 2 he has put the beginning of the descent into column III, so that the opening descent from *a* is deleted from column IV, based on a division of the vocative "Sol et luna" from the imperative main clause "laudate eum." In antiphon 3, conversely, he has (so to speak) moved the preparatory rise *F-G-a* out of its independent slot in column III, leaving that slot empty, and subordinated it to the descent phrase in column IV as a mere preparation, thus keeping the subject and predicate of the main clause in the direct quotation of the maid's words together as a single syntactic unit. The double *F-G-a* rise in antiphon 5 has been handled by attaching the second rise to the single descent phrase of column VII, on the pattern of the conflation of columns III and IV just discussed.[7]

Single chants built on a recurrent ordering of variant or substitutable phrases may as conveniently be displayed in this kind of graphic chart as multiple instances of melodic types. Treitler (1974:348–49) shows what he calls the "formulaic system" of the mode 2 Tract "Deus deus meus" with the staff notations vertically aligned so as to show the motivic paradigms for each of the four successive phrase units of the melodic type for mode 2 Tracts.[8]

Example 4 (after Hucke 1953)

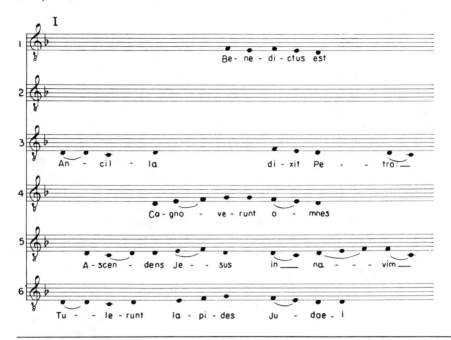

206

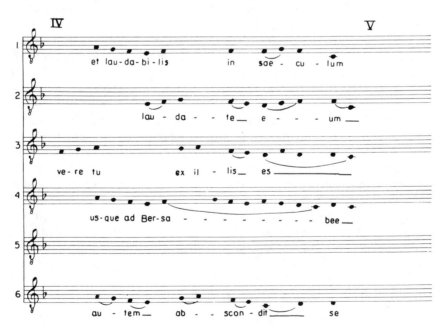

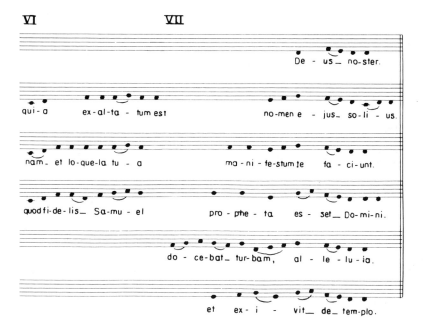

207

2.2 Representing and Displaying Subjects and Functions. A musical scholar might also have stopped to wonder why Ruwet thought that "it would clearly be very difficult to apply the same [notational chart] procedure to polyphonic structures," for matrix charts representing polyphonic music are by no means unheard of. Here Ruwet may have been misled by Lévi-Strauss's own misapprehension of the relationship between scores and music. Since the famous structural chart of the Oedipus myth that inspired Ruwet's musical charts has become a point of reference in the music-as-language metaphor, as it has in so many other semiologies, it is worth examining once more, in musicological terms. For just as Lévi-Strauss mistook the musical surface for the musical structure in his many analogies of Western polyphony with primitive myth, so also Ruwet mistook the graphic surface of Lévi-Strauss's mythic chart and failed to see that its design is as readily applicable to segmentable polyphony as it is to segmentable myth or monody.

The Lévi-Strauss chart to which Ruwet referred in 1966 was first published in 1955 and has been reprinted several times; Ruwet cited the version printed as Chapter XI of Lévi-Strauss's *Anthropologie structurale* in 1958. The analysis of the Theban myth cycle that the chart represents is the most often cited specific instance of Lévi-Strauss's use of the Saussurian linguistic model in the mythic field; not only are its elements more familiar than the South and North American repertory of his *Mythologiques* but also it occurs in his first and fullest description of the method. It was also, incidentally, his first explicit use of the metaphor of Western polyphonic music and the musical score, which so dominates *Le Cru et le cuit (Mythologiques I)* and which returns in the celebrated analysis of Ravel's *Bolero* that concludes *L'Homme nu (Mythologiques IV)* (for a discussion of this analysis in the context of Lévi-Strauss's music-myth metaphor see Hopkins 1977).

Lévi-Strauss began the description of his matrix arrangement as follows (1955:432):

> The myth will be treated as would be an orchestral score perversely presented as
> a unilinear series and where our task is to re-establish the correct disposition.

Certain "functions . . . predicated to a given subject" (ibid.:431) were then chosen from the Theban myths and set down in a vertical-horizontal matrix of the design shown in Table I below.[9] The Theban myth matrix as here shown gives only the "values" for the "functions" represented by the columns—that is, the "subjects" (the relationships) about which they are predicated. For some examples of the actual wording of entries in the matrix, see items I.1, I.8, II.3, II.5, and II.9 in Table I-B (omitting matter in square brackets).

Table I-A (after Lévi-Strauss's chart of the Theban myth cycle)*

	I	II	III	IV
1.	Cadmus/Europe			
2.			Cadmus/Serpent	
3.		Sown men/Sown men		
4.				Labdacus = lame?
5.		Oedipus/Laius		Laius = "gauche"?
6.			Oedipus/Sphinx	
7.				Oedipus = swollen-foot?
8.	Oedipus/Iocaste			
9.		Eteocles/Polyneices		
10.	Polyneices/Antigone			

* The horizontal and vertical coordination follows Lévi-Strauss
1958:236. The spellings of names follow Graves 1955. For further
reference to the stories used by Lévi-Strauss, see also Graves
no. 58 for lines 1-3, 105 for lines 4-8, and 106 for lines 9-10.
See also Leach 1970/74:63-71, and Pettit 1975:80-86, for discussions of Lévi-Strauss's model of the Theban myths and his use
of the metaphor of the orchestral score.

After the tabulation Lévi-Strauss's description continues (ibid.:433):

> Thus, we find ourselves confronted with four vertical columns each of which
> includes several relations belonging to the same bundle. Were we to *tell* the
> myth, we would disregard the columns and read the rows from left to right and
> from top to bottom. But if we want to *understand* the myth, then we will have to
> disregard one half of the diachronic division (top to bottom) and read from left to
> right, column after column, each one being considered as a unit. All the relations
> belonging to the same column exhibit one common feature which it is our task to
> unravel.

The "functions" then assigned by Lévi-Strauss to each of the four
columns are summarized under I-IV in Table I-B. The wording of items
listed for "functions" I and II has been translated from Lévi-Strauss's
matrix (1958:236) except for I.10, where "Antigone buries her brother
Polyneices, violating the prohibition" has been transformed from active
to passive, to simplify the formulation of the "function." Functions listed
for column III require only insertion of the "subjects" from Table I-A; for
column IV the "predicate" for each name is "father of [the name be-
neath]."

The metaphor of the orchestral score had great significance in Lévi-
Strauss's formulation of the gross constituents of structural analysis out-

Table I-B (see Table I-A and Lévi-Strauss 1958:235-42=1955:432-36)

I.   [man] [verb] [female relative]   [in context of transgression]

    1. Cadmus seeks his sister Europe, ravished by Zeus

    8. Oedipus marries Iocaste, his own mother

   10. Polyneices is buried by his sister Antigone,
       against [Creon's] command

II.   [man (men)] kills [male relative(s)]

    3. The Spartoi [warriors spring from the serpent's teeth]
      kill each other

    5. Oedipus [son] kills his father Laius

    9. Eteocles [brother] kills Polyneices [brother]

III.   [man]   kills   [monster]

IV.   Three father-son generations of men with deformities

210

side the purely linguistic frame.[10] As Leach put it, there is in a body of myths, as in an orchestral score, "a basic message which is manifest in the score as a whole rather than in any particular myth" (1974:64). But in structural analysis as elsewhere, there is a risk of mixing the metaphor with the message. The structures to be found in music, as in language and no doubt as in myth, are those which lie behind both what is apprehended by the recipient and what was intended for his apprehension. A multi-line score is merely a notated representation of multi-part music, and bears the same relation with the structure of the polyphonic piece that a notation on one staff bears with the structure of a monody.

    I shall suggest in the next division some real differences between the structural types likely to be found underlying polyphonic versus monodic repertories, but singly versus multiply notated representations of musical surface have no bearing on singularity versus multiplicity in the representations of an analysis of that music. For example, on the notated surface speech is monodic, but it can be analyzed and represented polyphonically. Ruwet (1972:211-14) employs a polyphonic analysis of a line of Racine, "Le jour n'est pas plus pur que le fond de mon coeur," to illustrate a linguistic analysis of "the famous question of the poetic role of sonorous elements." The sequence of key words "jour . . . pur . . . fond . . . coeur" is presented, as it were, in open score: a matrix in which binary oppositions in distinctive features of the "sonorous elements"— the vowel and consonant phonemes—are written out in eleven separate horizontal lines, one above another, so that the eleven phonemes of the four key words are represented not by eleven single symbols but by eleven columns of "simultaneous" symbols (+, −, or 0). The four lines displaying the main contrastive parameters (compactness, continuousness, diffuseness, and pitch) look like nothing so much as the four principal parts of a multi-part musical texture, and as Ruwet observes (ibid.: 213–14),

> there is in fact an analogy between the relations of equivalence and opposition that we have extricated and the relations that link the successive chords of a work of tonal music through common or different tones.

By the same token, graphic displays of polyphonic music need not necessarily use only staff notation in open score. Elements of musical structure, at whatever level, can always be represented by manipulable symbols, provided only that those symbols are indexed and keyed to the musical data to whatever degree of rigor is needful for the analysis.

In any case, Ruwet's *Geisslerlied* chart and others like it are not homomorphous with the Theban myth chart, since they illustrate altogether different levels of analysis. The *Geisslerlied* chart, like my Examples 4 above and 6 below, is simply a faithful copy of notated symbols for the surface of music, taken from a written source, with no change other than the rearrangement for vertical alignment of correspondences. Insofar as such a display is itself an analytical statement, it is a simple and direct statement about a corpus of otherwise uninterpreted data. What are entered in the rows and columns of the Theban myth chart, to the contrary, are catchword phrases, which themselves are already selected and interpreted summary representatives for narrated or printed episodes of myth. Each catchword phrase in itself represents an analytical judgment, and the particular choices of mythic episodes and the particular expressions chosen to stand for them are in turn consequent upon what is being said about them through their arrangement in the matrix.

In saying that "it would clearly be very difficult to apply the same procedure to polyphonic structures," therefore, "Ruwet I" seems to have taken Lévi-Strauss's metaphor too literally in two ways, first confusing analytical summaries with raw data, and subsequently confusing a metaphoric structural "score" with an actual representational score. The latter confusion at least is hardly to be wondered at, since Lévi-Strauss himself was none too careful about keeping metaphorical model and target structures separate, most notoriously in *Le Cru et le cuit* (1964:23):

> For if one has to recognize in Wagner the undeniable father of the structural analysis of myths . . . it is highly relevant that that analysis was first made *in music*. When we suggested, then, that the analysis of myths was comparable with that of a full score (Lévi-Strauss 1958:234), we were only drawing the logical consequence of the Wagnerian discovery that the structure of myths is unveiled by means of a score.

211

But to say that the "analysis of myths [is] comparable with that of a full score" is not the same as to say that the "analysis of myths . . . was first made in music." The two propositions, like most pairs of analogies, are not transitively related (and cf. Pettit 1975:104–06). The metaphor that individual performance parts are to a full score as mythic stories are to mythic structure is heuristically most effective. Likewise the notion that the mythic structure of a Wagner opera fully reflects and is reflected in its musical structure is freely granted (and see Table IV below and the accompanying discussion). But a full score is not itself therefore a musical structure; it is only a representation of the polyphonic surface of such a structure. The orchestral score of Wagner's *Tristan und Isolde* represents the musical events of the work; the structure of the work is something else again.

It would indeed be cumbersome to print full lumps of the orchestral score of *Tristan* one above the other in a chart for structural analysis, even more cumbersome than to print whole speeches from its libretto along vertical and horizontal axes in order to make a chart of its mythic relationships in terms of "subjects" and "functions" in the mode of the chart of the Theban myth cycle. But just as each "subject" relationship in the myth cycle was centered in the matrix by a summarizing salient catch phrase (presumably properly indexed and interpreted to the mythic narrative), so also the "subjects" and "functions" in a piece of music are customarily represented in an abbreviated form in musical charts. Of course, passages of polyphonic music to be compared can sometimes be set out directly in vertical alignment; it is simply a question of how complex the scores are to start with, to what extent they can be reduced to short score without losing the point to be made, and whether the graphic immediacy to be gained in aligning the surface representations outweighs the more cumbersome appearance. In Example 7 of "*Il Serse* Trasformato" (Powers 1962:89–90), for instance, I set out scores for an aria by Bononcini and an apparently very different setting of the same text by Handel in vertical alignment, with gappings and stretchings, in order to show that the later setting was, despite great differences in the musical surface, a straightforward *rifacimento* on the structure of the earlier one. This fact leaps out simply and vividly from the display in a way that neither verbal description nor a tabular representation could have made so convincing. But to have shown the similarly but more complexly related pair of arias whose notation appears in Example 5 of the same article (p. 83–5) in that way would have been impossibly cumbersome. Equivalences in motivic and harmonic detail had to be described separately, with references to the notation; then the large-scale formal equivalences could be set out symbolically, with symbols defined sufficient to the purpose, as shown in the quotation and Table II below (p. 86):

A summary of the two *prime parti* in tabular form will show the structural and thematic relations between them most clearly. Arabic numerals represent measure numbers, Roman numerals represent the tonal centers; the letter "R" represents instrumental *ritornello,* the letter "a" the line "*crude furie degl'orridi abissi*" and its [musical] subject, the letter "b" the line "*aspergetemi d'atro veleno*" and its corresponding [musical] settings.

In this layout of course, the roles of horizontal and vertical axis are reversed; the successive units of each piece separately are read downwards, while the equivalences claimed for the two pieces are horizontally aligned.

Table II: Two settings of "Crude furie" (__Serse__, Act III)
(after Powers 1962:86)

Bononcini				Handel		
I	1–16	R		I	1–8	R
I	16–19	a		I	8–10	a
I	19–21	R				
				I	10–19	b
V	21–34	b		V	19–30	b(a)
V	34–35	R		V	30–32	R
				V	32–34	a
				I	34–36	R
			modulates	36–40	a
I	35–51	b		I	40–48	b'
I	51–53	R				
I	35–51	b		I	48–53	b(a)
				I	53–56	b(coda)
I	54–58	R		I	56–60	R

213

Ruwet himself, like everyone else, has established and then manipulated alphabetic symbols not only for medieval monody but also for multipart music. For his analysis of the "Prélude" to Debussy's *Pelléas et Mélisande* in Ruwet 1962/72, the (piano-vocal) score is printed on p. 92–3 with measure numbers, which in an analytic chart on p. 91 are keyed to alphabetic symbols; these in turn are used in the subsequent discussion as names for the surface units in question.[11] Ruwet's segmentation of the passage to be symbolized was strict and mechanical, but the symbols are the same kind as those in my chart of the two settings of "*Crude furie,*" and his use of subscripts and superscripts on a given letter to separate claimed variants required simple music-analytic decisions no less than mine.

To use a letter of the alphabet to represent a formal division or theme is of course a commonplace convention. An equally commonplace convention is the designation of a pitch-class as "tonic" or "I" (or "i"), to denote that the harmonic relationships in a whole passage are claimed to form a system devolving ultimately upon that pitch-class. These two conventions are obvious instances of musical "subjects" and musical "functions" being represented by abstract symbols or catchwords for convenience of analytic discussion or chart-making. Once particular musical subjects or functions are established as such, by whatever combination of intuitive discovery and rigorous verification may be appropriate to the case at hand, then simple symbols standing in for those subjects or functions can be displayed so that "equivalent sequences are . . . written one under the other . . . [while] the text is read from left to right . . ." and so on, but now in symbols. For example, the aforementioned staff-notation chart displaying the melodic type for the Gregorian mode 2 Graduals (Suñol 1935: Table F) can be rewritten in a much smaller space if symbols are used for the various recurring units. Charts displaying the same melodic type with alphabetic letters (with ancillary marks), which are in turn keyed to an inventory of the melodic units in question, may be seen in Apel 1958:359–61. And as with monody, so also with polyphony. There is no need to display complete stretches of representational score in a metaphoric score so long as the structural units are properly established and clearly keyed to the notated score.

2.3 Metaphoric Scores. The musical illustrations in Edward T. Cone's "Stravinsky: The Progress of a Method" (1962), are an exemplary case in point. They are paradigmatic-syntagmatic charts of multi-part music, matrices like the Lévi-Strauss Theban myth chart. Their summary "catchword" entries are not verbal fragments, however, but fragments of staff-notation, which are then assigned to paradigmatic classes with alphabetic names. Rhythmic and melodic configurations in Stravinsky's music are generally expressed over relatively static harmonic, registral, and tone-color blocks, so that Cone was able in most cases to symbolize contrastive oppositions by simply writing out in register the pitches of the more or less static basic chords on one, two, or three staves, with instrumentation noted; for one element only (in stratum "B" of the *Symphonies of Wind Instruments*) he needed to identify an independent thematic contour.

Example 5 includes two excerpts from Cone's chart for the *Sympho-*

214

nies of Wind Instruments, representing the first 21 measures (Example 5-A) and 53 measures from later on in the first part of the piece (Example 5-B). Cone described his analytic purpose, the indexing of the chart to the score, the assignment of alphabetic names, and the display of paradigmatic equivalences, as follows (1962:21):

> The sketch of the *Symphonies of Wind Instruments* is not meant to serve as a complete linear and harmonic analysis but is rather intended to make clear to the eye the way in which the strata are separated, interlocked, and eventually unified. The thematic material represented by the capital letters is easily identifiable through the corresponding rehearsal numbers in the score; my own notation presents the minimum necessary for following the important lines of connection. These should be read first of all straight across—from the first appearance of A to the second, thence to the third, and so on. If this is done, the continuity of each layer should become immediately apparent.

Table III below is a homomorphous replica of Cone's sketch (his Example 1) up to rehearsal no. 44, which completes the first of the two main divisions of Stravinsky's composition. Cone's own alphabetic symbols have simply been substituted for the fragments of staff notation, for typographical convenience and to highlight the graphic design. The first three columns are equivalent to the beginning of his chart, shown in my Example 5-A. My Example 5-B shows Cone's staff-notation "catchwords" for the running music for flute and clarinet that forms the "E" stratum along with the simultaneous superimposition of references to the "B" and "D" strata in other instruments. Letters and lines A through F, with their corresponding staff-notation "catchwords," represent what Cone takes to be the six fundamental strata of the work; letters X and Y denote two classes of transitional block that can be associated with more than one stratum. Different levels in the vertical dimension, then, represent different structural strata; each level corresponds to a column in the Theban myth chart and represents a paradigm.

The horizontal orientation of the paradigms and the use of fragments of notation as "catchwords" make Cone's structural score at the same time a kind of shorthand "sketch" (as he put it) of the representational score. For whenever segmental blocks are successively juxtaposed, reading from a given level in one column to a different level in the next also includes horizontal movement from left to right, as though one were reading a representational score; and when segmental blocks appear in the same column they are to be read not successively but simultaneously. In this latter feature the "sketch" is not homomorphous with the Theban myth chart. Yet it is by no means merely an abbreviation of the surface of the music, since the contents of any given horizontal line are not extracted from the instrumental parts of the actual score but from combined features of instrumentation, harmony, register, and occasionally contour

215

Example 5-A (after Cone 1962, Example 1)

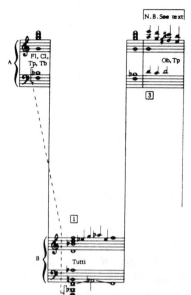

etc.

N.B.: "the little passage at No. 3 ... looks for-ward, both metrically and motivically, to the future F." (22)

216

Example 5-B (after Cone 1962, Example)

Table III: A chart of Stravinsky's **Symphonies of Wind Instruments**
up to rehearsal no. 44, modeled on Cone 1962, ex. 1.

```
[A]   A    A    X    X                          A      A    AX
[D]                       D   Y   D   D        D              Y    Y
[C]              C        (A+C)                   C      C
[B]   B    B         B    B---   B   B   BBX  B                    B
[E]                       E[E]E[E]EX       E
[F]
```

(compare for instance the representatives for the "B" stratum in my Examples 5-B and 5-A). The sketch therefore combines a shorthand surface representation of successive and simultaneous blocks of sound with the structural representation of their syntax and paradigms in a particularly powerful and elegant way.

That Cone's metaphoric score can come as close as it does to being a shorthand representational score, however, is a consequence of the Stravinsky compositional "method" that Cone was demonstrating, a "method" that results in a kind of music in which not only the underlying structure but also the surface of the music is one of direct, even abrupt, contrast. Both surface and structure comprise separate or simultaneous juxtapositions of strata of sonority whose underlying distinctive-feature parameters—instrumentation, harmonic type, tempo, and so on—are also the foreground of the music. Much of Debussy's music, including the "Prélude" to *Pelléas* and other music analyzed in Ruwet 1962, was composed with this "method" too. Few musical styles or languages, however, will lead to a chart of musical structure that is so much like a representation of the musical surface. The chain of links from surface to structure, from representational score to metaphoric score, is usually somewhat longer and less clear-cut.

One sees, at any rate, that it is irrelevant to the displaying of a musical structure whether musical notation or some other kind of symbols be used, and that the choice of dimensional orientations too is a matter of appropriateness to the task at hand. What particular graphic design is employed is purely a matter of heuristic efficiency, convention, even aesthetic preference. A completely different kind of geometry may be seen in Table IV, a translation of Alfred Lorenz's chart of the overall tonal/dramatic structure of Wagner's *Tristan und Isolde*. Some aspects of the temporal succession of events are represented by a circle; all other spatial orientations represent timeless structure. Rectilinear orientation denotes categories in structural opposition, diagonal orientation denotes categories in structural subordination, and distance from the center of the

217

circle denotes distance from the core level. The very elements represented in this chart are already at a level well below the surface, and the chart has the additional exemplary attraction of being a genuine structural chart based on a musical and mythic structure created by Wagner, Lévi-Strauss's "father of the structural analysis of myths."

A general concatenation of principal tonalities and correlated dramatic content is represented by the circular dotted line connecting "beginning/*a* minor/longing" [the "*Vorspiel*"] with "ending/*B* Major/ecstasy" [the "*Liebestod*"]. These two keys can be taken as the minor subdominant and the dominant of *E* Major, which Lorenz claimed as the underlying tonal center: "The whole *Tristan* is nothing but a phrygian cadence iv⁶ to V [of *E* Major] composed out on a gigantic scale" (1926: 179). This is a cogent instance of the structuralist notion that a fundamentally determining deep level need not manifest itself directly. The tonality of *E* Major rises only once to the musical surface, in Tristan's Act III vision of Isolde's journey to him ("wie sie selig . . . wie schön bist du"), roughly 50 measures out of 5500. Lorenz observed (ibid.:177) that

218

> the tonic in the work as a whole is as good as not sounded, but is only expressed through the subdominant of the beginning and the dominant of the end. But [Table IV] shows how the tonal relationships are all parallel with the meanings in the work if [and only if] one assumes *E* Major as central point and principal key.

Lorenz's structural chart is designed to show a pattern of distinctive feature oppositions underlying the tonal relationships, which include oppositions of mode (Major/minor) and subordinate relationships of key (tonic-dominant, tonic-subdominant) ibid.:177–79):

> The relative major/minor keys are oriented horizontally, the parallel major/minor keys vertically; the subdominants are half-left over the tonics, the dominants half-right . . . The meaning of a relative tonality is a certain negation of the condition expressed in the original tonality, while the parallel tonality sets up a direct opposition.

Still broader oppositions, such as "violent death/redeeming death" and "affirmation/denial," are aligned horizontally on opposite sides of the circle that denotes temporal succession. The tonalities of the former pair are connected in that their tonic triads have two common tones (as do the relative Major/minor and the parallel Major/minor oppositions), but the particular connection here is that the root (*A*♭) of the (*A*♭) Major triad is opposed by the fifth (*G*) of the correlated (*c*) minor triad, Hugo Riemann's *Leittonwechselklang* ("leading-tone-substitution-sonority"). The tonalities "affirmation/denial" are related only indirectly, through their relative-mode opposites "longing/ecstasy," which are in turn subordinated to the main tonality "image of love" [*Liebes-Idee*] in the center of the circle. Yet more remote levels of opposition and subordination appear still farther outside the circle, and more crucial ones inside the circle.

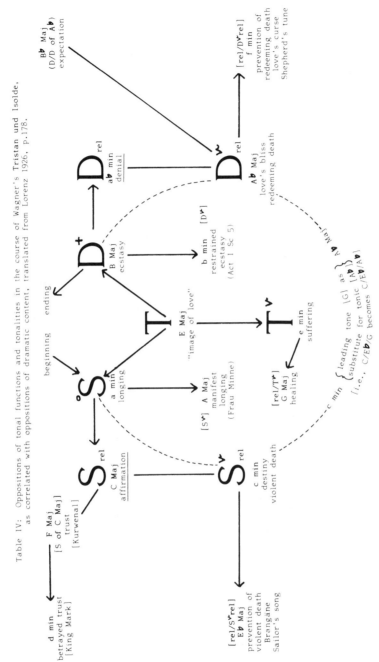

Table IV: Oppositions of tonal functions and tonalities in the course of Wagner's *Tristan und Isolde*, as correlated with oppositions of dramatic content, translated from Lorenz 1926, p.178.

T=tonic S=subdominant D=dominant D/D=dominant rel=relative major or minor ⌄=parallel major or minor
The dotted circle represents the temporal succession through the course of the opera as it occurs. Straight-line connections, and all vertical and horizontal relationships, are structural only. (o and + are symbols from Hugo Riemann's notation for functional harmony, attached to minor and major triads, respectively, reflecting his original "dualist" hypothesis that the "root" of a minor triad is really its fifth.)

219

Lorenz 1926, Hucke 1953, Cone 1962, and other studies mentioned in passing such as Ferretti 1938 on centonate chants or Bayard 1954 on tune-families, and many others not mentioned, can illustrate that the on-going 20th-century musicological and music-theoretical traditions had not been wanting in breadth of subject, variety of technique, or interesting and provocative results on the subject of musical structure. Musical scholars may well and profitably look to linguistics for suggestive notions, but the differences between music and language are great, and the special difficulties of working with music greater still, and no amount of even genuine sophistication and experience in linguistics can serve a musical scholar as substitute for an informed awareness of both the methods and the matter of musical studies themselves.

2.4 Melodic Types and Generative Grammar. By way of illustration, I conclude this division with an examination of Robin Cooper's "Abstract Structure and the Indian Rāga System." Cooper has worked out (1977:27)

> a simple and explicit grammar . . . which generates a large number of correct rāga scales and, as far as I know, no incorrect ones. It does not handle rāgas derived from mixed *thātas* [heptatonic collections] . . . [and] the nature of the melodic function which generates well-formed possible extemporizations from the final output trees of the grammar is not clear . . .

So far as it goes there is nothing wrong in this, though as "Ruwet II" has written in another connection, "it strikes me by the contrast between the *ampleur* of the means put to use and the *minceur* both of object and results" (Ruwet 1975:19). Even on the level of the "rāga scale" the ma-chinery cannot cope with required accidentals, nor without its "me-lodic function" can it deal with so called *vakra* "crooked" *rāga* scales, for *rāga*-s in which one or more scale degrees are regularly taken out of order in ascent or descent. In practice the majority of *rāga*-s show this latter feature to some degree; for instance the only actual Indian music dealt with in the article belongs to such a *rāga, sūhā.*

The real problem, though, lies in the mixture of uncritical enthusiasm for the generative-grammar fashion with uncritical reliance on secondary sources (such as Daniélou 1968) and second-hand ideas (such as those from Reese 1940:163, as cited on p. 9). A musical scholar—or for that matter a generative grammarian—ought to have been disturbed by the fact that "the melodic function which generates well-formed possible extemporizations . . . is not clear." It is not clear because it was elimi-nated in the grammar itself. Cooper's generative trees (p. 28–30) are right enough in starting from "*rāga*" at the top of the tree, like the generative grammarian's "S," and in putting "*pūrvānga*" and "*uttarānga*" in the first branch positions, those occupied by "NP" and "VP" in a phrase-marker. But at that point the term "tetrachord" is substituted for the term "anga," and the tree goes dead. Pitch-collections—partial scales—have been substituted for what in fact includes melodic content also, the anga-s, and the "melodic type" aspect of rāga has been thrown out. But there is no reason to suppose that rewriting out from the deep structure of a rāga to the surface structure of "well-formed possible extemporizations" is at some point going to give, so to speak, tones rather than tunes. One should start at the other end, with the tunes, with the surface, with the ad hoc informal local rules for how to handle this place or that, in short, with the language itself. The "melodic function" is where the research should begin, not end. Even and especially at the preliminary phases of research a generative grammar is supposed to be able to account for some well-formed utterance or other, even if only produced by the linguist himself. The essays in generative grammar that I have seen do not start from deep structure and fail to reach any surface at all. Yet Cooper's grammar is never brought to bear even on the musical "utterances" quoted earlier in the article. Nor could it have been—it would not work—not because of anything wrong with the existing machinery, not even because the machinery was incomplete and admittedly not expected to reach so far as an actual musical "utterance," but simply because none of the "utterances" were rightly understood in the first instance.

221

Cooper reproduces Ruwet's *Geisslerlied* chart as an instance of how "constituent breaks in musical syntax can be recognized from the repetition of certain formulas" (ibid.:16–18). After a brief criticism of this approach in general, Cooper continues (p. 18):

> Analysis in terms of repeated formulas fails completely with classical Indian music. (25) is the *sthāyī* (first part of the *ālāp* or non-rhythmic introduction to the extemporization) to the rāga *Sūhā* as transcribed in Jairazbhoy (1971:200f) from the recording by Vilayet Khan which accompanies the book.

The musical example as in Jairazbhoy's book follows immediately, then the following comment (loc. cit.):

> I do not see any clear constituent breaks that could be made on the basis of repeated melodic formulae here.

My Example 6 is Cooper's Example 25 rearranged with the corresponding melodic motives vertically aligned in columns, in the manner of the *Geisslerlied* chart, the tables from Hucke 1953, and so on. Clearly, even in this short stretch of *ālāp* two formulas are unmistakably repeated, with a notated exactitude somewhere between the literalness of recurrence in the *Geisslerlied* transcription and the transformed equivalences of the next example in Ruwet 1962, a trouvère song (p. 121–25). These formulas appear in my columns labeled II and III, at the extreme left and right of Example 6. The recurring rising formula of II.3 and II.4 (f-e b-f) is extended by repetition in II.6, where it is used as part of the basic descent; the g concluding the middle appearance of the formula of column III (g-bb a/g-bb-g) is extended by several alternations of f and g to which I have not here assigned a separate column.

The numbering of the columns follows the order in which recurrent material appears for the first time. The major interruption in the chart was allowed to fall between columns II and III because formula II has two distinct syntactic continuations and approaches, one for rising and the other for falling, and the falling pattern f-eb-f-d is not interruptable in the larger context of the *kānaḍā* group of *rāga*-s, to which *sūhā* belongs. The arrangement whereby the initial motion away from the drone-tonic *c* and the subsequent return to it appear in the middle of the page rather than at the left is a matter of expository efficiency. This chart is a visual model of the melodic recursions taking place in one instance of a type that can have other instances. The correct geometry for this kind of musical chart is a spiral stripe down the outer surface of a cylinder, like a barber-pole. That is, taking Example 6 as a specimen, one has to imagine the end of line 1 brought round the barber-pole to meet the beginning of line 2, the end of line 2 coming round to meet the beginning of line 3, and so on. Example 6 is simply the barber-pole with its surface cut once at right angles to the spiral staff-line, at a convenient and appropriate place, and laid flat.

The analytical decisions governing the alignment of the opening and closing material in the second column on the page—I.1, I.2, and V.6— were admittedly informed as well as intuitive; the material was included only to complete the chart for the demonstration, and the arrangement would probably have to be made a little differently in a display of the whole *ālāp*. But the existence of formulas II and III at least is verifiable (if not discoverable) even in this excerpt by the kind of methods and model mechanically outlined by "Ruwet I" in 1966, and more subtly in some earlier as well as later musicological and music-theoretical studies. And these two formulas, including and especially motive II (f-eb-f) in ascent, are all-pervasive in Vilayet Khan's *sūhā* as transcribed by Jairazbhoy, including the part reproduced by Cooper. The continuation of Cooper's *sūhā* discussion, therefore, is as puzzling as his inability or unwillingness to see the repeated formulas in the first place.

My Examples 7-A and 7-B are unmodified replicas of the first part of Cooper's Example 26 and of his Example 27; about these vis-à-vis his Example 25 (my Example 6) he had this to say (p. 19):

> It seems fairly hopeless to look for constituent analysis that would show that (25) and (26) (which appears in Daniélou 1968:297 . . .) are similar in a way in which extemporizations of two different rāgas are not. (26) is again the *sthāyī* to the rāga *Sūhā*.

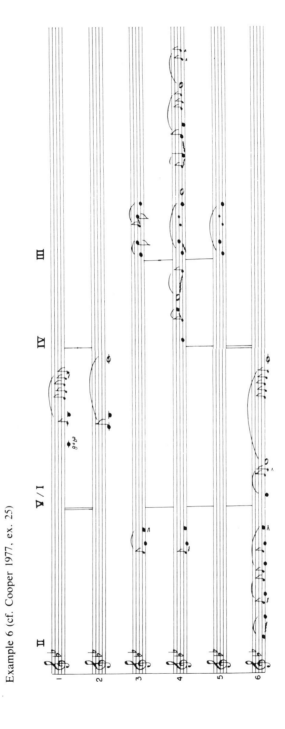

Example 6 (cf. Cooper 1977, ex. 25)

223

Example 7-A (after Cooper 1977, ex. 26)

Example 7-B (after Cooper 1977, ex. 27)

224

His Example 26 follows, whose first third is seen in Example 7-A here, and the discussion continues immediately:

> The problem here is similar to the one encountered in the Gregorian chant. What these two examples have in common basically is not observable surface phenomena, but rather the relationships between the notes they employ. The only way in which these relationships can be expressed is by abstracting them away from the music and representing them directly. By positing a rāga-mode such as (27) (which is the form given by Daniélou 1968:296), we can express very simply what no constituent analysis is seemingly able to do (i.e. what (25) and (26) have in common but no extemporization using different relationships shares).

Then follows his Example 27 (my Example 7-B), and the text continues:

> For the sake of simplicity in this paper I shall ignore differences between ascent and descent and simply regard rāga-modes as a set of pitch relations to the tonic which are represented in this case somewhat in the following manner:
>
> Sa(vādī) ri GaK Ma(samvādī) Pa NiK
> [c ("sonant") d eb f ("consonant") g bb]
>
> The relationship between this abstract mode and the actual extemporization is represented by the "melodic function."

Now the "rāga-mode given by Daniélou," Example 7-B here, had been (correctly) additionally labeled by Daniélou "*āroha* ascent/*avaroha* descent," though even without any such label the arrangement of the notes in rising and falling form is obviously making some kind of a statement about ordering. Before going still farther beneath the surface by eliminating that aspect of it, a musical scholar might well have wondered about the adequacy of the model even at that level. Daniélou's "ascent-descent" pattern omits e♭ between *d* and *f* in the ascent of the *pūrvâṅga*, a gap which Daniélou asserted in words as well (1968:296). Yet the rising pattern in his own actual example(s) for *suhā* is always as it appears in Example 7-A, *c-d-e♭-f-g*; no explanation is offered for the discrepancy between the abstracted "*āroha* ascent" and the instance presented as its embodiment.

In any case, whether the ascent of *suhā* as reported by Daniélou be taken as *c-d-f*, *c-d-f-g*, or *c-d-e♭-f-g*, it includes *d*, whereas Vilayet Khan's *suhā* invariably omits *d* in the *pūrvâṅga* ascent, throughout the excerpt transcribed by Jairazbhoy, and *a fortiori* in the excerpt quoted by Cooper. The "*āroha* ascent" of Vilayet Khan's *suhā* in its *pūrvâṅga* would have to be given as *c-e♭-f* or *c-e♭-f-g*. In short, what is left of Cooper's "melodic function" in Daniélou's ascent pattern for *suhā* (Example 7-B) has nothing to do with Vilayet Khan's *suhā* (Example 6), and the two instances of *suhā* given by Cooper are not at all "similar in a way in which extemporizations of two different rāgas are not." All they have in common is the pitch collection, which of course can be common to two different *rāga*-s as well as to two different instances of the same *rāga*.

Rather than retreat still farther into abstraction, a musical scholar having got so far might then begin to wonder if he had to do rather with a discrepancy in the sources, or perhaps even with two different entities altogether. And in fact this is the case. "A rāga-mode such as [Example 7-B]" would never be expected to "express . . . what [Example 6] and [Example 7-A] have in common" because they have no more in common than might two different *rāga*-s using the same pitch collection. They are not in fact really instances of the same *rāga* at all, in that no performer would have them both in his repertory and call them both *suhā*. They represent conflicting traditions, which is characteristic for minor *rāga*-s in general, and especially for those of the *kānaḍā* group. As Kaufmann has put it, "the performance rules in most *Kanada* ragas are often indistinct, and musicians have differing opinions about performance practice" (1968: 518). *Suhā*, in Vilayet Khan's version, is distinguishable from all other *kānaḍā* varieties precisely in formula II of my Example 6, the figure *f-e♭-f*, as used in ascending patterns such as *c-e♭-f* and *e♭-f-g*, and in the omission of *d* in the ascent.[12] This is the *suhā* with which I am familiar; it is common to the Agra and Gwalior traditions, as well as to the Jaipur and Rampur traditions represented in Bhatkhande's *Kramik Pustak Mālikā*. Daniélou's example for *suhā* in performance, "noted as played on the North Indian *Vīṇa* by the late Shivendranath Basu of Benares" (1968: Foreword), patently belongs to a different tradition altogether, a fact confirmed by his assignment of it to the "second quarter of the night" where in the other traditions *suhā* is taken to be a daytime *rāga*.

An exactly parallel situation arises in Cooper's discussion of Gregorian chant; anxiety to get to the supposed deeper layers of structure led him to overlook obvious discrepancies in surface features and make a premature incorrect generalization bearing on the musical system in question. As his Examples 7a-e appear five Gregorian chants transcribed from the *Liber Usualis*, in the liturgical categories (which Cooper did not mention) and with the finals and modal assignments shown in Table V here. Directly after the examples comes this observation (p. 9):

> An adequate analysis of Gregorian chant must account in some way for the musician's intuition that (7a-d) have something in common which they do not share with (7e).

After some discussion it turns out (p. 9–10) that:

> [it is] the relations between the different degrees of the scale (i.e. TSTTSTT) [which] is what (7a–d) have in common and where they differ from (7e), which is based on the mode . . . [STTTSTT]. If such abstract modes are not posited, the analysis cannot explain the relationships between the chants given in (7).

The scales in question are the so-called "Aeolian" octave-species with its lowest degree set at *D* (7a, 7b, 7c) or at *a* (7d) and the "Phrygian" octave-species with its lowest scale degree set at *E* (7e).

There are two curious points in this discussion. First, the distinction between the octave-species cited depends on the unstated assumption that in each of them one of the scale-degrees has primacy over the others, which turns out to be always the note occurring last in the chant in question; all scales cited by Cooper have those finals as their lowest degrees. Leaving aside the unexplained use of authentic octave-species having been cited for both plagal (7a–d) and authentic (7e) pieces, the assumption of the tonicity of the final must be made, for otherwise the octave-species cited are merely arbitrary segments of a single endless scale made up of groups of alternately two tones and three tones separated each time from one another by a semitone.

But granting the tonicity of finals for present purposes, Cooper's "musician's intuition" is in any case begging the question. Any intuition

Table V (cf. Cooper 1977, ex. 7)

Ex.	Category and chant	Final	Modal assignment in LU
7a	Communion Ego sum pastor bonus	D	2
7b	Antiphon Ante Luciferum	D	2
7c	Introit Veni et ostende	D	2
7d	Alleluia verse Confitemini	a	2
7e	Communion Gustate	E	3

that 7a–d belong to a single category that contrasts as a whole with another category to which 7e belongs must have been heavily influenced by a prior knowledge of the modal assignments of the five pieces in modern chant books. A properly functioning "musician's intuition," undistracted by foregone conclusions and abstract models, would have noticed that 7a, the Communion "*Ego sum pastor bonus,*" differs in some quite striking particulars from the other three pieces assigned to mode 2, considered as a group. This Communion appears as my Example 8-A, transcribed from the *Liber Usualis,* Cooper's source.

Cooper's Examples 7b, 7c, and 7d all show a strong emphasis on the final and the (minor) third above—these are *D* and *F*, or *a* and *c* in the case of 7d in mode 2 transposed—and this is in fact generally characteristic for pieces assigned to mode 2. But the final of "*Ego sum pastor bonus,*" the note *D*, is very weak, being used mostly as a passing or neighbor tone. The note *F*, a third higher than the final degree, occurs in the first phrase of "*Ego sum pastor bonus*" somewhat less weakly than the final, but in the second and third phrases it comes only once altogether, as a very weak lower neighbor tone in the second phrase. Most

227

Example 8: Two versions of the Communion for the feast of St. Thomas (modes 2, 8)

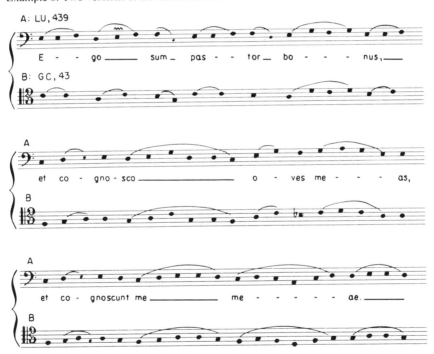

striking of all is the case of the next degree above the final (*E* in 7a–c, *b* in 7d). In Cooper's 7b-d this degree always occurs in subordinate positions, as a passing or neighbor tone, as is generally the case in pieces assigned to mode 2. In "*Ego sum pastor bonus,*" to the contrary, the degree next above the final—the note *E*—comes very strongly to the fore throughout, above all as pivot and medial final in the second phrase. In short, there seems to be a strong prima facie case for thinking there might be something wrong either with the piece or with the modal assignment.

So far might the musician's intuition go. Serious suspicion that verification of the intuitive analysis might be possible could be prompted by knowing in general that, as Apel had put it (1958:312):

> The most remarkable aspect of the Communions is their tonal behavior. No other type of chant includes such a large percentage of melodies showing tonal instability and, as a result, ambiguity of modal assignment.

Confirmation of the anomaly of "*Ego sum pastor bonus*" specifically can be found in Bomm 1929 (85–87), where one learns that this Communion is indeed one of those showing Apel's "tonal ambiguity and . . . ambiguity of modal assignment," having been given to mode 8 rather than mode 2 in a number of early sources. A mode 8 tradition for this Communion has been preserved in the Cistercian monastic liturgy; a transcription of it from the Cistercian Gradual may be seen in my Example 8-B, vertically aligned with the transcription of the mode 2 version from the *Liber Usualis.*

Apart from minor fluctuations around the half-step location in the first phrase, the differences between the two notations are a matter of mixed transposition, probably arising originally from notational-theoretical problems in writing the melody that are not relevant here. The two versions are notated a fifth apart in the first phrase, a fourth apart in the second and third phrases. The configuration type appearing in the third phrase, especially the concluding setting of "*meae,*" is frequently found in both mode 2 and mode 8 chants; it is of course the same intervallically whether placed to finish at *D* (for mode 2) or *G* (for mode 8). In any case, the relationship between the so-called "mode 8" melody and the so-called "mode 2" melody of "*Ego sum pastor bonus*" is much closer than the relationship between that Communion and the other mode 2 chants in Cooper's Example 7, which are mutually self-consistent. The historical evidence supports the "musician's intuition" that Cooper's Example 7a, "*Ego sum pastor bonus,*" has no more in common with the three unambiguously mode 2 pieces of his Examples 7b–d than they have with the unambiguously mode 3 Communion of his Example 7e.

I hasten to add that a chief reason why Cooper's article serves as so exemplary a warning against excessive enthusiasm for external models is much to its author's credit. The singular clarity of the exposition and the copious exemplification allow the inadvertent blunders in judgment to be seen by inspection, without any need for specialized knowledge; less attachment to the model and more attention to the music would alone have prevented them. Needless to say, however, an informed connoisseurship in the repertories, even a reasonable acquaintance with existing scholarship in the fields in question, would have made the avoidance of such blunders infinitely easier, a matter of educated intuition rather than laborious verification. The case for language models for musical analysis is not in itself weakened by its failure here, which is not in the machine but in its overzealous application to insufficiently prepared ground. The only case in point here is the case for knowing the traditions, both practical and scholarly, the case for critical attention to sources as well as systems. Whether and to what extent language models of this sort or of any sort might be useful in dealing with these repertories or with others is a different matter.

229

3. THE LINGUISTICITY OF MUSICS

If some scholars, seduced by well-formed linguistic models, have tended to underestimate the musicological and music-theoretical traditions, other scholars, in their eagerness to yield to the same seductions, have been tempted to oversimplify the data of comparative musical studies. I can testify to this from personal experience.

My long-standing hobbyist's interest in languages and linguistics for their own sakes has been powerfully reinforced by many years of work in Indic musicology. On the whole I have tried to avoid overt use of the music-as-language metaphor, but it has sometimes surfaced.[13] My underlying model in comparative-diachronic linguistics for a comparison of North and South Indian *rāga*-s, for instance, is occasionally betrayed by linguistic jargon of varying origins, such as "Lautverschiebung of accidentals" (1970:45) or "the signs m and n are in complementary distribution" (ibid.:68), and in another place there is a brief discussion of an Indian version of the music-as-language metaphor (ibid.:8). In viva voce lectures, to the contrary, I have never hesitated to talk freely (and no doubt loosely) of syntax versus paradigm, or of combination versus selection, in discussing melodic structures both foreground and background. And the fact is, there really are close resemblances between the way Indian classical music works and the way languages work, not just in hypothetical underlying "competence" but in "performance" too, literally as well as metaphorically.[14] Until a few years ago I took it for granted that I would find it easy enough to show that the parallels between music and language are as close and as deep elsewhere as they are for Indian classical music. But in recent years work with non-Indian Asian musics, and in the history of European music theory, has led me to think that the striking validity of the language-music analogy in Indian classical music is probably far from typical. It is not, though, that other musics are in no way formally like language. It is rather that few musics are as much like language as Indian music is.

When ''Ruwet II'' pulled back from some of the extreme and simplistic rigors of ''Ruwet I'' he made among others the following simple and obvious observation, so far as I know for the first time (1975:19):

> All human languages are apparently of the same order of complexity, but that is not the case for all musical systems.

If this be true—and I cannot imagine anyone would think otherwise once it is called to his attention—it highlights a fundamental deficiency in the general analogy of musical structuring with the structuring of languages. Put barbarously in terms of the analogy itself, the ''linguisticity'' of languages is the same from language to language, but the ''linguisticity'' of musics is not the same from music to music.

To Ruwet's telling observation I would add only that musical systems are much more varied than languages not only as to *order* of complexity but also as to *kind* of complexity. For instance, no two natural languages of speech could differ from one another in any fashion comparable to the way in which a complex monophony like Indian classical music or the music of the Gregorian antiphoner differs from a complex polphony like that of the Javanese *gamelan klenèngan* or of 16th-century European motets and masses. In monophonic musical languages we sing or play melodic lines more or less alone, just as we talk more or less one at a time in conversation, and our hearers follow accordingly. We do not all talk at once, saying different things, and expect coherently to be understood. Yet in ensemble musics with varied polyphonic lines we can (so to speak) easily make beautiful music together, which can be as easily followed by those who know how.

3.1 Ensemble Constraints and Linguisticity. A recently published essay by Alton P. and Judith O. Becker is entitled ''A Grammar of the Musical Genre Srepegan.''[15] This well-wrought study offers a generative grammar for the *balungan* ''skeletons'' of eight representative pieces of a simple Javanese *gamelan* genre used to accompany fighting in the *wayang* shadow puppet theatre. The analysis is thorough and complete; the

230

Beckers' generative grammar (unlike Cooper's) does reach to a musical surface, though that surface is both limited and simple, and the machinery (like Cooper's) seems rather big for the job at hand. But more to present matters, the authors point out (1979:42, n.4) that the

> contours which form the basis of this analysis are a kind of nucleus of a srepegan, played on only one kind of gamelan instrument. This is the rough equivalent of playing the theme of a symphony on one instrument.

And indeed, to have dealt with the other strata of the ensemble would have introduced into the analysis not so much a greater complexity—in *srepegan* both the other parts and the ensemble constraints are simple and quite reducible to rule—as rather a different kind of complexity altogether. As for the many elaborate and sometimes quite freely unfolding *panerusan* "connective-elaborative" strata of such as the *gamelan klenèngan* ensemble, individually and collectively, no linguistic theory can compensate for the absence of a theory of how the ensemble of parts is mutually controlled and constrained. And for this, language itself provides no parallel, as I said, since as a rule we do not speak different sentences in chorus.

Rules for simultaneous ensemble constraint cannot be assumed *a priori* to be the same kinds of rules or rest on the same foundations as rules for constraint on succession. They may well be similar, but they may well not be similar also. It seems to me that ensemble constraints must first be understood in their own terms, within musical cultures individually and comparatively, looking to what appear to be basic principles in each in light of the others. I would call such a study "comparative counterpoint." And though I am hardly qualified to provide an independent theory of ensemble constraints in Javanese *gamelan* music, I can suggest in this domain some curious seeming structural parallels between Javanese so-called heterophony and European Renaissance and medieval so-called polyphony.

The "heterophony" of Javanese *gamelan* music has often been said to be based on a *cantus firmus* "fixed melody" adorned with accompanying parts that move at a slower metric/structural pace and a faster melodic/ornamental pace; a middle stratum played by the metallophones called *saron*—or in small ensembles like *gamelon gadon* by the *slentem*— is taken to be the *cantus firmus*. At one time this *cantus-firmus*-like stratum was deemed to be itself the *balunganing gending* "skeleton of the piece"; this was the view of Kunst, Hood, and others. It seems more likely now that the *balungan* should be conceived as some rather more abstract "inner melody," to use Sumarsam's felicitous term (1975a), of which the *saron* (or *slentem*) part is merely the most regular and restricted cognizable embodiment. But in either case the *balungan* is the "subject" of the piece in the familiar instrumental genres. In some other genres the subject is not a *balungan* or "inner melody" but rather a definite "outer" melody to which the other parts serve as accompaniment. Instances are the *suluk* songs in the *wayang purwa* shadow plays, which accompany or are accompanied by *paṭetan* music, and *jineman* songs like "*Glatik glinding*" (= *Uler kambang*); where there is an overt *balungan,* as in "*Glatik glinding*" and many other well-known songs, it is a background to the vocal melody. Some instrumental *genḍing* are also based ultimately on an "outer" melody; the *balungan* of the *ketawang* called "*Pawukir*" for example, comes from its *gérong* (male vocal melody), which is in origin the tune used to recite the *macapat* verse meter named *Pawukir*.[16]

But whatever the "subject" may be, of whatever kind and by whatever name, and whether it is thought of as guide to the overall direction and tenor of the individual parts or merely as their underlying common content, it is that "subject" which gives each item in a *gamelan* genre its individuality, and it is the glue which binds the *panerusan* parts of the ensemble in this way rather than that. In short, even if the equation of Javanese *balungan* with polyphonic *cantus firmus* is a considerable over-simplification, the presence of a preformed subject of some sort, around and toward whose contours and (principal) tones the flow of the melodic ensemble is directed, is a feature of Javanese music as it is of European Renaissance and medieval polyphony. This seems to me quite in contrast with later European tonal-harmonic art music (and possibly African polyphonies?), where the flow is governed more abstractly, and from points and by principles farther in the background. Zarlino's 16th-century definition of "subject," *mutatis mutandis,* is not inappropriate to Javanese ensemble music too (Zarlino 1950:229–31):

232

> in every good counterpoint, or in every good composition, there are required many things . . . The first of these is the subject, without which one can do nothing. . . .
> The subject is that part from which the composer derives the invention to make the other parts of the work, however many they may be . . . such a subject may be of several kinds: it may be a tenor . . . whether of plainsong or of figured music; again, it may be two or more parts of which one follows the other in consequence or in some other way, for the various forms of such subjects are innumerable.
> When the composer has discovered his subject, he will write the other parts in the way which we shall see later on.

There are two principal ways in which the notes of a subject (Javanese or European) constrain the other parts of the ensemble. First, the particular simultaneity that can appear at any given point is selected according to the subject at that point. Second, and it follows from the first, the sequence of simultaneities in the ensemble is a function of the subject as a whole.

Though there are as yet no fully formalized rules governing simultaneities in Javanese *gamelan* music, there are much greater constraints on the simultaneities permissible at structural points than there are on those that may sound at points in between. At the fourth and final stroke of each *gatra* of a *balungan*, for example, the keyed metallophone *gendèr barung* normally sounds either a "fifth" (*kempyung*) or an "octave" (*gembyang*), whose lower tone (struck or held over) is of the same pitch-class as the *balungan* tone; the *gendèr* simultaneities that can occur with the first three strokes of a *gatra* are much less constrained by the *balungan* tones, and the simultaneities sounding on the *gendèr* alone between *balungan* tones are still less constrained vertically (see for instance Sumarsam 1975b:ex. 8ff.). This contrast between great vertical constraint at goal tones and two degrees of lesser constraint between them is of course not just analogous but precisely equivalent to the contrast between the usage of pefect consonance at cadence points and imperfect consonance and metrically weak dissonance between them in European contrapuntal polyphony.

In *gendèr* parts on the larger scale, constraints as to which of the permissible sonorities may appear at a given goal tone, as well as on the patterns that should be used to approach them, sometimes depend not only on the goal tone and the particular configuration of the *balungan* approaching the goal tone but also on the modal class—the *patet*—of the piece (Sumarsam 1975b:166–71, and McDermott & Sumarsam 1975:238–39); and the probability in turn of any particular tone occurring in the "subject" at a structural strong point in a piece is also strongly connected with its *patet* (see Becker 1972:183–87). This too has a European parallel, reflected in those Renaissance theories and practices that claimed that the Gregorian modes governed—or ought to govern—the composition of polyphony, as in Tinctoris's famous fifth rule of counterpoint (1961:135):

> that above absolutely no note, be it medium, superior, or inferior, should a perfection be taken by which a removal from its mode (*distonatio*) can happen.

This incipient linkage between modal structure and polyphonic structure was elaborately worked out later by German *musica poetica* theorists of the 16th century, such as Hermann Finck (1556) and Gallus Dressler (1563).

I find the ways of choosing and placing simultaneities in Javanese music sufficiently like the ways of choosing and placing simultaneities in European Renaissance polyphony—and (with less surety) sufficiently unlike the ways of using simultaneities in some other kinds of multi-part

music—to warrant looking at each of these ensemble musics in terms of
the other, rather than in terms of an exterior model, linguistic or otherwise.
And in general, I would expect to find that the more any musical practice
is subject to constraints of ensemble performance, the less easily amenable it will be to quasi-linguistic analysis.

3.2 Linguisticity and Extempore Musical Discourse. The language-
music structural analogy breaks down in another and rather more crucial
feature still. Languages begin, and linguistics began, with speaking. There
is a freedom-to-fixity parameter in language use that extends from conversation through such stages as story-telling, formal oratory, and formulaic poetic recitation on to literary composition (oral as well as written
down).[17] In musical languages this freedom-to-fixity parameter of use is
more often than not eccentrically skewed. For instance, there are individual musics (including Western classical music and many others) where
there is hardly anything corresponding with the spontaneous discourse of
language, where skilled performance is simply the rendition of more or
less set musical compositions. This contrasts very strongly with Indian
classical music, for instance, where spontaneous and flexible musical
discourse is as essential and almost as easy for the trained musician as
speech for the fluent speaker of a language. Indeed, the Indic term
ālāpă[na], denoting the principal genre for presenting a *rāga* (melodic
type) extemporaneously, simply means "discourse."

David Lidov has observed (1975:9–10) that

> in linguistics we need to account for the fact that everybody can speak original
> sentences . . . improvisation in particular, the usage in music which may be
> closest to spontaneous speech in function, may exhibit a special dependence on
> formula . . . a comparative study . . . of "formulas" in general . . . might be an
> important element in a semiotic theory of music.

Some very interesting and valuable notions about improvisation in music
have come out of recent work done by Bruno Nettl and some of his
students in Middle Eastern musics. Nettl's simple yet penetrating observation regarding improvisation in the Middle East and in South Asia
(1974:9) is that

> the improviser, when he performs a variety of versions of one mode . . . is really
> doing precisely that—performing a version of something, not improvising upon
> something. In other words, he is giving a rendition of something that already
> exists, be it a song or a theoretical musical entity.

Bringing this into the sphere of the linguistic analogy, we might say that a
musical improvisation in this sense is an extempore oratorical discourse,
on a traditional theme, which is elaborated and ordered using traditional
rhetorical forms and techniques. Of course these same themes and tech-

niques may just as well be used to make a precomposed set piece as an *ad hoc* oration. Nettl rightly points out (ibid.:10) that in South Indian music we

> find a given culture using essentially the same compositional techniques, whether the material is, by our standards, composed or improvised.

The analogy of music with language in its particular form of oratory also brings out clearly an essential distinction between set piece and extempore discourse in music, at least in South Asia, and I suspect in the Middle East as well. Nettl has rightly observed that there is no necessary distinction between composing and inprovising so far as the material and the procedures are concerned, and the oft made distinction between oral composition and written composition seems less significant still in principle, since fixed set pieces may perfectly well be orally composed and orally transmitted. But from the performer's point of view there is a very real difference between what is improvised and what is memorized. The analogy in oral language would be the distinction between speech that is spoken and a speech that is recited.

Nettl's piece on what is improvised in improvisation touches on the vastly variable improvisability of musics in many other thought-provoking ways. A certain carelessness in terminology, however, reflects a commonplace and disastrously oversimplified understanding of the actual material already available to comparative musical studies in this domain. Nettl's hypothesis (ibid.:11) is that

235

> The improviser . . . always has something given to work from . . . We may call it his model. In some cultures specific theoretical terms are used to designate the model: *raga* . . . and other, basically modal configurations—*patet* in Javanese and Balinese gamelan music, *dastgah* in Iran, *maqam* in Arabic and Turkish music.

The hypothesis is poweful, and surely correct. The instances, however, embody an unexamined cross-cultural generalization, which has time and again provoked frustrating comparisons that in fact cannot be made and obscured illuminating contrasts that can.

First, the inclusion of the Persian term *dastgāh* under the general rubric "modal configuration" is misleading, at least if an Arabic or Turkish *maqām*, an Indian *rāga*, or even a Javanese *paṭet*, is a "modal configuration." The modern Persian *dastgāh* is equivalent to the Azerbaijani "*mugam*" or the "*makom*" of the Central Asian *shashmakom*, but not to the *maqām* of Turco-Arabic usage. Jürgen Elsner (1975:233) has defined *dastgāh* as

> a succession of more or less fixed parts, variable in number but in an underlying definite order . . . each part of the *dastgāh* is characterized by a definite tonal structure and definite melodic characteristics . . . for each *dastgāh* there is one

particular part whose tonal-melodic character is definitive for the whole
dastgāh . . . So the *dastgāh* would be defined as a musical cycle that is in part
rhythmically and formally fixed and is characterized by a complex of tonal and
melodic characteristics.

The modal configuration from which each *dastgāh* takes its proper name
is the most important modal configuration in the *dastgāh*, and the returns
to its cadential pattern from time to time serve as binder to the whole
cycle, but the principal modal configuration in a *dastgāh*, more often than
not, is not the only one. The *dastgāh* cycle is a heterogeneous collection
of different kinds of items, some of which may function as models for
improvisation and some of which do not; but it is not a "modal configuration." The expression "*dastgāh-e Māhūr*" means "the system of items
headed by the modal configuration called *Māhūr*" and not "the modal
configuration called *Māhūr*."

These fine distinctions of naming are not so hair-splitting as may at
first appear. To notice that "*dastgāh*" means "system" and not "modal
configuration" can start one to wondering if there is any specific expression in modern Persian usage for "modal configuration" (other than the apparently obsolete terms "*maqām*" or "*pardeh*"), and if not, why not.
Certainly the cover term *gusheh* will not do. "*Gusheh*" can denote a
"modal configuration" (of limited compass) used as a model for improvisatory items, but it denotes not just those items but any item performable
in a *dastgāh* cycle, including items characterized by rhythmic style and
items that are fixed compositions.

Second, and more central to the question of oratorical discourse in
music, only some of the items in Nettl's list are models to work from.
Near Eastern modal entities—*maqām* in the Turco-Arabic sphere, certain
kinds of *gusheh* in the modern Persian terminology—are comparable to
Indian *rāga*-s as models for extempore oratorical discourse in music.
Javanese *paṭet* and European "modes" (*modi* or *toni*) most certainly are
not, for they are only tonal categories which at best constrain but do not
guide performance; as I have suggested above, the latter role is peformed
by something more like a "subject" specific to the item performed.
Maqām-s and *rāga*-s exist in completely open-ended systems of types
with dozens upon dozens of fluidly interrelated members. *Paṭet* and *modi*,
by contrast, constitute systems of classes that to all intents and purposes
are closed, each having a dozen or fewer members.

The reason for the confusion of these two general kinds of systems is
that the term "mode" has been used as a translation/equivalent for individual technical terms—*rāga, maqām, paṭet, chōshi, tiào, modus, échos*—
from many different musical cultures, not to mention its various adop-
tions as an investigator's "scientific" term in connection with musical

cultures less prolix with general musical terminology. Now an Indian *rāga* can indeed be thought of as a "mode" in certain respects; so too can a Javanese *paṭet*, but in very different respects. And if two things are each only in part equal to some third thing, they may well not at all be equal one to the other. To translate each of many terms singly with the word "mode" is not at all to say that all the things denoted by those terms taken together have in common some superordinate thing that is "mode." Yet "mode" is well on its way to becoming a reified cross-cultural universal, as Nettl's casual usage so neatly illustrates.

Insidiously consequent upon regarding such things as both a Javanese *paṭet* and an Indian *rāga* as "modes" is the fallacious generalization that because one of them is indeed a model for improvisation then both may be so regarded. This logical error regarding "mode" hopelessly muddles an absolutely fundamental distinction in peformance practice, and the same logical error is introduced with regard to improvisation. It may be reasonable to say that Javanese *gamelan* performers "improvise," but if so, it is an "improvisation" that has nothing to do with what an Indian performer "improvising" an *ālāp* is doing. A *gendèr barung* player, for example, has some choice as to what pattern he might play over a given four-beat *gatra* of *balungan*, but any of the patterns he might play are only versions, variants, or equivalent replacements of one another (see McDermott & Sumarsam 1975:234–35 for a perhaps even too strong statement of the case). Much about an individual pattern at a given point is constrained, as mentioned earlier, by the individual goal-tone of the *gatra* and by the point of origin from the previous goal-tone; the player may vary details here and there but not the general tenor. And more constraining still is the overall order of the sets of patterns to "choose" from or "elaborate" upon, which is of course not determined by the general modal category (the *paṭet*) but rather by the specific piece, from a fixed-rhythm *genḍing* with an "inner melody" *balungan* to a loose and flexible *paṭetan* that nonetheless corresponds at every point with the phrase of a shadow-play *suluk* song, as mentiond above. It is comparable with performance practices closer to home ranging between the ornamentally elaborating improvisations of a violinist on a Baroque adagio and the rendition by a traditional jazz ensemble of a "standard."

The Indian vocal or instrumental soloist rendering an *ālāp* is doing something very different indeed, something for which I know no such appropriately illustrative parallels in Western musical practices. There are loose general procedures in *ālāp*: one begins with lower lying material (where the *rāga* permits), coming to higher levels, and returning. The material itself consists of recognizable motivic types, to be stretched and compressed, added on to at head or tail or in the middle. The composite of

237

all the freely rendered and variously ordered tokens of these motivic types is a rendition of the melodic type, the *rāga*. As implied earlier, the closest European parallel is not musical at all, but rather extempore oratorical discourse on a prescribed general topic, following the pre-scribed general procedures of traditional rhetoric.

The difference between "improvisation" as elaboration on a specific item and "improvisation" using a stock of familiarly associated motives and turns of phrase is profound. Some musics feature the one, some the other, and some neither. I would suppose that the notion of "subject" or "item" or "piece"—the notion of the more or less fixed melody whether "inner" or "outer"—should be kept quite distinct from notions like "modal configuration" or "modal model" or "melody type," which im-ply freely manipulable melodic material available equally for improvised extempore musical discourse or for (oral) composition of fixed pieces. And not only "melodic subject" but also "melodic type" should be kept distinct from the notion of "mode" as a category in a classification sys-tem.

Among the differences between improvisation of details elaborating a fixed item and improvisation loosely guided by a modal model is that the latter has plentiful and obvious parallels in language use. The presence of modal models and the concomitant normal capacity for free extempore oratorical discourse in music characterize some complex musics, while other musics of equal complexity in musical product make no use of such models and have no such capacities. I would therefore expect to find that the less a musical practice lends itself to freely improvised musical dis-course, the less amenable it will prove to quasi-linguistic analysis.

4. LANGUAGE MODELS IN WESTERN MUSICAL THOUGHT

In each of the two preceding divisions of this essay I had occasion to comment on a generative grammar that had been proposed for an Asian music. In neither case was the generative grammar dealt with directly. In one instance I uncharitably pointed out how the author's unfamiliarity with the musical repertories in question and the scholarship dealing with them had led through gross misapprehension of surface features to unten-able preliminary generalizations. In the other instance I merely observed (following the authors themselves) that the generative grammar in ques-tion dealt with only one line of a multi-part texture, and I wondered to what extent rules for ensemble constraint would lend themselves to ex-planation in terms of transformational-generative grammar.

4.1 New Grammars for Tonal Music. Two currently ongoing amalgamations of transformational-generative grammar and music-analytical method are a preliminary study by Fred Lerdahl and Ray Jackendoff called "Toward a Formal Theory of Tonal Music" and the first part of "The Syntax of Prolongation" by Allan Keiler, both published in 1977.[18] Neither of my separate earlier reservations apply to these studies. Both studies deal with Western "tonal" music, a music with whose repertory and surface the authors are thoroughly familiar, and they deal with it as a multi-part music.

Lerdahl and Jackendoff have set up two pairs of analytical reduction conditions, four altogether. In the first pair, formal-rhythmic structure is derived through hierarchic levels, (first) of phrase-grouping boundaries and (second) of metric weight. In the second pair of reduction conditions "pitch hierarchization" is described, also on several levels in each of two domains; the first domain is "time-span"—that is, duration broadly speaking—the second comprises a quasi-Schenkerian "prolongation" of established pitch levels. As in Schenkerian analysis, and quite unlike transformational grammar, each of the four components of a Lerdahl and Jackendoff derivation analysis is not only hierarchically presented but also deals with acoustic substance at every level. These acoustic substances are shown visually with phrase-bows for phrase boundaries, columns and rows of dots representing stress pulses for metric levels, forks away from nodes in a tree representing relative durations in hierarchic levels of time-span, and notes on a staff representing pitches. This is in contrast with the analytic tree diagrams used by Keiler, which resemble those of transformational-generative grammar in the use of abstract immediate-constituent categories such as "tonic closure" (TC) and "dominant prolongation" (DP), like "noun phrase" (NP) and "verb phrase" (VP). When the "phrase-marker"—the tree or other diagram—is complete, then the "terminal" form must be rewritten substituting surface sounds.

Keiler does not so far seem directly interested in carrying his use of transformational-generative linguistics techniques beyond the sphere of "common-practice" Western tonal music. In his review of Leonard Bernstein's *The Unanswered Question,* however, he necessarily discussed the question of musical universals in a general way (Keiler 1978: 203–07), and was able to show in particularly telling manner, by reference to Bernstein's discussions, the more obvious pitfalls in making superficial musical analogies based on uninformed enthusiasm for linguistics (ibid.: 209–13).

Lerdahl and Jackendoff, to the contrary, have forthrightly claimed (1977:166–67) that the theory of musical syntax we have proposed here provides hypotheses about musical universals. Preliminary investigation has indicated that the theory can be modified to produce structural descriptions of pieces in styles as diverse as Macedonian folk music, North Indian music, and 14th-century French music . . . [though] a limited amount of the world's music, notably a good deal of 20th-century art music, would appear not to meet all four conditions.

I suspect that the expression "limited amount of the world's music" will ultimately read "substantial amount," and of course I look forward with interest to learning more about the preliminary investigations of the three styles mentioned. Given my present belief in the much greater range of variability as to both order and kind of complexity in the world's musics versus the world's languages, I can hardly imagine how a model developed really satisfactorily for the detailed structural explanation of one musical language is so easily to be modified to another, and all the more so if the original model be evolved from linguistics rather than from the musical disciplines.

4.2 Medieval Antecedents for Musical Grammar. But I do not mean to comment further on these studies now, and as before I am avoiding a close examination of the actual grammars proposed. My interest here continues to be primarily in the fact that linguistics is being used as a source for models, and in details of particular models and particular repertories only secondarily, for illustrative purposes. Lerdahl and Jackendoff's work, and Keiler's as well, originate in the question of whether and to what extent there is a valid analogy between the deep and surface levels of transformational-generative linguistics and the background-middle-ground-foreground *Schichten* of Schenkerian musical analysis. These studies still in progress represent but the latest phase of an ancient Western tradition for the discussion and analysis of music in terms borrowed from theories of language structure.

We now consider real music to be something performable as opposed to something theoretical. It would not be hyperbole to claim that the very idea that performable music might be susceptible to rational analysis was originally a consequence of making the analogy between language and music. As is well known, in classical antiquity the music of the philosophers and the music of the performers were separate; only the former was considered cognizable, and that as one of the sciences of number. During the Latin Middle Ages the desire of Carolingian and Ottonian learned clerics and monks to bring *musica* as a heritage of antiquity in line with Christian chant caused them occasionally to glance away from immutable and timeless quantitative relations to something more flowing, sequential, and hierarchic, to shift their musicological attentions from the numerical

240

arts of the *quadrivium* (including *musica*) to the language arts of the *trivium*, especially grammar and rhetoric. As Mathias Bielitz put it in the conclusion of his richly informative study *Musik und Grammatik* (1977: 241):

> Medieval music theory, to a not inconsiderable degree through reliance on the extramusical conceptual system of grammar, attained to the formulation as "music" of an orally transmitted "song" previously largely dependent on speech structures, and beyond that, to the notion of "music" as composition also obeying formal laws.

The fullest early articulation of the language-music parallel in the Western tradition occurs (so far as I know) in the anonymous 9th-century *Musica Enchiriadis*. The treatise begins as follows (Gerbert 1784:I, 152A):

> As the elementary and individual parts for the speaking voice are letters—syllables composed of them form nouns and verbs and they [in turn] the text of complete speech—so *phthongi*, which are called *soni* ["sounds"] in Latin, are the bases of the singing voice; and the content [*continentia*] of the whole of music comes down to them in the final analysis. From the coupling of *soni* [are formed] *diastemata* [= Latin *intervalla*], and from *diastemata* are formed *systemata* [= Latin *constitutiones*]. But *soni* are the first foundations of the chant.

Bielitz has found a model for this passage in Chalcidius's fourth century commentary on Plato's *Timaeus* (1977:31), which in turn he found to be derived from a second century Greek source (ibid.:30, 336).

241

Later on in the *Musica Enchiriadis* the analogy of music and language is made at the level of clause and sentence structure. The syntactic levels of speech, as marked off by the *positurae*—the punctuations—of the Latin grammarians are likened to the greater and lesser registral spans of melodic flow within a mode (Gerbert 1784:I, 159B):

> Modes are the species of melodies . . . Their lesser parts are the *cola* and *commata* of singing, which mark off the song at its endings. But *cola* are made by two or more *commata* coming together, although there are cases where *comma* or *colon* can be said interchangeably. And the *commata* are made by *arsis* and *thesis*, that is, rising and falling. But sometimes the voice rises and falls in *arsis* and *thesis* just once in a *comma*, at other times more often.
>
> The distance between the high and the low pitch in a *comma*, moreover, is called *diastema*. These *diastemata* in fact are now lesser, like the one we call a tone, now greater, having an interval of two or three on up to however many tones. Furthermore, as *cola* consist of *commata*, just so we call the compasses [*spatia*] of *commata*, *diastemata*; but the compasses that are in *cola*, or in any whole melody, we call *systemata*.

The connecting of temporal flow with registral space that is made here has not just its analogy but its precise equivalent in the Indian concept of *aṅga*, which likewise has both temporal and registral aspects, as part of a *rāga*.

A good specific illustration tying all together is to be found in the treatise of Johannes, ca. 1100 (Gerbert 1784:II, 242–43). (Note, however, the partial reversal in hierarchic order in the roles of *colon* and *comma*.)

> For just as there are three *distinctiones* (which can also be called pauses) namely *colon* or *membrum*, *comma* [or] *incisio*, and *periodus* [or] *clausura* [or] *circuitus*, so [it is] also in the chant. In prose of course, when something is read inconclusively [*suspensive legitur*] it is called *colon*; when a sentence is divided by a proper stop, *comma*; when the sentence is brought to an end, *periodus*. For instance, at "In the fifteenth year of the reign of Tiberius Caesar" [Luke 3.1] and at each of the [five] following [stopping] points there is *colon*; then where "under the high priests Annas and Caiaphas" is set down it is *comma*; but at the end of the verse, where "the son of Zachary in the desert" is, there is *periodus*. Likewise, when the chant pauses, raised up to the fourth or fifth note above the final, it is *colon*; when it is brought down to the final medially it is *comma*; when it reaches the final at the end, it is *periodus*, as in this antiphon [Example 9, after the Worcester and Lucca antiphoners, *Paléographie musicale* vols. 12 and 9]:

Example 9: an antiphon in mode 1, two versions

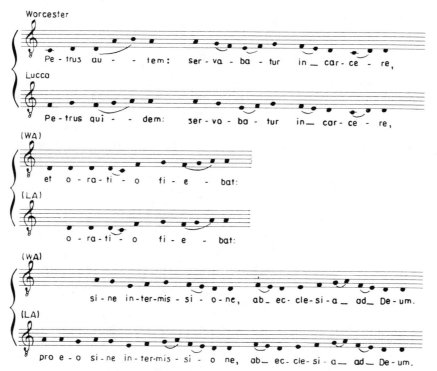

> "*Petrus autem*," colon; "*servabatur in carcere*," comma; "*et oratio fiebat*," colon; "*pro eo sine intermissione*," comma; "*ab ecclesia ad Dominum*," *periodus* . . . What the grammarians call in prosody *colon*, *comma*, *periodus*, moreover, some musicians call *diastema*, *systema*, and *teleusin*. *Diastema*, moreover, signifies distinctive figuration [*ornatus*] that occurs when the chant

pauses not at the final but suitably at another [pitch]; *systema* indicates figuration conjoined as often as a suitable pause in the melody is made at the final; *teleusis* is the end of the chant.

4.3 Musical Grammar in German Theory. A much better known and fully systematic application of language arts to musical structure, but modeled on rhetoric rather than grammar, was developed by German humanist musical theorists beginning around 1500. To the traditional medieval categories of *musica practica* and *musica theorica,* which were the ancient arts of the *cantor* and the *musicus*—the performer and the speculative theorist—they added a third category, *musica poetica,* to denote the relatively new art of the polyphonic composer. Foremost among the 16th-century writers who have actually shown what they meant by *musica poetica* in analytical terms were Gallus Dressler (1563) and Joachim Burmeister (1606). Their composition manuals pursue the analogy of music as oratorical discourse in a fashion which, literal-minded as it sometimes appears, nonetheless succeeds in integrating with admirable concision the disparate kinds of rules for vertical combination of tones, successions of vertical sonorities, and overall plan of entrances and cadences.[19]

The German rhetorical-verbal tradition for musical analysis thereafter never died out, though it has gone through several evolving phases. It was comprehensively developed in the 18th century, above all by Johann Mattheson (1737, 1739, and see Lenneberg 1968 for some translated excerpts). "Rede-Kunst" is also the model for the compositional prescriptions of Heinrich Christoph Koch's *Versuch einer Anleitung zur Composition* at the end of the 18th century. Koch's doctrine of composition is founded on a theory of musical phrase which, like the medieval Latin constructions many centuries earlier, turns not just on language but on the hierarchic levels of punctuation. The resemblance in detail as in principle is striking, and inherent in a certain characteristically European mode of thought, since Koch (as his discussion shows clearly) had no inkling of his medieval forerunners (1787:342–6):

> As certain more or less marked "pauses in thought" [*Ruhepuncte des Geistes*] are necessary in speech generally, and thus also in the products of those fine arts that attain their ends through language, namely poetry and oratory, just so are certain "pauses in thought" necessary in melody if it is to work on our sensibilities . . . By means of these more or less marked "pauses in thought" the products of these fine arts permit of being resolved into greater and lesser sections. Through the most marked, for example, speech falls into separate periods, and through the less marked in turn the periods fall into individual sentences [*Sätze*] and segments of speech [*Redetheile*]. And as with speech, the melody of a piece of music permits of being resolved into periods, and these again into individual phrases [*Sätze*] and melodic segments [*melodische Theile*] by means of similar "pauses in thought." . . . If we consider in the products of the art of music the

243

different parts of which periods consist, we find chiefly two characteristics through which they are distinguished as parts of the whole: first, the manner of their endings . . . and second, the length of the parts . . .

The endings of the phrase are certain formulas which allow us perceptibly to distinguish the more or less marked "pauses in thought," and there is yet no generally accepted technical term at hand . . . in the absence of a completely suitable expression, we will name this subject "melodic punctuation" [*melodische Interpunction*], on account of the similarity it expresses with the larger and smaller pauses in thought in language . . . for example, the full stop closes the periods of speech as the cadence the *Period* of melody, and the *Absatz* and *Einschnitt* ["segment"=Latin *incisio*=Greek *kómma*] distinguish the melodic parts of the *Period,* just as the semicolon and comma [distinguish] the smaller parts of the period of speech.

The extent of the melodic phrases and their proportion—or the relationship they have to one another from the point of view of the number of measures—will be designated by the expression "rhythm."

Koch then provided some concocted instances to illustrate the music-as-language metaphor, adding for them some aspects of the third language art of the *trivium,* logic, to the already present aspects of grammar and rhetoric. Alongside the familiar metaphor of the musical "subject" appears the notion of predication, and added to the metaphor of coordinate clauses appears the notion of restrictive subordination, or in more modern linguistic terms, embedding (ibid.:350–56):

If subject and predicate in melody could be as definitely distinguished as in speech . . . then an incomplete sentence [*Satz*] or "incise" [*Einschnitt*] would be a melodic part such that it was lacking either a subject or a predicate. The completeness of a simple sentence [*enger Satz*] would be expressed through the linking of a predicate with a subject; and an expanded sentence [*erweiteter Staz*] would then be either one in which more than one predicate would have been linked to the subject, or one in which either the subject or the predicate or both at once would have been more precisely defined by subordinate ideas.

I want to pursue this comparison of melodic passages [*Sätze*] with sentences [*Sätze*] of speech for a moment. For instance, if we want to consider the following *Satz* from this logical point of view:

Example 10

it would be a simple complete *Satz,* because the main idea or subject contained in the first two measures gets a certain orientation [*Richtung*], a certain definition [*Bestimmung*], in the two subsequent measures. Let him to whom this seems to be too subtle or sophistic try reshaping the last two bars in different ways, that is, linking other predicates with the subject, for instance:

Example 11

Example 12

and it will be found that through the alteration of this predicate the subject has another definition, another orientation . . .

If such a simple *Satz* should be expanded, and the predicate, for instance, more strictly defined, then perhaps the *Satz* would appear in the form of Fig. 1; if more than one predicate were linked with the subject, it might appear as in Fig. 2.

Example 13

Figure 1.

245

Figure 2.

In Fig. 3 the *Satz* would be expanded by a tighter definition of the subject, and in Fig. 4 subject and predicate as well would be more strictly defined . . .

Figure 3.

Figure 4.

> However, I am abandoning the comparison because, as already said, subject and predicate cannot be determined distinctly enough. We must therefore use the presence or absence of "pauses in thought," and learn to distinguish the peculiarity of a phrase, in regard to its completeness, through feeling.

By the concluding observation of course, Koch meant to convey that the metaphor of music as language was after all only a metaphor. For him and his time, a subject and predicate were not merely syntactic categories, they were logical categories, and therefore had to have contents, meanings in the ordinary sense, in order to be manipulated further. So even though the composition system in the rest of the *Versuch* is built up from these fundamental sectionings taken from language, the elaboration of the system is carried out by musical means, in terms of a purely musically defined syntax.

Other late 18th- and early 19th-century theories of musical form, such as Reicha's *Cours de composition musicale,* also used sentence analysis as a metaphorical source of terms and categories for musical analysis, and of course such common musical terms as "subject," "phrase," "cadence," and many others are survivals from one or another phase of the music-as-language metaphor. And so the ancient habit continues. Koch himself was one of the principal models for Hugo Riemann's much misunderstood normative theory of musical phrase (cf. Riemann 1903:199–200, 270–71), and Riemann's theory in its turn has recently come in for sympathetic attention again in David Lidov's recent studies on the semiotics of the musical phrase (1975), which I quoted earlier in connection with improvisation in music and spontaneous versus memorized speech.

5. CONCLUSION

In this essay I have urged that in applications of the music-as-language metaphor we should attend to diverse musical traditions in musical terms, including not only traditions of the musics we study but also traditions of how we study music. By the same token, modern analytical theorists of Western music can do worse than reflect on theories and studies of other musical practices. These things are begining to happen, and it augurs well for what may emerge as a genuine and revitalized ''comparative musicology.'' Language models for musical analysis used circumspectly can contribute fundamentally and not superficially to the musical disciplines, as they have more than once over the past millennium or so. Bielitz's characterization of the upshot of the medieval phase in this ongoing tradition can hardly be improved on for our own time (1977:9):

> Thus grammar, with its well-known terminology, provided section-categories for music theory, which then sought to define the actuality of musical articulation by its own methods, and thus (as it were) struggled to fill out the expressions taken over from grammar. But grammar, with its defined expressions for articulations, is thereby also an outward model and stimulus for the aforesaid conception of an autonomously manipulable musical substance.

NOTES

247

1. This is apart from the slow and dignified, metrically and rhythmically free *ālāp* style, also of purely Indian origin, also taken into *sitār* playing from vocal music via the *bīn*.

2. This matter is demonstrated in full in my forthcoming essay *The Structure of Musical Discourse: A View from Madras.*

3. A philosophical critique of this aspect of the metaphor may be read in Boretz 1969:34–36, 51–64 (''Linguistic Models as Musical Models''), and 70–71. A recent general discussion of the metaphor may be seen in Narmour 1977:21, 167–69, 193, and 203–08 (''Music Versus the Study of Language''), as well as Chapter 9 ''The Linguistic Analogy''; see also Keiler's review (1979). For an introductory survey in plain language of the broad structuralist context and musicology, see Turnstall 1979.

4. Ruwet's segmentation chart of the *Geisslerlied* reappears from time to time in the literature of musical semiology (e.g. Nattiez 1975:244–45, Cooper 1977:16–17, and most recently in Keiler 1980a), rather like Lévi-Strauss's chart of the Oedipus myth (see Table I-A below) in literature about structuralism.

5. Lidov has commented briefly on a transformation in one of the analyses (1975:62–63); Ruwet has himself quoted and expanded on Lidov's criticism (1975:27ff.), following Lidov's lead also in using an example by Mozart taken from Rosen 1972 to illustrate his rejoinder.

6. Part B of Hucke's table, which purports to show that melodies belonging to other liturgical classes are also members of the type, is omitted here.

7. In Ferretti 1938:113–16, many other mode I antiphons are similarly analyzed by means of paradigms in syntactic categories, likewise in connection with their texts, but the presentation is not in the form of a chart but rather in the form of an inventory, in which each motivic type is shown once in notation and assigned a number which is thereafter simply noted by the textual segments of those antiphons in which it appears. See also example 9 below for a mode 1 antiphon in two versions whose opening gestures have the same neumes, both establishing *a*, but with different actual pitches.

8. Compare this with the surface analysis of mode 2 Tracts by segmental distribution of fixed formulas in Apel (1958:323–29)—which however is expressly superimposed (324) upon Peter Wagner's original analysis of the mode 2 Tracts (Wagner 1921:353–57), in which they were laid out as ''free variations of a free psalmody'' (357).

9. The disposition of the matrix varies in the printed versions: that of Table I is based on the French version of 1958, both because the last item in column IV of the original English version and its many descendants seems to have been typeset too low, and also because this is the version Ruwet cited.

10. The musical score also furnished the basic metaphor in Nelson Goodman's formulation of the constitutive requirements of a work of art in his *Languages of Art* (1968), a linguistic philosophy of art in nominalist terms very different from semiology.

11. See also Nattiez 1975:250, 260–61, where Ruwet's derivation of an alphabetic symbol code for the "Prélude" is reproduced and then the symbols alone are rearranged in a tree branching diagram. See Nattiez and Hirbour-Paquette 1973 on the analysis of the *Pelléas* "Prélude."

12. In both these respects it resembles the *rāga bhīmplās,* and the effect of *bhīmplās* must soon be counteracted in rendering *sūhā* by the use of either *e♭-f-d* or *b♭-g,* both of which are alien to *bhīmplās* and reestablish the *kānaḍā* quality of *sūhā.* See Powers 1977: 318–(upper left corner)–19, and 328–29.

13. For references in my dissertation, written in the mid-1950's, see Powers 1977:309.

14. See my forthcoming *The Structure of Musical Discourse: A View from Madras* and also Powers 1977.

15. Becker 1979. The first version of this paper is summarized in Nattiez 1975:370–74.

16. Not all *gending* named after Javanese verse meters are so clearly connected with conventional recitation tunes for those meters, *Pangkur* being the most familiar case in point.

17. For a stimulating drawing of the parallels between formulaic poetic recitation and the corpus of Gregorian chant, see Treitler 1974; Treitler 1975 continues the story, but undervalues the aims and underestimates the methods of traditional chant scholarship.

18. Lerdahl is a composer and theorist, Jackendoff a linguist, and Keiler a linguist turned theorist. Keiler's "Music as Metalanguage" (in press b) came to my attention too late to be considered for the body of the essay. His discussion of Rameau's use of musical notation for both object language and metalanguage bears significantly on the matter of "acoustic substance" versus "abstract. . . categories" mentioned in the second paragraph of this section.

19. A translation of Burmeister's formal analysis of a Lassus motet was published in 1972 by Claude Palisca, with commentary.

REFERENCES CITED

Apel, Willi
    1958   *Gregorian Chant.* Bloomington: Indiana Univ. Press.

Bayard, Samuel P.
    1954   "Two Representative Tune Families of British Tradition," *Midwest Folklore* 4: 13–33.

Becker, Alton P. and Judith O. Becker
    1979   "A Grammar of the Musical Genre Srepegan," *Journal of Music Theory* 23(1):1–43.

Becker, Judith O.
    1972   *Traditional Music in Modern Java.* PhD dissertation, Univ. of Michigan, Ann Arbor.

Bhatkhande, V. N.
    1952   *Kramik Pustak Mālikā.* (Hindi version) IV. Hathras.

Bielitz, Mathias
1977   *Musik und Grammatik: Studien zur mittelalterlichen Musiktheorie.* Munich: Musikverlag Katzbichler.

Blacking, John
1973   *How Musical is Man?* Seattle: Univ. of Washington Press.

Boilès, Charles
1967   "Tepehua Thought-Song," *Ethnomusicology* 11(3): 267–92.

Bomm, Urbanus
1929   *Der Wechsel der Modalitätsbestimmung in der Tradition der Messgesange im IX bis XIII Jahrhundert,* Einsiedeln.

Boretz, Benjamin
1969   "Meta-variations: Studies in the Foundations of Musical Thought (I)," *Perspectives of New Music* 8(1):1–74.

Bright, William
1963   "Language and Music: Areas for Cooperation," *Ethnomusicology* 7(1):26–32.

Burmeister, Joachim
1606   *Musica Poetica.* Rostock: S. Myliander.

Cone, Edward T.
1962   "Stravinsky: The Progress of a Method," *Perspectives of New Music* 1(1):18–26.

Cooke, Deryck
1959   *The Language of Music.* London: Oxford Univ. Press.

Cooper, Robin
1977   "Abstract Structure and the Indian Rāga System," *Ethnomusicology* 21(1):1–32.

Daniélou, Alain
1968   *Northern Indian Music.* 2 ed. London.

Deva, B. Caitanya and K. G. Virmani
1968   "Meaning of Music: An Empirical Study of Psychological Responses to Indian Music," *Sangeet Natak* 10(Oct.–Dec.):54–93.
1974   *Semantic Descriptions and Synesthetic Relations of Raga-s.* Research Report II, New Delhi: Sangeet Natak Akademi.

Dressler, Gallus
1916   *Praecepta Musicae Poeticae. In* Bernhard Engelke, *ed., Geschichts-Blätter fur*
(1563) *Stadt und Land Magdeburg* 49–50:214–49.

Elsner, Jurgen
1975   "Zum Problem des Maqām," *Acta Musicologica* 47(2):208–39.

Feld, Steven
1974   "Linguistic Models in Ethnomusicology," *Ethnomusicology* 18(2):179–217.

Ferretti, Paolo
1938   *Esthétique grégorienne.* (trans. from Italian). Solesmes.

Finck, Hermann
1656   *Musica Practica.* Wittenberg.

Gerbert, Martin (ed.)
1784   *Scriptores Ecclesiastici de Musica Sacra Potissimum.* 3 vol., St. Blaise.

Graves, Robert
1955   *The Greek Myths.* 2 vol., Baltimore: Penguin Books.

Hopkins, Pandora
1977   "The Homology of Music and Myth: Views of Lévi-Strauss on Musical Structure." *Ethnomusicology* 21(2):247–61.

Hucke, Helmut
1953 "Musikalische Formen der Officiumsantiphonen," *Kirchenmusikalisches Jahr-buch* 37:7–33.

Jairazbhoy, N. A.
1971 *The Rāgs of North Indian Music: Their Structure and Evolution.* Middletown, Connecticut: Wesleyan Univ. Press.

Kaufmann, Walter
1968 *The Ragas of North India.* Bloomington, Indiana: Indiana Univ. Press.

Keil, Charles and Angeliki Keil
1966 "Musical Meaning: A Preliminary Report," *Ethnomusicology* 10(2):153–73.

Keiler, Allan
1977 "The Syntax of Prolongation (I)," *In Theory Only* 3(5):3–27.
1978 "Bernstein's *The Unanswered Question* and the Problem of Musical Compe-tence," *Musical Quarterly* 64(2):195–222.
1978 "The Empiricist Illusion: Narmour's *Beyond Schenkerism*," *Perspectives of New Music* 17:161–95.
in press a "Two Views of Musical Semiotics," *Proceedings of the International Confer-ence on the Semiotics of Art* (to appear 1980).
in press b "Music as Metalanguage: Rameau's Fundamental Bass," *in* Richmond Browne, *ed., Topics in Music Theory,* New York (to appear 1980).

Koch, Heinrich Christoph
1782 (I) *Versuch einer Anleitung zur Composition.* Leipzig: A. F. Böhme.
1787 (II)
1793 (III)

Labov, William
1972 *Sociolinguistic Patterns.* Philadelphia: Univ. of Pennsylvania Press.

Lenneberg, Hans
1958 "Johann Mattheson on Affect and Rhetoric in Music," *Journal of Music Theory* 2(1,2):47–84, 192–236.

Leach, Edmund
1974 *Claude Lévi-Strauss.* 2 ed. New York: Viking Press.

Lerdahl, Fred and Ray Jackendoff
1977 "Toward a Formal Theory of Tonal Music," *Journal of Music Theory* 21(1):111–71.

Lévi-Strauss, Claude
1955 "The Structural Study of Myth," *Journal of American Folklore* 68(270):428–44.
1958 *Anthropologie structurale.* Paris: Plon.
1964 *Le Cru et le cuit (Mythologiques I).* Paris: Plon.
1971 *L'Homme nu (Mythologiques IV).* Paris: Plon.

Lidov, David
1975 *On Musical Phrase.* (Monographies de sémiologie et d'analyses musicales I. Faculté de musique, Université de Montréal). Montréal: Les Presses de l'Université de Montréal.

Lorenz, Alfred
1926 *Das Geheimnis der Form bei Richard Wagner.* II (Tristan). Berlin.

Mattheson, Johann
1737 *Kern melodischer Wissenschaft.* (contents reprinted in Mattheson 1739)
1739 *Der vollkommene Capellmeister.* Hamburg: Herold.

McDermott, Vincent and Sumarsam
1975 "Central Javanese Music: The Patet of Laras Sléndro and the Gendèr Barung," *Ethnomusicology* 19(2):233–44.

Merriam, Alan P.
1964 *The Anthropology of Music*. Evanston, Illinois: Northwestern Univ. Press.

Narmour, Eugene
1977 *Beyond Schenkerism*. Chicago: Chicago Univ. Press.

Nattiez, Jean-Jacques
1975 *Fondements d'une sémiologie de la musique*. Paris: Seuil.

Nattiez, Jean-Jacques and Louise Hirbour-Paquette
1973 "Analyse musicale et sémiologie: À propos du Prélude de *Pelléas*," *Musique en jeu* 10:42-67.

Nettl, Bruno
1974 "Thoughts on Improvisation: A Comparative Approach," *Musical Quarterly* 60(1): 1-19.

Palisca, Claude
1972 "*Ut Oratoria Musica*: The Rhetorical Basis of Musical Mannerism," *in* F. W. Robinson and S. G. Nichols, Jr., *eds.*, *The Meaning of Mannerism* (Hanover, New Hampshire: Dartmouth Univ. Press, 37-59).

Pettit, Philip
1975 *The Concept of Structuralism: A Critical Analysis*. Berkeley: Univ. of California Press.

Powers, Harold S.
1961- "*Il Serse* Trasformato," *Musical Quarterly* 47(4):481-92, 48(1):73-92.
1962
1968 "*L'Erismena* Travestita," *in* H. S. Powers, *ed.*, *Studies in Music History: Essays for Oliver Strunk* (Princeton, New Jersey: Princeton Univ. Press, 259-324).
1970 "An Historical and Comparative Approach to the Classification of Ragas (With an Appendix on Ancient Indian Tunings)," *Selected Reports of the Institute of Ethnomusicology* 1(3):1-78.
1977 "The Structure of Musical Meaning: A View from Banaras," *Perspectives of New Music* 14(2)/15(1):308-34.
unpublished "The Structure of Musical Discourse: A View from Madras."

Reese, Gustave
1940 *Music in the Middle Ages*. New York: Norton.

Riemann, Hugo
1903 *System der musikalischen Rhythmik und Metrik*. Leipzig: Breitkopf & Härtel.

Rosen, Charles
1972 *The Classical Style*. New York: W. W. Norton.

Ruwet, Nicolas
1972 *Langage, musique, poésie*. Paris: Éditions de Seuil. (The first five articles are on music, originally published in 1959, 1961, 1962, 1966, and 1967.)
1975 "Théorie et méthodes dans les études musicales: quelques remarques rétrospectives et préliminaires," *Musique en jeu* 17:11-36.

Sumarsam
1975a "Inner Melody in Javanese Gamelan Music," *Asian Music* 7(1):3-13.
1975b "Gendèr Barung, its Technique and Function in the Context of Javanese Gamelan," *Indonesia* 20:161-72.

Suñol, Gregorio Maria
1935 *Introduction à la paléographie musicale grégorienne*. Paris: Desclée et cie.

Tinctoris, Johannes
1961 *Liber de Arte Contrapuncti*. (Trans. by Albert Seay, American Institute of Musi-
(1477) cology). n.p.

Treitler, Leo
   1974 "Homer and Gregory: The Transmission of Epic Poetry and Plain-Chant," *Musical Quarterly* 60(3):333–72.
   1975 "'Centonate' Chant: *Übles Flickwerk* or *E Pluribus Unus*," *Journal of the American Musicological Society* 28(1):1–23.

Turnstall, Patricia
   1979 "Structuralism and Musicology: An Overview," *Current Musicology* 27:51–64.

Wagner, Peter
   1921 *Gregorianische Formenlehre.* Leipzig.

Wellesz, Egon
   1919- "Die Struktur des Serbischen Oktoechos," *Zeitschrift fur Musikwissenschaft* 2(3):
   1920   140–48.

Zarlino, Gioseffe
   1950   *Istituzioni Armoniche.* Excerpts translated in Oliver Strunk, *ed., Source Readings*
   (1558) *in Music History: From Classical Antiquity Through the Romantic Era* (New York: Norton), p. 229–61.

Art Has Its Reasons

Five Graphic Music Analyses
by Heinrich Schenker,
with a new Introduction and Glossary
by Felix Salzer.
Dover, 61 pp., $2.50

La Poétique, la Mémoire
Change No. 6, 1970,
Editions du Seuil (Paris)

Shakespeare's Verbal Art
in *Th' Expence of Spirit*
by Roman Jakobson and
Lawrence G. Jones.
Mouton (The Hague),
Humanities Press, 32 pp., $3.25

Charles Rosen

I

"It is equally fatal intellectually to have a system and to have none. One must decide to combine both."

—F. von Schlegel

Heinrich Schenker claimed that if you did not hear music according to his system, you could not be said to hear it at all. Moreover, his system was not elaborated with much consideration for more traditional ways of looking at, or listening to, music. He swept away as trivial and insignificant not only such notions as "modulation" and "sequence" but even "melody," the common man's way of recognizing and appreciating music.[1] Schenker's contempt for the layman is exceeded only by his contempt for all previous theoretical work before his own except that of Karl Philipp Emanuel Bach.

Schenker was the musical heir of the great Romantic literary critics of the early nineteenth century, like Friedrich von Schlegel, who conceived the task of the critic as being to convey the unity of the work of art. At the time of his death in Vienna in 1935 at the age of seventy-eight, he was ignored by most of the world of music except for a small group of distinguished pupils and admirers. Before Schenker, the analysis of a musical work was largely an articulation of its parts. Even today the most common method is still to identify the succession of themes and to note which ones appear more than once. A more technical analysis may articulate the harmonic scheme, listing the different keys to which the music moves and their relation to the main key of the piece (the tonic).

Schenker tried instead to show not how the piece may be divided up, but how it held together. A beginning was made toward this end in music criticism as early as E. T. A. Hoffmann, who observed how a work of Beethoven seemed to derive from a single motif, and traced this technique of composition back to Haydn and Mozart. For later nineteenth- and twentieth-century critics, however, analysis of motifs became only a new way of atomizing a work of music, and matters remained at this relatively primitive level until Schenker revived Romantic aesthetics and combined it with an anticipation of certain aspects of structuralism.

Schenker's analyses contain the most important and illuminating observations made in this century about the music written between 1700 and 1880. Until now only the earliest and weakest of his books, a treatise on harmony, was available in English. A translation of the central theoretical work, *Der Freie Satz*, has never been published, nor are there any English versions of his analyses of Beethoven's Third, Fifth, and Ninth Symphonies and the last piano sonatas.

For this reason two recent publications are welcome: this *Five Graphic Music Analyses* and, in *Music Forum*, Vol. II, a discussion of the Saraband of Bach's C Major Cello Suite, one of the essays (and by no means the most significant one) from the volumes called *Der Meisterwerk in der Musik*.[2] The *Five Graphic Music Analyses* is particularly important, although—since the book contains almost no text at all—it can hardly be said to make a beginning with the task of translating Schenker into English. These reductions of music by Bach, Haydn, and Chopin to skeletal graphs are Schenker's last works.

In his excellent Introduction Felix Salzer maintains that, although Schenker was a specialist in eighteenth- and nineteenth-century music, his theory has much to contribute to the understanding of other periods as well. Schenker, however, was no mere specialist in these two centuries, but a firm believer that musical art of any consequence was confined to that period, when a developed and sophisticated form of tonality was the basis of music.

His book on Beethoven's Ninth Symphony was dedicated to "Brahms, the last great master of German music." "German" was an unnecessary qualification for Schenker, who considered the ability to sustain musical expression a proof of membership in the German race, even if one had foreign blood in one's veins. Chopin, whom Schenker used to illustrate his theories almost as often as Beethoven, would, I presume, be an honorary German. This is like Schle-

gel's "They say that the Germans are the greatest people in the world for their sense of art and scientific spirit: no doubt, but there are very few Germans."

That the music after Brahms did not fit Schenker's theories was only a proof to him of its inferiority. Stravinsky and Reger are both easily disposed of in this way and outside tonality was the outer darkness into which the degenerate composer was forever consigned.[3]

In Schenkerian analysis, every work of music is reduced to a simple line which is a step-by-step descent to the central or tonic note, and under each note of the line the harmonic functions are indicated by a bass. This line always outlines one of the intervals of the tonic triad (third, fifth, or octave). (In C Major, for example, the line may descend from E to C or from G to C; the octave descent C to C is rarely encountered.)

The fundamental line constitutes, for Schenker, the structure of every tonal work at the deepest level, and music that cannot be reduced to this structure must be judged incoherent and, indeed, ungrammatical. The "idea" of each work is not, emphatically, this fundamental line, but the elaboration of the line into the rich and individual superstructure that we actually hear. It is implied by all of Schenker's writings that only genius can arrive at a musical work that is both grammatical and interesting; and within the terms set by Schenker himself, this is an inescapable conclusion.

What Schenker did was to extend the idea of dissonance from the individual moment to the level of the piece as a whole. Dissonance is simply an interval that requires resolution into a consonance, and the only consonances accepted in Western music since the fifteenth century are the intervals of the basic triad (third, perfect fifth, and octave) and the inversion of the third, or the sixth.[4] All other intervals

---

[1] This point is somewhat obscured by Schenker's occasional use of the term "melody" to describe the linear working out of his deep structure. But in his article on sonata form, he insists that the layman's and the theoretician's general conception of melody, theme, and motive only serve to hide the true musical process.

[2] *Music Forum*, II, also contains Lewis Lockwood's essay on the manuscript of Beethoven's Cello Sonata, in its intelligence and sympathy the most illuminating description of Beethoven's method of revising and sketching I have read. This was certainly the most important musicological contribution to the Beethoven year.

[3] This is not an argument against Salzer's adaptation of Schenkerian analytical methods to medieval and contemporary music, and his work merits independent consideration.

[4] The ambiguous historical role of the fourth may illuminate this: theoretically it fluctuated between consonance and dissonance with theorists unable to decide; practically, it was a dissonance after 1400 except when it functioned as an inversion of the fifth.

254

are, by convention, dissonant, and demand to be resolved into one of the consonances.

This concept was already extended in the eighteenth century when the chord and not the interval became the basis of harmonic thought. Dissonance now implied resolution into a triad, and the final resolution of every work of music was, of course, into the tonic triad.

The basis of Schenker's system is that every note of a piece, whatever its immediate function, is considered as dissonant to the notes of this final, tonic cadence (except, naturally, for the notes of the cadence itself). Each note has therefore ultimately to be resolved into the tonic triad. An unresolved note is considered as in suspense, the tension it creates lasting until its resolving note finally appears in a context that emphatically displays its role in the large plan. The context is defined by the harmonic significance at each point of the basic line.

What is most striking about Schenker's analytical system is his insistence that both listener and composer—consciously or unconsciously—have a sense of tonal forces that overrides the immediate, small-scale event and allows them to hear "at a distance" so to speak. For example, the basic phrase (Ursatz) underlying the whole of Chopin's Etude in F Major, opus 10, no. 8, is:

Resolution at a distance would require enormous space to illustrate properly, and the shortest example will have to suffice. Measures 10 to 15 of the original

are represented in the most complex of the series of Schenker's analytic graphs by:

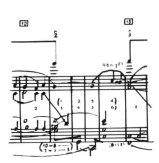

We can see here not only all the notes of the original resolved into the basic phrase (or its octave doublings), but also the relation of the high G of measure 11 to the high A that occurs four measures later. This is a relationship that a pianist with a sense of line naturally sets in relief, and is a direct

part of musical experience. The large-scale resolutions take place according to the strict rules of counterpoint derived from the practice of J. S. Bach.

Schenker assumed that the contrapuntal technique of voice-leading (in which each note is part of an independent vocal or instrumental "horizontal" line in addition to combining into a simultaneous harmony with other notes) was valid not only on the level of the single phrase but underlay the general harmonic structure as well. He found that he could connect what he considered the basic notes at the points of structural importance, and that they formed a series of lines that conformed to the tradition of voice-leading as it had been elaborated in the fifteenth and sixteenth centuries, and systematized in the eighteenth.

These lines constitute the most complex of Schenker's analytic graphs, the *Urlinie Tafel*. These in turn can be reduced in a series of stages to the simple cadential phrase outlining the tonic triad. This latter phrase is not to be understood as the structure of the work being analyzed, but as the structure of the tonal language.

In other words, for Schenker every tonal work is the elaboration of a simple cadence. Historically this point has much to be said for it (although Schenker's way of thinking was pre-eminently anti-historical). The cadence is the determining element in Western music, at least from Gregorian chant until the early twentieth century. Not only classical tonality but the medieval modes are defined by the cadence, and the basic impulsive force of both Renaissance and Baroque music—the harmonic sequence—is generally a repetition of cadential formulas. The cadence is a framing device, and it isolates and defines a piece of Western music as the frame defines a Western painting. Unlike much of the music of Africa and Asia—and much of what is being written today from John Cage to rock—a work of European music from the twelfth to the twentieth centuries is conceived as a determinate isolated event, and the cadence fixes each performance in time.

If a work is essentially a cadence magnificently expanded, then it may be seen as a delaying action, or, in Schenker's own terms, a tension sustained until the final resolution. What was original in Schenker's approach was his insistence that the means of sustaining the tension be intimately related in all details to the simple cadence which defines the work. In this way, he was able to explain that sense of unity and integrity of the great works of eighteenth- and nine-

teenth-century music. A quartet of Mozart holds all its most violent and dramatic contrasts in one characteristic whole, while a quartet by Dittersdorf —with much more uniform material and texture—falls into a series of separate sections, jolly and tuneful as they may be.

It is a waste of time to ask if this unity that we seem to perceive really exists, or if the composer knew that he created this unity, whether or not he was able to put his awareness into words. These are not, of course, answerable questions even if the composer is on hand to incriminate himself. The unity of a work of art is the oldest critical dogma that we have, and every piece of music demands a perception of its unity in the absolute sense that that is precisely what listening to it means. That is, the unity is neither an attribute of the work nor a subjective impression of the listener. It is a condition of understanding: the work reveals its significance to those who listen as if even its discontinuities correspond to hold it together.

Some sort of symmetrical correspondence between detail and large structure is therefore integral to all Western art, and Schenker locates the basic correspondence in music between those tonal forces that enable a listener without perfect pitch to realize that the original key has returned and the rules of counterpoint that govern the individual phrase. Bach did conceive a saraband as an immense, single phrase, and Haydn could, indeed, think musically at a much longer range than any of his contemporaries except Mozart.

The reduction of a Chopin Etude to a simple contrapuntal graph that often resembles nothing so much as a phrase of Bach is not surprising when we remember how much Chopin revered Bach and how much he depended on him for his conceptions of harmony and form. Schenker considered tonality as God-given and established for all eternity (so much the worse for those heathen on other continents beyond the pale of revelation), but this should not obscure his discovery of how sensitive the greatest composers were to the implications of their musical language.

The limitation of Schenker's approach is as evident as its cogency (although most musicians are capable of appreciating only one or the other, and discussion is blindly partisan). The most crippling omission is the rhythmic aspect: harmony and melody can be entirely reduced, convincingly, if at times somewhat speciously, to the simpler lines of the *Urlinie*, but rhythm plays not only a subordinate role but often none at all. This falsifies the musical thought of all the works with which Schenker dealt, most evidently those of Beethoven.

Resulting logically from the neglect of rhythm is the total disregard of proportions. Schoenberg once looked at Schenker's graph of the *Eroica*, and said, "But where are my favorite passages? Ah, there they are, in those tiny notes."[5] It is not merely that one

[5] Schoenberg had a great admiration for Schenker's work, and he was one of the few to appreciate it during Schenker's lifetime, in spite of his inevitable disagreement with many of its aspects. Schoenberg's music, indeed, develops on its surface many of the relationships that Schenker was later to read under the skin of classical works.

note of Schenker's basic line may last one second and another a full minute in the complete piece, but that Schenker often minimizes the salient features of a work. This implies that there are important forces in musical composition that Schenker takes no account of, and they may often supersede the aspects of music with which he is concerned.

Basically these limitations arise because his thought—his way of looking at music—was ruthlessly linear, and while this may be an understandable and fitting mode for an age that saw the development of the twelve-tone technique and the serial music that Schenker so hated, it radically distorts the music of any period, including Schenker's own. His neglect of rhythm, too, has only accentuated the nonsensical separation in theory of the elements of music, as if a tonal melody could exist without a rhythmic contour.

These limitations, however, would not account for the extraordinary distaste that his work often provokes, chiefly among musicologists, and for the absurd disregard of his achievements that still lames critical writing on music. Nor would his manner of writing, brutally and repulsively arrogant, and his insistent German chauvinism explain why work of that importance should have remained relatively unknown and ignored except by an unhappy few during Schenker's lifetime, and should continue to excite hostility during the more than thirty years since his death in 1935.

It is hard to take offense at Schenker's suggestion that a new Beethoven would have to appear among the Germans just as Nature places elephants and crocodiles only where they will find the conditions to sustain life. Absurdities like this have been excised from the more recent edition of *Der Freie Satz*, and Schenker's disciples tend to gloss over, and even dismiss, these aspects of his thought, but a true Schenkerite ought to insist that Schenker's work hangs together as an organic whole. The paranoiac style of Schenker's essays along with his insistence that his theory was a form of monotheism does reflect an essential characteristic of his ideas.

Schenker's method is the uncovering

of a hidden and secret form underlying the explicit one. He does not deny that the explicit forms exist (sonata form, rondo form, ternary form are almost as real for him as they were for d'Indy); he denies their importance. The implicit form is the only one that brings salvation, and it alone reveals the way the music was composed. The explicit form was imposed almost as an afterthought.

This absolute rejection of the explicit in favor of the implicit is a classic method of interpretation: the Marxian analysis of ideology, the Freudian theory of dreams and slips of the tongue, and the structuralist doctrine of myths. For Marx (in the *18 Brumaire*, for example) the ideology of the different political parties was a mask for their allegiance to a particular class; for Freud, and for Lévi-Strauss, the dream or the myth is a disguise for an irresolvable and unacknowledgeable tension. In each case, the explicit meaning is generally false, and only the implicit meaning systematically revealed is given any weight. The initial reaction to each of these systems was one of rejection by the academic establishment: the Marxian dialectic met as much resistance from orthodox economists as psychoanalysis from the medical profession, and Lévi-Strauss is regarded by many of his fellow anthropologists as something between a charlatan and a poet.

The style of religious paranoia that occasionally appears in all these movements is both an answer to this ostracism and a provocation of it. Their organization into quasi-conspiratorial sects[6] is related to the rejection of explicit meaning, and, in every case, this rejection is presented as a scandal. The scandal may be political, sexual, or purely intellectual, but it is always construed as an ethical attack on a

---

[6] Structuralism is the great mandarin conspiracy of the 1960s, and no other recent intellectual movement has so insisted upon the need for an hermetic vocabulary and a set of sacred texts (Mallarmé, Sade, and Lévi-Strauss). A counterrevolutionary movement is rising, however, and it is now becoming fashionable in Paris and New York to claim proudly to be unable to understand *Tel Quel*.

conspiracy of silence. The explicit meaning which is to be cast out is conceived not only as mistaken or trivial, but as having been deliberately designed to mislead. The symbols of a dream are there to hide what they unconsciously betray, as ideology is intended not to enlighten but to conceal. For Schenker, all musical theory before his own was a deliberate conspiracy between mediocrity and non-Germanic musicians to betray the great tradition of music from 1700 to 1850 by concentrating only upon the superficial, explicit aspects of the great German classics. Even the works themselves, indeed, are conceived not as revelations, but as concealments of the underlying structure.

In Schenker's analyses, this creates a difficulty when moving from the implicit to the explicit.[7] He tried to cover the difficulty with an interesting and provocative theory of "improvisation," but the awkwardness is always present. Schenker continued to use old-fashioned concepts like "first theme," "counter statement," and "bridge passage" in writing about sonatas, and even accepts these terms with all their nineteenth-century crudity. What remains unclear, however, is the transition from Schenker's graph to the music itself with its admitted tunes, modulations, and so forth.

The transition from implicit to explicit always presents this difficulty, which is naturally less obvious when going in the other direction. It is easy enough to see the implicit meaning hidden within the exterior shell once the methodology has been learned, harder to decide why the inner sense should have taken just this outer form.

It should be emphasized that it is neither the truth nor the importance of Schenker's deep structure that is in question but its *status*—its nature and its relation to the work as a whole. What does a Schenkerian graph represent? We cannot call it the form of a piece because it omits too many major forces of musical importance. We cannot even call it an adequate representation of the purely linear element of the form unless we are willing to claim that this is not essentially affected by proportion and rhythm. Nor is it, as Schenker claimed, a method of composition, although it plays a definite role in this process.

This ambiguity is a stumbling block found in any artistic analysis that takes the form of a hidden pattern, and yet it is hard to conceive of an analytic approach that could remain interesting while claiming that the meanings it uncovers are less significant than the explicit ones that have been evident all along. Such humility would appear to be self-defeating. The problem becomes clearer when we leave the isolatable world of music for literature, composed in a medium that connects at every point with a language used for everyday speech.

II

Ferdinand de Saussure, even while giving the lectures at the University of

---

[7] He was, himself, aware of this, and his article on sonata form begins amusingly, "To bring the general into line with the particular is one of the most difficult tasks in human experience."

The New York Review

Geneva which are the foundation of structural linguistics, spent many years investigating the possibility of hidden anagrams in Latin poetry. When he died in 1912, he left ninety-nine notebooks filled with his speculations, but never published anything on the subject. (He was also never able to bring himself to publish—or, indeed, even to write—the great *Course in General Linguistics* on which his immense reputation rests. It is a compilation of students' notes.)

The notebooks have been largely withheld from publication, perhaps because their character is as embarrassing as it is fascinating and provocative. A few selected passages of a general nature were published in essays by Jean Starobinski in 1954 in the *Mercure de France*, in *Tel Quel* No. 37, and in the *Festschrift* volume of 1967 for Roman Jakobson.[8] In *Change* No. 6, which appeared a few months ago, Starobinski has edited Saussure's analysis of lines 1-52 and 1184-1189 of Lucretius's *De Rerum Natura*.

The origin of Saussure's researches was an investigation into the phonetic structure of that early, primitive, and mysterious form of Latin verse called Saturnian. He became convinced that there was a regular repetition, a coupling, in fact, of the phonetic elements. Alliteration (the repetition of an initial sound) and rhyme (the repetition of a final) were only particular cases of a more general phenomenon, in which the interior syllables also had a function. His attempts to work out a regular law for these couplings in Saturnian verse proved unfruitful, but they suggested to him that the basis for them was a proper name (a number of the fragments of Saturnian verse that have come down to us are commemorative and taken from the sepulchral epitaphs of the Scipios).

From the proper name it was only a step to the idea of any word, its phonetic elements isolated, freely distributed and combined, providing the basis for verse, and Saussure turned to a study of Virgil, only to find the same couplings and the same musical suggestion of a hidden word influencing and even determining the phonetic structure of any given series of lines. This seemed to Saussure, as to anyone else, a deplorably and absurdly burdensome method of writing poetry, but the hypothesis explained the intricate phonetic symmetries that are a regular characteristic of poetry, and even—though less markedly—of prose.

The assumption that Saussure made was that the manifold phonetic symmetries of a passage in verse, including those not required by the rules of versification, were not determined at random by the sense, but combined into an ordered unity. This would correspond to the feeling shared by many readers of poetry that each part of a poem, closely read, has a specific and individual phonetic character of its own. This individuality of sound is the source of the most direct, most immediately sensuous pleasure that verse can give.

Saussure made the further assumption, a natural if more dubious step,

that the unity obtained by the combination of the dominant assonances within a short passage had itself a clearly definable meaning—in other words, that the various syllables made up a word. This word was his "anagram," a term with which he was eventually dissatisfied, substituting, in turn, "paragram," "hypogram," "logogram," "paramorph," and "anaphony"; the last named best expressed Saussure's insistence that the game was played not with writing but with sound.

In all of his speculations on this subject, he relied principally on his ear, and his analyses constantly stress the setting-in-relief of his phonetic couplings by the accent of the verse and the stress of meaning within the line. He made it a condition not only that the different phonetic elements of his theme words should appear clearly emphasized within a very few lines, but that these lines should contain a definite model of the theme words in the form of a short phrase that began and ended as the word did. For example, "*Āëriae prīmum vŏlucrēs tē*" is one model, or mannequin, as Saussure called it, for "Aphrodite."

The analyses are fascinating to read because of this sensitivity: they represent the spontaneous reactions of a reader of poetry systematized and rationalized almost to a point of insanity. Almost—because at every point Saussure stopped to ask himself whether the whole investigation was not a magnificent delusion like the hunt for a Baconian cypher in Shakespeare.

In the first fifty-two lines of Lucretius's poem, which contains the invocation to Venus, Saussure finds that the phonetic emphases combine to form the syllables of the Greek word "A-phro-di-te." This is striking enough to shake any doubts of Saussure's approach. Lucretius was a poet so steeped in Greek verse that it is more than probable that the composition of his invocation to Venus was accompanied by innumerable souvenirs of Greek verses to Aphrodite, echoes of lines and phrases remembered and half-remembered.

It is also reasonable that a poet should be almost pathologically sensitive to the suggestiveness of the purely phonetic aspect of words. The inherent improbability of Saussure's theory begins for a moment to evaporate. In fact, if we accept Saussure's analysis of Lucretius, we do not even have to ask whether the poet was conscious of his use of an underlying theme word; an unconscious intent is as natural and as credible in this case as a planned strategy.

Nevertheless, Saussure felt impelled to ask just that question: was the anagram a consciously applied technique of Latin verse? At this point, the latent paranoia of his program of research comes to the surface. If Saussure's conjecture is right, the conspiracy of silence on the part of the whole body of classical literature is frightening. Finally, in desperation, Saussure wrote to a contemporary Italian who composed Latin verses, hoping to learn that the tradition of anagrams had been handed down secretly to the present day. We do not know if there was a reply, but Saussure never spoke again of his researches

To conceal a word phonetically

within a set of different words is a legitimate poetic effect; there is a famous example in Valéry's *Cimetière Marin*:

La mer, la mer, toujours recom-
mencée
O récompense après une pensée
Qu'un long regard sur le calme des
dieux.

The second line literally illustrates the preceding word *"recommencée"* by hiding it and expanding it over the entire line, like a larger wave that builds itself up and breaks after a moment's tension, broadening the faster and more regular rhythm that preceded it.

Such effects, based on the quality of the individual sounds, are more crucial in French verse, with its relatively uniform syllabic weight, than in English, which relies on the force of the rhythmic accent. They are perhaps even easier to achieve in Latin, with a syntax that permits so much greater freedom in the order of words. Both in French and Latin verse, passages are often emphasized by being constructed out of a specific nexus of sounds, and the importance given to such peculiar refinement is one of the reasons non-French-speaking readers find French poetry so difficult at first to appreciate. One classical scholar has remarked on the intricate patterns of sound that arise in Latin poetry from repeating the phonetic elements of the most expressive word in a passage, so that the sense of the word seems to radiate phonetically into those that surround it.[9] With this explicit "radiating word" we are not far from Saussure's implicit anagram.

In all of his work on the anagrams, Saussure continued to ask whether his results were due to chance. To this question, and also to the question whether the procedure was intentional or unconscious, no answer could in principle be given, whatever statistics were compiled. Alliteration, assonance, rhyme, rhythmic pattern—any form of phonetic repetition, in general, is part of the essence of poetry. Each system of versification sets up those repetitions which are obligatory (sometimes called canonic), and the others are freely used in subsidiary contrapuntal patterns with the main one. Accent and, sometimes, rhyme are obligatory or canonic in English; assonance and alliteration are subsidiary and, in a sense, free, but they are nonetheless a deeply ingrained part of English poetic tradition. That anagrams may be derived from these subsidiary systems is not surprising; phonetic repetition is not just by chance in a poem.

Or in prose, either, for that matter. Saussure found his anagrams, somewhat unwillingly, even in Latin prose (artistic prose, however, that of Cicero and Julius Caesar). But, as Starobinski pointed out, they may be a part of ordinary speech as well. How often do we not find a word or even an idea suggested by alliteration or rhyme, and allow our thoughts to be guided by sound as well as by sense? Saussure's anagrams grow as much from language itself as from literary technique. The

[8] Saussure's published correspondence with Antoine Meillet largely treats of these anagrams.

[9] N. I. Herescu: *La Poésie Latine-Etude des Structures Sonores* (Paris, 1960). The first of Herescu's studies precedes by many years the first publication of any quotation from Saussure's notebooks.

significance of Saussure's ninety-nine notebooks is to show the intimate relationship between poetry and the processes of language and, above all, to demonstrate the power of a phonetic pattern to demand a meaning, the right to exist as a truly functioning part of language. It is difficult to read Saussure without hoping that he will prove to be right.

An ordered structure is a provocation, and we instinctively refuse to admit its lack of meaning. What Saussure was claiming was a significance for the structure of language independent of the message it contains. Saussure thought he was investigating not an attribute of language, but an esoteric technique of poetry. Ironically, what he found was an attribute of language which is a necessary condition for the existence of poetry.

We may rephrase Saussure's questions so that neither intention nor chance will muddy the waters. Can the subsidiary, non-canonic techniques of phonetic repetition in a poem have a meaning of their own independent of the explicit poetic discourse? If Saussure's own philosophy of language is right and meaning can only come into existence given an arbitrary convention that unites sound and sense, then the answer must be No. Can the non-canonic repetitions interact with the poetic discourse to form new meanings? That would mean taking the phonetic structure of poetry very seriously indeed. It would also entail defining the relation of implicit to explicit in a work of art.

258

III

The explicit, canonic structure of one of Shakespeare's sonnets is fourteen lines of iambic pentameter with a rhyme scheme of three quatrains (each *abab*) and a final couplet. In his pamphlet on Sonnet CXXIX (*Th'expence of Spirit in a waste of shame*). Roman Jakobson (in collaboration with Lawrence G. Jones) has identified a considerable series of subsidiary patterns of a phonetic, syntactic, and semantic nature.

In his literary criticism, Jakobson relies largely on the principle of binary opposition which played so fundamental a role in his systematization of the study of the sound structure of a language. Completing Troubetzkoy's work, he reduced the phonetic structure of any language to ten and only ten possible oppositions so that each elementary unit of sound, or phoneme, is analyzed as nasal or non-nasal, consonantal or non-consonantal, and so on. This principle of binary selection is essential to information theory, which conceives the transmission of a message as dependent on a series of successive choices between alternatives.

For this reason, perhaps, he prefers to analyze short poems that divide into four or five parts. He can then contrast the stanzas individually, pitting odd against even, inner against outer, anterior against posterior. The points he considers are of a precise technical nature often brushed aside by critics. The contrast of grammatical and nongrammatical rhymes (rhyme words with the same or different grammatical function) has been treated in English previously only by W. K. Wimsatt, I believe, although the relation of grammatical rhymes to the poetic language was already raised in the section drafted by Jakobson of the Theses of

1929 of the Prague Linguistic Circle. In the Theses, too, we find the principle developed later by Jakobson that the "purely" phonetic patterns in poetry are strongly bound to the semantic structure.

Here is the sonnet as Jakobson and Jones have arranged it for analysis:

I   1 *Th'expence of Spirit / in a waste of shame*
    2 *Is lust in action, / and till action, lust*
    3 *Is perjurd, murdrous, / blouddy full of blame,*
    4 *Savage, extreame, rude, / cruel, not to trust,*
II 1 *Injoyd no sooner / but dispised straight,*
    2 *Past reason hunted, / and no sooner had*
    3 *Past reason hated / as a swollowed bayt,*
    4 *On purpose layd / to make / the taker mad.*
III 1 *Mad[e] In pursut / and in possession so,*
    2 *Had, having, and in quest, / to have extreame,*
    3 *A blisse in proofe / and provd / a[nd] very wo,*
    4 *Before a joy proposd / behind a dreame,*
IV 1 *All this the world / well knowes / yet none knowes well,*
    2 *To shun the heaven / that leads / men to this hell.*

What Jakobson calls the "poetry of grammar" is most brilliantly shown in this great "generalizing" sonnet on lust by the remarks he and Jones make on the only two nouns that refer to man: *taker* in *a swallowed bait that makes the taker mad*, and *men* in *the heaven that leads men to this hell*:

Both . . . function as direct objects in the last line of the even strophes: II *taker* and IV *men*. In common usage the unmarked agent of the verb is an animate, primarily of personal gender, and the unmarked goal is an inanimate. But in both cited constructions with transitive verbs the sonnet inverts this nuclear order. Both personal nouns characterize human beings as passive goals of extrinsic, nonhuman and inhuman actions.

It is upon details such as this "grammatical metaphor" (as Jakobson has called it elsewhere) that the authors build their reading of the poem with its "semantic leitmotif" of "tragic predestination." The ability of the grammatical structure of language to assume a poetic life of its own is fundamental to music, which imitates this aspect of language above all.

In their description of the verbal art of the sonnet, the authors are concerned to show the inner correspondences that work against the simple division into three quatrains and final couplet. Most convincing in this respect is the light shed on the central verses in this scheme. Lines 7 and 8 stand out in relief, as they are the only ones without grammatical parallelism, and line 8 is "built of five totally unlike grammatical forms." This partially elucidates the means by which Shakespeare achieves the remarkable change of tempo in the center of the sonnet, with its sudden breadth and complexity of movement.

The prejudice against linguistic criticism of this kind is solidly, and to some extent reasonably, founded on a distaste for learning a new vocabulary, one which is at times unnecessarily technical for one's purposes. But Shakespeare's art consists—at least in large part—in an extraordinary feeling for the very stuff of language in all its aspects, and criticism has need of the tools that Jakobson offers. It is melancholy to read the pious horror (mostly British) at the invasion of an urbane humanistic discipline by the linguistic barbarians. Syntax is as relevant as

irony for the understanding of literature, and Jakobson's microscopic examinations come out of a long life's delight in literature, and a breadth of interest unsurpassed since the deaths of Erich Auerbach and Leo Spitzer.

Those of us who cannot read a Slavic tongue must be content with Jakobson's essays on English and French poetry. The most famous of these is the analysis of Baudelaire's *Les Chats* (done in collaboration with Claude Lévi-Strauss), the most satisfying perhaps the closely reasoned treatment of Baudelaire's *Spleen*. Equally important are the theoretical papers, above all the article "Linguistics and Poetics,"[10] in which the largeness of vision is balanced by its clarity. In all this work, social and biographical interpretations are excluded. Jakobson has always insisted that language and literature must be understood as systems in their own terms before their interaction with other systems can be apprehended. It is doubtful whether, as a matter of fact, this is a possible or even desirable goal in all of the purity with which Jakobson has invested it, but it is unquestionably the best practical starting point for criticism.

As appears in one minor aspect of the Shakespearian pamphlet, Jakobson has been considerably influenced by Saussure, and he and Jones tentatively suggest an anagrammatic signature worked into the opening line:

Th'expence of Spirit in a waste of shame
ksp   sp.r   Sha

in addition to a pun on *Will* in the concluding couplet, *All this the world well knowes yet none knowes well,/ To shun the heaven that leads men to this hell*; and in support of this suggestion they cite Shakespeare's tendency to equate "will" and "well" in puns. (For a sonnet on lust, they might have added the Elizabethan sense of "will" as "carnal desire.") This is not Jakobson's first use of Saussurian anagrams. He finds anagrams for *Spleen* in all four of Baudelaire's poems with this title, and an anagrammatic influence of the title throughout the poem called *Le Gouffre*.

The difficulty—at least in the Shakespeare—is not an inherent improbability, but the lack of coordination with the rest of the analysis. Sonnet CXXIX, written on the most personal of themes—fornication and its bitter aftermath—is "the only one among the 154 sonnets of the 1609 Quarto which contains no personal or corresponding possessive pronouns." Nor is a fornica-

[10] In *Style in Language*, edited by T. Sebeok (New York: Wiley, 1961).

tor even referred to except in a dependent clause as part of a simile and there in a passive role (see remarks on *taker* above), and in the superbly general word "men" in the last line. The entire sonnet is not only "generalizing," but absolutely and even repressively impersonal.

If we accept the anagram and the pun on *Will*, they are—if conscious—sardonic jokes, and—if unconscious—the revenge of suppressed nature.[11] In either case, we are left with a specifically personal meaning which deliberately undercuts the explicitly generalizing form of the sonnet. We need a very superior sort of irony to integrate the two.

The most disappointing part of Jakobson and Jones is the section "Odd Against Even." They list every binary correspondence that comes to hand, and we sometimes have the impression of reading a series of notes left unused after an analysis was written. (There is even an apologetic note in the presentation, when they write, "By the way, the preposition *in* appears only in the odd strophes.") It would be unfair to suggest that much of this detail has an interest more linguistic than literary: poetry rejects no aspect of language. But the presentation of this section does not establish throughout its relevance to Shakespeare's verbal art.

All this would not matter if the significance of the odd-even opposition were acceptable. It is suggested that the odd strophes contain "an intensely abstractive confrontation of the different stages of lust (*before, in action, behind*), whereas the even strophes are centered upon the metamorphosis itself." I do not believe that a reading of the sonnet bears this out: the heaven and hell of the fourth strophe, for example, are as abstractive a confrontation as anything in the first, although one leads to the other; and the opening line already describes the metamorphosis of "in action" into its aftermath.

In fact, the treatment of the three stages of lust is beautifully balanced, and the movement from one to the other is subtly modulated. Jakobson and Jones do not study this movement, so they miss the balance of the opening quatrains, in each of which the first two lines present two states and the last two lines characterize one at length (*before action* in lines 3 and 4, *after* in 7 and 8). They also miss the remarkable backward slide in time of line 10:

Had, having, and in quest, to have extreame,

which is prepared by the retrospective glance of lines 7 and 8, where the third stage is described by its horrified view of the first.

Jakobson has called upon Saussure's authority to justify taking "the elements out of the order in time" in which they are presented in the poem. But to be effective, the correspondences so discovered should not be invalidated by an actual reading in time. A detail found in both the first and third strophes cannot be isolated when it is found in the second as well, and in linking the odd strophes Jakob-

son and Jones cite as correspondences some features which are pervasive; they bring together: I, *Spirit* (sp.r.t) *in*; III, *In pursuit* (p.rs.t). But they themselves later call attention to the paronomastic chain which unites the odd and even strophes and which pairs *In pursuit* with *Past reason* (the latter occurring twice in the second strophe, both times in the prominent initial position). Their neglect of this pervasive character makes the analysis of the expressive sound structure of the final couplet uncertain as well.

On the other hand, if we eliminate the opposition of odd and even, we can see that the four consonants of *Spirit* dominate the first twelve lines:

1 *expence, Spirit, waste*
2 *lust. lust*
3 *Is perjurd* (sp.r.rd)
4 *Savage, extreame* (str), *trust*
5 *dispised straight*
6 *Past reason hunted* (p.str.s))
7 *Past reason hated,*
8 *On purpose layd* (p.rp.s'....'d).
9 *In pursuit* (p.rs.t)
10 *in quest, to have extreame*
11 *A blisse in proofe*
12 *proposd*

This concentration is emphasized by the phonetic symmetries of the verses (e.g., the first word of line 7 is *past*, the final word *bayt*; *pursuit* of line 9 is balanced by *possession*; in line 6 *reason* and *sooner* exchange their three consonants).

In the last two lines, on the other hand, this particular nexus of sounds disappears, and the contrast of sonority is striking. The final couplet has no "p," only one "r" (in *world*) and its three "t"s are all on weak beats and two of them are finals (*yet* and *that*), which further weakens their emphasis. The dominant sounds of the last two lines are the alliterations on "w," "n," "th," "h," the recurrence of "l," "s," and "n" in final position, and the prominent "sh" of *To shun,* a remarkable concentration of aspirates and soft consonants.

Jakobson and Jones remark on the density of texture in the final couplet[12] but not on its hushed quality and on the almost complete absence of the explosives that pervade the first twelve lines. If one were to construct anagrams, it might justly be said that *Spirit* determines the sonority of the quatrains, and *shame* of the final couplet.

Jakobson and Jones do not convey

the richness of meaning in the opening line and the extent to which it announces the tragic theme of the whole sonnet. They note double meanings in the opening line for *shame* (chastity and genitalia) and for *Spirit* (a vital power of both mind and semen), but do not give for the latter the common meaning in Shakespeare's time of the soul, in particular at the moment of death as if leaves the body. This is a sense enlisted by the word *expence* which had for Shakespeare the now obsolete meaning of "loss," as in Sonnet XXX:

Then can I drowne an eye (un-us'd to flow)
For precious friends hid in deaths dateless night,
And weepe afresh loves long since canceld woe,
And mone th'expence of many a vannisht sight.

Th'expence of Spirit is a metaphor for death, which is itself the oldest and most common of all rhetorical images for sexual intercourse. This philological background is a necessary supplement to Jakobson's and Jones's linguistic detail.

Jakobson has held with Empson that "the machinations of ambiguity are among the very roots of poetry," as of any message centered on itself, and Jakobson and Jones remark that Shakespeare's *double-entendre* does not interfere with the firm thematic construction of the sonnet. The double meanings they sketch are, as they say, only a kind of double-talk. But Empson's stand is more powerful and more interesting, and his machinery enables us to integrate ambiguity into the sonnet as a whole instead of presenting it as a suggestive but unessential decoration. He claims that when the poetic context calls up two meanings of a word, it enforces a relation between the two which is understood in the context of the poem.

In *Th'expence of Spirit* this relation is, in fact, the theme of "tragic predestination" that Jakobson and Jones clarify. The grossly physical sense (semen) of *Spirit* is identified with the spiritual (soul) by the degradation of lust. The religious overtones of the last line (*the heaven that leads men to this hell*) take this up again: man loses his soul through the expense of *Spirit* and is damned. The paradox of a heaven that leads to hell mirrors the opposition compressed into *Spirit*.

IV

As we have seen from Saussure, a formal pattern must signify something, but to achieve this significance, it needs a context. The context of a poem can only come from a "reading," and many of Jakobson's and Jones's correspondences do not submit to—or, better, do not acknowledge submission to—their own specific "reading" which is essentially the thematic structure they assess so convincingly.

In other words, there is a hierarchy of significance in all poetry before Mallarmé, and an explicit sense to which all the other interpretations must pay homage. This central, explicit sense is generally not subject to much controversy. It is the meaning established by a reading in time, in a simple linear[13]

---

[11] Acrostic signatures (like Villon's) and joking titles (like *Mr. Eliot's Sunday Morning Service*) cannot be equated with hidden allusions. The latter stake a claim to greater significance—else why were they hidden?

[12] The final couplet is actually less dense than lines like

Is perjurd, murdrous,
ur urd   urd
            bloody full of blame
            bl   f. l   bl

Savage, extreme, rude,
        kstr   rue
            cruel, not to trust
            krue   t   tr. st

[13] I do not mean linear in Schenker's sense, which distorts the actual movement in time, but in Saussure's, in which the order from past to future is essential to the comprehension of a message.

fashion starting from the beginning. This explicit meaning is the literal reading of Aquinas, and, when summarized, it is the simple thematic structure affirmed by Jakobson.

This is not to claim that non-linear interpretations and subsidiary, implicit patterns do not exist. On the contrary, their existence and their interaction with the explicit structure is the source of poetic strength, the verbal art of Jakobson's and Jones's title. But the criterion of relevance for these implicit patterns is the possibility of integration into the explicit one.[14]

Unfortunately for critics, some of these patterns will always prove to be irrelevant. In every sonnet, the phonetic structure is partially set in advance and therefore gratuitous. The semantic structure is mapped out to fit the rhyme and the meter. In a line like

Is lust in action, and in action, lust

the ideas are arranged to reveal the balance of the ten syllables and to isolate them: to some extent the content signifies the form and illuminates it, holds it up for inspection. The poet works to make the gratuitous form seem to be determined by the meaning. By definition he cannot completely succeed: if the phonetic structure seems totally dependent on the meaning, the work ceases to be poetry—that is, it ceases to be a privileged message, protected by its prosody from being confounded with an ordinary statement. The form must remain overdetermined.

The subsidiary, non-canonic phonetic patterns, in harmony with the principal one, are also partially gratuitous, can never completely fulfill the criterion of relevance. Their interaction with the semantic structure can never be complete. Above all, the semantic pattern itself will inevitably reveal the workings of organizing forces that are partially gratuitous: it, too, is set up like the rules of a game. These patterns also demand interpretation and yet cannot be made to yield absolutely to coherence. An analysis will always leave a residue, arabesques of phonetic and semantic patterns that imply a meaning and yet elude interpretation.

This gives art its privileged position. We are not allowed to claim, because of Sonnet CXXIX, that Shakespeare thought sexual intercourse disgusting, immoral, or degrading. This would be like rushing onto the stage to warn Othello that the handkerchief was planted. The sonnet is not a personal communication, however much feeling and experience went into it. The richness of meaning in the sonnet depends on the partial release of language from its normal function of conveying information. A poetic "message" is not tied to a specific receiver, and. its direction remains open; in Schlegel's words, "A poem is written for everyone or no one—the poet who writes for someone in particular deserves to go unread." If, however, the significance of the "message" is now tied asymmetrically to the sender, this freedom is equally menaced. A personal message to everyone or to no one is a voice crying in the wilderness, and

excites an absurdly misplaced pathos.

This privileged status makes. art dangerous: these arbitrary conventions that struggle into significance and that signal to the reader that the message is a fiction allow things to be written that would be otherwise intolerable. The unspeakable may be whistled. A characterization of fornication that has the intimate emotional power of Shakespeare's would have been unthinkable in late sixteenth-century prose, even in a sermon.

When the poetic "message" is freed from too intimate a tie with a specific sender or receiver, the latent meanings in the text are released and come alive, and the sonnet is open to the reader to interpret as irresponsibly as he pleases. No control is possible. But if the status of a work of art is threatened by being taken too seriously, it is also endangered by being reduced to "a superior amusement," as T. S. Eliot modestly called poetry. Unless the implicit patterns, the intricate correspondences that Jakobson delights in uncovering take their place within a "reading," they lose the significance that only that framework can give, and, in turn, cease to contribute to that framework. They tend to become facts of language, not of poetry. The analysis of the most complex and various patterns can only impoverish a work if they do not come together, if there is no focus.

Jakobson has, indeed, always insisted that the apparently autonomous phonetic and grammatical structures must be related to the structure of meaning. But the relation he generally proposes is a static one, less dynamic than a simple reading. His implicit correspondences sometimes add emphasis to the thematic structure, or at other times are a decorative counterpoint to the explicit form. Rarely do they substantially affect or alter the explicit reading; we start from the text and move to the discovery of the interior symmetries. What is lacking is the continuous movement back and forth between the whole text and the interior forms, a movement which makes possible the fullness of poetic criticism.

As we read, we create—by imagination, instinct, reason, or whatever—a frame from which the poem takes its meaning. Criticism is only an extension of this process, and is therefore, as Walter Benjamin said, the necessary completion of a work of art. The fundamental critical tradition since the sixteenth century, philology, is the creation of a historical context. It appears inevitable that linguistics, with its new-found power, will replace philology, and Jakobson prefers a context as little tied to history as possible. This releases Jakobson's correspondences from any fixed relation with tradition for the most part, and the new freedom is welcome: not all poetic technique is founded on convention, based on precedent. But the loss of historical significance is not easy to accept. It makes the poetry paradoxically less immediate, less likely to disturb.

Like literature, music can disturb and even shock. It has all the attributes of language except one. It has a grammar, a syntax, accent, tone of voice, syllables, and phonemes; it, too, is formed into sentences, paragraphs, chapters—what it lacks is a vocabulary. Musical phonemes act directly without first being strained through an abstract system of denotation. Music is a mimetic art in so far as it imitates language and

language's poor relation, gesture. It may be called pre-verbal but post-lingual. (What rudimentary vocabulary music has is mostly one of gesture, not of language.)

Most accounts of the expressive character of music have been largely attempts to identify the vocabulary; that is why they appear so simple-minded. The expressive force of music rests principally in its grammar. The capacity of the grammatical structure of a language to assume a meaning of its own (described by Jakobson), the power of any ordered pattern to appear significant, to demand interpretation (which fascinated Saussure)—these attributes of language are annexed by music and developed with an intensity unparalleled in any other art. Music is made up in great part of relationships like those that Jakobson analyzes as Shakespeare's verbal art, but the musical structures are far more sophisticated, efficient, and powerful.

The relation between explicit and implicit in music is therefore more difficult to clarify. For example, the distinction between canonic and non-canonic organization necessary for prosody is almost useless in music. Those conventional forms so often taught in music courses are largely a fiction, invented long after the fact. The fugue was a free form for Bach, and Mozart and Haydn never heard of sonata form and certainly had no idea of the standard pattern that has been taught under that name since the middle of the nineteenth century. Schenker was correct in maintaining that (at least since 1600) the most important "rules" of music are simply the rules of counterpoint and the laws of tonality. It is to these rules that Schenker reduces a work of music, ignoring the phrase-structure—which for most listeners contains the explicit sense of the work, and he turns his principles of organization into a hidden, esoteric form.

This is so because his method takes the form of a gradual reduction of the surface of the music to his basic phrase,[15] and the analysis moves in one direction, away from what is actually heard and toward a form which is more or less the same for every work. It is a method which, for all it reveals, concentrates on a single aspect of the music and, above all, makes it impossible to bring the other aspects into play. The work appears to drain away into the secret form hidden within itself. That is the impasse of every critical method which places the source of vitality in an implicit form.

Criticism cannot do without these implicit forms, inner relationships, hidden significances. But they must be so presented that they not only reflect the work but also reflect back upon it, and at an oblique angle so that they can receive more in return than their own images. Criticism is not the reduction of a work to its individual, interior symmetries, but the continuous movement from explicit to implicit and back again. And it must end where it started—with the surface. □

[14] For this reason, *Les Chats* is a more impressive analysis than *Th'expence of Spirit*. The reader can forgive the mass of detail heaped indiscriminately upon him for the sake of the elucidation of the large movement from extrinsic to intrinsic, which dovetails with the progression real to surreal.

[15] The presentation of the analysis by Schenker as starting with the *Ursatz* and moving to the finished piece does not disguise the principle, which is always that of reduction.

Addendum

The musical section of this review is an attempt to explain the importance of Schenker to a public whose appreciation of musical examples is primarily visual. Schenker was of interest here only as one form of criticism that claims to discover a hidden pattern. On one point, this article does him a grave injustice: it is true that rhythm is skimped in *Der freie Satz* and treated in the *Five Graphic Music Analyses* largely by counting the number of bars in a phrase, but other analyses of Schenker, particularly those in *Das Meisterwerk in der Musik*, are filled with the subtlest observations on rhythm.

4. Méthodes d'analyse en musicologie *

A André Souris.

1

Dans tout système sémiotique, le rapport entre le code et le message peut être décrit de deux points de vue différents, selon que l'on va du message au code, ou du code au message [1].

Dans le premier cas, la démarche est analytique; elle s'impose en principe chaque fois que, s'agissant d'une langue inconnue, d'un mythe ou d'une musique exotiques, etc., le message est seul donné. Le travail de l'analyste consiste alors à décomposer et manipuler le corpus (l'ensemble donné de messages) de diverses manières, de façon à dégager les unités, classes d'unités et règles de leurs combinaisons, qui constituent le code. Le problème crucial est ici celui des procédures de découverte, c'est-à-dire des critères d'analyse. La linguistique structurale s'est — du moins au Danemark et aux États-Unis — préoccupée pendant vingt ans presque exclusivement de ces problèmes, et a élaboré divers modèles analytiques, basés sur des critères explicitement définis, tels que le principe de commutation dans l'école glossématique, ou celui de substitution dans des environnements identiques de l'analyse distributionnelle améri-

* *Revue belge de Musicologie*, 20 (1966), p. 65-90. *Liber amicorum André Souris.*
1. Dans cet article, je traiterai la musique comme un système sémiotique, partageant un certain nombre de traits communs — tels que l'existence d'une syntaxe — avec le langage et d'autres systèmes de signes. Je laisserai complètement de côté l'aspect proprement esthétique, et notamment la question de savoir si l'esthétique peut se réduire à une sémiotique. Par ailleurs, sur le plan terminologique, à cause de la référence à la notation impliquée nécessairement dans l'emploi du mot « texte » en musique, j'utiliserai, de préférence à la dichotomie hjelmslévienne du système et du texte, celle, jakobsonienne, issue de la théorie de la communication, du code et du message.

caine [1]. On trouve une esquisse de procédure de découverte appliquée au mythe chez Claude Lévi-Strauss [2] et, plus récemment, divers chercheurs ont abordé le problème en sémantique ainsi qu'en stylistique [3].

Une fois le code dégagé, une démarche inverse permet d'engendrer (*to generate*) des messages à partir de ce code, selon des règles de dérivation qui peuvent, elles aussi, être explicitées rigoureusement [4]. Ainsi, en face d'un modèle analytique, on dispose d'un modèle synthétique, qui part des éléments les plus abstraits et les plus généraux pour aboutir aux messages concrets. De ce point de vue, la grammaire d'une langue, formulée synthétiquement, apparaît comme une sorte de machine capable d'engendrer toutes — et rien que — les phrases admises, ou « bien formées », ou « grammaticales », dans cette langue. A première vue, le modèle synthétique n'apporte rien de nouveau; il implique le modèle analytique, dont il donne simplement l'image en miroir. Il sert seulement d'épreuve de la validité du modèle analytique : il permet de vérifier si celui-ci donne bien une image fidèle des faits, et, surtout, d'éprouver sa productivité : si le modèle analytique est bon, sa transformation synthétique engendrera des messages qui ne figuraient pas dans le corpus initial (limité par définition) mais que les sujets reconnaîtront comme également bien formés.

A vrai dire, cette conception du rapport entre les deux modèles — c'est à peu de chose près celle de Hjelmslev — est trop simplifiée, et le modèle synthétique a des raisons d'être plus fondamentales. Comme l'ont montré les théoriciens de la grammaire générative, il semble très difficile de formaliser complètement les procédures de

1. Cf. L. Hjelmslev, *Prolegomena to a Theory of Language*, tr. angl. 2e éd., Madison, 1961; K. Togeby, *Structure immanente de la langue française*, Copenhague, 1951; Z. S. Harris, *Methods in Structural Linguistics*, Chicago, 1951, et *Discourse Analysis Reprints*, La Haye, 1963; P. L. Garvin, *On Linguistic Method*, La Haye, 1964.

2. Cf. *Anthropologie structurale*, Paris, 1958, chap. xi, « La structure des mythes ».

3. Cf. notamment A. J. Greimas, *Sémantique structurale*, Paris, Larousse, 1966; M. Riffaterre, « Criteria for style analysis », *Word* 15, p. 154-174 (1959) et « Vers la définition linguistique du style », Word 17, p. 318-346 (1961).

4. Cf. les travaux de l'école de grammaire générative-transformationnelle aux États-Unis, et notamment N. Chomsky, *Syntactic Structures*, La Haye, 1957, et *Current Issues in Linguistic Theory*, La Haye, 1964; ainsi que E. Bach, *An Introduction to Transformational Grammars*, New York, 1964.

découverte, et l'application rigoureuse de critères tels que la commutation ou la distribution laisse toujours des restes; ceux-ci ne peuvent être réduits qu'à condition de faire intervenir des considérations d'un tout autre ordre — comme le principe de simplicité, appliqué à l'ensemble du système (du code). D'un autre côté, il paraît erroné de tenir que les *données* initiales de l'analyse se ramènent à un corpus de messages (au « texte encore inanalysé » de Hjelmslev, au recueil d'énoncés enregistrés des Américains) qui constituerait la seule voie d'accès au code. A partir du moment où l'on renonce à un objectivisme assez primaire, on s'aperçoit que l'analyste dispose de données plus variées, par exemple de toutes sortes de jugements métalinguistiques portés par les sujets sur le code, jugements qui, traités avec précaution, fournissent toute une série d'indices sur la structure du code [1].

Aussi, si la constitution du code continue à reposer sur l'existence de procédures analytiques, celles-ci seront nécessairement fragmentaires et multiples, et ce sera seulement au niveau de la formulation d'un modèle synthétique que le code pourra être décrit sur un mode unifié, avec le maximum de cohérence interne et de simplicité. Ajoutons que, comme l'expérience l'a montré, les modèles analytiques les plus élaborés ont toujours eu un caractère statique, qui les préparait mal à rendre compte de deux types de problèmes fondamentaux, celui de la créativité, de la productivité, des systèmes linguistiques ou sémiotiques, et celui des lois universelles qui gouvernent ceux-ci. Un code comprend essentiellement deux parties : des inventaires d'éléments, et des règles de combinaison et de fonctionnement de ces éléments. Or, les modèles analytiques tendent à privilégier le côté de l'inventaire, laissant dans l'ombre la question des règles.

264

---

1. Cf. Chomsky, « Some methodological remarks on generative grammar », *Word* 17, p. 219-239 (1961). Chomsky rejoint, d'une certaine manière, la conviction, exprimée par Cl. Lévi-Strauss, que l'analyse des mythes n'est possible qu'à partir de deux sortes de données : les textes, et leur contexte ethnographique; l'analyse interne du texte est nécessaire, mais elle ne suffit pas (cf. « La structure et la forme », *Cahiers de l'I.S.E.A.*, 1960). En musique, on voit assez bien à quoi peuvent correspondre certaines de ces données additionnelles : l'analyste ne dispose pas seulement d'un corpus de pièces enregistrées, mais également de descriptions d'instruments, de renseignements sur la manière d'en jouer, de données sur les conditions d'exécution, de commentaires divers — ne fût-ce que les titres des œuvres — qui sont autant d'indices directs ou indirects sur la structure du code.

D'où leur côté statique, d'où aussi leur manque d'universalité : c'est au niveau de l'inventaire des éléments que les langues (ou les systèmes musicaux) divergent le plus, tandis que les règles qui mettent en œuvre ces éléments présentent un caractère beaucoup plus général.

Il était nécessaire d'indiquer brièvement les limitations des modèles analytiques. Si on entreprend d'établir des procédures de découverte en musicologie, on risque de s'attarder sur des problèmes méthodologiques apparemment très difficiles, mais dont l'intérêt est en définitive restreint : au niveau du modèle synthétique, ces problèmes ne se posent plus. Ainsi, une question — qui peut concerner les musiciens — a longtemps préoccupé les linguistes : l'analyse doit-elle être menée en allant « de haut en bas » ou au contraire « de bas en haut »? Pour Hjelmslev, ce qui est donné, c'est le texte inanalysé (qui peut être très vaste, à la limite l'ensemble des énoncés émis dans une langue donnée) dans sa totalité, et l'analyse prend la forme d'une division progressive de ce tout en parties de plus en plus petites, définies par leurs relations mutuelles, — cette division aboutissant aux éléments ultimes indécomposables. Harris, au contraire, part d'énoncés relativement brefs et dégage d'abord les unités minimales — les phonèmes — qu'il groupe progressivement en classes d'unités plus vastes, morphèmes, syntagmes, phrases, pour s'attaquer en dernier lieu à l'analyse du discours. Les résultats des deux types d'analyse, appliqués aux mêmes matériaux, se recouvrent partiellement, mais, comme de toute façon une procédure unique ne peut jamais suffire, l'alternative des deux procédures cesse d'être cruciale : dans la pratique, les deux se mêlent constamment. Bien entendu, il est très utile d'avoir envisagé de façon précise les conséquences de l'emploi de telle ou telle procédure particulière.

Ces réserves faites, il reste que des procédures de découverte explicites, même partiellement insuffisantes, sont indispensables, ne fût-ce que pour garantir que le modèle synthétique ne se muera pas en système normatif. L'histoire de la linguistique témoigne de leur nécessité : elle n'aurait jamais atteint le stade actuel des grammaires génératives si vingt ans de recherches analytiques intensives ne l'avaient dégagée à tout jamais des systèmes, synthétiques, mais normatifs, de la grammaire traditionnelle.

103

2

Considérons maintenant l'état présent de la musicologie du point de vue de la distinction des deux modèles. On peut constater : *a*) que le problème théorique de la distinction n'a jamais été posé; *b*) qu'aucun modèle analytique n'a jamais été explicitement élaboré; *c*) que les analyses musicales, même les meilleures — par exemple celle donnée par Pierre Boulez du *Sacre du Printemps*[1] — ne formulent pas les critères de découverte sur lesquels elles reposent. D'une manière générale, la plupart des traités d'harmonie, de fugue, etc., présentent une situation analogue à celle offerte par les grammaires traditionnelles : le modèle est synthétique, partiellement explicite seulement, et entaché de normativisme. Ceci est bien connu. Il y a plus frappant : les réussites les moins contestables de la musicologie, tant dans le domaine de la tonalité occidentale — Gevaert[2] — que dans celui des échelles ou des rythmiques exotiques ou populaires — Braïloïu[3] — ont reçu une formulation synthétique : les matériaux sont toujours présentés en partant des éléments les plus abstraits (le système des quintes par exemple chez Gevaert) et en reconstituant progressivement toute la diversité des messages concrets. De toute évidence, cette formulation synthétique présuppose de nombreuses démarches analytiques préalables, correctes à en juger par la valeur de ces travaux. Mais ces démarches ne sont pratiquement jamais explicitées[4].

266

1. Cf. Pierre Boulez, « Stravinsky demeure », *Musique russe*, t. I, Paris, P.U.F., 1953.
2. Cf. F. A. Gevaert, *Traité d'harmonie*, Paris, 1907. Je dirai en passant ma gratitude à André Souris d'avoir attiré mon attention sur cet ouvrage capital, devenu presque introuvable, et dont il est un des seuls à avoir apprécié toute la valeur.
3. Cf. C. Braïloïu, « Le giusto syllabique bichrone », *Polyphonie* 2 (1948), p. 26-57; « Sur une mélodie russe », *Musique russe*, t. II, Paris, P.U.F., 1953, p. 329-391; « Le rythme enfantin », *les Colloques de Wégimont*, Bruxelles, 1956, p. 64-96.
4. Sans doute trouve-t-on dans les ouvrages de Gevaert ou de Braïloïu bien des matériaux qui permettraient dans certains cas de reconstruire un modèle analytique. Voir par exemple Gevaert, Quatrième Étude, 2ᵉ section, p. 64 s. Dans « Sur une mélodie russe », Braïloïu donne un certain nombre d'indices auxquels on reconnaît analytiquement les *pyens* (p. 339 s.), mais il ne les groupe

J'illustrerai la nécessité de recourir à des procédures de découverte en considérant deux types de problèmes — d'ailleurs intimement liés — : celui des échelles et des modes, d'une part, et celui de l'articulation d'une œuvre en unités de différents niveaux hiérarchiques, d'autre part.

Gevaert et Braïloïu donnent tous deux des tableaux, l'un des modes diatoniques, l'autre des systèmes prédiatoniques, engendrés déductivement. Ils les illustrent à l'aide d'exemples, mais ne se posent pas la question cruciale : étant donné un corpus quelconque de mélodies modales, à quoi reconnaît-on qu'une de ces mélodies appartient à tel mode déterminé? Ou encore : à quoi reconnaît-on qu'une mélodie passe successivement de tel mode à tel autre, ou qu'elle présente une organisation hiérarchique de divers modes? Les premiers spécialistes du chant grégorien avaient décidé, par ce qui apparaît comme un embryon de procédure de découverte, qu'une mélodie appartient au mode dont sa dernière note est la « tonique »[1]; mais cette procédure est par trop simpliste. En fait, malgré l'insistance de divers musicologues sur le rôle des formules mélodiques, par exemple, dans la détermination des modes[2], il reste un grand trou entre, d'une part, les messages concrets (le corpus grégorien par exemple) et, d'autre part, le système des modes, qui ne constitue que la partie la plus abstraite du code. Il manque tout l'ensemble des règles qui feraient passer de ceux-là à celui-ci (et vice versa).

Autre problème : pour tout le monde, il semble aller de soi qu'une œuvre musicale ayant un minimum de complexité est soumise à une

267

---

pas en une procédure ordonnée systématiquement — ce qui le conduit à certaines erreurs d'interprétation, cf. l'exemple 10, p. 343.

Ajoutons toutefois que le problème des procédures de découverte commence à préoccuper les musiciens — il est posé, au moins implicitement, chez André Souris (cf. par exemple l'article « Phrase », in *Encyclopédie Fasquelle*) — et les ethnomusicologues, qui y sont amenés inévitablement par le biais de la transcription (cf. des travaux en cours de Gilbert Rouget, ainsi que les actes d'un symposium sur la transcription, publiés dans *Ethnomusicology*, vol. VIII, n° 3 (1964)).

1. Cf. notamment G. Reese, *Music in the Middle Ages*, New York, 1940, p. 161 s.

2. Cf., pour le pentatonique, Braïloïu, « Sur une mélodie russe », p. 351 s. Il est clair que les formules — divers types d'*incipit*, etc., — sont utilisées seulement à titre illustratif. Le problème se pose d'ailleurs de savoir comment l'autonomie de ces formules a été établie, ce qui pose de nouveau la question des procédures de découverte, sur un autre plan (voir ci-dessous, problèmes de la division).

organisation hiérarchique, se divise en parties de différents niveaux. Ainsi, d'après Ferretti [1], les mélodies grégoriennes se divisent en *périodes*, celles-ci à leur tour en *phrases*, les phrases en *membres* et ceux-ci en *incises*. De telles analyses, cependant, soulèvent une multitude de questions, dont la moindre n'est pas celle de la validité de la conception taxinomique de la structure musicale qu'elles semblent impliquer (voir plus loin). On peut aussi se demander si ces notions de période, de phrase, etc., sont susceptibles de recevoir des définitions générales ou universelles, ou si au contraire il ne faut les tenir que pour des notions *ad hoc*, valables seulement pour telle pièce déterminée. Mais la question cruciale, préliminaire à toutes les autres, est la suivante : *quels sont les critères qui, dans tel cas particulier, ont présidé à la division?* Or, cette question, personne ne prend la peine d'y répondre, comme si l'évidence des critères sautait aux yeux [2].

Cette question en entraîne une série d'autres. En voici quelques-unes. Si je divise une section A en deux segments *a* et *b*, est-ce en me basant sur les pauses, sur les différences de timbres, l'opposition des registres, les cadences mélodiques et/ou harmoniques, l'identité ou le contraste des rythmes, la durée égale ou inégale des segments, etc.? Ou est-ce une combinaison de ces critères qui joue? Les divisions reposent-elles sur les identités ou sur les différences entre segments? Certains critères sont-ils substituables? Est-ce que, par exemple, j'obtiens les mêmes résultats si je fonde la division sur les pauses et ensuite sur les cadences — coïncidence qu'on trouve notamment dans le choral — ou au contraire le recours à des critères différents instaure-t-il des divisions différentes, qui introduisent des ambiguïtés dans la structure? Ce cas est certainement très fréquent, et son étude serait fondamentale pour rendre compte, entre autres, des variantes d'interprétation. Est-il possible d'introduire une hiérarchie entre les divers critères, l'un n'intervenant que si l'autre laisse subsister

1. Cf. Reese, *op. cit.*, p. 169, et les articles d'André Souris dans *Encyclopédie Fasquelle.*
2. Dans mes propres analyses de Debussy — cf. ici-même, chap. III — la division des fragments analysés est tenue pour une donnée acquise : voir par exemple l'analyse du passage de *Fêtes* en sections et sous-sections (p. 75 s.). Je donne toutefois une ébauche rudimentaire de procédure de découverte à propos du Prélude de *Pelléas* (p. 90).

106

des ambiguïtés? Peut-on établir des procédures permettant de vérifier la validité d'un critère choisi [1]? Existe-t-il des critères universels? Serait-il utile de distinguer des critères essentiellement syntagmatiques (les pauses) et des critères paradigmatiques (fondés sur l'équivalence interne et/ou externe des éléments), ou encore des critères relevant surtout de la substance (les pauses encore une fois, les timbres) et des critères essentiellement formels (la répétition, la variation)?

Ces questions risquent de paraître futiles aux musiciens et musicologues. Pourtant, leur importance dans l'étude des musiques non européennes n'est guère contestable. D'un autre côté, l'application de procédures de découverte explicites à des systèmes musicaux plus familiers peut très bien n'aboutir qu'à des conclusions banales, déjà reconnues intuitivement. Mais cela même est loin d'être négligeable. Il est en effet très utile de pouvoir vérifier pas à pas l'élaboration d'une procédure par le recours à l'intuition; cette procédure une fois déterminée complètement, pourra ensuite être appliquée à l'étude de matériaux moins connus. D'ailleurs, même dans des domaines aussi connus que celui de la fugue, des procédures de segmentation bien définies aboutiront à réviser les analyses traditionnelles (confirmant en cela l'intuition des meilleurs musiciens) [2].

Je disais plus haut que le problème de la division (de l'articulation) d'une pièce et celui de la détermination des échelles et des modes étaient liés. En effet, la structure modale peut servir d'indice dans la procédure de division, et inversement. Il y a donc un danger d'introduire un cercle vicieux dans la procédure. Considérons les prin-

---

1. Par exemple : supposons que, en me fondant sur la pause, j'ai divisé une section donnée en deux segments A et B, cette division a de grandes chances d'être confirmée si, recherchant des équivalences dans la structure interne de A et de B, je découvre que A et B ont la même longueur absolue (en termes de temps, de mesures, etc.) et/ou que $A = a + b$, et que $B = a + c$ (donc que A et B sont équivalents d'un certain point de vue).

2. L'application aux fugues du *Clavecin bien tempéré* d'une procédure analogue, dans ses grandes lignes, à celle basée sur le principe de répétition qui est exposée ci-dessous, permet de dégager des unités de divers niveaux, correspondant souvent aux unités définies par la théorie traditionnelle (exposition, divertissement, sujet, etc.). On peut cependant déterminer d'une manière purement formelle qu'il est impossible, dans le cas de telle fugue particulière, de parler, par exemple, de contre-sujet, ou de tête du sujet, etc.

cipaux critères retenus par Bruno Nettl [1] pour déterminer la tonique d'une pièce donnée. Ce sont : *a*) la fréquence et la durée plus grandes de tel son par rapport aux autres; *b*) la position finale de ce son dans des sections et phrases individuelles; *c*) sa position terminale dans le chant. Ce qui nous intéresse ici, c'est le point (*b*). Il présuppose que l'on dispose déjà de critères de division de la pièce en « sections et phrases individuelles » et que, sauf cercle vicieux, ces critères excluent toute référence à la structure scalaire et modale (Nettl ne fournit pas de critères explicites de division). Je ne suggère d'ailleurs pas que la seule procédure de découverte possible ira de la division aux échelles. On peut au contraire imaginer l'utilisation successive de deux procédures, l'une allant de la division aux échelles, l'autre des échelles à la division, et la seconde servant à vérifier la validité de la première; j'ai bien souligné au début de cet article qu'il n'existe sans doute pas de procédure de découverte entièrement satisfaisante : plus donc on disposera de procédures indépendantes, mieux cela vaudra pour la constitution finale du code. Mais il est essentiel que l'une des procédures ne suppose pas acquis les résultats de l'autre.

270

3

Je m'intéresserai surtout, dans cet article, aux procédures de division, quitte à signaler, à propos d'un exemple donné, leur incidence sur l'analyse modale. Deux voies s'offrent pour dégager une procédure. On peut soit partir d'analyses déjà faites, et essayer de reconstruire les critères, pas nécessairement homogènes, qui y ont présidé, soit choisir *un* principe donné, parfaitement explicite, quitte à s'apercevoir qu'il est insuffisant, qu'il demande des aménagements,

---

1. *Music in Primitive Culture*, Cambridge, Mass., 1956, p. 46. Je ne reprends pas nécessairement à mon compte l'idée qu'il est possible de déterminer une tonique dans les musiques non tonales — cf. Brailoïu, « Sur une mélodie russe », p. 346 s., sur l'instabilité de la tonique dans les systèmes pentatoniques. La discussion est ici purement de méthode. On remarquera d'autre part que Nettl mêle les critères quantitatifs (*a*) et qualitatifs (*b, c*). Peut-être conviendrait-il de les séparer plus nettement, et d'essayer de définir les échelles en termes purement structuraux, c'est-à-dire qualitatifs. De toute façon la fréquence relative de tel ou tel son ne me paraît pas du tout décisive.

voire qu'il est à rejeter. C'est cette dernière voie que j'essayerai de suivre.

Laissons tout d'abord de côté la référence aux pauses, certainement insuffisante si la segmentation est poussée assez loin, ainsi que le recours à la structure linguistique des paroles [1], dans le cas de la musique vocale. Posons en principe que l'on n'aura recours à ce type de données que subsidiairement, soit pour confirmer des segmentations fournies par ailleurs, soit à titre d'indices suggérant des segmentations possibles, dans les cas où l'analyse proprement musicale se heurte de prime abord à de grosses difficultés (quand par exemple le critère de répétition n'est pas immédiatement applicable). Il s'agit donc avant toute chose de formuler des procédures basées sur des critères spécifiquement musicaux.

D'un autre côté, il est utile d'introduire une distinction théorique entre deux types d'éléments musicaux, que j'appellerai, respecti-

---

1. Il est évident que la structure linguistique des paroles doit entrer en ligne de compte dans l'analyse de la musique vocale. Mais cette évidence n'autorise pas à mélanger les deux niveaux, comme cela est courant dans l'étude des « formes » de la chanson médiévale. Reese (*Music in the Middle Ages*, p. 224) analyse *Por conforter ma pesance* de Thibaut de Navarre en :

1) $a + b + a + b + c + d + E$

Si on laisse provisoirement de côté le contraste entre le chœur (E) et le soliste, une analyse musicale, basée sur le critère de répétition, donne une première division en $A + A + X$; à un second niveau, A se décompose en $a + b$, et X en $a' + c$ ($a' = a$ transposé). D'où :

2) $a + b + a + b + a' + c$ (c se divise ensuite à partir d'un tout autre principe, l'opposition chœur/soliste).

L'analyse linguistique donne une structure différente; au point de vue des rimes (qui n'en est qu'un aspect), on a 3., qui peut se superposer à 2. de la façon suivante :

3) $m + n + m + n + n + m + p$
2) $a + b + a + b + a' + c$

Cette analyse n'a qu'une valeur indicative; elle veut surtout réagir contre une tendance à aplatir la réalité musicale et linguistique en projetant sur un seul plan des structures multidimensionnelles. Ajoutons que, sur le plan purement linguistique, la distinction de plusieurs niveaux s'impose : les divisions obtenues en termes de syntaxe ne correspondent pas nécessairement à celles obtenues en termes de phonologie ou de métrique. Cf., pour des illustrations, l'analyse des « Chats » de Baudelaire par R. Jakobson et Cl. Lévi-Strauss, *l'Homme* 2.1 : 5-21 (1962) et mon article « Sur un vers de Charles Baudelaire », ici-même, chap. VIII.

Enfin, il est inutile de rappeler que bien des éléments linguistiques peuvent intervenir dans l'analyse musicale *en tant qu'ils sont des éléments musicaux :* ainsi la rime peut agir comme timbre, ou l'opposition syllabique/mélismatique comme opposition staccato/legato, etc.

vement, paramétriques et non paramétriques [1]. Un élément paramétrique peut se présenter sous deux formes. Dans le premier cas, il s'agit d'un élément qui est constant pendant toute la durée d'une pièce, comme par exemple le tempo dans certains Allegros de Bach, ou le caractère monodique et le timbre dans une mélodie vocale chantée en solo. Ici, évidemment, cet élément n'est d'aucun recours dans la segmentation de la pièce. Dans le second cas, l'élément se manifeste sous la forme d'une opposition binaire, qui divise la pièce en sections caractérisées par la présence tantôt de l'un et tantôt de l'autre terme de l'opposition; cf. l'opposition soliste/chœur dans l'antiphonaire, l'opposition *piano* (= « séparés ») / *forte* (= « ensemble ») dans les doubles chœurs vénitiens, celle entre l' « original » et l'écho (= « proche » / « lointain », plus, souvent, « complet » / « tronqué ») dans certaines musiques de l'époque baroque, l'opposition mineur/majeur dans le mouvement lent de la 3e Symphonie de Beethoven, l'opposition de registre, grave/aigu (c'est aussi une opposition de timbre), dans la Marche initiale de *Renard* de Stravinsky, etc. Comme ces exemples le montrent, beaucoup de ces oppositions sont composites, et mêlent plusieurs dimensions; celles-ci peuvent très bien être dissociées, et en ce cas, le découpage de la pièce sera différent selon que l'on considérera l'une ou l'autre. Mais, en chaque cas, le principe du découpage sera le même : des sections successives sont délimitées en termes de contrastes, et ceux-ci reposent sur la présence ou l'absence dans la section d'un des deux termes d'une opposition binaire.

Un élément non paramétrique, au contraire, ne se laisse pas ramener à une opposition binaire; il se caractérise plutôt par un assez grand nombre de distinctions à l'intérieur d'une même dimension (cf. les nombreux intervalles différents engendrés par la gamme diatonique ou chromatique, ou encore les séries de durées, d'intensités, de modes d'attaque, dans les œuvres sérielles). Comme l'a montré — dans un autre langage — André Souris [2], il n'est pas possible

272

1. Cette distinction n'est pas absolue, et toute une gamme de transitions est possible. Soulignons que le mot *paramétrique* est ici utilisé dans un sens légèrement différent de celui qu'il a dans les écrits des musiciens sériels. Pour désigner ce que ceux-ci entendent par *paramètres*, je parlerai simplement de *dimensions* de la substance musicale.
2. Cf. en particulier l'article « Forme », in *Encyclopédie Fasquelle*.

de déterminer *a priori* que telle ou telle dimension musicale a une vocation paramétrique ou non paramétrique. Des dimensions, paramétriques dans telle culture, ou à telle période de l'histoire, sont non paramétriques dans telle autre.

Dans cet article, je laisserai complètement de côté les éléments paramétriques, qui seront donc considérés constants dans toute la durée des pièces analysées. Je m'en tiendrai aux éléments non paramétriques, et choisirai, comme principal critère de division, la *répétition*. Je partirai de la constatation empirique du rôle énorme joué en musique, à tous les niveaux, par la répétition, et j'essayerai de développer une idée émise par Gilbert Rouget [1] :

> ... Certains fragments sont répétés, d'autres ne le sont pas; c'est sur la répétition — ou l'absence de répétition — qu'est fondé notre découpage. Lorsqu'une suite de sons est énoncée à deux ou plusieurs reprises, avec ou sans variante, elle est considérée comme une unité. Corollairement, une suite de sons énoncée une seule fois, quels que soient sa longueur et le nombre apparent de ses articulations (notamment les silences) est considérée elle aussi comme une unité...

Avant d'aller plus loin, il faut préciser ce que l'on entend par répétition, et délimiter quelles données l'application du critère de répétition suppose connues. Répétition signifie identité entre des segments répartis à divers endroits de la chaîne syntagmatique. Mais qui parle d'identité soulève la question : identité à quel point de vue? En effet, du point de vue purement physique, deux événements concrets ne sont jamais complètement identiques. Une certaine abstraction est donc inévitable, et la question devrait se poser de savoir sur quoi elle repose. Nous ne nous poserons pas ici cette question, et considérerons comme des données certaines identités élémentaires. D'autre part, il s'agit de savoir du point de vue de quelles dimensions — hauteur, durée, intensité, timbre, etc. — deux segments différents seront considérés comme des répétitions l'un de l'autre. Ici, étant donné que les exemples seront empruntés à la tradition écrite occidentale, et seront monodiques, on ne retiendra que la hauteur et la durée. Mais il faut rappeler que des segments, variables quant aux hauteurs

1. Gilbert Rouget, « Un chromatisme africain », *l'Homme*, I. 3 (1961), p. 41.

et aux durées, peuvent être considérés comme des répétitions pourvu qu'ils soient identiques à d'autres points de vue.

On considère donc comme données les identités élémentaires, minimales, de hauteur et de durée. Plus précisément, on peut se représenter les choses en disant que l'on dispose au départ d'un mécanisme quelconque, qui est capable de reconnaître une hauteur, un intervalle, ou une unité de durée déterminée (pour ce mécanisme, un *do₃* sera partout un *do₃*, une tierce mineure sera partout une tierce mineure, et une blanche une blanche). De plus, dans la procédure particulière ici choisie, les identités de hauteur et de durée sont considérées *ensemble*, du moins au début : ne sont considérés comme identiques que les segments identiques à la fois du point de vue des hauteurs et des durées. A un stade ultérieur de la procédure, les deux dimensions seront éventuellement dissociées, pour fournir des unités qui, répétitions l'une de l'autre à un seulement des deux points de vue, seront considérées comme des transformations l'une de l'autre (ou des variations). Cette procédure a semblé convenir au type de matériau utilisé (elle y fait gagner du temps : une procédure qui séparerait les deux dimensions aboutirait aux mêmes résultats, mais par un plus long chemin), mais elle n'est pas obligatoire; il est des musiques — les motets isorythmiques du xiv⁰ siècle notamment — qui exigent que l'on sépare dès l'abord les deux dimensions.

274

4

Ceci dit, voici, dans ses grandes lignes, la description d'une procédure de division, fondée sur le principe de répétition, et appliquée à des monodies.

a) Notre « machine à repérer les identités élémentaires » parcourt la chaîne syntagmatique et repère les fragments identiques. On considère comme des unités du niveau I les séquences — les plus longues possibles — qui sont répétées intégralement, soit immédiatement après leur première émission, soit après l'intervention d'autres segments. Cette première opération fournit des structures telles que A + X + A, A + A + X, A + X + A + Y + A, A + A + B + B + X, A + B + A + X + B + Y, etc. (les sections répétées, unités de niveau I, sont représentées par les premières lettres, les « restes » par les dernières lettres, de l'alphabet).

b) Le ou les restes sont considérés provisoirement comme des unités du même niveau I (cf. la citation de G. Rouget); cette analyse est confirmée ou infirmée par le recours à d'autres critères. La durée globale des segments peut fournir un premier indice : si, par l'opération (a), on a dégagé une structure A + A + X, X sera en principe considéré comme une unité de même niveau que A si sa durée globale est approximativement la même que celle de A (en ce cas, pour montrer que (b) a eu lieu, on peut, dans la notation, remplacer X, Y, Z, etc., par B, C, D, etc., et A + A + X est écrit A + A + B). Notons que, en recourant à l'équivalence des durées des segments, nous ne faisons qu'appliquer le principe de répétition à un niveau plus abstrait : X est, du point de vue de sa durée absolue, et toutes choses égales d'ailleurs, une répétition de A.

b_1) Les résultats de (b) peuvent ensuite être consolidés par le recours aux indices fournis par les pauses, ou par l'analyse linguistique des paroles s'il s'agit de musique vocale.

c) Si les opérations (b) et (b_1) n'ont pas abouti, et si les restes ne sont pas assimilables à des unités de niveau I, deux cas se présentent : 1) X, Y, etc., sont beaucoup plus brefs que A, B, etc.; on transmet alors ces restes à un stade ultérieur de l'analyse, en attendant les résultats des opérations suivantes (d); 2) le reste est beaucoup plus long que A, B, etc.; dans ce cas, ou bien, grâce aux opérations de (b), (b_1), (d) il apparaît segmentable [1] en unités de niveau I, qui seront des transformations de A, B, etc. — et alors, par exemple, A + A + X sera décrit comme A + A + B + C — ou bien il se réduira ultérieurement — après une nouvelle application de (a) aux unités dégagées au niveau I — en unités de niveau II, ou, enfin, il doit être considéré comme unité inanalysée de niveau O (voir ci-dessous, (e)).

d) Souvent, on sera amené à considérer diverses unités — aussi bien parmi les A, B, etc., que parmi les X, Y, etc. — comme étant

1. Avec, éventuellement, de nouveaux restes brefs, à transmettre à un stade ultérieur de l'analyse; par exemple, A + A + X = A + A + B + C + y (on représentera les unités de niveau I par des majuscules et celles de niveau II par des minuscules).

113

des *transformations* (des variantes, rythmiques et/ou mélodiques) les unes des autres. C'est ainsi que, par exemple, A + A + X sera réécrit A + A + A', ou encore A + B + A + B sera réécrit A + A' + A + A'. Il serait essentiel de dresser la liste des types de transformations possibles, et de décrire les procédures qui permettent de les dégager. Je me bornerai à quelques remarques (en laissant de côté la question des transpositions, transformations particulières qui ne posent guère de problèmes).

d_1) Une première classe de transformations sera dégagée si on applique, comme on l'a déjà suggéré plus haut, le principe de répétition, *séparément* aux hauteurs et aux durées. On obtient alors des transformations rythmiques des mêmes structures mélodiques, et inversement.

d_2) D'autres transformations feront intervenir des opérations plus compliquées, telles que permutations, ajouts ou suppressions de certains éléments. Je n'entrerai pas ici dans le détail de ces opérations, quitte à en signaler quelques-unes au cours de l'analyse des exemples.

d_3) Il importe de remarquer que, pour qu'une section, B ou X, soit considérée comme une transformation d'une autre section A, il est souvent nécessaire de passer par une nouvelle application, à un niveau inférieur, de l'opération (a); celle-ci dégage alors des unités de niveau II, telles que, par exemple, A = $a + b$, et X = $a + c$. Ainsi, une partie de X apparaît comme une répétition stricte de A, et, pour peu que, à d'autres points de vue — durée absolue, pauses, structure des paroles, etc. — X soit équivalent à A, X sera considéré comme une transformation de A : X = A'. Nous voyons ici un exemple de la nécessité, au cours de la procédure, de *shunter*, c'est-à-dire de procéder tantôt de haut en bas, tantôt de bas en haut. Un autre exemple en était donné dès le début, puisque, partis du « bas » — les unités élémentaires de durée et de hauteur — nous avons ensuite, avec l'opération (a), procédé à partir du « haut ».

d_4) Souvent, en dégageant des transformations — notamment par l'opération (d_1) — on est amené à réviser une première segmentation, fournie par (a) et (b). Supposons que ces deux opérations ont abouti à une structure A + x + A + y (avec des restes très brefs). Si (d_1) montre que A + x est, du point de vue des durées par exemple, identique à A + y, et si d'autres raisons interviennent également

114

— telles que l'absence de pause entre A et *x*, A et *y*, et la présence au contraire d'une pause entre *x* et A — on posera que A + *x* est une seule unité, dont A + *y* est une transformation, et on réécrira la structure comme A + A′.

e) Nous pouvons maintenant aborder un problème dont (d_4) n'offre qu'un cas particulier. Supposons que l'opération (a) ait fourni des structures telles que

1) A + X + A + Y...

ou

2) X + A + Y + A...

Une question se pose, que nous avions tout d'abord laissée de côté : ne peut-on pas considérer que, en (1) A + X et A + Y, et, en (2), X + A et Y + A, constituent des unités d'un niveau supérieur au niveau I (appelons ce niveau le niveau O)? L'opération (a) ne donne aucun moyen de répondre à cette question, et on est obligé de recourir à des critères subsidiaires. Voici les deux plus importants; tous deux me paraissent également nécessaires pour décrire (1) comme (A + X) + (A + Y), et (2) comme (X + A) + (Y + A).

e_1) La terminaison de X et de Y en (1), celle de A en (2) — par contraste avec celle de A en (1), celles de X et de Y en (2) — est marquée d'une façon spéciale, par la pause et/ou l'allongement de la finale (en face de l'absence de pause et/ou d'allongement dans les autres unités).

e_2) L'analyse ultérieure — c'est-à-dire, essentiellement, les opérations groupées sous (d) — montre que Y est une transformation de X.

Il reste à dire que, une fois dégagées les unités de niveau I, la procédure doit être appliquée de nouveau, en commençant par l'opération (a), de manière à dégager des unités de niveau II, et ainsi de suite, jusqu'à ce qu'on arrive à des unités qui se confondent avec les unités élémentaires dont on était parti.

115

5

Illustrons maintenant la procédure par des exemples, en commençant par les plus simples. Les difficultés qu'elle rencontre, les problèmes qu'elle pose, apparaîtront progressivement. Soit d'abord un *Geisslerlied* allemand du XIVe siècle, « Maria muoter reinû maît » (cf. ex. 1)[1]. Quelques mots tout d'abord sur la représentation graphique des exemples. Il m'a paru éclairant, dans l'étude des monodies, de reprendre un procédé que Claude Lévi-Strauss applique à l'analyse des mythes — en s'inspirant d'ailleurs lui-même de la notation musicale des partitions d'orchestre[2]. Les séquences équi-

278

exemple 1 (a) : Geisslerlied

1. Cité d'après Reese, *Music in the Middle Ages*, p. 239, qui le reprend lui-même à Paul Runge, *Die Lieder und Melodien der Geissler des Jahres 1349* (1900), p. 9. Comme je ne m'intéresse pas ici aux problèmes de transcription, je traite les transcriptions comme des données, sans préjuger de leur validité.
2. Cf. *Anthropologie structurale*, p. 234 s.

valentes sont, autant que possible, écrites au-dessous les unes des autres, dans une même colonne, et le texte doit se lire, en faisant abstraction des blancs, de gauche à droite et de haut en bas. Ainsi, certains traits de structure sont immédiatement apparents, de même d'ailleurs que certaines ambiguïtés. Il serait évidemment très difficile d'appliquer le même procédé à la représentation des structures polyphoniques.

Il faut insister sur le fait que, dans l'analyse telle qu'elle est effectivement menée, les diverses étapes de la procédure ne se suivent pas nécessairement dans l'ordre donné. La procédure est beaucoup plus une procédure de vérification, destinée à veiller à ce que l'analyse soit cohérente, qu'une procédure de découverte au sens strict du terme. Sans doute, il serait toujours possible de l'appliquer rigoureusement dans l'ordre donné, et on obtiendrait les mêmes résultats, mais il est beaucoup plus économique et plus rapide de s'en servir pour vérifier les résultats d'une analyse obtenue, très rapidement parfois, d'une manière purement intuitive. C'est là une situation que les linguistes connaissent bien [1]. Aussi, dans l'analyse des exemples, et pour ne pas allonger démesurément la démonstration, je me permettrai souvent d'être assez elliptique, sûr que le lecteur pourra reconstituer lui-même la série des opérations effectuées.

Considérons notre *Geisslerlied*. Un premier parcours de la procédure dégage, au niveau I, la structure A + A' + B + B, sans reste (A' pour rendre compte des légères variantes, en *b* vs *b'*, *si bémol* vs *la*, et ensuite, le *la* noire subdivisé une fois en deux croches) [2].

La série explicite des opérations aurait en fait donné :

a) X + B + B;

279

1. Cf. Z. S. Harris, *Methods in Structural Linguistics*, p.l. : « These procedures also do not constitute a necessary laboratory schedule in the sense that each procedure should be completed before the next is entered upon. In practice, linguists take unnumbered short cuts and intuitive or heuristic guesses, and keep many problems about a particular language before them at the same time... The chief usefulness of the procedures listed below is therefore as a reminder in the course of the original research, and as a form for checking or presenting the results... »
2. Pour simplifier, dans la suite de l'analyse, je ne tiendrai plus compte que de la première variation, la seconde s'expliquant très bien comme une variante combinatoire due à la structure syllabique et métrique des paroles (deux syllabes, accentuée et inaccentuée respectivement, vs une seule syllabe accentuée); je ne retiens donc ici que deux unités de niveau II, *b* et *b'*.

117

b) résultat négatif : pas d'équivalence en durée absolue entre X et B, (pas plus qu'entre A et B) ;

c), d) : X = A + A'; A' est une transformation mélodique (durée constante) de A (cf. d_1); il est certain que, intuitivement, on aura déjà dégagé des unités de niveau II, et que c'est en termes de *b* et de *b'* — plutôt que de A et de A' — que l'on aura repéré les transformations.

Si, malgré le résultat négatif de (b), A, A' et B sont considérées des unités de même niveau (I) c'est surtout à cause des résultats de (d), et parce que au stade ultérieur, A, A' et B apparaîtront constitués en partie d'éléments identiques (cf. d_3).

Une seconde application de la procédure donne des unités de niveau II, obtenues par exemple de la façon suivante :

a) A' = *x* + *b* + *y* + *b*;

b) A' = *a* + *b* + *c* + *b* (durées de *a*, *b*, *c*, identiques);

d) A = *a* + *b* + *c* + *b'* (*b'* = T^m — abréviation pour transformation mélodique — de *b*);

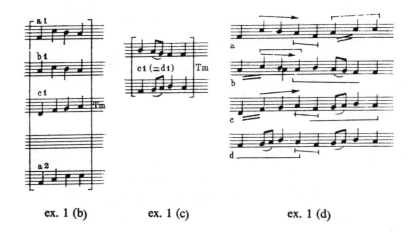

ex. 1 (b)   ex. 1 (c)   ex. 1 (d)

a) B = *z* + *b'* (*b'*, identifié en A, se retrouve ici);
b) B = *d* + *b'*.

Une troisième application de la procédure donne des unités de niveau III (désignées au moyen de nombres souscrits aux désignations des unités de niveau II, ex. a_1) :

a) $d = d_1 + d_1$;

a) $c = c_1 + d_1$;

b) $a = a_1 + a_2$, $b = b_1 + b_2$, $b' = b' + b_2$ (toutes ces unités étant équivalentes en durée à d_1); de plus :

d_1) (cf. ex. 1 (b) et 1 (c) : a_1, b'_1, b_1, c_1, a_2 sont toutes des transformations mélodiques d'une même structure rythmique (quatre noires); de même b_2 est une T^m de d_1.

Enfin, une quatrième application de la procédure permet de dégager un certain nombre d'unités qui sont, soit des répétitions, soit des transformations de divers types (transpositions, renversement, récurrences, T^m) (cf. ex. 1 (d). Ce qui empêche ici de parler d'unités de niveau IV, outre qu'elles sont de longueurs très inégales (certaines sont aussi longues que des unités de niveau III), c'est le fait que ces unités empiètent les unes sur les autres de diverses manières. Le caractère discret des unités et des niveaux — qui semble essentiel à une conception taxinomique de la structure musicale — y apparaît donc obscurci. Si, d'autre part, on pousse plus loin encore la segmentation, on aboutit aux unités minimales postulées au départ, et la procédure a épuisé ses effets.

Retenons comme un des résultats essentiels de cette analyse la dissymétrie qu'elle dévoile, à tous les niveaux : dissymétrie entre A (varié en A', et composé de trois sous-unités) et B (non varié à sa reprise, et composé de deux sous-unités), dissymétrie entre a, b, c (composés de deux segments différents) et d (composé de deux segments identiques), dissymétrie plus subtile entre a (dont les deux segments ne sont que des T^m l'un de l'autre) et b, c (dont les deux segments sont variés à la fois mélodiquement et rythmiquement), dissymétrie, enfin, due aux empiétements des « unités de niveau IV ».

5.1

Cette analyse n'a eu recours, à aucune de ses étapes, à des données relatives à l'échelle ou au mode. En revanche, il est possible d'utiliser ses résultats pour dégager la structure modale de la pièce. Une hié-

281

rarchie très nette des différents sons utilisés résulte de l'analyse en unités de différents niveaux, et cette hiérarchie ne fait pas intervenir, du moins pas directement, des critères quantitatifs. Le principal critère retenu est celui de la position, initiale, finale, ou de transition, que les sons occupent dans les diverses unités. Les positions initiale et finale sont considérées comme privilégiées [1], et on admet que la position initiale et/ou finale dans les unités de niveau supérieur a plus de poids que la même position dans les unités de niveau inférieur.

1. *fa* est initial et final de A, A′ et B; *fa* est également initial de a_2 et de d_1;

2. *do* est final de a;

3. *la* est initial de b, final de c, final de a_1, b_1, $b′_1$, c_1, d_1;

4. *ré* est initial de c, et absent partout ailleurs;

5. *si bémol* est initial de b_2; partout ailleurs, il est en position de transition (notons d'ailleurs que b est la plus « soudée » des unités de niveau II, à la fois parce que *si bémol* y va du *la* au *la*, et à cause de l'empiétement de b_2 et de l'unité de « niveau IV », qui est une transformation rétrograde de d_1; aussi, même là, la position de *si bémol* est très proche d'une position de transition);

6. *sol* n'apparaît qu'en position de transition.

Un critère secondaire — pratiquement dérivé du premier, — fait intervenir le rôle des différents sons comme notes de passage, broderies, etc., leur place dans des mouvements conjoints vs disjoints, et le fait qu'ils sont ou non immédiatement répétés;

7. *fa, do, la, ré*, sont les seuls sons à être enchaînés — à l'intérieur d'une unité, ou à la frontière de deux unités — par mouvements disjoints;

8. *si bémol* et *sol* ne sont jamais donnés que par un mouvement conjoint, ascendant-descendant ou descendant pour *si bémol*, ascendant ou descendant pour *sol*;

9. *fa* (à la finale de A et de B), *do* (à la finale de a) et *la* (à la frontière de c ou d et b ou $b′$) sont les seuls sons à être répétés immédiatement;

10. la variante b vs $b′$ accentue le caractère de note de passage de *si bémol* et la position plus forte de *la*.

---

1. Ce critère, suffisant sous cette forme pour la pièce en question, demanderait à être raffiné. Il faudrait au moins tenir compte de la structure rythmique (anacrouses, etc.).

Tous ces traits permettent de dégager une hiérarchie modale très nette, que l'on pourrait caractériser comme un fa majeur, avec oscillation vers le relatif mineur en *c*, et des relents de pentatonisme. Mais il faut bien noter que ces aspects — fa majeur, pentatonisme — n'ont de signification que si l'on replace cette pièce dans un contexte plus large. Si l'on s'en tient au système particulier dont notre *Geisslerlied* est le message unique, parler de majeur (sans sensible, *mi*) ou de pentatonisme (*fa-sol-la-do-ré*, alors que rien ne nous autorise — au contraire — à donner plus de poids à *sol* qu'à *si bémol*) revient à déformer les faits. C'est seulement si on replace cette pièce dans un corpus plus vaste qu'elle apparaîtra comme un cas de majeur ou de pentatonisme, et son système sous-jacent comme un sous-code du système tonal ou un sous-code d'un système pentatonique.

6

Soit un autre exemple, une chanson du trouvère Guiot de Provins, « Molt me mervoil[1]... » (cf. ex. 2).

1. Une analyse basée sur le mètre et les pauses donnerait tout de suite huit unités distinctes de niveau I; notre procédure aboutit au même résultat par le chemin suivant[2] :

a) X + B + Y + B;

b) X = A (durée égale à celle de B);

c) et (d) : Y se décompose en unités de longueur égale à A ou B (j'abrège la procédure, qui implique shuntage — référence aux unités de niveau II — et recours aux transformations : C = C'), d'où la structure :

$$A + B + C + D + E + F + C' + B$$

1. D'après F. Gennrich, *Troubadours, Trouvères, Minne- und Meistergesang*, coll. Das Musikwerk, Cologne, 1951, p. 25.
2. Que ce chemin soit plus long ne signifie pas nécessairement qu'il est moins économique. Non seulement il est plus rigoureux, mais il apporte une information qui est absente dans l'autre cas : par exemple, il indique que, d'un certain point de vue, tout ce qui est compris entre les deux émissions de B constitue une seule unité.

284

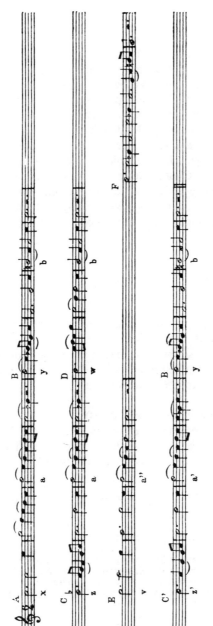

exemple 2 (a) : Guiot de Provins

2. L'application de (a) — et éventuellement de (d) — à un niveau plus bas livre une série d'unités de niveau II, selon le tableau suivant :

$$
\begin{aligned}
A &= x + a & B &= y + b \\
C &= z + a & D &= w + b \\
E &= v + a'' & F &= ? \\
C' &= z' + a' & B &= y + b
\end{aligned}
$$

Ce tableau appelle deux remarques. Tout d'abord, F est la seule unité qui ne se laisse pas décomposer, ce qui introduit une dissymétrie, d'autant plus frappante que F est la seule unité à se terminer sur le *sol* (*vs. do*, ou *do* + *si bémol*, dans les autres unités). D'autre part, on doit se demander s'il faut considérer les restes, x, y, z, etc., comme étant des unités de second niveau au même titre que a et b. Il existe en effet une différence de durée entre ces restes et les autres unités, et d'autre part, les restes ne représentent pas des transformations simples de ces autres unités; par ailleurs, il existe des rapports de transformation entre certains des restes — tous ont la même durée — mais ces rapports ne sont pas toujours simples. Aussi il me semble mieux rendre compte de la structure en leur conservant une notation différente.

3. On peut maintenant se poser la question de savoir si les unités de niveau I : A, B, etc., ne se groupent pas en unités de niveau supérieur (niveau O). Les critères retenus en (e) sont inopérants, mais un autre critère — qui correspond en un sens à une élaboration de (e₂) — apparaît, si on reconnaît que (A + B), (C + A), (C' + B), sont autant de manifestations d'une même structure abstraite, définie en termes de relations entre unités de niveau II; cette structure est décrite par la formule suivante (où les accolades indiquent qu'il faut choisir entre les unités qu'elles renferment)[1] :

$$
\left\{ \begin{array}{c} x \\ z \end{array} \right\} a \left\{ \begin{array}{c} y \\ w \end{array} \right\} b
$$

1. Cette notation est empruntée aux linguistes transformationnistes; cf. par exemple E. Bach, *An Introduction to Transformational Grammars*, New York, 1964. Je néglige ici la différence entre a et a', z et z'.

285

123

Le cas de F pose un problème. Comme E a une structure interne qui correspond à la première partie de la formule, $(v + a'')$, on dira que F est, d'un point de vue externe (distributionnel), équivalent à la seconde partie de la formule, mais qu'il en diffère par sa constitution interne.

4. Si on veut pousser plus loin l'analyse, on peut se demander s'il faut poser un niveau intermédiaire entre le niveau II et celui des unités minimales. Dans la perspective choisie dans cet article, un niveau se définit par l'existence de segments, n'empiétant pas les uns sur les autres, et dont certains au moins sont répétés dans des environnements différents. Si l'on a, par exemple, une succession $a + b$, et si ni a ni b n'apparaissent séparément — c'est-à-dire si on ne rencontre ni $a + c$ ni $d + b$ — il est inutile de poser un niveau dont a et b seraient des unités; $(a + b)$ doit être considéré comme une unité unique. Or, dans la chanson de Guiot de Provins, on ne trouve plus, en dessous du niveau II, de segments autonomes répétés, mais seulement, parfois, des segments qui sont des transformations simples les uns des autres. Je laisse ouverte la question de savoir si c'est là un élément suffisant à la position d'un niveau autonome. (On trouvera quelques-uns de ces cas de transformation dans l'exemple 2, cf. notamment 2 (b). En revanche, il est très important de noter que, dans la mesure où ces rapports de transformation lient, soit des segments immédiatement successifs, à l'intérieur d'une même unité, soit des segments appartenant à des unités de niveau I différentes, mais ne se trouvant pas « à la même place » dans ces unités, ces rapports de transformation ont pour effet de créer entre les unités de niveau I des relations en quelque sorte « obliques » (par rapport aux relations d'équivalence représentées selon un axe vertical). Dans le tableau 2 sont indiquées quelques-unes de ces transformations, qui ont pour effet de brouiller les frontières entre unités de niveau II. Particulièrement notables sont celles : (i) qui relient B et D à C (cf. 2 (e), introduisant une relation oblique par rapport au contraste A, C *vs* B, D, et (ii) qui relient F respectivement à B, C′ et E (cf. 2 (d), rattachant ainsi F au reste de la pièce, dont, en termes d'unités de niveau II, F semblait se dissocier.

exemple 2 (b)

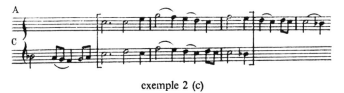

exemple 2 (c)

exemple 2 (d)

exemple 2 (e)

125

288

exemple 3 (a) : Raïmbaut de Vaqueiras

7

Voici encore un autre exemple, la célèbre *Estampida* « Kalenda maya » de Raïmbaut de Vaqueiras (d'après Gennrich, *op. cit.*, p. 16) (cf. ex. 3).

1. Par l'application de (a) est dégagée sans difficulté une unité A, répétée immédiatement; puis, par (a) et (c) sont dégagées deux séquences B + x et B + y, qui, en vertu de (d_4), sont réécrites B et B′ — dans un rapport de transformation : B = suspensif, B′ = conclusif; ensuite se pose un problème : faut-il considérer les séquences représentées, dans le tableau, respectivement par c et par D (ou D′), comme des unités distinctes de niveau I, ou au contraire, partant du principe que l'on essaie d'abord de dégager des unités les plus longues possibles, faut-il les grouper en une seule unité ($c + c + $D, puis $c + c + $D′) que l'on réécrirait C (C′ à sa seconde apparition)? En fait, il n'est pas possible de donner une réponse univoque à cette question, et on a certainement ici affaire à un cas d'ambiguïté inscrite dans la structure même. Sans doute, par sa longueur (critère (b)), c est assimilable à des unités de niveau inférieur, d'autant plus que c apparaît effectivement comme une T^r (= transformation rythmique) du « motif » final de A et de B′. D'un autre côté, c partage avec les unités de niveau I, A et B, le privilège d'être réitéré immédiatement après sa première apparition, ce qui, en un sens, le met sur le même pied que ces unités. Enfin, D commence et finit de la même manière que A et B, et nous allons voir que ces trois unités sont dans un rapport de transformation; fondre D avec c en une seule unité C lui ferait perdre ce caractère. C'est pourquoi je pense qu'on peut représenter une première segmentation de la pièce par la formule suivante, qui sauvegarde l'ambiguïté :

$$A + A + B + B′ + c + c + D + c + c + D′$$

2. Nous avons négligé une autre ambiguïté. En durée absolue, A est deux fois plus long que B. Ce fait, joint à cet autre que B est la seule unité dégagée jusqu'à présent à ne pas se terminer sur le *do* (d'où son caractère suspensif), amène à penser que, en un sens, A est équivalent à (B + B′) — d'où une éventuelle division de A en $A_1 + A_2$.

127

Mais (cf. ex. 3 (b) un autre rapport de transformation, qu'on peut qualifier de réduction « par le milieu », lie A à B et à D. En se transformant en B puis en D, A se trouve, en deux étapes, réduit à ses « motifs » initial et final, *a* et *b,* dont l'autonomie se trouve par là

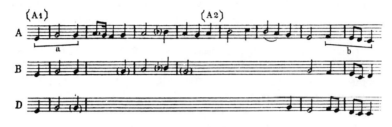

exemple 3 (b)[1]

290

exemple 3 (c)

1. Dans ce tableau, comme dans le suivant, certains segments sont reproduits deux fois — dont une entre parenthèses — dans une même rangée mais dans des colonnes différentes. Dans ce cas, les deux occurrences valent pour un seul élément, et signifient que cet élément pourrait également figurer dans deux unités, mais qu'on l'a — plus ou moins arbitrairement — assigné à l'une des deux.

même mise à nu. Enfin, des transformations (surtout mélodiques), d'une part, relient ces motifs *a* et *b* à d'autres éléments (notamment, *c* est une T^r de *b*), et, d'autre part, dessinent les contours de segments de niveaux intermédiaires (cf. ex. 3 (c).

En résumé, si l'analyse livre assez nettement — à deux niveaux extrêmes, supérieur et inférieur — des unités qui satisfont aux critères de répétition, de non-empiétement et d'autonomie, elle révèle aussi de multiples ambiguïtés structurales, non seulement aux niveaux intermédiaires, mais même dans les rapports entre les unités des deux niveaux extrêmes (cf. le cas de *c*). Le résultat est que, si la notion d'unité garde de sa valeur, celle de niveau (i.e., celle de niveaux distincts) tend à s'oblitérer.

8

Un dernier exemple, qui est également une chanson de troubadour, la chanson « Be m'anperdut... » de Bernard de Ventadour (Gennrich, *op. cit.*, p. 13) (cf. ex. 4).

Une première application de (a) livre aisément la structure A + A + X. Les difficultés commencent toutefois dès que l'on essaie, soit de réduire le reste X, soit de segmenter A en unités plus petites. Dans ce dernier cas, une nouvelle application de la procédure à un niveau plus bas ne fournit que des unités très brèves, réduites à une, deux ou trois notes (ex. 4 (c) ; aux niveaux intermédiaires, on ne trouve que des segments aux contours assez mal délimités, liés seulement par des rapports de transformation et non d'identité simple, et dont l'autonomie est faible.

Quant au reste X, l'application de (a) et de (d) livre un long segment final (A$_{1.2}$) qui est une répétition, avec de légères transformations, d'une grande partie de A. Mais ce segment est lui-même précédé d'un segment plus court, de cinq blanches (A$_{1.1}$), qui est dans un double rapport de transformation avec le début de A (cf. 4 (b) : d'une part, il est équivalent, en longueur absolue, à tout le début (tout ce qui précède l'équivalent de A$_{1.2}$), et, d'autre part, il représente une transformation mélodique, par « remplissage diatonique » du motif de blanches *la-do-ré-fa*. L'absence d'autonomie de ces

129

292

exemple 4 (a) : Bernard de Ventadour

deux segments $A_{1.1}$ et $A_{1.2}$, ainsi que la grande longueur de $A_{1.2}$ par rapport à A, empêche de les considérer comme des unités constitutives d'un niveau intermédiaire. On peut les grouper en un segment A_1, qui, à certains points de vue, pourrait être mis sur le même plan que A — durée absolue, toute la fin ($A_{1.2}$) identique — mais qui, à d'autres points de vue, l'absence du motif initial notamment, ne semble équivaloir qu'à une fraction seulement de A.

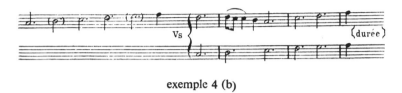

exemple 4 (b)

Ayant soustrait A_1 de X, il nous reste, au début de celui-ci, un segment ($A_{1.2}$) qui, avec des transformations un peu plus complexes [1] que dans le cas de $A_{1.2}$, correspond à une partie plus courte de la fin de A. L'autonomie relative de ce segment pourrait aussi amener à postuler une division de A en deux parties de longueur à peu près égale ($A = Y + A_{1.2}$), mais ce serait poser là une unité (Y), qui, empiétant partiellement sur $A_{1.2}$, n'a, pas plus que celui-ci, une existence bien déterminée.

Finalement, c'est le tableau 4 (c) qui donne l'image la plus claire (quoique non exhaustive, il n'indique pas les rapports de transformation entre petites unités, faciles à déceler d'ailleurs) de la structure de la pièce. Les segments entre accolades correspondent à de « grandes unités », s'emboîtant partiellement les unes dans les autres, les brefs segments qui se trouvent dans les mêmes colonnes verticales correspondent aux petites unités, et, enfin, les segments représentés sur une même portée, dans une même rangée horizontale, représentent des unités intermédiaires. Ce tableau dévoile aussi assez nettement un procédé de composition qui consiste à intercaler — ou à supprimer — de brefs segments à l'intérieur de segments plus vastes.

1. Celles-ci, avec l'insistance sur le *la* qu'elles introduisent, ont surtout pour effet de donner à cette section une allure suspensive, qui la fait contraster avec la section correspondante en A.

294

exemple 4 (c)

9. *Résumé et conclusion.*

Parti de la distinction entre modèle analytique et modèle synthétique, j'ai insisté dans cet article sur la nécessité de développer le point de vue analytique en musicologie, autrement dit, sur l'urgence qu'il y a à élaborer des procédures rigoureuses destinées à découvrir le code à partir des messages. En même temps, j'ai souligné les limitations de ce genre de démarche. J'ai esquissé principalement une procédure de segmentation, basée sur les critères de répétition et de transformation, et j'ai essayé de l'appliquer à quelques monodies médiévales.

Il est trop tôt pour tirer des conclusions d'une étude qui ne représente que le début d'une recherche. Bien des choses ici énoncées seront à reprendre et à élaborer : c'est le cas de la distinction entre éléments paramétriques et non paramétriques, ainsi que de la notion même de transformation. En particulier, il sera nécessaire d'inventer des procédures de découverte destinées à reconnaître, précisément, les rapports de transformation entre éléments. Ces rapports, sauf dans des cas très simples, ont ici été souvent considérés comme allant de soi.

Je voudrais cependant attirer l'attention sur deux des résultats de cette étude.

1. Il semble bien que, au moins dans certains cas (ceux où la segmentation en unités de niveaux distincts est aisée) (cf. le § suivant), une procédure de segmentation du type présenté ici peut avoir d'importantes conséquences pour l'analyse scalaire et modale. Elle peut servir d'alternative ou de contrôle aux analyses plus traditionnelles. Par manque de place, je n'ai guère insisté sur ce point, mais, par exemple, l'application, même rapide, de la procédure esquissée au § 5.1 aux mélodies analysées du point de vue modal par E. Costère [1], dévoile immédiatement la fausseté de ces analyses. D'autre part, on peut entrevoir une procédure de découverte applicable à la question des *pyens*, procédure qui, faite en termes de distribution des intervalles, compléterait et systématiserait l'apport de Braïloïu.

1. Cf. article « Mélodie », in *Encyclopédie Fasquelle*.

133

2. Précisément parce qu'elle essaie de définir rigoureusement les niveaux et les unités, la procédure suivie nous a amené — par des chemins différents de ceux suivis par André Souris — à mettre en question une conception purement taxinomique de la structure musicale. Même dans un cas aussi simple que celui de l'exemple 1 (cf. § 5), il est impossible de se représenter complètement la structure sous la forme d'une série d'emboîtements, les unités de niveau I se décomposant intégralement en unités discrètes de niveau II, celles-ci à leur tour en unités discrètes de niveau III, etc. La principale raison de cet état de choses tient évidemment au fait que la syntaxe musicale est une syntaxe d'équivalences : les diverses unités ont entre elles des rapports d'équivalence de toutes sortes, rapports qui peuvent unir, par exemple, des segments de longueur inégale — tel segment apparaîtra comme une expansion, ou comme une contraction, de tel autre — et aussi des segments empiétant les uns sur les autres. La conséquence de tout ceci est, comme on a pu le constater, qu'il est impossible de représenter la structure d'une pièce musicale par un schéma unique.

Janvier 1965.

PRESCRIPTIVE AND DESCRIPTIVE MUSIC-WRITING

By CHARLES SEEGER

THREE hazards are inherent in our practices of writing music. The first lies in an assumption that the full auditory parameter of music is or can be represented by a partial visual parameter, i.e., by one with only two dimensions, as upon a flat surface. The second lies in ignoring the historical lag of music-writing behind speech-writing, and the consequent traditional interposition of the art of speech in the matching of auditory and visual signals in music-writing. The third lies in our having failed to distinguish between prescriptive and descriptive uses of music-writing, which is to say, between a blue-print of how a specific piece of music shall be made to sound and a report of how a specific performance of it actually did sound.

I shall deal here with the writing of only the simplest kind of music — unaccompanied melody. All three hazards have combined to render probable that speech conceptions of melody have played an important part not only in the development of the technique of writing but also in the composition and performance of melodies in writing. And the conditions of the musicological juncture, in which we attempt to communicate in the art of speech relative to the nature of the art of music and what it communicates, render certain that speech-conceptions of melody may sometimes outweigh music-conceptions of it, particularly in any discussion of the problem of music-writing. We cannot, therefore, dismiss with a wave of the hand the questions 1) to what extent do our speech-conceptions of melody correspond to our music-conceptions of it, and 2) to what extent does the visual representation of melody condition both conceptions of it? While it is risky to think we can answer these questions definitively, we can at least bear them in mind and set ourselves seriously to consideration of ways and means of evading or offsetting the hazards of the task. I shall refer only briefly to the problem of multidimensional visual representation of melody. For technological advance, upon which we must depend for aid in this respect, has not yet overcome the difficulties in the visual representation of the composite melodic functions of tone-quality and accentuation. And since we cannot conceivably escape from the limitations of the musicological juncture, I shall single out two speech concepts of melody, not as comprehending the total range of the problem, but as underlying the two methods of music-writing now available to us — the one prescriptive and subjective, the other descriptive and objective.

On the one hand, let us agree, melody may be conceived (verbally, it must be remembered) as a succession of separate sounds, on the other, as a single continuum of sound — as a chain or as a stream. Conception as a chain tends to emphasize structure and entities that move; conception as a stream, function and movement itself. Neither, of course, tells the whole story as the musician knows it. Both distort this knowledge to extents we cannot precisely gauge. For many of the links of the chain may be fused together; and the stream may run through successions of comparatively stable levels. And there may be breaks in both. Like so many speech constructions, these verbal constructions are not mutually exclusive opposites, but can be shown to have possibilities of serving as complements to each other. And the truth may lie somewhere between them.

Visual representation of melody as a chain is comparatively easily done by a chain of symbols; as a stream, by a curving line. Symbolization inevitably results in sharp distinction between music space (tone) and music time (rhythm) as separate, independent factors; lineation, in non-separation of the two, as overlapping, interdependent factors. Within the incomplete frame of the two-dimensional page, both symbolization and lineation depend upon certain graphic conventions of obscure origin. One, identification of elapse of time with occurrence from left to right on the page, possibly borrowed from speech-writing, underlies both factors. Another, identification of height in pitch with height on the page underlies some symbolic and all linear music-writing. Uniform vertical coordinates for elapse of time (indicating tempo) and uniform horizontal coordinates for height of pitch form the basic chart for the most recent developments of linear music-writing known as "graphing."

The history of the European fine art of music shows that our conventional music-writing was first a predominantly symbolic, second a predominantly linear, and third a mixed symbolic-linear notation. The Greek tradition, as made known to us most clearly by Alypius, was based upon the convention of representing elapse of time from left to right. Separate symbols for pitches of tones and for meter were placed accordingly. The accents and neumes of the early Christian era added the convention of identifying height of pitch with height on the page, but were linear in character, expressing movement rather than the points moved to and moved from. They seem first to have come into use to describe an existing practice of recitation. The notation became, however, more and more used for prescriptive purposes. First, ecclesiastical authorities and, later, composers began to specify exactly from where and to where movement was to go, and how long it was to take to do so. Addition of the lines of the staff and of the stems and barlines (prototypes respectively of the horizontal and vertical coordinates of the graph chart) were major steps towards the graph; standardization of the note-head and the metrical flags and beams was a reversion to symbolism.

300

As we find it today, our conventional notation is still a mixed symbolic-linear music-writing in which the symbolic element is the more highly organized and therefore dominates. It is practically entirely prescriptive in character. Emphasis is upon structures — principally of pitch and meter. It does not tell us much about the connection of the structures. It does not tell us as much about how music sounds as how to make it sound. Yet no one can make it sound as the writer of the notation intended unless in addition to a knowledge of the tradition of writing he has also a knowledge of the oral (or, better, aural) tradition associated with it — i.e., a tradition learned by the ear of the student, partly from his elders in general but especially from the precepts of his teachers. For to this aural tradition is customarily left most of the knowledge of "what happens between the notes" — i.e., between the links in the chain and the comparatively stable levels in the stream.

In employing this mainly prescriptive notation as a descriptive sound-writing of any music other than the Occidental fine and popular arts of music we do two things, both thoroughly unscientific. First, we single out what appear to us to be structures in the other music that resemble structures familiar to us in the notation of the Occidental art and write these down, ignoring everything else for which we have no symbols. Second, we expect the resulting notation to be read by people who *do not carry the tradition of the other music*. The result, as read, can only be a conglomeration of structures part European, part non-European, connected by a movement 100% European. To such a riot of subjectivity it is presumptuous indeed to ascribe the designation "scientific."

There are three ways out of the dilemma, for that is what it is, so rare is the carriage by any one person of more than one music tradition and so difficult the correction of the bias typical of that one.[1] On the one hand, we may increase the already heavy over-load of symbols in the notation, with a resulting increase of difficulty in reading and but little, if any, gain in accuracy or objectivity. On the other hand, we may dispense with many of the symbols and extend the graphic potentialities of the notation. The hand-made graph based upon the notation has its uses. But for purposes of formal description — our main concern here — the objectivity of the electronic reduction of the oscillographic curve, especially of the sound-track of high-fidelity sound-recording, is vastly superior. As Bartók has rightly said, "The only true notations" (music-writing is what he might have said) "are the sound-tracks on the record itself."[2] These, unfortunately, are legible only through laborious mathematical calculation. For when large enough to be seen in detail by the human eye they are several feet long per second. Electronic analysis can reduce or compress them automatically, as desired. Compression within a range of about 2.5 to 25mm per second produces a graph legible by anyone who can read conventional notation and is willing to do a little practice.

The time has not yet come, of course, for abandonment of our conventional notation. It has come, I aver, for development of the graph. Structure and function are equally important methodological concepts. Prescriptive and descriptive uses of music-writing are equally necessary and not necessarily incompatible. Musics surely differ from one another in their adaptability to one or the other kind of music-writing. But surely, also, we may hope, they resemble each other in this respect. The important thing for study is to know objectively wherein they differ and resemble, regardless of their being written one way or another. Furthermore, as a means of communication among people, music must be expected to have its subjective aspects. The least we should expect of the scholar is that he will not be a party

[1] E. von Hornbostel, *Fuegian Songs*, in *American Anthropologist*, XXXVIII (July-Sept., 1936), 357, note.
[2] Béla Bartók and Albert B. Lord, *Serbo-Croatian Folk Songs*, New York, 1951, p. 3.

to the passing off of his own subjectivity as someone else's or that he will fail to report objectively upon the subjectivity of that someone else. My recommendation for the foreseeable future, then, is to employ the notation and the graph concurrently.

Correlation of the graph and the notation depends in great measure upon recognition of their relative capacities and limitations. Both are based upon the conventions of identifying elapse of time with left to right on the page and height in pitch with height upon it. They differ in that spacing is irregular in the notation, but uniform in the graph. The comparative efficiency of the two methods of writing in handling the six principal functions of the single melody may be summarized as follows:

TONAL FUNCTIONS. 1) *Pitch* is only roughly indicated, i.e., within a half tone by the notation. The attempt to increase accuracy by superscription of additional symbols such as cents numerals, arrows, plus and minus signs, modifications of accidentals, etc., found in many ethnomusicological works is severely limited by the decrease in legibility. My present fundamental frequency analyzer, which is a mere Model T in the way of graphing devices, has a top discrimination of about 1/14 tone.[3] 2) *Amplitude* (dynamics) is only roughly indicated by the notation. My present amplitude graphs show changes in dynamics far beyond what the ear can detect. 3) *Tone-quality* cannot be shown at present by either method of writing. Ample acoustic research has been completed and engineering applications are already in use permitting rough but meaningful graphs of tone-quality. A practical device is still to be designed and manufactured.

RHYTHMIC FUNCTIONS. 4) *Tempo* is only roughly indicated in the notation, even with the aid of the metronome. It is very accurately indicated upon the chart in both frequency and amplitude graphs by the analyzer I am using. The margin of error seems to be about 1/100 second. 5) *Proportion* is easy to read in the notation, but difficult, in the graph. 6) *Accentuation,* for the present, is problematic in both notation and graph — in the notation, because of the multiplicity of symbols; in the graph because of its representation of stress solely in terms of amplitude. The notation can lay down an unheard basic pulse, certainly as prerequisite to the perception as to the performance of some musics. This the graph can do only by manual superscription of

[3] Charles Seeger, *Toward a Universal Music Sound-Writing for Musicology,* in *Journal of the International Folk Music Council,* IX (1957), 63.

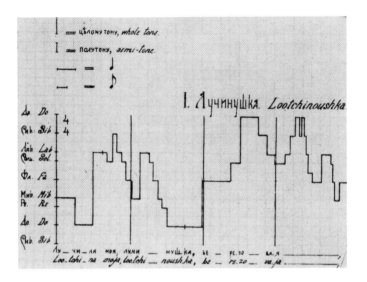

Hand Graph, made by ear from phonograph recording. Excerpt of Diagram 1, in *The Peasant Songs of Great Russia,* by Eugenia Eduardovna (Paprik) Lineva. Moscow, 1912. The vertical lines are music bars. Rectangular chart, in color, not reproducible.

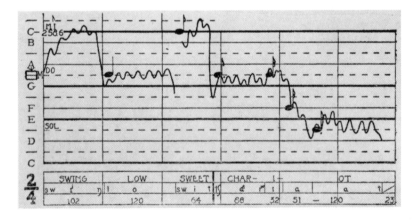

Hand Graph, made by mathematical reduction of a "sound wave photograph." Fig. 29, in *Phonophotography in Folk Music,* by Milton Metfessel. Copyright 1928 by the University of North Carolina Press. Reprinted by permission. The light vertical lines are seconds; the heavy one, a music bar.

Plate I

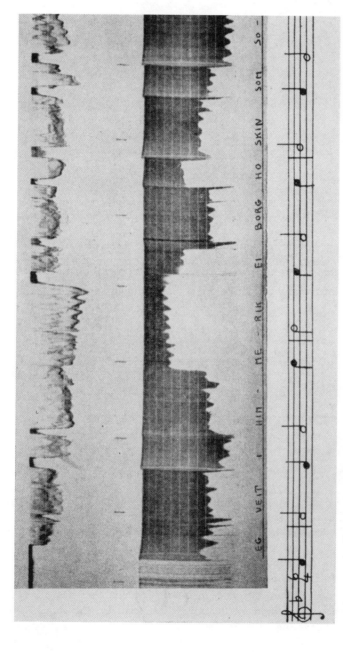

Automatic Graph (oscillogram) made by electronic-mechanical reduction, photographed on film, of Norwegian folksong, sung by woman's voice. Excerpt of Fig. 3, in *Photography as an Aid in Folk Music Research*, by Olav Gurvin, in *Norveg*, III (1953), 181-96. Reprinted with permission. Upper, shaded, outline shows intensity (amplitude); lower, white, outline, pitch (fundamental frequency) upon ruled, semitonal staff, with seconds marked by timer. (Enlarged?)

Plate II

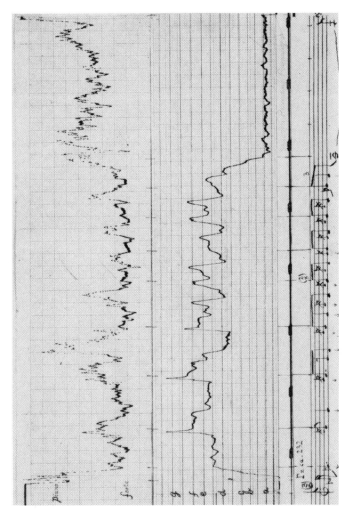

Automatic Graph (oscillogram) made by electronic-mechanical reduction written directly on paper (see footnote 3), of Abatutsi Traditional Song, sung by man's voice. Excerpt of Band 16, in *Voice of the Congo, Riverside World Folk Music Series*, RLP 4002, recorded in Ruanda by Alan P. and Barbara W. Merriam, 1951-52. Upper, broken, line shows amplitude; lower, continuous, line, fundamental frequency, upon rectangular millimeter chart (green) with ruled, semitonal staff, and with seconds marked by timer. (Reduced)

Plate III

notational symbols, as, for example, of meters, bars, etc. But it can show, with surprising accuracy, the fluctuation of a basic pulse so symbolized. And this, the notation cannot do.

On the whole, the student will find the pitch and the beat more accurately shown in the graph than in the notation, but less independently delimited. As conceptions of verbal thinking, he will find both becoming less rigid and absolute. Also, he will find the gross formal aspects of melody more readily perceivable in the graph. But he will have some difficulty in fitting conventional terminology with what he sees in the graph. The problem is most clearly presented in all its complexity in the sung melody. For it is there that the tonal factor of vibrato meets the rhythmic factor of rubato head-on, in the most diverse and subtle manners.

First, let us consider the sung melody as a chain. From this viewpoint, vibrato and rubato are separate, unrelated factors.

Surely, all students of Occidental music know that the actual variance of the vibrato is an alternation of adjacent pitch frequencies customarily perceived, i.e., musically thought of, by us as one salient pitch about the mean of the variance.[4] (Variance of loudness and of tone-quality in the vibrato are secondary and need not detain us for the moment.) It is this mean, not the actual, variance that we identify as a "note" and relate to a norm of our music theory such as a degree of a scale and, so, as a link in the chain.

Surely, also, all students of this music know that the actual variance of the rubato is an alternation of anticipation and delay (or delay and anticipation) of successive beats customarily perceived by us as one salient deviation from the mean of the variance, or tempo. (Variance of accentuation need not detain us for the moment.)

Operation of the vibrato is mostly below the threshold of deliberate control. That is, it is largely autonomic, customarily thought of as a characteristic of voice-production, as, for example, of the single note or link in the chain. It can be modified — even acquired — by conscious effort, but not so much in terms of its actual as of its mean variance. Once acquired, it is set in its pattern and persists throughout the process of rendition, regardless of changes of pitch or loudness. The singer does not, and perhaps cannot, change its rate, span, or regularity as we are accustomed to change the rate or regularity of divisions of a beat, by deliberate control.

[4] Carl E. Seashore, ed., *The Vibrato,* Iowa City, n.d., p. 369.

Operation of the rubato, on the other hand, is mostly above the threshold of deliberate control. It is thought of as a characteristic of the sequence of notes or links in the chain. While factors of which we are largely unconscious are constantly deflecting it in minute ways, our deliberate control of it is mainly in terms of its actual variance with respect to whole beats and, in slow tempos, of divisions of beats. As to its mean variance, the Grand Tradition, as I received it from my most admired teachers, requires that it be 1) continuous in all but very strict tempos and 2) compensatory, for "the music should come out with the metronome at the end" — a quaint, but tenaciously held bit of musical folklore. The notation does not even attempt to show this; but the graph can submit it to an acid test. It can also show any unevenness in vibrato or rubato that is musically significant.

Now, the attack upon the next succeeding note in any melodic process, the more so if it is accented, long held, dissonant, or unusual in some respect, is very much a matter of deliberate attention and control on the part of the executant. But according to the Iowa and other students of the vibrato, we customarily vastly underestimate 1) the extent of its actual variance, which may be commonly 40-200 cents, i.e., from one-fifth to a whole tone, 2) its rate, which may be 4-10 per second, and 3) its irregularity in both respects. Such variances might be expected to modify the expectations of the singer, automatic as they are and occupied as he may be with the mean variance of the tone he is producing with the intention of arriving within the mean variance of beat required in the rendition of the melody he is carrying. Seashore and others have pointed out that singers — even the best — habitually over- or under-shoot both upward and downward melodic progression. The fundamental frequency analyzer that I have been using shows this also. I would like, therefore, to advance the hypothesis that when the phase of the actual vibrato is in the direction of the melodic progression the establishment of the mean variance of the new note upon the beat expected is more likely to occur, whereas if it is contrary the new note may not be established until after the beat, a slide being interposed.

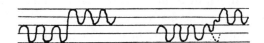

Schematic diagram of vibrato and upward melodic progression, in phase (left) and out of phase (right)

If the slide, which is typical of legato singing, is fairly slow or covers a wide interval, the graph may show little jagged points where the continuation of the vibrato may have forced an interruption of the progression. Over- and under-shooting may also involve or be involved in difference in phase and progression. Thus, rubato may be influenced by vibrato.

Conversely, if the attack upon a higher or lower note is anticipated or delayed by rubato, a vibrato that might have facilitated a decisive attack may be upset. A slide or over- or under-shooting may result. Thus, vibrato may be influenced by rubato.

It is not only in the attack or release of substantial notes (links in the chain) that vibrato and rubato may meet head-on. A very common complication seems to result within the beat when the rate of actual variance of the vibrato and a division of the beat by articulated notes are within the 4-10 alternations of the vibrato and the 2-16 (approximately) of the beat division. For example, a vibrato of five actual variances per second will produce a very different rendition of a group of four sixteenth notes at a quarter $= 60$ from that of a vibrato of seven per second.

305

Next let us consider the melody as a stream, broken only by the necessity to take breath, as at the end of a phrase, or by the briefer closures of the vocal apparatus in enunciation of certain consonants, or the making of exceptional effects such as staccato, etc. From this viewpoint, vibrato and rubato are closely related factors in a continuum. For here, melody is not viewed as a jagged rising and falling but as a sinuous flowing along a course. In what may be the vast majority of cases, the glide between levels, their over- and under-shooting, and the various inflections given them are not exceptions to theoretical norms but integral characteristics of the stream, intentional and cultivated. Except in the most strict *tempo giusto* and marcato, which are rare in singing, the manner of proceeding between levels and of modifying the levels themselves are, then, often quite as important data for the student as are the levels themselves.

In instrumental performance, the collision (in the chain) or interplay (in the stream) of vibrato and rubato is modified or even broken variously by movements of fingers, changes in bowing or embouchure, etc., peculiar to each technique. Approximation of many of the devices of singing style above mentioned can, however, be noted in instrumental playing — as on the vina and sitar, the ch'in and koto, and even in our own banjo and guitar playing — where slide-fretting, pressing down on strings and pulling them sidewise are common, as are tightening, relaxing, and shaping the embouchure on the trumpet, clarinet, and other wind instruments in our jazz bands. The almost infinite variety of this interplay between and within beats defines more closely the fault so often found with the unskilled performer: that he rendered the notes correctly but "left out what should have come between them," which is to say, he did not connect them in accordance with the appropriate aural tradition. Each of the many music traditions in the world probably has its own distinctive ways of connecting or "putting in what should come between the notes." Conventional notation can give no more than a general direction as to what these ways are, as, for example, by the words and signs for portamento, legato, détaché, staccato, spiccato, crescendo, diminuendo, accelerando, rallentando, etc. In the graph they are all there for anyone to see, in clear detail. If it causes us some trouble to find out just what the notational equivalents are, we must not complain that the performer did not render notes. Rather, we should be glad that instead of rendering notes he rendered music, and that we may set ourselves with greater assurance to the task of finding out what he did sing, without preconceptions that he meant to, or should, have sung notes.

At this point it is necessary to say a word of warning about the fetish of extreme accuracy in the writing of music. Physics can determine and engineering can reproduce incredibly small difference of pitch and time. Psychology (and rare musical experience) can prove that human beings — not necessarily with talent or training in music — can perceive differences beyond 1/100 of a tone or of a second.[5] But the great music traditions, their practice by those who have carried them, and the phenomenological and axiological norms[6] incorporated in them were not determined by the exceptional human being. He contributes to them. We may never cease the controversy how much.

[5] See, for example, one of the most valiant attempts at descriptive accuracy using conventional notation (Bartók-Lord, *op. cit.*), in many of whose transcriptions there are passages in which it is difficult or impossible to decide to what extent the notes represent 1) unequal articulated divisions of a beat sung in strict time, 2) equal articulated divisions sung with rubato, 3) either of these with written out or partly written out vibrato, 4) an uneven vibrato, or 5) a vibrato that a less sensitive ear would hear as a single tone, i.e., whose mean, instead of actual, variance would be the musical fact.

[6] The elasticity with which our notational norms are actually made to sound by competent professionals has recently been measured with great accuracy by Charles R. Shackford in his doctoral dissertation (Harvard, 1954), *Intonation in Ensemble String Performance—An Objective Study.*

The same is true of our notation, which is, *par excellence,* a matter of norms determined by the vast aggregate of practice and codified by generations of workers. The graph, on the other hand, shows individual performance. Each graph, whether of the exceptional performer or the merest tyro, is unique. Norms can be arrived at by comparative studies of large numbers of graphs. But these norms may differ in many important respects from the norms embodied in the notation. Or they may confirm them. In any event, where the individual notation may give too much norm and too little detail, the individual graph may easily give too little norm and too much detail. It is well, therefore, especially in these pioneer stages of the development of the graph not to look for too much detail or, better, detail too far beyond the norms of general practice, except for most carefully considered ends. For the present, I am inclined to set 1/10 of a tone (20 cents) and 1/10 of a second as fair margins of accuracy for general musicological use. Detailed study may go beyond these at the discretion of the student.

As a strictly musicological tool, the graphing apparatus brings to our existing notational techniques the needed complement to show "what happens between the notes" and what any departures from their theoretical norms really are in terms of actual hearing — and what these norms should be in terms of musicological thinking. For lexicographical and many classificatory uses, the pitch-time graph will probably be the most useful. Used side by side with the amplitude-time graph, a beginning can be made in the all-important exact study of performance style, especially of singing-style, without which the infant discipline of comparative melodic research cannot hope to do more than half a job. But as yet, this can be only a beginning. For its full study, graphing of tone-quality and "visible speech," both now in advanced stages of development, will be necessary.

We are, then, at last nearing the time when scientific definition of the world's musics and comparative studies of them can, and should, begin in earnest. Extrinsic contributions in terms of culture history, of geographic extent, and of social depth are being made by anthropology, sociology, psychology, physiology, physics, and other non- or extra-musical disciplines. Musicology is hardly ready yet to attack the necessary definition and comparative study in intrinsic terms. We have not more than coined a word when we speak of the concept "music" or even "a music." We do not even know whether our basic categories of music "idiom" — fine, folk, popular, and primitive arts of music — hold everywhere outside of the Occidental culture community.

The volume of data now already at hand shows that in the near future we shall be compelled to adopt statistical techniques such as those being developed by anthropology.[7] These will increasingly employ the kind of thinking and operating that depends upon precise visual representation of the most detailed observation as well as of the most generalized synopsis or synthesis. Musicologists will have to learn to read the graphs of non-musical sciences. And it is not impossible that non-musical scientists might learn to read the music-graph more readily than the conventional Occidental notation.

As a descriptive science, musicology is going to have to develop a descriptive music-writing that can be written and read with maximum objectivity. I believe that the graphing devices and techniques, above referred to, show the way towards such an end. But it must be remembered that technological aids of this sort report only upon the physical stimulus to the outer ear. At present, too, it is possible to put into visual form only fractioned aspects of this, such as pitch and time, amplitude and time, etc. One can conceive, though scarcely imagine, an automatic music-writing that would comprehend the total physical stimulus in a single, continuous process of writing or reading. But even if this present impossibility were to be realized, we would still have to take pains lest the visual representation of the stimulus were mistaken for the full sensory and perceptual reaction of a person conditioned by the particular music-cultural tradition of which the stimulus were a product. For perception does not accept sensation without change. Put bluntly, "we do not hear what we think we hear." Just what is the nature of the change is one of the things we most want to know. For culturally unconditioned listening to music, unless by "wolfboys," congenital idiots, or the like, is not known to us. If the stimulus is a product of the particular music tradition that we carry, we perceive it as such. If it is a product of a tradition we do not carry, we perceive it as we would a product of the one we do carry, making such changes as we are accustomed to. Therefore, automatic music-writing by such aids as those referred to must no more be taken for what we think we hear than most conventional notation. But even in its present pioneer stage of development, such writing must be accepted by us as a far truer visual portrayal of what we actually hear than is the notation. By comparing the two, we may achieve several useful ends: 1) we may learn more about the divergence of

7 Linton G. Freeman and Alan P. Merriam, *Statistical Classification in Anthropology: An Application to Ethnomusicology*, in *American Anthropologist*, LVIII (June, 1956), 464-72.

sensation and perception in our own music; 2) we may take steps towards the discovery of how a music other than our own sounds to those who carry its tradition; 3) we may begin to correct our misperception of other musics than our own by cultivating "bi-musicality" — surely, one would think, a prerequisite for musicological work. For the automatic graph can serve as a bridge between musics — a common denominator, as it were. The physical stimulus constituted by a product of any music tradition is identical to those who carry the tradition and to those who carry another. It is the perceptions of it by the respective carriers that are different. Is there not a clue here to the vexing problem of form and content in music, and perhaps an indispensable guide to the present almost abandoned effort to develop a world-wide philosophy of music upon a rational rather than a mystical base?

The Living Work:
Organicism and Musical Analysis

RUTH A. SOLIE

> Every linear progression shows the eternal shape of life—birth to death. The progression begins, lives its own existence in the passing tones, ceases when it has reached its goal—all as organic as life itself.
>
> Heinrich Schenker

> Every culture passes through the age-phases of the individual man. Each has its childhood, youth, manhood, and old age.
>
> Oswald Spengler

311

The notion that human history, society, and experience may be viewed˙and described in organic terms has been a pervasive one in Western culture. The use of the organism and its life as metaphors specifically for works of art can be traced back at least as far as Plato and Aristotle, and has recurred periodically in the history of philosophy and aesthetics, but its most recent incarnation can be thought of as belonging quintessentially to the critical language of the late eighteenth and nineteenth centuries. The metaphor has not been without significance for music theory and criticism; since, as linguists have been telling us for some time now, language is not merely reflective but actually constitutive of our awareness, constellations of language like that surrounding the

figure of the organism tend to shape and control the observations of the analyst using them. To borrow a few phrases from the literature on melodic analysis, for instance, in "the embodied will to motion" one might be inclined to perceive characteristics not so readily apparent in "a pitch-time trajectory" or "a stochastic process with sequential dependencies"—notwithstanding the possibility that all three phrases might refer to the same melody. Similarly, the analyst dealing with a "musical organism" will likely respond to it differently from one studying a "linguistic structure" or perhaps "fluid architecture."

For this brief study I will take as illustrative certain aspects of the work of Heinrich Schenker and Rudolph Reti. They are by no means alone in their reliance on organic language, but neither is their selection arbitrary. I choose them simply as loci of two now familiar impulses in analysis, especially of music of the common-practice period; that is,

0148–2076/80/030147+10$00.50 © 1980 by The Regents of the University of California.

147

both exemplify methodologies which have to some degree become "standard." Both reductive or layer analysis and notions of thematic unity are, in their several ways, offspring of the same metaphoric orientation in nineteenth-century aesthetics.

The characteristic of biological systems most commonly invoked in aesthetic evaluation is their "organic unity," a notion which lies at the center of a whole network of related ideas. The use of such unity as a primary criterion for excellence in works of art is hallowed by time and tradition, so much so that in recent decades it has often been taken utterly for granted. Generally, the principal canon of an organic aesthetic can be formulated in the following deceptively simple terms: a work of art should possess unity in the same way, and to the same extent, that a living organism does. Such a criterion, however, raises more questions than it answers. A more concrete and helpful definition has been formulated by Stephen Pepper:

312

There are two qualitative dimensions that yield organistic standards of beauty—the degree of integration and the amount of the material integrated. . . . The maximum of integration is a condition where every detail of the object calls for every other. . . . Or negatively, it is a condition where no detail can be removed or altered without marring or even destroying the value of the whole. Such a whole is called an organic unity.[1]

The terms of Pepper's definition originate in the organistic school of literary criticism as found in the writings of its first major exponent, Samuel Taylor Coleridge. Under the influence of the German organicist philosophers of the late eighteenth century, and in an era in which biology was gradually replacing mechanics as the central intellectual paradigm, Coleridge applies organic explanatory categories to a wide variety of areas of investigation, including history, a theory of mind, and aesthetics. Indeed, in his posthumously published *Theory of Life*, Coleridge de-

fines life itself as "the power which discloses itself from within as a principle of unity in the many," or "of unity in multeity"; this power "unites a given all into a whole that is presupposed by all its parts."[2] A work of art considered as living being, then, will be evaluated similarly, in terms of multiplicity-and-unity. Coleridge is particularly fascinated by the possibility that the multeity of traits assimilated in a work might include quite sharp contrasts, whose artistic unification will thus be all the more powerful. The task of poetic imagination, he says, is

the balance or reconciliation of opposite or discordant qualities: of sameness, with difference; of the general, with the concrete; the idea, with the image; the individual, with the representative.[3]

Not only is the balance of disparate qualities to be considered in an organic aesthetic, but also the reciprocal relationship of part and whole. The problem, as Coleridge sees it, is to create not the greatest possible amount of unity but the optimum amount consistent with preserving the separate character of the components—that is, to maintain the creative tension between whole and parts.

A poem is that species of composition which . . . is discriminated by proposing to itself such delight from the whole as is compatible with a distinct gratification from each component part.[4]

In literary criticism since Coleridge the organic idea has become so widely known and applied that there is a certain tendency for its language to be taken for granted and for certain fundamental questions to go unasked. Why do works of art need such unity? what sort of organism can serve as the model? what are the relevant characteristics of life forms and, in fact, is there any evidence to suggest that they can support the weight of aesthetic justification which has been erected upon them? That is to say, a cardinal assumption of organicist

---

[1]Stephen Pepper, *The Basis of Criticism in the Arts* (Cambridge, Mass., 1946), p. 79.

[2]Pointed out by M. H. Abrams, *The Mirror and the Lamp: Romantic Theory and the Critical Tradition* (London, 1953), p. 220.
[3]Samuel Taylor Coleridge, *Biographia Literaria*, ed. George Watson (London, 1965), p. 174.
[4]Ibid., p. 172.

criticism is that the form as given is "necessary"—parts cannot be removed, added, or rearranged without, as Pepper says, "marring or even destroying" the whole. As genuine organisms go, however, this view seems a bit sentimental. The customary neglect of these speculations in organicist criticism can largely be explained by considering that for Coleridge himself—and for many later nineteenth-century writers as well—the organic idea had much more than a metaphoric force. For the theory as Coleridge used it originated in the tenets of German and English idealist philosophy, where it had a far more concrete significance.

From its origins with Leibniz in the seventeenth century to the work of the neo-Hegelians of the twentieth, the tradition of idealistic philosophy has included a number of differing schools of thought. Common threads among them can be found, however, including especially an emphasis on mind-spirit values as opposed to material ones and the basic hypothesis that reality exists in the ideal realm and not in the finite world of objects. There is also the suggestion of a strong interrelationship between all things: in Bosanquet's words, "every finite existence necessarily transcends itself and points toward other existences and finally to the whole."[5] Concrete objects, to the early idealists, were merely the time-space relationships between the "real" (ideal) substances. Leibniz was much concerned with defining and characterizing these substances in such a way that concrete bodies could be explained.

Assuming that the human being, consisting of mind and body, is a true unity he [Leibniz] extended the notion of organism to cover all beings endowed with substantial forms. A substantial form, for Leibniz, was something analogous to a mind and capable of "perception" (the lowest degree of mental activity, not involving either self-consciousness or thought). It is through its perception that any individual "expresses" what goes on in the universe.[6]

An organism, then, is an ideal substance which expresses the universe in a wider sense. Not an unlikely definition for a work of art!

With the philosophy of Kant, the transcendental aspect of idealism was given increased emphasis. It is interesting that this particular branch of the tradition, which flourished in both Britain and the United States, was closely associated in both countries with literary men and especially poets. The American transcendentalists, with their poetic vision of one Soul shared by all living creatures, are first cousins to the exponents of organic literary criticism. While the organism model itself is not particularly stressed by the idealists, they do dwell on the mystical relationship of parts and wholes in the universe—as we have seen, an important article in the organicists' creed as well.

The clearest explication of the relationship of idealism to organicism is found in the aesthetic writings of Hegel. For Hegel, the transcendence of the finite characterizes the highest human achievement, and at this summit he places art, religion, and philosophy. The arts in turn are ranked according to their degree of ideality, with architecture and sculpture at the bottom and poetry, closely followed by music, at the top. An art work, he writes, is "an individual configuration of reality whose express function it is to make manifest the Idea in its appearance." Such manifestations of Idea occur first in nature, and provide models of aesthetic beauty:

We must . . . conceive Nature as herself containing in potency the absolute Idea. She is that Idea in *apparent shape*, which mind, in its synthetic power, posits as the object opposed to itself.[7]

Beauty is in turn defined by Hegel as the *union* of idea and objective reality; that is, the success of this unification is the measure of the degree of beauty. It follows, then, that the unity most like nature's unity produces the highest beauty.

---

[5]Quoted by H. B. Acton in *The Encyclopedia of Philosophy*, ed. Paul Edwards (New York, 1967), s.v. "Idealism," p. 115.

[6]L. J. Russell, in *The Encyclopedia of Philosophy*, s.v. "Leibniz," p. 428.

[7]Georg Wilhelm Friedrich Hegel, *The Philosophy of Fine Art*, trans. F. P. B. Osmaston, vol. I (London, 1920), pp. 100, 127.

Note, however, that when in subsequent generations literal notions of "organic unity" are applied to the analysis or evaluation of particular works of art, a paradoxical reversal occurs of the values originally at the root of the concept. For the philosophers, the point of calling something "organic" was not to describe the arrangement of its physical attributes but, on the contrary, to elevate it to a status transcendent of the physical. They stressed that the ideal quality of living organisms was the element of soul or *Geist*, and wished to attribute this quality to works of art. For this reason Hegel placed considerably more emphasis on defects of content or Idea than on defects of executive skill in his discussions of art. That is, he never suggested a clinical accounting for the fingers and toes of a poem; his own writing about particular works of art makes this quite clear.

This particular manifestation of idealism, then, places much emphasis on the transcendence of the multifarious, diverse substances of the apparent world in a higher and unified reality. It suggests that, as Leibniz puts it, every small thing mirrors the whole universe.[8] A gradual reorientation of philosophical and analytical attention occurs during this period, from a consideration of the part-to-whole construction of the world which prevailed in mechanistic pre-Romantic times to a construction in which the whole is primary and its constituent parts derived therefrom. It appears first as a salient characteristic of the organism—

The difference between an inorganic and organic body lies in this: In the first . . . the whole is nothing more than a collection of the individual parts or phenomena . . . while in the second, the whole is everything, and the parts are nothing[9]

—but is eventually applied to historical and aesthetic evaluation as well. "Depend on it, whatever is grand, whatever is truly organic

and living, the whole is prior to the parts."[10] The general trend toward philosophical and intellectual holism which is apparent in nineteenth-century criticism is, then, intimately related to the fundamental biological orientation of thought in the period, since holism is an easily-observed property of organisms.

Further, biology is itself moving during the nineteenth century away from its earlier dependence or concentration on anatomy. An increased interest in physiology led to a new focus on process rather than structure. The study of functional interrelationships of the many parts of a complex organism calls for a new paradigm of thought, fundamentally different from the old linear cause-and-effect model. A branch of research in the life sciences which came to be called "organismic biology" characterized the physiological behavior of whole organisms in this way: "The whole acts as a causal unit on its own parts"—a quixotic invocation of *a posteriori* causality which, however illogical in terms of eighteenth-century rationalism, appears quite compelling in a climate of rampant organicism.

In keeping with this general shift of focus, the characteristic of the organism which first and foremost drew the attention of philosophers and artists was its status as a single complete entity. This self-contained unitary quality stands in direct opposition to the nature of machines or of inorganic matter. The problem for literal interpreters of the metaphor, then, is how the artwork may be "analysed"—a threatening word to organicists, with its implication of division into component parts.

The fact that we divide a work of art into parts, a poem into scenes, episodes, similes, sentences, or a picture into single figures and objects, background, foreground, etc. . . . . *annihilates the work*, as dividing the organism into heart, brain, nerves, muscles and so on turns the living being into a corpse.[11]

[8]Harold Osborne, *Aesthetics and Criticism* (London, 1955), p. 193.
[9]Coleridge, *Table Talk*, quoted in Abrams, p. 171.
[10]Coleridge, *Philosophical Lectures*, quoted in Abrams, p. 171.
[11]Benedetto Croce, *Aesthetic as Science of Expression and General Linguistic*, trans. Douglas Ainslie, 2nd edn. (London, 1929), p. 20. Emphasis added.

Or, as Hutchings says admiringly of Reti's *Thematic Process in Music*, "One observes living organisms; one dissects dead bodies."[12] If the critic must fear for the literal annihilation of the work, then meaningful analysis of its constituent elements is in fact not possible. The only clear path for investigation is the monistic one, which leads solely to the pursuit of unities, commonalities, ultimate one-ness.

Perhaps the most significant achievement of Heinrich Schenker was the creation of models and procedures for treating a musical composition as a whole. It has become a commonplace to compare his work to that of Gestalt psychologists, so directly does it address itself to the recognition of a whole work "greater than the sum of its parts." Unlike the Gestaltists, however, Schenker predicates his notion of totality not upon perceptual mechanisms in the observer, but upon the work of art itself. Wholeness stems from a central generative force to which everything else is subordinate. It is at this juncture that the reliance of Schenker's holistic aesthetic upon traditional concepts of organicism is most clear: the generative force which brings forth the composition—an entelechy or *élan vital* to which I shall return below—is music's origin in nature, in the major triad or *Naturklang* as found in the overtone series.

Even the octave, fifth, and third of the harmonic series are a product of the organic activity of the tone as subject, just as the urges of the human being are organic.[13]

These natural urges of the tone are concretized in the *Ursatz*, a sort of anti-taxonomic device whose effect is to put all pieces in the same category by a Leibnizian transcendence of their multifarious surfaces. Like Leibniz's monads, the *Ursatz* is elemental stuff, mystical/musical

protoplasm. Schenker himself draws the parallel:

All transformations presume a final unalterable nucleus: in man, it is character, and in composition it is the urlinie.
Just as there is only one line, there is only one consummation of it. The urlinie is, to employ a concept of Leibniz, the pre-stabilized harmony of the composition.[14]

Needless to say, here as in other critical realms the organism becomes by literal or metaphoric extension the validator of the work. In one of Schenker's discussions of the *Urlinie*, for example, he explains that no progression of $\hat{8}-\hat{5}$ can be an independent *Urlinie* since the fourth is not given in the harmonic series: it must be part of an $\hat{8}-\hat{1}$ progression. Similarly for musical languages as a whole: "the quest for a new form of music is a quest for a homunculus."[15]

It is nothing new to point out that Schenker is the organicist *par excellence*. He is everywhere explicit about the use of metaphoric figures, warning that "music is never comparable to mathematics or architecture"[16] and introducing his final work, *Der freie Satz*, as an antidote to such mechanistic approaches:

I here present a new concept, one inherent in the works of the great masters; indeed, it is the very secret and source of their being: the concept of organic coherence.[17]

What is worth noting, however, is that for Schenker no less than for the organismic biologists of an earlier generation the passionate commitment to a holistic view leads inevitably to an intense singularity of focus. In defining the quality of "organic structure" he says the following:

315

---

[12]Arthur J. B. Hutchings, "Organic Structure in Music," *British Journal of Aesthetics* 2 (1962), 339.
[13]Heinrich Schenker, *Free Composition (Der freie Satz)*, trans. Ernst Oster (New York, 1979), p. 9.

[14]Schenker, "Resumption of Urlinie Considerations," in Sylvan Kalib, *Thirteen Essays from the Three Yearbooks Das Meisterwerk in der Musik by Heinrich Schenker: An Annotated Translation* (Ph.D. diss., Northwestern University, 1973), II, 144–45.
[15]Schenker, *Free Composition*, p. 9.
[16]Ibid., p. 5.   [17]Ibid., p. xxi.

This characteristic is determined *solely* by the invention of the parts out of the unity of the primary harmony—in other words, by the composing out of the fundamental line and the bass arpeggiation.[18]

And again:

All musical content arises from the confrontation and adjustment of the indivisible fundamental line with the two-part bass arpeggiation.[19]

Thus Coleridge's interest in the paradox of irreducible unity-in-variety has been skewed sharply to one side, in the transcendental manner. As Sonia Slatin writes,

[Schenker's] ultimate criterion of musical value is that of a totality of integration in which all of the musical elements function actively and completely toward the necessities of the whole.[20]

Strikingly different is Rudolph Reti's invocation of organic models in his studies of "thematic process" and "thematic patterns."[21] For one thing, he concentrates less upon the synchronic view of an individual organism, preferring metaphors of growth, development, and evolution—upon which I shall elaborate a bit farther on. For another, the Coleridgean paradox interests him more: the composer, he argues, "strives toward *homogeneity in the inner essence* but at the same time toward *variety in the outer appearance.*"[22] The purpose of his analytic work is to resolve this paradox.

Notwithstanding these differences, it becomes clear that the two views of music spring from a common source. The starting point for Reti's work, he is fond of pointing out, is in a question he asked as a student:

Why is it that we cannot produce a convincing musical composition by taking a group or a section from one work and linking it to that of another—even assuming an affinity of key, rhythm, and tempo?[23]

The question rests, of course, on the assumption that we *cannot* do so—by no means a foregone conclusion—and as such it reflects one of the fundamental tenets of nineteenth-century organicism. And Reti is very much concerned with extending thematic relationships beyond the boundaries of the individual piece or movement toward a kind of transcendent one-ness; he says, like an echo of Bosanquet, that

thematic connections account not only for the structural detail of a work but also for its larger shaping and gradually even for its widest architectural plan.[24]

As these thematic connections are stretched to include key relationships between movements, "the whole [work], through its key relationships, *becomes one great expression of its basic motiv.*"[25]

Not only does the organism display exemplary unity and coherence, but it is, to use an anachronistic term, genetically coded. That is, barring catastrophe its final state is inevitable from the moment its first cells are formed. Leibniz generalized this characteristic to all substances (which, remember, he called organisms) in his metaphysics. "Each substance contains in its nature the law of continuation of the series of its own operations and all that has happened to it and all that will happen to it."[26] An organism, that is, *grows*, and it grows in a *teleological* or goal-oriented manner.

The metaphor of organic, developmental growth is of course quite a different thing from organic unity. As growth has to do with change occurring in time, it has had particular rele-

---

[18]Schenker, "Organic Structure in Sonata Form," *Das Meisterwerk in der Musik II* (1926), trans. Orin Grossman, *Journal of Music Theory* 12 (1968), 166. Emphasis added.
[19]Schenker, *Free Composition*, p. 15. Emphasis added.
[20]Sonia Slatin, *The Theories of Heinrich Schenker in Perspective* (Ph.D. diss., Columbia University, 1967), p. 495.
[21]See Rudolph Reti, *The Thematic Process in Music* (London, 1961) and *Thematic Patterns in Sonatas of Beethoven*, ed. Deryck Cooke (New York, 1967). The latter was published posthumously from analyses done in the late 1940s and early 1950s.
[22]Reti, *Thematic Process*, p. 13.

[23]Ibid., p. 348.
[24]Reti, *Thematic Patterns*, p. 45.
[25]Reti, *Thematic Process*, p. 223.
[26]Quoted in Russell, p. 428 (see fn. 6).

vance for the study of music. Schenker, for example, saw the musical work quite literally as an organism with a life of its own, making its own demands in accordance with its own inner needs. He wrote in *Der freie Satz:*

The origin of every life, whether of nation, clan, or individual, becomes its destiny. . . . The inner law of origin accompanies all development and is ultimately part of the present. Origin, development, and present I call background, middleground, and foreground; their union expresses the oneness of an individual, self-contained life.[27]

There is more than an accidental resonance here with the words of a contemporary Viennese phenomenon, Sigmund Freud—"biology is destiny"—and in turn with Rudolph Reti's deterministic characterization of the "Tristan" chord: "compressed into one chord, the musical story of the whole opera is latent in this initial harmony."[28]

Elsewhere in his final book Schenker reiterates the idea in a vivid image:

The hands, legs, and ears of the human body do not begin to grow after birth; they are present at the time of birth. Similarly, in a composition, a limb which was not somehow born with the middle and background cannot grow to be a diminution.[29]

One notices about such statements a certain confusion of modality between the temporal and spatial. Clearly, the existence of a human child in complete (albeit small) form is not properly analogous to the unheard but everpresent background of a piece of music. Schenker is not simply suggesting that the beginning of a piece predestines its outcome, but is conflating ideas of temporal and logical priority. This very confusion, however, is endemic to the use of organic growth metaphors—witness the two epigraphs at the head of this essay, with their proclivity for not-quite-analogies suggesting that ontogeny recapitulates phylogeny in art and culture as

well as in genetics.[30] Furthermore, the same confusion is typical not only of distinctions between Schenker's work and Reti's, but of the development of the former's own thought.

In his early writings, when he still used the notion of musical motives, Schenker explained that the continuity of a piece arises from the fact that motives reproduce themselves as men beget men and trees beget trees.[31] Here the temporal organization of the metaphor is congruent with the "growth" of the piece of music as it is heard—the beginning of the piece begets its end. Some of his early analyses make use of this "seminal" version of organic explanation, in a rather familiar way. Of the beginning of Mozart's Symphony in G Minor, he writes:

A sixth-leap is thrown into the filling voices like seed into clod; see b-flat–g¹ in the viola part in bars 1–2; this seed is seen in the upper voice in bars 3, 7, etc. . . . In bar 10, through a²–f-sharp², the [actual] downward arpeggiation, which was still obscure in bars 3 and 7 because of the sixth-leap upward, is clearly recognized here. In this new, merely rectified form basically, the third-leap of bar 10 becomes the assumption for the fourth-leap g²–d² in bar 11 (seed→harvest).[32]

But later on, as Schenker's formulation of the *Ursatz* nears completion, his application of organic growth metaphors changes. Now the growth direction does not mirror the perceptual progress of the piece, but rather its conceptual progress from background to foreground. He explains, for example, that free composition arises from elements which were "lying budlike" in strict contrapuntal technique—by which he means the prolongations of passing tones, neighboring tones, and so forth. A piece originates in the *Urlinie* which is the *Keim*, or seed, from which the piece grows, ". . . as man, animal and plant are

---

[27]Schenker, *Free Composition*, p. 3.
[28]Reti, *Thematic Process*, p. 338.
[29]Schenker, *Free Composition*, p. 6.

[30]Ibid., p. 44; *The Decline of the West*, trans. Charles Francis Atkinson (New York, 1939), I, 107.
[31]Wilhelm Keller, "Heinrich Schenkers Harmonielehre," in *Beiträge zur Musiktheorie des 19. Jahrhunderts*, ed. Martin Vogel (Regensburg, 1966), p. 204.
[32]Schenker, "Mozart: Symphony in G minor," Kalib, pp. 345, 347.

figurations of the smallest seed. . . ."[33] The *Urlinie* is of course a particular arrangement of the Chord of Nature; the beginning of its growth process is the "awakening to life" of the chord through the layers in their increasing complexity. This natural motion, Schenker says, "wills to persist and increase on its own." He uses the Chord of Nature in much the same way that Hegel uses the Idea, that ultimate source of content which is concretized in the external artwork by its own power.

The Idea, which is essentially concrete, carries the principle of its manifestation in itself, and is thereby the means of its own free manifestation. . . . But inasmuch as in this way the Idea is a concrete unity, this unity can only enter the artistic consciousness by the expansion and further mediation of the particular aspects of the Idea; and it is through this evolution that the beauty of art receives *a totality of particular stages and forms.*[34]

As the foreground is reached, the seed continues to grow by its own teleology and in an inevitable, foreordained direction.

The content of the second and subsequent levels is determined by the content of the first level, but at the same time it is influenced by goals in the foreground, mysteriously sensed and pursued.[35]

Reti's conception of organic growth remains much like the early Schenker of the *Harmonielehre* and thus, as his analytic demonstrations of individual musical "cells" make clear, his theoretical apparatus is not hierarchically but linearly organized.

Music is created from sound *as life is created from matter.* In the organic sphere one cell engenders the other in its own image, yet each of the innumerable cells is different from all the others. . . .
In an astoundingly analogous way one musical motif, one theme releases another as an expression of its own innermost idea, yet the latter is a being entirely different from the first.
. . . and the act of creation is centered on this very process by which a musical idea emerges as a

consequence of another, as a thing which is a part of the given world, yet which has never existed before.[36]

The very instinct which draws analogies between organic life and musical works impels the theorist to see the history of music as a determinate, developmental process. Evolution, especially as viewed within nineteenth-century intellectual history, has an organic life —a teleology—of its own, and invites still further ontogenetic/phylogenetic entanglements.

The *Grave* [of the "Pathétique" sonata], like all slow introductions in the symphonies of Haydn, Beethoven, Brahms, etc., or the toccatas and preludes of Bach, symbolizes *the improvisational stage of a composition at the moment of its creation.* In these cases, the following allegro or fugue represents *the organized result* of that former quasi-instinctive activity.[37]

The slow introduction foretells, as an embryo, the form and content of the mature individual. As regards history, Reti tells us that the thematic principle did not appear in the early stages of Western music, but

Gradually . . . in the course of the evolution, since it obviously corresponds to an inborn sense of musical formation, such affinities between the voices [of counterpoint] emerged in the compositional design, at first sporadically and perhaps instinctively, later more frequently and clearly intentionally.[38]

The notion is familiar—the sense is "inborn," and it "emerges" in the history of the art.

It has been clear by implication all along that if a musical work shares with animal or plant its teleology, its goal-oriented pattern of growth, it must share also in whatever mysterious force or wisdom guides that predestined course. This entelechy, what old-fashioned biologists used to call the "vital force," plays an acknowledged role in Schenker's musical cosmos:

---

[33]Quoted by Walter Riezler in "Die 'Urlinie'," *Die Musik* 22 (1930), 508.
[34]Hegel, p. 102. Emphasis in original.
[35]Schenker, *Free Composition*, p. 68.

[36]Reti, *Thematic Process*, p. 359.
[37]Reti, *Thematic Patterns*, p. 30.
[38]Reti, *Thematic Process*, pp. 59–60.

The fundamental structure shows us how the chord of nature comes to life through a vital natural power. But the primal power of this established motion must grow and live its own full life: that which is born to life strives to fulfill itself with the power of nature.[39]

Reti likewise defines his subject matter as the "inner force" of music, as opposed to the more obvious "outward" aspects of form. This expressive core of the piece "certainly . . . cannot grow from the harmonic or contrapuntal mechanism"[40]—a statement which, despite its violent rejection of Schenkerian principles, is no less firm a commitment to the idealist's belief in the autonomous inner life of the organism and his instinctive distrust of the mechanical. Like Schenker's *Ursatz* fleshing out from layer to layer, Reti's thematic pattern "moves by transformation toward a goal."[41]

Belief in an autonomous vital force at the heart of a musical work, whether explicit or tacit, has interesting consequences in the contemporary depiction of both artist and critic. For one thing, such goal-oriented behavior on the part of works of art—teleology and entelechy combining to give every sonata movement what can only be described as a mind of its own—renders the composer's role somewhat ambiguous. The organism grows and takes shape by itself: the artist need only give it birth. Coleridge repeatedly uses the phrase *"ab intra"* with reference to a very few poets of the highest genius, notably Shakespeare. It suggests that they worked with natural forces coming from within, not "with prescience" and rational planning. The role of the artist as problem-solver in the modern view—or even as creator in any craftsmanlike sense of the word—is distinctly minimized. Jean Paul Richter wrote in his *Vorschule der Aesthetik* (1804) that the genius is "in more than one sense a sleep-walker; in his clear dream he is capable of more than in waking, and in darkness does he mount every height of reality."[42] William Blake testifies to his own

inspired composition, "I have written this Poem [*Milton*] from immediate Dictation, twelve or sometimes twenty or thirty lines at a time, without Premeditation and even against my Will. . . ."[43]

Furthermore, since the artist was regarded as a sort of midwife to this immanent life force, rather than a maker-of-things, a sharp and absolute distinction grew up between the genius and the non-genius, the poet *ab intra* and the poet manqué *ab extra*. There is much to ponder here for students of music in the nineteenth century. The idea is faithfully reflected in Schenker,

Musicians are distinguished [i.e., can be divided] into those who create out of the background, that is to say, from tonal space, the urlinie, who are the geniuses, and those who move only within the foreground, who are the non-geniuses. . . . A perennial barrier lies between them.[44]

and makes its presence felt as well in the restricted repertoire of compositions he considers in his analyses. As we have noted above, Hegel's aesthetic concern focused on the quality of Idea, not execution, because only the natural ability of the artist of genius to perceive and formulate the Ideal was really at stake. It is important, though, that however one characterizes this artistic genius it has nothing to do with intelligence or rationality. On the contrary, "the organic poet, as it were, does not know very clearly what he is doing until he has done it."[45] The forces of nature are at work in him.

The fundamental line and bass-arpeggiation governed him [Haydn] with the power of a natural force, and he received from them the strength to master the whole as a unity.[46]

319

[39]Schenker, *Free Composition*, p. 25.
[40]Reti, *Thematic Process*, p. 109; pp. 136–37.
[41]Ibid., p. 139.
[42]Quoted in Abrams, p. 212.

[43]Quoted in Abrams, p. 215.
[44]From "Clarifications," Kalib, pp. 161–62.
[45]James Benziger, "Organic Unity: Leibniz to Coleridge," *PMLA* 66 (1961), 28. Some artists were uneasy about this dismissal of their responsibilities; in his poem "Individuality," Sidney Lanier asks:
    What the cloud doeth   What the artist doeth
    The Lord knoweth,   The Lord knoweth;
    The cloud knoweth not.   Knoweth the artist not?
[46]Schenker, "Organic Structure in Sonata Form," trans. Grossman, p. 168.

Organicism was, of course, intimately involved with the whole development of the romantic notion of the genius as a being apart from and essentially unlike other men, a law unto himself. Genius was indeed considered organic itself, born and not made. Blake put it this way:

I do not believe that Raffael taught Mich.Angelo, or that Mich.Angelo taught Raffael, any more than I believe that the Rose teaches the Lilly how to grow or the Apple tree teaches the Pear tree how to bear fruit.[47]

The connection between the work of art and the artist's personal consciousness once severed, the artistic genius becomes a kind of vessel for the life forces of art or inspiration. Since the vital element or entelechy of artworks as well as organisms appears quite mysterious to the onlooker, a certain amount of magical power becomes attached to the artist who then is revered as the prophet or revealer of hidden unities, relationships, or meanings in his work—what Carlyle called the "secret and silent growth" of the organism. This quasi-priestly function of the artist is even shared, by extension, with the critic, who serves as a kind of acolyte or substitute revealer, and to whose advantage it therefore is to dwell upon hidden and obscure aspects of a work. "I was given a vision of the urlinie, I did not invent it!"[48] The very mysticism and obscurantism which organicist criticism invites puts it in sharp contrast to present-day ideas about the role of perception and of understanding by a more "democratic" audience in designing an adequate critical theory. Too, the desire for an explanatory theory for idiosyncratic events and for individual elements within the work of art has led theorists in re-

cent decades to explore a variety of approaches more phenomenologically oriented and borrowing insights from disciplines as disparate as anthropology and engineering. Still, the romantic legacy of the critic or analyst as priestly oracle is very much with us, perhaps at its most noticeable in our endemic uncertainty about the role of perception and "musicality" in the theorist's work. More than one school of contemporary analytic thought relies upon somewhat cabalistic symbology accessible only to a closed circle and prompting inevitable analogies to "discipleship."

In another respect, however, organic aesthetic beliefs have been useful for musical criticism insofar as they have helped to steer the course of analysis away from the purely mechanistic and simplistically structural. A comparative view of the analytic traditions born from the work of Tovey and Riemann shows clearly enough that their preference for the languages of architecture, logic, and rhetoric entails a restriction to morphological, low-level observations. There is no question that the crucial role played by the passage of time in music, and its ineffable sense of motion (whether "real" or "imaginary") are better dealt with in terms of growth and development metaphors than additive, static ones. Many commentators have noted that organic theories tend toward a view of music as process, and it is of course precisely this new orientation that is most enthusiastically greeted in Schenker's work. Its source, as Hegel reminds us, is in the life process itself. "[The] affirmation and resolution of the contradiction which obtains between the ideal unity and the material juxtaposition of the members, constitutes the appointed *process* of life itself. And Life is simply *process*."[49]

320

---

[47]Quoted in Benziger, p. 38.
[48]Schenker, "Resumption of Urlinie Considerations," Kalib, p. 218.

[49]Hegel, p. 166.

ON HISTORICAL CRITICISM

By LEO TREITLER

There is a rattling of skeletons in the halls of humane learning.

It is natural that in the conduct of our daily work we avoid direct and interfering contact with its fundamentals. But it is clear, too, that there must come times of reflection about the goals that are defined and the ways that are marked. If sharp attacks upon tradition are symptomatic, then this is such a time.

The most trenchant criticisms have reached for the widest audience: the wholesale denunciation of humanities and humanists in William Arrowsmith's essay *The Shame of Our Graduate Schools*[1] and the radical curative proposals offered by Eric Larabee in his essay *Saving the Humanities*[2] ("shattering the sanctity of jealously-guarded department boundaries, strangling the Ph.D. octopus, punishing pointless research, abolishing tenure, lowering inflated salaries...").

In the field of musical scholarship acrid exchanges in the pages of *Perspectives of New Music* and the *Journal of the American Musicological Society*[3] have been only the sharp edge of a series that includes

---

[1] *Harper's Magazine*, March 1966, pp. 51-59. Symptomatic though it may be, Arrowsmith's broadside is not altogether well informed. Thus his linking of classics and musicology as the most backward of the humanistic disciplines is surely ill-advised, considering the enormous differences in the background and current state of the two.

[2] *Commentary*, December 1966, pp. 53-60.

[3] Charles Rosen, *The Proper Study of Music*, in *Perspectives*, I (1962), 80-88; Joseph Kerman, *The Proper Study of Music: A Reply*, in *Perspectives*, II (1963), 151-59; Kerman, *A Profile for American Musicology*, in *JAMS*, XVIII (1965), 65-69; Edward E. Lowinsky, *Character and Purposes of American Musicology; A Reply to Joseph Kerman*, ibid., 222-34; Communication from Kerman, *ibid.*, 426-27.

some rather more reflective writing.[4] The field of art history has seen some serious theorizing in the work of James Ackerman, E. H. Gombrich, Erwin Panofsky, and Meyer Schapiro.[5]

A recurrent theme in this new round of questioning and defining stems from a unique condition of historical studies in the arts. It is that the central object of study is an artifact born into a special, that is an esthetic, relationship with the culture of which it is a part, and which continues through its survival to be both a historical record and an object of esthetic perception. It is a work of art, and the historian is obliged to come to terms with it as such; "the curse and the blessing," Panofsky wrote, "of art history."[6] There is a repeated show of concern whether we have met that obligation, whether our history is sound from the standpoint of what is called "criticism." Ackerman, Arrowsmith, and Kerman, especially, have argued that a more prominent place for criticism in our methodology is the most pressing need, and I shall take that assertion as a point of departure in the present essay. But I shall suggest that the diagnosis on which it rests can be misleading, that certainly in music-historical literature critical assessments abound, and that the issue is not "how much?" or "how central?" but rather "what kind?" and "on what premises?" I shall offer an alternative view, not that history and criticism are too widely separated but that they have been, in a sense, too closely confounded. The cry for criticism has had something in it of the cranky, nagging child who does not articulate what it is he wants. We need to know what a critical account of an art-work may be, or what it may seek to do;

323

[4]Warren Allen, *Philosophies of Music History*, New York, 1962; Frank Ll. Harrison, Mantle Hood, Claude V. Palisca, *Musicology* (The Princeton Studies: *Humanistic Scholarship in America*), Englewood Cliffs, N.J., 1963; Lewis Lockwood's review of the latter in *Perspectives*, III (1964), 119-27; Harold S. Powers, review of Allan Merriam, *The Anthropology of Music*, in *Perspectives*, V (1966), 161-71.

[5]Some principal writings: Ackerman, *A Theory of Style*, in *Journal of Aesthetics and Art Criticism*, XX (1961), 227-37; Ackerman, with Rhys Carpenter, *Art and Archeology* (The Princeton Studies; see note 4), 1963; Gombrich, *Art and Illusion*, 2nd ed., revised, New York, 1961; Gombrich, *Meditations on a Hobby Horse and Other Essays on the Theory of Art*, London, 1963; Panofsky, *Das Problem des Stils in der bildenden Kunst*, in *Zeitschrift für Aesthetik*, X (1915), 460-67; the discussion of the latter is continued in *Der Begriff des Kunstwollens*, in *Zeitschrift für Aesthetik*, XIV (1919-20), 21-39; Panofsky, *Meaning in the Visual Arts, Papers in and on Art History*, New York, 1955; Schapiro, *Style* (reprinted in Morris Philipson, ed., *Aesthetics Today*, New York, 1961, from A. L. Kroeber, ed., *Anthropology Today*, Chicago, 1953); Schapiro, *On Perfection, Coherence, and Unity of Form and Content*, in Sidney Hook, ed., *Art and Philosophy*, New York University Institute of Philosophy, New York, 1966, pp. 3-15.

[6]*Der Begriff des Kunstwollens* (see note 5).

and we need to know how it relates to a historical account.

I have raised the first of these questions elsewhere and attempted a number of formulations of the objectives of criticism, as the basis for a series of arguments for the relevance of the historian's evidence to the interpretation of musical works.[7] I argued there that in the analysis of art-works we seek to distinguish the fortuitous from the significant, and the uniquely significant from the conventional, and that the evidence of the historian is directly relevant to that task. This is the "historical point of view," in one sense of that expression.[8] My object here is to explore another sense by asking whether there is a special "historical account" of art-works.

How does the historian understand a work of art? To begin the investigation of this question I should like to set forth one point of view about how it is to be answered, a point of view that has had great influence on the discipline of musicology and related fields. It distinguishes, first, between a commonplace meaning of "understand" that suggests a sense of empathetic or intuitive familiarity, and the scientific understanding of natural or historical phenomena; "I understand how you feel," as against "Learn to understand the principles of the internal combustion engine." In the second of these meanings — and it is only the second that is relevant to the systematic study of anything, according to this point of view — to *understand* something is to be able to *explain* it, and to *explain* a thing is to give its *causes*. Briefly, *understanding* is knowledge of *causes*.[9]

---

[7] *Music Analysis in an Historical Context.* College Music Society *Symposium*, VI (1966).

[8] This point of view has been newly represented by Edward Lippman in *The Problem of Musical Hermeneutics: A Protest and Analysis*, in *Art and Philosophy* (see note 5), pp. 307-35.

[9] This apparently innocent distinction in meanings for our word "understand" rests on the ancient epistemological split between subjective and objective knowledge, that is to say the dissociation of the knower from what is known. It harbors issues of great importance and ultimate relevance that must be mentioned here, even though these remarks may not appear to be immediately basic to the argument that is to follow. From the point of view that I have been sketching above, statements must derive their validity either from factual correctness (verifiability) or formal consistency (as in a definition or mathematical equation). "Subjective" statements can do neither, and are therefore disqualified from the status of knowledge and relegated to the category of expressions that includes also cries of pain and ecstasy. The language of formal logic represents, then, a distillation of the substantive content of rational, "objective" statements, and, by corollary, statements that are not reducible to the notation of formal logic are not "objective." These remarks apply with equal force to long-term intellectual processes, such as experimentation and theory development, and, relevant to this discussion, causal explanation. This canon forms

To complete the exposition of this point of view it is necessary to clarify what is meant by *causes*. They are of two kinds: precipitating conditions—conditions that must obtain in order for a given event to occur—and general laws under which the given event must occur whenever the specified conditions obtain. If I wish to explain some phenomenon, for example the production of ice cubes in my home freezer, I must show that certain conditions prevail—the tray of water has been placed in an enclosure in which a temperature below 32 degrees F. is maintained—and I must cite a general law that is in effect—"At sea level the freezing-point of water is 32 degrees F." It follows that the power to *explain* is tantamount to the power to *predict*, for, given the precipitating conditions, the general law tells us that the event in question will ensue. If I can explain my ice cubes, I can also predict that whenever I place another tray of water in the same enclosure under the same conditions I shall have more ice cubes.[10] Each case in which the same train of events is set in motion is covered by

---

the basis of the scientism to which the humanities and social sciences have aspired since the 19th century, and it now informs a good deal of music-historical and music-theoretical writing. That being the case, it is necessary to note at once that, as a model for rational discourse, this bipartite reduction of knowledge, with its methodological consequences, has come to be widely regarded as an oversimplification and even as a delusion. I quote Michael Polanyi: "I start by rejecting the ideal of scientific detachment. In the exact sciences, this false ideal is perhaps harmless, for it is in fact disregarded there by scientists. But we shall see that it exercises a destructive influence in biology, psychology, and sociology, and falsifies our whole outlook far beyond the domain of science." (*Personal Knowledge*, Chicago, 1958, p. viii.) And on the principal subject of this discussion, Mario Bunge wrote: "The reduction of lawfulness [orderliness] to causality is a mistake in scientific method and, like other mistakes of this sort, it is liable to have noxious consequences for every general world outlook that claims to be based on science" (*Causality*, Cambridge, 1959, p. 262). The opposition is voiced in diverse fields—linguistic and analytic philosophy, the philosophy of history, the philosophy of science, gestalt psychology, the theory of art—and it is not coordinated. It is impossible to formulate alternative views in this space, but a number of central principles should be mentioned: 1) Knowing is an active process of assimilation that incorporates an act of appraisal. It is like skill and connoisseurship in being partly inarticulate and inarticulable. 2) Theory—seen as interpretative patterns or structures—is in effect a screen between the knower and the things known. We do not regard facts as being true except as they have a place in some theoretical framework. Particulars are meaningless if we lose sight of the pattern they jointly constitute. Observation and theory are related in an interplay, not a hierarchy or a strictly ordered time-sequence. 3) Verifiability as the measure of lawfulness yields ground to intelligibility, coherence, potential explanatory power. 4) The knower finds himself within a continuous matrix that connects the world of "objective" reality, directly given through experience and activity, with consciousness. 5) Formal logic is not identical with meaningful discourse; it is one—highly specialized and selective—among several varieties thereof.

[10] This is one of the most vulnerable points in this view of explanation. It has been argued that, although explanation and prediction may show parallel formal structures, they do not always turn out to be reversible. The basis for the argument is the assertion that each of the terms "cause," "law," "explanation," and "prediction" in fact covers a wider range of referents than

the same general law, and this paradigm for explanation is therefore known as the "covering law model."

The general viewpoint that I have briefly outlined here is known as the Neo-Positivist position. Its central thesis is that scientific study means systematic investigation of causes, in the sense of the covering law model for explanation. While this doctrine took form earliest in the context of the natural sciences, its wider application to all fields of knowledge is the subject of continuing and urgent discussion. For the study of history the central Neo-Positivist document is Carl Hempel's well-known essay *The Function of General Laws in History*.[11] In his address to the New York meeting of the International Musicological Society in 1961, Arthur Mendel affirmed the correctness of Hempel's position and formally extended its application to the discipline of musicology.[12] In the course of his exposition Mendel distinguished, in terms of levels of generality, between two phases of the musicologist's work: his establishing of lower-order facts, such as the date and place of birth of some composer, and the relating of higher-order facts, such as musical styles. The first has to do with the treatment of evidence, the second with what I shall call, rather loosely for the moment, the writing of narrative history.

For the remainder of this essay I shall confine myself to the second of these subjects, and I shall raise these fundamental questions:

1) Does causal explanation according to the covering law model

---

is recognized by the covering law model. See William Dray, *Laws and Explanation in History*, London, 1957, Chap. III (pp. 58-85) and Bunge, *op. cit.*, pp. 307-32. A minute example: the statement "Lions are fierce" provides the basis for a prediction on which one's life may depend, but it would not explain a single manifestation of a particular lion's fierceness. I shall want to consider the status of such "explanations" in music history further on.

As students of music especially, we should not be surprised by this lack of symmetry between explanation and prediction. The analysis of music, even as the analysis of narrative or dramatic fiction, comes down very much to a detailed demonstration of the way in which the events of the work are motivated. Being convinced by such a demonstration we do not, however, go on to claim that it was all predictable. On the contrary, we would say that it is just within this gap between explanation and prediction that artistic excellence is located.

[11] *Journal of Philosophy*, 39 (1942), reprinted in Feigl and Sellars, eds., *Readings in Philosophical Analysis*, New York, 1949, and Patrick Gardiner, *Theories of History*, New York, 1959.

[12] *Evidence and Explanation*, in *International Musicological Society Report of the Eighth Congress, New York 1961*, Kassel, 1962, pp. 3-18. The reader will find there a far more detailed and thoughtful exposition of this point of view than space allows here.

adequately represent what historians do when they explain historical phenomena?[13]

2) What are the consequences of the placement of causal knowledge at the center of music-historical study?

It might be well to reflect first on the special problems that may be encountered when the historical facts we seek to explain are art-works or classes of art-works. If we wish to explain how it happened, say, that Haydn composed twelve symphonies for performance in London, we can readily refer to a chain of events and conditions that lead up to the fact in question. But suppose we seek to explain why it is that in the next-last of those symphonies (No. 103) there is a return near the conclusion of the first movement to the tempo and music of the introduction. Now we seem to enter a different realm, for it is hardly possible to imagine such an explanation in terms of precipitating conditions and covering laws. This would suggest that there are at least two kinds of explaining of art-works: explaining the *causes*, but also explaining the *quality* of their being.

In music history we often explain one work or style by reference to another, antecedent work or style. The establishing of the relationship of antecedence is a necessary and illuminating part of history writing,

---

[13] This question is not raised here for the first time. The following brief review incorporates some of my own arguments, but it owes much to the selections from a very extensive literature that I list here and cite specifically in the context of my discussion.

H. Butterfield, *The Whig Interpretation of History*, London, 1931.

Arthur Child, *Thoughts on the Historiology of Neo-Positivism*, in *Journal of Philosophy*, LVII (1960), 665.

Benedetto Croce, *Historical Determinism and Philosophy of History*, reprinted in Gardiner, *Theories*.

Alan Donagan, *Explanation in History*, in Gardiner, *Theories*.

William Dray, *Laws and Explanations in History* (see note 10), *Explaining What*, in Gardiner, *Theories*, and *Explanatory Narrative in History*, in *Philosophical Quarterly* (1954), pp. 15-27.

Charles Frankel, *Explanation and Interpretation in History*, in Gardiner, *Theories*.

Patrick Gardiner, *The Nature of Historical Explanation*, London, 1952.

Michael Scriven, *Truisms as the Grounds for Historical Explanation*, in Gardiner, *Theories*.

W. H. Walsh, *The Intelligibility of History*, in *Philosophy* (1942), pp. 129-43.

Mendel supports Hempel's thesis, and in rejecting the arguments presented by the latter's opponents he shows that the conditions of history that are alleged to stand in the way of a scientific methodology — e.g. the uniqueness of historical events, the elusiveness of causal laws — obtain in science as well. Indeed the following arguments are not intended to support the doctrine that history is *sui generis* in its methods. But then the general conclusion must be that "it is desirable to dispense with a nomenclature attached to an outdated philosophy of science, namely that asserting the coextensiveness of science and causality" (Bunge, *op. cit.*, p. 277). This is to say that the identification of all knowledge as *causal* is as unsatisfactory in science as it is in history.

but as causal explanation it can, in most cases, hope to rely only on the thin paste of *post hoc ergo propter hoc*.

Another form of explanation frequently encountered in music history is that in which an individual work is identified with a class or type about which some general characteristic is alleged. As an example we may take the following sentence: "Four-part writing was of course no novelty *c.* 1300...; but its appearance in several English compositions..., when considered together with the attempt at six-part writing in *Sumer is icumen in*...seems to show a predilection on the part of the English for greater fullness of sound..."[14] Associations of this type increase our power of understanding particulars. As soon as we are able to say that the particular in question is a such-and-such, we have taken hold of it. But we have by no means given a causal explanation of it.

Among the criticisms that have been raised against Hempel's thesis, some do not question the historian's interest in causes, but nevertheless deny both the possibility of collecting enough information about the circumstances under which his events took place and the possibility of formulating satisfactory general laws.[15] With respect to conditions, in order to make a scientific explanation of Napoleon's decision to invade Russia the historian would need to know far more about the Emperor's public and private life than he could ever hope to learn (more, no doubt, than Napoleon himself knew). And with respect to laws in history, they must be of such generality as to be trivial, or of such specificity as to apply to only a single case.

We may take as an example the statement "Louis XIV was unpopular because his policy was detrimental to France."[16] The general law on which this explanation rests might take this unimpressive form: "Rulers whose policies are detrimental to their countries become unpopular." Or we might fill out the statement of the law with a complex of factors including Louis's expansionist foreign policy, his heavy taxation, and his religious persecutions. But as it gains in explanatory power it narrows in its applicability, until the conditions it specifies are met only by the case of Louis XIV. Then it might resemble general laws in form, but it would be, in fact, an explication of the particular

---

[14] From Gustave Reese, *Music in the Middle Ages*, New York, 1940, p. 403.

[15] This is Donagan's thesis, although most critics express the same concern in one form or another.

[16] The example is from Dray, *Laws and Explanations*, p. 39 ff.

case. And herein lies the thrust of an altogether different notion of explanation.[17] In this view the explanations that satisfy historians are indeed explications, detailed unfoldings of the case under consideration, in the context of all that can be discovered about the attendant circumstances. These may be related through an interpretative transformation of facts, so that they manifest a recognizable pattern or theme. In this view explaining is a kind of ordering process, like explaining the functioning of a sentence. To be sure, somewhere in the background there are ultimate regularities and correlations on which it all depends, but they are of an extremely general and fundamental sort, like the broadest generalizations about human behavior. It is not from these that the explanation derives its power. It is, rather, from the coherence of the pattern that the historian has recognized. He is credited, not with discovering that a particular phenomenon falls under a general law, but for finding that a number of elements may be brought together into a single pattern in such a way as to be made intelligible in terms of one another. This view rejects the ultimate artificiality, the belief in the separability in practice of observation and theory—as Taine had it, "Après la collection des faits, la recherche des causes."[18]

These criticisms are made on logical grounds and from reflection about what historians in fact *do*. Others stem from consideration, not of the truth, but of the usefulness of the covering law hypothesis. It is useful to the pure scientist, for he is principally interested in the laws themselves; he values them for the fact that they explain. It is useful to the applied scientist, for his chief business is making predictions. And it is useful to the geologist, say, or to the musicologist working with his evidence, for both are concerned in reasoning from present evidence through laws to past facts. But none of these statements describes the principal purpose of the historian writing narrative history, for his objective is to establish connections among facts of which he is already in possession.[19]

The question of value may be approached from still another direction. The covering law hypothesis, and indeed the general movement

---

[17] Walsh, Child, Butterfield, Dray, *Explaining What*; (Gardiner, *The Nature of Historical Explanation*, Chap. 2.

[18] Quoted by Croce, p. 239. As an antidote to Taine's maxim I refer the reader to Norwood Hanson's *Patterns of Discovery*, Cambridge Univ. Press, 1958.

[19] Child, p. 665; Butterfield, p. 22; Frankel, p. 411.

towards "scientific" procedure in historical studies of which that hypothesis is a late and quintessential manifestation, answered a pressing need. It was the need to bring to light the assumptions that are, as Hempel wrote, "buried under the gravestones 'hence', 'therefore', 'because', and the like," and to erect a standard against which it would be possible to show that explanations thus offered are often "poorly founded or downright unacceptable."[20] It was to affirm that the responsibility for logical, deductive reasoning, to the limits of the evidence, was not to be *circumvented* by recourse to "intuitive conviction" and "historical sensitivity." I believe that Hempel's argument is best interpreted in that light, and *not* as a demand for strict adherence to the letter of the covering law model. For Hempel himself recognized the impossibility of meeting such a demand in history; thus he spoke of "explanation *sketches*," as others have spoken of "loose laws" and "probability hypotheses."[21] With this interpretation, then, the covering law model is but a maximal formulation for the sort of reasoning to which the historian is obligated, and for his recognition that events are orderly rather than capricious. The need for such an orientation is hardly to be denied.

It is in the leap from that emphasis to the central placement of causal knowledge in historical inquiry that the difficulties are to be located!

And now I have returned to my principal subject. For it seems to me that in the practice of musicology the explaining "what" has been heavily prejudiced by a preoccupation with explaining "why." The historian's account of what the work *is*, is conditioned by his habit of inquiring how it came to be. This is the second "historical point of view." The historical fact is understood principally through its antecedents and consequences, and the sequence of historical facts is linked in a geneological chain of cause and effect. This view is supported, as we have seen, by the Neo-Positivist approach to explanation. But it is also reinforced by a number of inherited beliefs about the nature of historical change and historical necessity that come, paradoxically, from another direction altogether. It is to those that I turn now.

We may begin by considering Guido Adler's propaedeutic postulate for musicology, given in his *Methode der Musikgeschichte*: "The task

[20] *Op. cit.*

[21] Dray, *Laws and Explanation*, pp. 25-31.

of music history is the investigation and the setting forth of the developmental paths of music.'[22] The *Shorter Oxford English Dictionary* offers two families of meaning for the word "develop"; as technical term in mathematics, photography, and warfare, and then this group: "To unfold or unroll, to unfurl, to unveil, to disclose, to bring out all that is contained in, to bring forth from a latent or elementary condition, to cause to grow what exists in the germ, to grow into a fuller, higher, or more mature condition." These definitions have in common the notion, either of disclosure of what is already present, or of realization of a stored potential. In either case a process is suggested for which the course is charted, and the end-point determined. Now the context for these definitions is largely biological, and we shall probably object that no such determinist ideas underlie our notions of development in history. Yet in the history of art, and in political and social history, there is a strong tradition for just such a concept.

It goes back, in any case, to Aristotle. He wrote, in the *Physics*, "Those things are natural which by a continuous movement originated by an internal principle arrive at some completion" and "Each step in the series is for the sake of the next." In the *Poetics* he wrote, of the development of tragedy, "It was in fact only after a long series of changes that the movement of Tragedy stopped on its attaining to its natural form.'[23]

From Leo Schrade's essay *Renaissance, the Historical Conception of an Epoch*,[24] we learn of the scheme of cultural development in terms of which the men of the 15th and 16th centuries saw their age. Writers in all disciplines rejoiced in their participation in a "restoration," "renovation," "return to the light," "rebirth." The original, or model, was, of course, antiquity, in some versions together with the early Christian era. The two epochs—the original and the rebirth—had been separated by an "immense interval," a "lacuna," an "exile," an "abyss," a "dark ignorance," or "middle age." The rebirth was followed by a period of growth that, as Schrade observed, "stimulated the assumption of the biologic process of passing through the phases of infancy or youth, mature manhood, and old age. It seems but natu-

[22] Leipzig, 1919, p. 9.

[23] Quoted from the Oxford translation, edited by W. D. Ross. *Physics*: Bk. II, Ch. 8, p. 199b, 11. 15-19; p. 199a, 11. 15-16. *Poetics*: Ch. 4, p. 1449a, 11. 14-15.

[24] *International Musicological Society, Report of the 5th Congress, Utrecht, 1952*, Kassel, 1953, pp. 19-32.

ral that the biological idea of an organic growth toward fullest ripeness suggested the principles of progressiveness and perfection to the summit of potentialities."

This scheme of history again held a central position in the self image of 18th-century artists and scholars. Immanuel Kant wrote in 1784:

> All the capacities implanted in a creature by nature are destined to unfold themselves, completely and conformably to their end, in the course of time...In man, as the only rational creature on earth, those natural capacities which are directed toward the use of his reason could be completely developed only in the species and not in the individual, for reason requires the production of an almost inconceivable series of generations in order that Nature's germs, as implanted in our species, may be at last unfolded to that stage of development which is completely conformable to her inherent design.[25]

(Hegel, not long after, took the same doctrine, and nearly the same language, as a central tenet of his philosophy of history: "The principle of development involves the existence of a latent germ of being—a capacity or potentiality striving to realize itself.")[26] In a work begun also in 1784, Johann Gottfried Herder put it this way: "As a botanist cannot obtain a complete knowledge of a plant unless he follow it from the seed through its germination, blossoming, and decay, such is Grecian history to us."[27] That this doctrine should find expression within the context of a discussion of Greek civilization is, of course, especially meaningful. For once again that civilization, at its height, represented to the men of the second half of the 18th century a perfection, a standard that was to be emulated.

All this is explicit in the work of the influential archeologist Johann Joachim Winckelmann. In his monumental *History of Ancient Art*, published 1764, he distinguished three stages: "The arts which are dependent on drawing have, like all inventions, commenced with the *necessary*; the next object of research was *beauty*; and finally the *superfluous* followed." Here is his summary of the course of Greek art:

> The earliest attempts, especially in the drawing of figures, represented, not the manner in which a man appears to us, but what he is; not a view of his body, but the

[25] Kant, *Idea of a Universal History from a Cosmopolitan Point of View*, reprinted from the translation of W. Hastie in Gardiner, *Theories*, pp. 22-34.

[26] Hegel, *Lectures on the Philosophy of History*, excerpted in J. Loewenberg, ed., *Hegel Selections*, New York, 1929, p. 409.

[27] *Ideas Toward a Philosophy of the History of Man*, reprinted from the translation of T. Churchill in Gardiner, *Theories*, pp. 35-51.

outline of his shadow. From this simplicity of shape the artist next proceeded to examine proportions. This inquiry taught exactness (and) gave confidence and success to his endeavours after grandeur, and at last gradually raised art among the Greeks to the highest beauty. After all the parts constituting grandeur and beauty were united, the artist, in seeking to embellish them, fell into the error of profuseness; art consequently lost its grandeur, and the loss was finally followed by its utter downfall.[28]

This evaluation is important, for it shows that "dread of corruption," as Gombrich recently termed it,[29] through which the new "classicism" of the 18th century was to be purified. It implied an appeal for the perpetuation of ideal forms that Winckelmann had already made explicit in his *Thoughts on the Imitation of Greek Works in Painting and Sculpture*, published in 1755.[30] The economy and incisiveness that are asked for here became and have remained, as we know, synonymous with both the notion of "perfection" and the concept "Classical."

Just as our conception of the "Renaissance" as a historical epoch follows, and continues to reinforce, the self image of Renaissance men, so our continued designation of the second half of the 18th century as the era of "Classicism" rests ultimately upon, and preserves, ideals that were given expression at the time. And a single view of history—the developmental view — underlies both cases.

The active role that this theory of history plays in the practice of musicology is most apparent in textbooks of music history, although these do not by any means constitute its only sphere of influence. I shall cite a characteristic passage, and let it evoke others like it. And by way of preface to all the quotations that follow, I should like to make it quite clear that it is not my purpose to take issue with them or their authors directly, but rather to relate them to a framework of theory.

Here, then, is a passage from a widely read introductory textbook: "When Emma's spectral funeral music...announced in its transformation at the end of the opera [*Euryanthe*] that the sinner is redeemed, the seed was planted from which, at Wagner's hands, the whole form of Music Drama was to grow."[31] We may read this sort of language

333

[28] The quotations are from the translation of G. Henry Lodge, Boston, 1873, pp. 191-92.

[29] Public lecture, *Philosophies of History and their Impact on Art; I. Platonism and the Dread of Corruption.* University of Chicago, 1966.

[30] *Gedanken über die Nachahmung der griechischen Werke in der Malerei und Bildhauerkunst,* available to me in the edition of B. Seuffert, Heilbronn, 1855.

[31] Alfred Einstein, *A Short History of Music,* 4th American ed., revised, New York, 1956, p. 164.

as literary gift wrapping, enclosing less theoretical meaning than appears on the surface. But then here is a less picturesque statement by a different author which is, nevertheless, informed by the same doctrine: "Instrumental music in the early 17th century was in a different stage of development from vocal music. Vocal music had to assimilate the new technique of monody...; but instrumental music for the most part had only to continue along the path that had already been marked out before the end of the Renaissance."[32] Here is the same view again, expressed in one of our most recent textbooks of history, and this time stated quite explicitly as theory: "Musical materials have to be 'used up', their potential fully exploited, before style can move ahead on the long line of history. As in a development section by Beethoven, the material already introduced has to be shredded down to its constituent fibers, all its meaning extracted, before new meaning will seem meaningful."[33]

There can be no question that the developmental doctrine is a prominent feature in the philosophical background of historical musicology. Before asking how it manifests itself in the evaluation of musical works I shall need to make one final digression.

The concept of historical development falls squarely in the field of a fundamental and recurring philosophical controversy, that between the positions of "Nominalism" and "Realism." To the Nominalist, categories of particulars are constructs: artificial, arbitrary, and practical. The general terms by which we designate them are *names* only, and the study of categories amounts to the study of the linguistic rules that govern the use of the terms that represent them. For the Realist particulars are grouped together because of properties held in common, and general terms derive their meanings from the real features of the objects to which they refer — not the other way about. For the Nominalist categories are hypothetical and are valued for their usefulness in the management of data. For the Realist the common features of particulars by which they are set off in categories are independently "true" and are to be discovered. Whether a particular belongs to a certain category is for the Nominalist a formal question of definition, of the use of the terms in the case, but not so for the Realist.

[32] Donald Jay Grout, *A History of Western Music*, New York, 1960, p. 297.

[33] Richard Crocker, *A History of Musical Style*, New York, 1966, p. 525.

For a concrete example from music history of the approach to a single problem from these opposed points of view we may consider the controversy over the status of the concept "Baroque." The Nominalist position was represented by John Mueller in his essay, characteristically entitled *Baroque—Is it Datum, Hypothesis, or Tautology?*[34] In answering the rhetorical question of his title Mueller treated the style-category "Baroque" as an invention of historians, thereby denying the first of his alternatives, and then challenged its soundness because, he argued, the integrity of the category could not be demonstrated. But Manfred Bukofzer claimed for the Baroque the status of "period in its own right"—not a construct, but a collection of real attributes.[35] In the following statement by Paul Henry Lang the Realist position is taken a step further, in that the particulars belonging to the category *owe* their characteristics to the circumstance of their having been born into the category: "The Baroque stands vividly before us for its power to mold all the arts according to its own eloquent spirit."[36] Here "Baroque" is no longer a designation for the common attributes of Baroque art-works; it denotes a distillation of these attributes in ideal form, a generative principle, an essence. Baroque works are no longer particulars that share certain properties; they are individual embodiments of a single essence. In the light of that distinction Karl Popper has introduced the term "Essentialism" for this extreme form of the Realist doctrine.[37]

The historical theory in which the causes of events are sought in developmental processes is an Essentialist theory. For at the core of each process of development—whether it is of a genre, of a school, or of a technique—there must be something that is recognizably the same even while it changes with respect to its outer form. We affirm this in our willingness to name what it is that is undergoing development— "music drama" and "instrumental music," in the textbook passages that I cited above. Those names refer to essences or universals, and to trace the development of such genres is to follow the successive embodiments of their essences. But the study of individual embodiments

---

[34] *Journal of Aethetics and Art Criticism*, XII (1954), 421-37.

[35] *The Baroque in Music History*, in *Journal of Aesthetics and Art Criticism*, XIV (1955), 152-56.

[36] *Music in Western Civilization*, New York, 1941, p. 529.

[37] *The Poverty of Historicism*, 3d ed., New York, 1961, pp. 26-34.

is undertaken as means, not as end, for they reveal the different forms that the essence may take; i.e. they reveal its *potentials*. Indeed, an essence may be regarded as the sum of its potential forms, and to really know an essence we must follow it through all of those forms. This is the sense, once again, of Herder's figure: "The botanist cannot obtain a complete knowledge of a plant unless he follow it from the seed through its germination, blossoming, and decay." From this point of view the study of anything is necessarily historical.

Goethe warned once: "Too much inquiring after the sources of things is dangerous. We should rather concentrate on phenomena as given realities."[38] What a curious and unexpected thing it is that an Idealist position—"All knowledge is historical"—and one that arises from a Positivist orientation—"All knowledge is causal knowledge"—should come together in the doctrine of historicism that is the antithesis of Goethe's meaning!

We can anticipate three characteristics in the approach to the musical work from the developmental point of view. It will be regarded as the embodiment of an essence; it will be understood in terms of its antecedents and consequences; and it will be seen in the context of a process that culminates in the fulfillment or perfection of the essence that it informs. The following selections of music-historical writing are all taken from a single field of inquiry, the study of music of the Classic era. This is done in the interest of maintaining a consistent framework, not because that field is unique in its theoretical bearing. And this time I quote, not from general textbooks but from scholarly publications intended for a professional audience.

First, passages from an article on *The Symphonies of Padre Martini*[39] (the title is significant, for its form suggests that the author means to give a *general* account of his repertory). Martini's works are repeatedly considered in terms of their embodiment of the Baroque and Classic styles. Thus, "The first book of Sonatas marked Martini's farewell to the Baroque," and "The Symphony 2 illustrates Martini's approach to the new [i.e. Classic] style." In the following passages the evaluation of musical works depends upon a comparison with past

[38] "Allzuvieles Fragen nach den Ursachen sei gefährlich; man solle lieber an die Erscheinungen als gegebene Tatsache halten." Quoted by H. J. Moser in *Zur Methodik der musikalischen Geschichtschreibung*, in *Zeitschrift für Aesthetik*, XIV (1920), 130-45.

[39] By Howard Brofsky, in *The Musical Quarterly*, LI (1965), 649-73.

and/or future counterparts: the slow movement of Symphony 22 is "retrospective, for it begins with the Baroque chromatic descending tetrachord in the bass," and "Oddly enough, Martini reverts in the late symphonies to the descending chromatic tetrachord," or "Martini disappoints us, for while the symphony dated 1736 is *au courant* with the conventions of the day his later stylistic progress is small, and does not keep pace with the important changes taking place around him." Finally, in the polarity of a "nascent Classical style" on one hand, and a "full-fledged Classical style" on the other, we have the familiar image of birth and development to maturity.

Next I quote passages from an encyclopedia article on the symphony.[40] Regarding the music of Florian Gassmann, "his orchestral treatment...points to the future," and that of Mozart, "Although Mozart did not consciously seek new and surprising effects, he was a pioneer with respect to the greater independence of the winds." "Massoneau's *Symphonie la Tempête et la Calme* (1794) may be regarded as preparing the way for the *Pastoral Symphony*." These passages, again, make their reports in terms of past and future. Characteristic too is the tendency to make no distinction between *forerunner* and *progenitor*, i.e. to require no further evidence that forerunner *is* progenitor. This tendency seems always to carry with it the attributing of the greatest significance to the earliest occurrence of a phenomenon or trait.

The growth image is projected in this passage: "In the early years of the [18th] century the overture is important as the cradle of the new Classic tone language...With composers of the first generation the sonata form of the first movement is only rudimentary...The second generation of overture composers shows greater mastery of sonata form." In this last passage, too, it must be plain that "sonata form" is an ideal, an essence. For how is it otherwise possible to speak in terms of degrees of mastery of a technique that has nowhere yet been fully defined or worked out? Of course we know the experience of the conscious quest for the solution of an intellectual or artistic problem. We are unable to specify the solution while we seek it, but we recognize it once it is presented to us. What I wish to observe here is the tendency to assume such a structure for all historical processes, and to derive from it every judgment about works of art.

There is an apparent difference between these last quotations and the passages about Padre Martini. Those were phrased in a heavily value-

---

[40] *MGG*, article *Symphonie*.

laden language; these seem objective and noncommittal. We might say that the first are *interpretative*, the second *descriptive*. But herein lies an issue of the first importance. The single criterion of value for the interpretative statements is the same developmental framework that gives form to the descriptive statements. The question is whether a descriptive statement on these lines can ever be bare of value connotations. Can we say "ripe Classical style" without implying a higher order of musical achievement than is suggested by "nascent Classical style"? Surely not, for all statements of this type are supported by a theory of history that imposes a hierarchy on their subjects. Every stage in a developmental process is a step nearer to the realization of potentials, hence what *is* is an improvement over what *was*. That is the spirit in which Hegel could write "The real world *is* as it *ought to be*" (italics mine).[41] The only difference between the passages on Martini and those on the symphony is in the degree to which their assessments are made explicit.

Let us return to the encyclopedia article: in the treatment of Philipp Emanuel Bach the interpenetration of historical position and artistic position is complete:

> Although he was among the most respected and influential personalities of the 18th century both as theoretician and composer, he did not always succeed in coordinating all the musical factors in the full Classical sense...A conflict arises from Bach's breadth of background in the traditions of the past, which is coupled with a striking futuristic tendency. He combined Baroque, Classic, and Romantic characteristics in a mixture that rarely resulted in a satisfying synthesis. In Bach's symphonies sensitive and striking details often interrupt the flow and balance of the over-all conception, which is evidence of the basic opposition between *Empfindsamkeit* and ripe Classicism.

The assessment of the man's position as an artist is truly indistinguishable from his location on the historical continuum. If his music is unsuccessful, it is *because* he occupies an awkward position historically. (We know of other composers, of course, whose mark of artistic achievement is their position not between, but in advance of, scheduled historical developments.)[42]

----

[41] *Lectures on the Philosophy of History*, transl. from the 3d German ed. by J. Sibree, London, 1894. The passage quoted is from the author's introduction.

[42] Oswald Spengler marked the beginning of the decline of Western music with Beethoven, on grounds very like those laid down by Winckelmann: profusion and the consequent disruption of form. Alfred Einstein argued that, on the contrary, Beethoven represents a peak in that he brought about the full realization of the potentials of sonata form. They assess their man differently, but only because he occupies different positions in their respective schemes of development. (Spengler, *The Decline of the West*, authorized transl. by Charles F. Atkinson, New York, 1926 and 1928, I, 291 ff.; Einstein, *Oswald Spengler und die Musikgeschichte*, in *Zeitschrift für Musikwissenschaft*, III [1920], 30-32.)

Finally I quote from a monograph on *The Symphonies of Joseph Haydn*.[43] Once again, measurement is taken in terms of the past and future: "Thus, the Salomon Symphonies sum up and synthesize all [Haydn] has achieved in the field, and at the same time look far forward into the future, to the orchestral world of Beethoven and Schubert, of Mendelssohn and Schumann."[44] Defined goals are achieved through a gradual development: "The first six [Salomon Symphonies] show a steady progress in the direction of the 'English Taste'."[45] And what lies at the end of the development is the perfection of the form, the full realization of its potentials; "last" is "best": "As the London period progresses, this tendency [i.e. the dramatic function of the slow introduction] emerges ever more clearly, and by 1794-95 [Symphonies 102-104] the formal and emotional necessity of the introductory slow sections is quite apparent. In no. 104 the profundity of the introduction reaches its height."[46] Given the now familiar theoretical framework we might have anticipated that judgment, if not its paradoxical wording.

In this philosophy art is a collective, impersonal enterprise; tracings of the passage of time, now more, now less distinct, now leading, now trailing behind. Art works are but manifestations of an Idea, like the shadows in Plato's cave, whose value is measured by the closeness with which they approximate their models, and whose necessities are imposed from without.

In our quest for the sources of art we neglect its quality. We do so to the disadvantage of our faculty for judging art works, for our standards of judgment have little to do with the ways in which we apprehend works. Then we are left with a history in which esthetics and hermeneutics play no significant part. But it may yet be that the same obsession with causality that yields such a curiously one-sided history is responsible also for distortions in the narrative for which so much is sacrificed; that our categorical prejudgments effect not only the interpretation and assessment of art works, but even those matters that we take to be open to "objective," "scientific" treatment: the reading of art works and the attribution of authorship, chronology, and provenance. That is a question for further inquiry.

339

---

[43] By H. C. Robbins Landon, London, 1955.

[44] *Ibid.*, p. 552.   [45] *Ibid.*, p. 552.   [46] *Ibid.*, p. 573.